Fan Fiction and Fan Communities
in the Age of the Internet

Fan Fiction and Fan Communities in the Age of the Internet

New Essays

EDITED BY KAREN HELLEKSON
AND KRISTINA BUSSE

McFarland & Company, Inc., Publishers
Jefferson, North Carolina, and London

ALSO BY KAREN HELLEKSON

The Science Fiction of Cordwainer Smith
(McFarland, 2001)

LIBRARY OF CONGRESS CATALOGUING-IN-PUBLICATION DATA

Fan fiction and fan communities in the age of the Internet : new
essays / edited by Karen Hellekson and Kristina Busse.
        p.   cm.
Includes bibliographical references and index.

ISBN-13: 978-0-7864-2640-9
softcover : 50# alkaline paper ∞

    1. Fan fiction — History and criticism.   2. Literature and the Internet.
I. Hellekson, Karen, 1966– .   II. Busse, Kristina, 1967– .
PN3377.5.F33F36   2006
809.3 — dc22   2006014823

British Library cataloguing data are available

Cover photograph ©2006 Brand X Pictures.

Manufactured in the United States of America

McFarland & Company, Inc., Publishers
Box 611, Jefferson, North Carolina 28640
www.mcfarlandpub.com

Contents

PART I—DIFFERENT APPROACHES:
FAN FICTION IN CONTEXT

PART II—CHARACTERS, STYLE, TEXT:
FAN FICTION AS LITERATURE

Preface

This book was built on the meeting of two worlds, the fannish and the academic, and was also built on the collision of two different kinds of fan worlds and fan experiences. Kristina and Karen first met at the 2004 International Conference for the Fantastic in the Arts, an academic conference that both science fiction academics and writers attend — itself a kind of world-colliding. Our shared scholarly interests, academic backgrounds, and investment in fan texts and fan media sources provided a common ground, but while working on this book, we discovered that although we were both active in fandom, whatever that term means, our activities took quite different forms. Both of us have PhDs in English, but whereas Kristina teaches, Karen does not. Both of us enjoy slash fan fiction: Karen writes it and runs a mailing list and a related fan archive, and Kristina reads and critiques it. Kristina is a fannish butterfly, lurking in every fandom and reading voraciously; Karen is a monofannish, selective reader. But since we've met, and especially since we've worked on this project together, we've changed too: Kristina has begun to engage with the texts more creatively; Karen has moved into the LiveJournal.com blogsphere and into other fandoms. Our worlds have merged and we are both the richer for it.

This meeting of worlds relies on an extension of experience through relationships and community, and this has become a central theme in this volume. When assembling papers for this volume, we were certain of one thing: we wanted to situate it at the intersection of the fannish community and academic discourses on fan culture. As a result, all the writers tend to be fans as well as academics; all are conscious of the difficulties surrounding those positions and their interactions. We come from a variety of fandoms and a variety of theoretical backgrounds, yet we all share an intersection of fannish and academic approaches and interests. Fandom as we find it now is quite different from the mostly zine-based, often hidden, monolithic fandoms of the 1970s and 1980s. The Internet alone has changed the size of fandom and its demographics and has created new forms of reader-author interaction. Rather than trying to make universalizing statements that are bound to be false, the writers in this volume focus on specific issues, subsets, and genres. No single essay can be seen as the truth about fandom: the sum total of these essays, in all their contradictions, is closer to an actual account of fandom.

The entire creation of the book was a virtual process. From the call for papers and the related inquiries to the brainstorming sessions and all the way to the various drafts and revisions, all communication occurred online. This process was appropriate, of course, considering our focus on how the technological changes of the past decade and a half have altered the fan community and its artistic creations. We describe in the introduction how the lived and affective experience of fandom parallels that of putting together this volume. Central to this is the idea of an always ongoing, always renegotiated work in progress — the creation of a text that can never reach closure — but for us, the very activity of its creation achieves the same status of the text itself, and this creation is the product of a community. Yet we don't want to unduly valorize the idea of *community* by assuming it has only positive connotations, because it doesn't. Implicit in community is dissent, but there are also discussion and mediation — strategies we used quite a bit as we worked through building this text. Because there is a community behind this book, the word *we* is used frequently (and deliberately) throughout this text. The authors who wrote the individual essays worked closely with us and, sometimes, with each other. Some of us knew each other before the project began, but many did not. We acknowledge the help of all members of the community that formed to create the book. Karen oversaw the project, handled formal correspondence, copyedited the book, kept people on schedule, acted as liaison with the publisher and peer reviewers, and dealt with the technical and organizational sides of publication. Kristina worked closely with authors to get papers into shape, laid out the book's organizational structure, and drafted the outline of the introduction, which was then reworked and rewritten alternately by Karen, then Kristina, and so on.

We thank our families, who suffered through a year of frantic work schedules and late-night writing: Michael Johnson and Ryan, Gabriel, and Matthias Simm. Megen Duffy copyedited the introduction and the bibliography. We thank the contributors to this volume for their patience through tight deadlines and endless revision: Francesca Coppa, Catherine Driscoll, Abigail Derecho, Robert Jones, Deborah Kaplan, Angelina I. Karpovich, Eden Lackner, Barbara Lynn Lucas, Robin Anne Reid, Mafalda Stasi,

Louisa Ellen Stein, Ika Willis, and Elizabeth Woledge. The insights we garnered from correspondence with Jane Glaubman, Matt Hills, Henry Jenkins, Melissa Lipscomb, Christine Mains, Rachel McGrath-Kerr, Juli Parrish, Margaret Rogers, Franziska Schmitt, Cynthia W. Walker, and Shannon White proved invaluable as we shaped the volume, and we thank them as well. Most importantly, we acknowledge all the friends within the fan community who not only created the fannish texts we are discussing and produced many of the theoretical discussions that often were the catalysts for our thinking process, but also provided feedback and encouragement along the way.

Introduction
Work in Progress
Kristina Busse and Karen Hellekson

It starts like this. Somewhere in cyberspace, someone complains: "I had a lousy day! Need some cheering up." Soon after, a friend posts a story dedicating the piece: "This is for you, hon — your favorite pairing and lots of schmoopy sex. Hope it'll cheer you up!" A third person chimes in: "I can't believe it! What a great fic! I mean, who would have thought of gay penguin sex? It totally works! I love it!" "Gay penguin sex?" someone else adds, finding it hilarious, and in response, she posts a poem she knocked off in five minutes flat, all about gay penguins having sex. "I'm taking two lines of that to add to my signature," someone informs her in a comment and goes on to write a three-paragraph snippet of fiction based on the poem, which in turn results in — well, you get the idea.

It starts like this. In a private e-mail, someone writes: "I want to edit a volume about fan fiction that better describes the current climate, one that takes into account online experience." She checks with her publisher to see if they'd consider it and finds that yes, they will. "Want in?" she asks her friend. "What a great project!" reads the e-mail reply. "I have so many ideas for what we could include." A call for papers appears online, and the responses begin. One author proposes: "I have an idea that fan fiction is more performative than literary." Another inquires: "I heard about this volume from a friend, and I want to talk about role-playing games. Interested?" "I heard a paper on a similar topic at a conference," the coeditors respond; "we love your idea, here are our comments on your draft, and you should also contact this person who is writing on RPGs." And so a book begins.

These illustrations — one an example of the creation of fan fiction and the other an account of the impetus of this book — highlight the dense intertextuality found in the creation of fan works of art and in fan academic

5

discourse. The community-centered creation of artistic fannish expressions such as fan fiction, fan art, and fan vids is mirrored in the creation of this book, with constant manipulation, renegotiation, commenting, and revising, all done electronically among a group of people, mostly women, intimately involved in the creation and consumption of fannish goods. As the examples above indicate, the creator of meaning, the person we like to call the *author,* is not a single person but rather is a collective entity. Furthermore, that collective, what we might call *fandom,* is itself not cohesive. It is impossible, and perhaps even dangerous, to speak of a single fandom, because fandoms revolving around the TV program *Due South* have rules different from those of fandoms revolving around the *Lord of the Rings* books and movies, and fandoms that are centered around face-to-face meetings, exchange of round-robin–style letters, or generation of hard-copy fan fiction fanzines (say, the experience described by Camille Bacon-Smith in *Enterprising Women* [1992])[1] are each different from the kind of online fandom that is our primary focus here.

   Work in progress is a term used in the fan fiction world to describe a piece of fiction still in the process of being written but not yet complete. This notion intersects with the intertextuality of fannish discourse, with the ultimate erasure of a single author as it combines to create a shared space, fandom, that we might also refer to as a *community.* The appeal of works in progress lies in part in the way fans can engage with an open text: it invites responses, permits shared authorship, and enjoins a sense of community. In *S/Z,* Roland Barthes (1974) distinguishes between readerly and writerly text, with the former denoting a text whose interpretation is solidified with little room for the reader to enter the text. In contrast, the latter is "a perpetual present, ... is *ourselves writing,* before the infinite play of the world (the world as function) is traversed, intersected, stopped, ... which reduces the plurality of entrances, the opening of networks, the infinity of languages" (5). If the fan is a reader in the Barthesian sense, then serial production is the ultimate writerly text. It invites the viewer to enter, interpret, and expand the text. In so doing, the open-source text in particular invites fan fiction as an expansion to the source universe and as interpretive fan engagement where the fan not only analyzes the text but also must constantly renegotiate her analyses.

   Every fan story is in this sense a work in progress, even when the story has been completed. To create a story (or, indeed, almost any other fan artifact; we just speak of stories here for convenience), some writers compose and post the story, with or without so-called *beta readers* who critique, read, and help revise on various levels, including spelling and grammar, style and structure, and canonicity and remaining in character. Others post versions and parts of the story publicly and revise according to comments. Still others cowrite, at times taking turns in voices and points of view. In most cases, the resulting story is part collaboration and part response to not only the source text, but also the cultural context within and outside the fannish community in which it is produced. Most writing has gone through some form of critical reading, followed by revision. However, when the story is finally complete and published, likely online but perhaps in print, the work in progress among the creators shifts to the work in progress among the readers, and a whole new level of discourse begins that provides engagement and both positive and negative feedback (comments, critiques, and letters of comment).

On a more abstract level, fan academics have begun to think of the entirety of fan fiction in a given fannish universe as a work in progress. This *fantext*, the entirety of stories and critical commentary written in a fandom (or even in a pairing or genre), offers an ever-growing, ever-expanding version of the characters. These multitudes of interpretations of characters and canon scenes are often contradictory yet complementary to one another and the source text. Nevertheless, working with and against one another, this multitude of stories creates a larger whole of understanding a given universe. This canvas of variations is a work in progress insofar as it remains open and is constantly increasing; every new addition changes the entirety of interpretations. By looking at the combined fantext, it becomes obvious how fans' understanding of the source is always already filtered through the interpretations and characterizations existing in the fantext. In other words, the community of fans creates a communal (albeit contentious and contradictory) interpretation in which a large number of potential meanings, directions, and outcomes co-reside.

The notion of a work in progress is thus central to fandom and the study of fandom. The source texts in many cases are serial, in progress, and constantly changing, as are the fan stories set in these universes. Fans' understanding of the characters and the universes the characters inhabit changes, just as scholarly understanding of fans and their relationship to one another, to the source text, and to the texts they generate is constantly being revised and rewritten. As fan academics, we inhabit a fluid space that needs to be continuously revised and reconsidered, where new influences, both internal and external, change not only the object of study, but also our theoretical and methodological frameworks. Like the fantext, with its complementary and contradictory readings of the source text, the academic text seeking to describe and understand fandom also creates a work in progress as it attempts a larger understanding of fan culture.

In both fandom and academia, the debates about such issues as defining

fans, understanding their motivations, and debating fandom's sociopoliti-
cal effects and limitations are often more important than any provisional
answers or solutions. Fan and academic discourses can contain mutually
exclusive readings and are not primarily focused on synthesis.[2] The concept of looking at fannish and academic practices as works in progress thus
foregrounds not only the similarity in what fans and critics do to the texts
they study and create, but also the similarities between writing and revising a particular piece and the discipline as a whole. The convergence
between the academic and the fan and between the work in progress of
scholarship and the work in progress of fan texts is central because all the
contributors to this volume are both fans and academics who are invested
in both worlds and are able to speak both languages. But in connecting fannish and academic practices here, it is important to emphasize that we are
not trying to colonize fannish spaces with an academic value system. In
fact, if anything, it's the reverse: we use our fannish knowledge and values
and apply them to academic practices. Rather than privileging a particular
interpretation as accurate, we have learned from fandom that alternative
and competing readings can and must coexist. We thus use fannish practice as a model for academic practice.

Many of the thoughts expressed here may bear the name of a single
author but could not have been conceived or written without the support
of the fannish community in which the bylined author is embedded. Much
of the interaction during the creation of the book occurred within fannish
spaces and with the constant feedback of other fans; all of it occurred online.
Whereas Matt Hills (2002, 11) accuses academics of valuing only those
aspects of fandom that are most like academia, we would like to foreground
the places where academic disciplinary practices can learn from fandom.
We want to emphasize fandom's communal spirit, what fandom itself often
refers to as its collective "hive mind," and fandom's constant awareness that
every reading is provisional and that every characterization yields one variation among a nearly countless number of others while still maintaining
the rigor of argumentation so crucial to the academic sphere. We look at
and build on two decades of collective insight into fandom studies, and we
situate ourselves not in opposition to but in dialogue with the work that
has come before us.

Fandom is fragmented and fragmentary, just as it is self-perpetuating,
itself a continual work in progress that cannot be shut down. The work in
progress represents not only the activity that creates fandom, but also this
book. When the book goes to press, it will not shut down the discourse
when it appears in unchangeable print. Instead, it will spawn a series of
new lines of discussion. We thus set forth a variety of highly personalized,

individual experiences and readings, with each essay told from a unique point of view, and draw connections among them. Yet because fandom is continuously created, it is continuously changing, and any discussion of it is always already obsolete. Thus, rather than trying to create a homogenous reading or attempting to essentialize fandom and the artworks that spring out of it, we hope to mirror the discussions and vitality of differences that characterize fandom. This collection is thus by necessity a snapshot and by definition incomplete and transitory. The central notion of the book indicates some of the strengths of fan culture, such as self-reflection, collective production, and acceptance of conflict; it strives to exhibit an awareness of the similarities and differences between subsets of fandom. The specific essays speak to one another, at times disagreeing with but more often complementing one another's insights into fan fiction and fan culture.

After a brief definition of terms, needed to create a consistent vocabulary for what follows, we discuss the role of media and related tools in online fandom; outline past research in media/fan studies and place ourselves in relationship to these studies; and provide an overview of the organization of the book and the essays' place in that organization.

Definition of Terms

The essays in this volume all use a common terminology; however, such terminology should be understood as provisional because terms continue to evolve, often depend on fandom, and are always in dispute. Although many readers will at least have a passing familiarity with the specific terminology used in media fandom, the constant debates and attempts at correctly defining and delineating fannish expressions suggest that it may be useful to clarify some of the more commonly used terms.

Most important to treatments of fan texts are understandings of *canon*, the events presented in the media source that provide the universe, setting, and characters, and *fanon*, the events created by the fan community in a particular fandom and repeated pervasively throughout the fantext. Fanon often creates particular details or character readings even though canon does not fully support it — or, at times, outright contradicts it. Complete agreement on what comprises canon is rarely possible, even with repeated viewings of the primary source, because of the range of individual interpretation. Furthermore, what comprises canon can be called into question: for *Lord of the Rings,* for example, the canon may include any combination of the books (including or excluding Tolkien's supplementary

work such as *The Silmarillion*), the animated movie directed by Ralph Bak-
shi released in 1978, and the 2001–2003 blockbuster Peter Jackson films. For
Star Trek fandom, usually any of the four TV series and any of the movies,
but not the animated TV show or the novelizations, may be considered
canon. An understanding of canon is particularly important for the creators of fan texts because they are judged on how well they stick to or depart
from canon.

Within the field of fan fiction, the three main genres are *gen, het,* and
slash. Gen denotes a general story that posits no imposed romantic relationships among the characters. *Het* stories revolve around a heterosexual
relationship, either one invented by the author or one presented in the primary source text. *Slash* stories posit a same-sex relationship, usually one
imposed by the author and based on perceived homoerotic subtext. *Archives*
of fan fiction, or online libraries that categorize and house fan fiction, use
these three genres as organizing principles, with slash often housed in separate archives. The archives' software imposes a way of presentation and
thus a way of reading, because most archivists do not create their own software or fully customize existing software, instead opting to use the software as presented by the creator with only minimal fandom-specific
tweaking. Most archives are very similar in the way they organize and present fiction, usually allowing different search functions, such as title, author,
date, pairing, or genre.

The *header* appears on virtually all posted fan fiction and contains
information about the story. It is used by fic archivists to properly categorize and upload the story without having to read it, and it is used by readers to decide whether or not they want to read it. The header traditionally
provides the title, author, e-mail address, romantic *pairings* (if applicable),
and rating. Often the author uses a rating system, supposedly to warn readers, although the higher ratings often function as advertisements as well.
The header often includes the story's genre or story type (slash or action/
adventure); *spoilers,* or identification of episodes of the media source that
have plot elements given away; acknowledgments to *betas,* who read the
story and make suggestions before the author posts it; *disclaimers,* or an
acknowledgment that the author does not own the characters and universe;
and author's notes, where extra information relevant to the story is provided.

Within fan fiction itself, a number of subgenres are well recognized —
far too many to include here, particularly because many fandom-specific
categories exist. Still, most fans will have heard of the following categories.
These include *hurt/comfort,* or *h/c,* stories, which, as the name implies,
revolve around a character being injured and another character comfort-

ing him; *Mpreg,* where a man gets pregnant; *deathfic,* where a major character dies; *curtainfic,* or fic so domestic that the main characters, often a male slash pairing, shop for curtains together; *episode fix,* a rewriting of an event provided in canon to a deliberately noncanonical, preferred conclusion; *episode tag* or *missing scene,* a continuation of a canonical scene that provides more information; *AU,* or *alternate universe,* where familiar characters are dropped into a new setting (which, depending on the media source, may or may not be canonical, because many of the source texts have fantastical components and not a few have played with multiverses); *crossover,* combining two different sets of characters from two media sources into a single story (as in a *Buffy the Vampire Slayer/X-Files* crossover); *fluff,* an often light story that usually seeks to make a tender emotional impact rather than put forward a plot; *PWP,* which gets spelled out either as "porn without plot" or "plot? what plot?"; and various forms of sexually explicit stories that revolve around *kink,* such as *BDSM* (bondage and discipline, dominance and submission, and sadomasochism). Some subgenres trouble readers and are presented with clear warnings so that readers will not be unpleasantly surprised or perhaps *squicked* (grossed out).

Many authors write their fandom's *OTP,* or "one true pairing," exclusively — that is, they have such an investment in the romantic relationship of that particular pairing that they will write and read to the exclusion of all other pairings. Some authors deliberately write *badfic,* or bad fiction, which is often parodic; such badfics may play with the well-known *Mary Sue/Marty Stu* story, in which an *original character,* or OC, all too often an avatar of the author herself, is presented as the beautiful, smart heroine who saves the day and then gets the guy, all to the virtual exclusion of the canonical characters, who generally have very little do with Mary Sue on the case. Of course, these genres are not exclusive: one could write a crossover AU BDSM PWP, for instance.

In addition to terms that are descriptive of fiction, fans use a variety of terms to describe themselves. There's the *Big Name Fan,* or BNF, a fan with a large following; the term may sometimes be pejorative, but regardless, BNFs are usually far too modest to claim such status themselves, allowing others to categorize them. BNFs are surrounded by worshipping *fangirls,* although this term is also used in a nonpejorative sense for fans of the media source. *Fangirl* has also become a verb, as when one *fangirls* another writer or an actor, perhaps by *squeeing* (a squeal of uncontained appreciation or excitement). There are *newbies,* who are new to the fandom but eager to learn the ropes; this term may be pejorative, depending on the fandom. *Lurkers* watch the fannish activity but rarely, if ever, interact with other fans. *Listmoms* or *list owners* own online communities and maintain control over what can be posted. They set rules and guidelines, thus setting the tone for the community and outlining appropriate action. *Vidders* create fan video artworks, short videos in which scenes from the canon source are set against a particular musical piece carefully chosen for its thematic meaning. These *vids* use selection and juxtaposition to highlight particular moments in the source text to tell a story that is or is not present in the text or to analyze a particular character, often playing with visual aesthetics. Whereas formerly vidders would create *songvids* by using their VCRs to splice together scenes, now *vids* are more sophisticated, with vidders using complex authoring software to manipulate electronic files.

The advent of LiveJournal.com and other *blog* (Web log) spaces—an important force in fandom and in the construction of fandom communities—has led to a vocabulary unique to this space. Most terms revolve around descriptions of aspects of the blogging software, which permits the user to create diary-like dated entries that others may then comment on. Central to LJ is the *friends list,* also known as the *flist.* The user defines her flist, generally comprising people with similar interests, and this, in turn, allows her to view all her flist's recent posts. Moreover, *friending* also allows the *user* to limit her posts to that particular group of people by *flocking (friendslocking)* her post; as such, LJ creates a space that hovers at the border of public and private. A central function for fannish interaction is LJ *communities,* where people with similar interests can join to post on the community's topic. Fan communities fulfill a variety of functions, from simple news gathering to in-depth discussions. Many exist as de facto fic archives, share images or other media, or allow discussion about the shows, actors, or related fannish topics; some host *RPGs* (role-playing games); and others simply gather links to interesting stories or fannish discussions, called *meta.* Also central to LJ is the *icon,* an image chosen to represent oneself. Unlike other LJ users, fans rarely use their own images. Instead, they choose actors or scenes that comment on the show or fannish debates. In fact, icon making has become a new form of textual poaching, with its own set of aesthetic sensibility, fannish rules, and network.

In addition to the terms outlined above, regular online and e-mail abbreviations and emoticons are also used: *LOL* for "laugh out loud," smileys to indicate emotion, and **g** or ::snuggle:: to indicate performative action. This use of acronyms and cryptic terms deliberately excludes those unaware of their meaning. Part of the task of a newbie is to sort through the unfamiliar terms and come to an understanding of their meaning. The exclusionary nature of the discourse enculturates the newbie and cements the online community.

Fan Communities Move Online

We focus primarily on online fandom in order to supplement earlier discussions of media fandom that mostly addressed zine culture. After all, technological tools affect not only dissemination and reception, but also production, interaction, and even demographics. The history of fan fiction makes clear that technology is complicit in the generation of fan texts. Perhaps the most important technological advance, the one with the farthest-reaching implications, is the advent of the Internet. The transition of fandom to the Internet occurred during the early 1990s. Before then, fandom was a face-to-face proposition: fan clubs formed, and fans wrote newsletters, zines, and APAs ("amateur press association" add-on circuit newsletters) and got together at conventions. This meant that fandom was transmitted from person to person through enculturation. Fan artifacts were physical, and geographical boundaries were often an issue. The movement online has changed all this. Fans may write and post fan fiction, for example, without even knowing what it is or knowing that there are forums to do this in, and such fans naturally have no idea that they are part of a wider community. In turn, fans can remain *lurkers* who consume fannish artifacts without interacting with other fans. For those who find an online fannish space in which to interact with others, rules that seemed important in the old-model enculturation stage—for instance, the admonition to never, ever write slash based on real people rather than characters (known as *real person slash*, or *RPS*)—have lost their meaning. Although hard-copy zines are still being created and sold, most fan fiction is made available on the Web for free. Fan texts are now overwhelmingly electronic, and many are transient. Moreover, demographics have shifted: ever-younger fans who previously would not have had access to the fannish culture except through their parents can now enter the fan space effortlessly; financial resources have become less of a concern because access to a computer is the only prerequisite; and national boundaries and time zones have ceased to limit fannish interaction.

Early online fandom occurred via first GEnie, which permitted electronic correspondence, and then via Usenet, an electronic discussion board to which one subscribed (for example, rec.arts.startrek). As new content-delivery technology became available, fans adopted it: ListServ technology efficiently delivers messages from a central server to individual people via e-mail. The content of the posts to Usenet and boards has tended to focus on a particular topic, such as a particular TV show. If the topic is fan fiction, then fiction and comments to that piece of fiction may be posted for everyone to read, in addition to general chatter related to the program. Related to lists are bulletin boards, fixed Web sites that focus on a large general topic (say, a TV show) that is in turn divided into smaller, related topics (episode discussion, character analysis, fan fiction, news, and actors). Individual users log in and post comments in the appropriate forum, and others comment on the comments.

In the early '00s, fandom expanded into the blogsphere, and its widespread and enthusiastic adoption has had interesting consequences for the fan-created space. Whereas Usenet, ListServs, newsgroups, and bulletin boards all focus on a particular fan topic — a television program, for example — people who blog are just that: people (who are fans) who blog. As a result, individual journals become a mix of fannish and other topics about that fandom, thus including not only fiction, fan art, and commentary on the source text, but also real-life *(RL)* rants, political discussion, and non-fannish musings. This, along with the threading, hypertextual nature of the blogsphere, where it's easy to click to another page, replaces targeted content delivery with interpersonal interaction. In some ways, the blogsphere has provided what other delivery systems could not: a return to the sense of interaction with a person with a variety of interests, only one of which happens to be fandom. In that, it resembles the kind of more personal and less topic-driven interaction fans enjoyed before the advent of the Internet. At the same time, however, online-constructed identities allow users to shield their names and other features, thus constructing a level of remove that is fundamentally different from pre–Internet fannish interactions.

LiveJournal.com has its own cultural idiosyncrasies that have affected and been affected by fannish discourses. This dialogue has been enabled by the nature of the software that powers LJ itself: it is free, it is available to anyone with a computer and a Web browser, and, perhaps most importantly, it is simple to use. LJ has created a new culture of visibility, where much fannish interaction previously restricted to mailing lists becomes public. As such, it has allowed easier entry into fandom at a time when the numbers of new fans are ever increasing — the result, perhaps, of fandom's pervasive presence online, which, by its mere existence, invites others in. The constant intrusion of personal information between fannish discussions and fiction presents a different mode of interaction in which a writer's personal impression may influence the way we read her fiction and vice versa. One benefit of this is that the mix of fiction and other material allows fans who are not creative writers to interact more fully. Fans whose central fannish function is to post fan fiction reviews or *rec lists* (recommendations of noteworthy fan fiction, with links) or to produce meta may be friended for these contributions to fandom.

More importantly, however, LJ has splintered fandom into nearly innumerable factions. Certainly there is fragmentation in ListServs and mailing lists, which spawned not only general fic-related lists and general actor-related lists, but also pairing- or character-specific lists. To keep up to date in a fandom, one might have to subscribe to several lists. This fragmentation has continued apace on LJ, in part because it is both free and easy to start up such a list. Now even a brand-new show in its first season may easily have ten to fifteen fiction communities devoted to it, some of which may be set up before the show even airs. As a result, it is easier to avoid stories, styles, or pairings that one does not like, but it is harder to get a comprehensive sense of a fandom and harder still to build a truly inclusive sense of community. In addition, because LJ's technology permits posts to be filtered by the user to a carefully targeted audience, content is further constrained. Fans counter such segregation with tools like rec journals, announcement communities, and newsletters, all of which allow LJ users to monitor interesting posts from journals not on their flist. This customization makes LJ a convenient — although not necessarily the best — tool for fannish interaction. The nature of LJ's software makes it easy to invite people in, but it also makes it easy to shut them out.

Some fans like the individualized discourse that allows for multifannish interaction and more personal conversation; others dislike it for those very reasons. Most agree that the signal-to-noise ratio is higher with blogs like LJ than with lists and that it is more difficult to keep up sustained discussions. The software permits instantaneous deletion of individual entries or of entire blogs and leaves no archival traces. Also, fans disagree about whether they like or dislike the fact that LJ is much more visually intensive; the software permits customization of pages with images and icons, and some fan pages are so densely customized that they are virtually unreadable or take a long time to load. Likewise, LJ has affected the types of writing produced and how such writings are presented. Many have bemoaned the increase of short pieces, *drabbles* (fics exactly one hundred words long) in particular. Little fic snippets often are written in lieu of actual comments, as in comment porn, for example, where an argument may be phrased fictionally or the writer may simply offer a whimsical fictional gift. This has changed the way readers and writers interact. Much of the beta process, in which the beta reader offers editorial help, has remained the same. But after the fic is posted, the reader/writer interaction has changed: often the writer will post the story or a link to it in her LJ, which allows readers to offer feedback directly in the comments and which usefully archives all comments to a fic in a single place. Many writers have noted that the amount of feedback has increased, yet it has become less detailed and critical. It is easy to hit the comment button and type a one-liner, but the public nature of LJ comments makes it hard for many to offer serious criticism.

Although it's tempting to provide a continuum (in-person fandom to GEnie to Usenet to ListServs to bulletin boards to blogs), this continuum is false. Usenet, ListServs, bulletin boards, and blogs are all still currently in use, and all have thriving fan communities. Also, of course, fans still get together in person in big groups for conventions and in little groups for fun. For many fans, the online fan experience is a way to meet people with similar interests who may become friends and whom one may, or may not, ever meet in RL. Rather than inhabiting a space and then moving out when a new space comes open, the spaces are continuously inhabited, with fans moving in and out of the spaces as their inclination and technological limitations dictate. Fans without broadband Internet access, for example, may avoid graphics-heavy blogs because of bandwidth constraints. They may prefer a community where they can go online just long enough to download content to their computers. Longtime fans may also continue with the Usenet groups because all their friends are there and not in the blogsphere.

Fans have migrated to new spaces as the new spaces have become available, and this is in part the result of fans' use of tools. For people who edit, print, and sell fanzines, knowledge of how to run a ditto machine has given way to knowledge of how to use desktop publishing programs with output generated by a professional printer. Similarly, as new tools have become available, fans have co-opted them and bent them to creative fannish uses. The artifacts that are most associated with fandom, zines and vids, have themselves changed: hard-copy zines are still being produced and sold, but so are online, subscription-only zines, CDs, or .pdf files. Online fan fiction archives provide megabytes of content for free, all carefully indexed and uploaded by volunteers. VCR tapes of fan vids have given way to sophisticated, perfectly synched, high-quality electronic files. Fannishly informational Web sites have been supplemented with the hyperlink intertextuality of *wikis*, a medium perfectly suited to providing factual, cross-referenced data. And whereas before a fan was content to choose a fan name to be known under or to publish fan fiction under, now she must not only choose her name, but also illustrate it with icons, the creation of which requires the acquisition of a whole new skill set, not to mention appropriate graphics software.

The driving force behind the movement online has, of course, been the Internet's far more widespread availability, but the creation of free, easy-to-use online tools that permit easy authoring of beautiful and accessible sites with little technical expertise cannot be emphasized enough. Yet despite the proliferation of online fan activity, the movement of fandom from a physical space to a virtual one has not adequately been addressed in the academic literature. Most of the academic research in fan studies began in the late 1980s and early 1990s, before the movement online, and subsequent research has built on this base. We aim to fill this gap. To that end, we now turn to a review of the literature in the field of fan studies so that we can build on it and explain how this volume fits within and complements the literature.

Fan Fiction and Fan Studies

The history of fan fiction studies, for the most part, is a history of attempting to understand the underlying motivations of why (mostly) women write fan fiction and, in particular, slash. As a result, *m/m* (male/male) slash fiction has received disproportionate treatment in both academic and mainstream journalistic representations. The earliest academic work suggests two possible explanations. Both texts are situated in the feminist pornography debates of the 1980s and clearly take differing stances. Joanna Russ's "Pornography by Women, for Women, with Love" (1985) reads fan fiction's explicit aspects as a feminist pornography; Patricia Frazer Lamb and Diane Veith's "Romantic Myth, Transcendence, and *Star Trek* Zines" (1986), conversely, suggests that even explicit sexual content must be metaphorically understood as a way for women to write their desires for equal relationships between equal partners. They argue that slash can depict a love between equals that does not fall prey to notions of hierarchical gender roles and that explores both the male and female sides of the characters. In fact, they suggest that the homosexual relationship actually signals a displaced idealized heterosexual one that valorizes inner compatibility, true love, and deep friendship over sexual object choices.

Russ and Lamb and Veith concur that slash is a liberatory practice for the women writing it and that such female sexual fantasies must be distinguished from classic "male" porn because of the emphasis on character, commitment, and nurture and because of the awareness that women may want different things in their sexual fantasies than either romance or porn can provide. April Selley (1987) offers more source text–based analysis to suggest what it is about the Kirk/Spock dynamic in particular that makes it appealing to slash authors. Drawing from Leslie Fiedler's 1960 study of the homoerotic, racialized tension in many American novels, she argues that Kirk and Spock's relationship follows a similar pattern, so that slash readings become extrapolations of this obvious textual tension.

The early 1990s established the central readings and theoretical approaches to fan fiction with three studies that remain tremendously influential. The most important is Henry Jenkins's *Textual Poachers* (1992b), which comprehensively theorizes the field, drawing from audience studies with a particular emphasis on popular culture and television and including not only fan fiction and fannish interpretive practices, but also songvids and filking. Theoretically, Jenkins does not fully embrace Stuart Hall's notion of "Encoding and Decoding" (1980), with its incorporation/resistance paradigm, instead choosing to use Michel De Certeau's (1984) more ambiguous notion of "poaching": "Hall's model, at least as it has been applied, suggests that popular meanings are fixed and classifiable, while de Certeau's 'poaching' model emphasizes the process of making meaning and the fluidity of popular interpretation" (34). Of course, given the scope and purpose of *Textual Poachers,* it is difficult to not place the fan in a position of subversiveness and resistance to the seemingly all-encompassing force of commercial media. Nevertheless, Jenkins tries to remain careful of differentiating and acknowledging the complexity of any given fan's subject positions, as well as the diversity and complexity of any fan community as a whole. In so doing, he is often more careful than were many of the scholars who used his work in the years to come.

Methodologically, Jenkins clearly situates himself as a fan who writes "*both* as an academic (who has access to certain theories of popular culture, certain bodies of critical and ethnographic literature) and as a fan (who has access to the particular knowledge and traditions of that community)" (1992b, 5). In fact, he addresses the danger of overidentification but suggests that any position creates dangers and limitations of understanding and insight. He also addresses the responsibilities to the community itself, a concern that has been crucial to us in the creation of this collection: "Writing as a fan means ... that I feel a high degree of responsibility and accountability to the groups being discussed here" (7). There is little we wish to add to these points except to emphasize that rather than choosing fans as collaborators, we *are* the fans—we are not in "constant movement" (5) between these identities; rather, they are inseparable from us.

In contradistinction to Jenkins's clear identification and immersion in fan culture is Camille Bacon-Smith's *Enterprising Women* (1992), in which she consciously constructs herself as an outside observer. Her methodological self-positioning intends to assure her reader that she is removed from her object of study and is thus not unduly invested in it, a move that trades fan approval for the academic value of objectivity. She uses ethnography, an anthropological approach, to emphasize the community of women and their interaction and ties in a way few other scholars had done or would do for a long time to come. The central problem with her study, from both the fannish and the academic position, is her overly privileged positioning of the hurt/comfort genre, which she reads as the emotional heart and secret of fandom. Perhaps because she draws from a limited set of fandoms and stories, Bacon-Smith fails to accurately depict the diversity of fandom as she tries to impose universal interpretive models; indeed, it seems clear that her ethnographic approach worked all too well as she embedded herself into a very particular fannish world. Her emphasis on community and the friendship between the female fans is powerful, even if her self-chosen outsider status prohibits her from fully understanding the bonds she observes.

The third important text, published in 1992, is Constance Penley's "Feminism, Psychoanalysis, and the Study of Popular Culture," later expanded in *NASA/Trek* (1998). Penley's essay uses a psychoanalytic approach to complicate notions of identification. She argues that, especially for heterosexual readers, slash allows female readers to have and be either and both of the characters. This identification with the characters is supplemented by an identification with the scene and fannish universe in its entirety, thus affording the reader multiple entry points and modes of identification. Although she does not draw any real conclusions, Penley raises questions about the sexual orientation of slashers and about class issues. She draws attention to her ambiguous situation as both participant and observer and as both fan and academic, although in this essay she refuses to occupy a particular subject position, as Bacon-Smith does.

These three texts set the stage for more than a decade of fan fiction studies that mostly used their various approaches — media studies, anthropology, and psychoanalysis — to apply their theories to particular texts or fandoms. These critics' source texts were mostly limited to the fandoms they engaged in personally or through their fan networks and were mostly restricted to pre–Internet culture. In fact, neither Bacon-Smith's nor Jenkins's full-length book treatment on fan fiction addresses Internet fan culture much, and even Penley's later *NASA/Trek* describes a fan culture that is "enthusiastic yet thoughtfully cautious about the new Internet culture" (1998, 116).

The year 1992 also saw the publication of the most centrally important collection of fan studies itself, which addresses the various ways fans engage with the source material, the psychology of their interaction, and the studies of the communities they create. Lisa Lewis's edited volume *The Adoring Audience* (1992) includes central essays on fans and fan culture alike. One essay in this volume, "Fandom as Pathology," by Joli Jenson, analyzes traditional (academic and popular) representations of fans and relates these predominantly negative portrayals to a critique of modernity. As such, a cultural unease with modern life gets projected onto fandom that functions as a symptom for modernity's failures. John Fiske's essay discusses the "Cultural Economy of Fandom" and the way fans "invest and accumulate capital" (30–31) within this economy. He defines a model of cultural capital within fan culture as well as a materialist model in the interaction between fans and the culture industries. Lawrence Grossberg's essay "Is There a Fan in the House?" focuses on what he terms the "affective sensibility of fandom" to determine how and why fans function (50). He emphasizes the active status of audiences and how pleasure and affect must be seen as crucial, not only in determining a group's relationship to popular culture but also in constructing individual fan identities. All three essays delineate various forms of theoretical approaches to fan studies that clearly tie in with cultural studies, in particular media and audience studies, and situate fan studies as one aspect of a larger disciplinary cultural phenomenon.

Over the next decade or so, most essays in fan fiction studies focused on fanfic as an interpretive gesture, thus using fan fiction to gain further insight into a particular source text. At the same time, of course, the issues raised by previous scholars regarding the particular appeals of slash, the sexual dynamics explored, and its identificatory practices were usually addressed in passing. Examples of such close readings of particular source texts include Christine Boese (1998) and Jeannie Hamming (2001) for *Xena: Warrior Princess,* Atara Stein (1998) for *Star Trek: The Next Generation,* Mirna Cicione (1998) for *The Professionals,* Christine Scodari and Jenna L. Felder (2000) and Robin Silvergleid (2003) for *X-Files,* Kurt Lancaster (2001) for *Babylon 5,* Esther Saxey (2001) and Kristina Busse (2002) for *Buffy the Vampire Slayer,* Will Brooker (2002) for *Star Wars,* Victoria Somogyi (2002) for *Star Trek: Voyager,* Sharon Cumberland (2002) for Banderas fan sites, Christine Scodari (2003) for *Farscape* and *Stargate SG-1,* Rachel Shave (2004) for *Harry Potter,* and Anna Smol (2004) for *Lord of the Rings.*[3] Most of these essays clearly focused on the source text and often used particular fan stories in an exemplary fashion. Many reiterated the concept of poaching, the subversiveness of women writing erotic fiction against the mainstream media, and the contentious relationship of slash to romance fiction.

Likewise, fields related to media fiction studies have done their own work that is influential to fandom and fan fiction studies, such as Nancy Baym's defining study of soap opera fans, *Tune In, Log On* (2000); John Tulloch's and Henry Jenkins's *Science Fiction Audiences* (1995); and Camille Bacon-Smith's *Science Fiction Culture* (2000). At the same time, a variety of books and essay collections have been published that focus on a particular source text and that usually address fans' relationship to specific TV series. Examples of this include David Lavery's *Deny All Knowledge: Read-*

ing the "X-Files" (1996), Roz Kaveney's *Reading the Vampire Slayer* (2001), David Lavery and Rhonda Wilcox's *Fighting the Forces: What's at Stake in "Buffy the Vampire Slayer"* (2002), and Rhiannon Bury's *Cyberspaces of Their Own: Female Fandoms Online* (2005).

Meanwhile, some fanfic scholars tried to use different paradigms and methodologies to address the widening field of fan fiction. Catherine Salmon and Don Symons's *Warrior Lovers* (2001), for example, uses human evolutionary biology to argue that slash is simply another version of women's erotic fiction. They contend that there exist differences between male and female mating psychology; as a result, women want nurture and monogamy rather than sex, so that romance novels, rather than pornography, fulfill women's erotic needs. Women's romance is characterized by a desire to "form a permanent monogamous union," and they argue that slash fulfills these exact needs. The main reason why women read slash rather than romance, according to Salmon and Symons, is that it presents both protagonists as "co-warriors" (82, 89), an idea that grows out of Lamb and Veith's (1986) contention that slash offers a love between equals.

In "'Normal female interest in men bonking': Selections from the *Terra Nostra Underground* and *Strange Bedfellows*" (1998), Shoshanna Green, Cynthia Jenkins, and Henry Jenkins create an interesting cowriting experiment that relies heavily on fan quotes and tries to reproduce the discussions and debates that occur within the community. In so doing, they try to avoid some of the more typical errors in academic fan studies, namely, the universalizing interpretations, homogenizing of fannish discourses, and the lack of contextualization. By letting fans speak for themselves, the essay presents fandom as a contradictory and contentious space where intelligent women can and do think about their practices as well as fandom's inherent problems, such as misogyny and homophobia, and find a variety of answers or explanations. Likewise, Sheenagh Pugh's *The Democratic Genre* (2005) draws heavily on fan writers and their thoughts about writing in favor of academic treatments. She foregrounds the similarities between fan fiction and other literary texts in order to focus on the texts themselves, often citing extensively and letting the fans and fan texts speak for themselves.

Even more fan centered are two more recent essays in which fans themselves analyze their own writing practices and use their experiences and texts to draw tentative conclusions: Kylie Lee (2003) and Susanne Jung (2004). Kylie Lee's text, a personal essay, is introductory in nature, but it stands out as a result of its informal, conversational style. It clearly situates the author as a fan writer (even in choosing to use her fannish pseudonym rather than her real name, with its academic credentials) and draws attention to the sexual aspects of fan fiction, not only by theoretically stating it but by providing extensive examples. In fact, the entire essay is predicated on the personal and contingent: "I make no claim that my research has any kind of statistical or scientific rigor. Rather, the responses can serve as a snapshot of a particular moment in time of members of the slash community" (81). Her repeated emphasis on her own affective relation to slash is indicative of a move in fan studies to acknowledge and address the unanalyzable, unexplainable, and often unspeakable excess of pleasure that fans experience.

In contrast, Susanne Jung, in "Queering Popular Culture: Female Spectators and the Appeal of Writing Slash Fan Fiction" (2004), reads her own story as implicated in current gender politics and consciously traces her political impetus in writing it. She describes how in her story she intended to "depict a utopian society which had overcome our current straight/gay divide, a society beyond heterosexual norms" (¶7). Although Jung's essay is important in showing how fanfic writers are often very familiar with current gender and queer theories and quite consciously use this theoretical framework when creating their fiction, her own subject position remains untheorized throughout.

A central theoretical shift occurs with Sara Gwenllian Jones's "The Sex Lives of Cult Television Characters" (2002) and Roberta E. Pearson's "Kings of Infinite Space: Cult Television Characters and Narrative Possibilities" (2003). Both essays follow Nicholas Ambercrombie and Brian Longhurst's critique in *Audiences* (1998), in which the researchers suggest that the incorporation/resistance paradigm of audience responses to media should be replaced by a so-called spectacle/performance paradigm: "a more positive view of consumption, which is seen no longer as a more or less enforced product of a capitalist economy but as a set of choices made by consumers anxious to construct an identity. This new model of the consumer is isomorphic with the new model of the active audience" (32–33). In so doing, fan fiction and the discourses surrounding it become less of a uniform force of resistance and instead much more differentiated — in parts even compromised.

This more contentious and complex relationship between producers and audience is also at the heart of Henry Jenkins's interest in media convergence. Jenkins (1998, ¶6) defines media convergence as "the fact that the technological convergences being discussed in the information and entertainment industries, the bringing together of all existing media technologies within the same black box in our living room, actually build upon a complex series of cultural and social shifts which are redefining how we relate to media and popular culture." In his 2004 essay "The Cultural Logic of Media Convergence," Jenkins describes a variety of effects of convergence, including "revising audience measurement," "rethinking media aesthetic," "redefining intellectual property rights," and "renegotiating relations between consumers and producers" (39–40). In fact, the recent main-streaming of fan fiction, at times not only tolerated but also invited and endorsed by producers, is just one of the effects Jenkins is describing. Sim-ilarly, Simone Murray's "'Celebrating the Story the Way It Is'" (2004) describes the way producers engaged with the *Lord of the Rings* fans before releasing the movies in order to ensure its positive reception. The fact that these discourses are available (that producers can and do interact with fans) negates more simplistic one-directional models. Other essays that address the interaction between fans and media at large include Sharon Cumber-land's "Private Uses of Cyberspace: Women, Desire, and Fan Culture" (2000), Mia Consalvo's "Cyber-Slaying Media Fans" (2003), and Cathy Cupitt's "A Space for Sex" (2003).

Concurrently, the other central shift in fan studies is a move away from studying the community to studying the individual fan, in particular her underlying motivations and psychology. Veering from the earlier interest in media fandom as a particular case study and creative community in its own right, several more prominent recent studies have appeared that widen the field of research and the definition of *fan*. In so doing, the research foregrounds the relationship of one particular fan to the object of her fan-nish affection. Matt Hills, in particular, in his essay "Media Fandom, Neo-religiosity, and Cult(ural) Studies" (2000) and the more comprehensive *Fan Cultures* (2002), has focused on these concerns. Cornel Sandvoss's *Fans: The Mirror of Consumption* (2005) likewise focuses on the specific emotional investment of the individual fan and the relationship between a fan's invest-ment in her fannish objects of desire and her psychological and cultural identity construction. Sandvoss's study widens the concept of fandom to include any "regular, emotionally involved consumption of a given popu-lar narrative or text" (8). Although such an approach allows the study of varying degrees and forms of fannish behavior, the specific particularities of the fannish community tend to be sidestepped. Because we are more con-cerned with the collective nature of fandom, its internal communications, and the relationship between fans that arises out of a joint interest in a par-ticular text, the psychology of the individual fan is not the focus of this book, even though many of the essays do address the fan as individual.

Finally, fans themselves have continued to produced a corpus of liter-ature that is often more insightful and current than much academic work. the Fanfic Symposium (http://www.trickster.org/symposium, accessed June 1, 2006), for example, hosts a collection of essays, and *Whoosh* (http://www. whoosh.org, accessed June 1, 2006) is a fandom-specific site with a similar host of writers. Moreover, every day, LiveJournal.com produces meta, including theoretical essays discussing specific shows and episodes, fan fiction, and fan writing, culture, and interaction. Although these are usually written in a nonacademic style, many are clearly influenced by literary theory, such as gender and queer studies, easily citing and referencing Sedgwick (1985), Butler (1990), Halberstam (1998), and Doty (2000), for example. As part of fandom, such essays reflect the community and its concerns far better than any outside observer ever could.

Autoethnography

With all of this in mind, and following Green, Jenkins, and Jenkins (1998), this collection merges fan and academic discourses, but it does so not by placing fans' quotes and voices next to our analyses, but rather by gathering together fans who are already academics and academics who are already fans. The trend in academic discourse to the personal and the realization that no subject position is completely outside the field of study, as well as the work that has gone before of well-known and well-regarded scholar-fans such as Jenkins, have permitted us to take a subject position that melds the fan and the academic without implying a lack of insight or intellectual rigor. We think that being embedded in a community — which we nevertheless study critically — can provide a useful approach, and a sketch of our subject position is necessary to situate this text among those we have just listed.

Hills (2002) defines *autoethnography* as an exercise in which "the tastes, values, attachments, and investments of the fan and the academic-fan are placed under the microscope of cultural analysis" (72) and suggests it as a useful tool to situate writers in their scholarly and fannish contexts. However, whereas Hills regards this as a "voluntary self-estrangement" (72), we think of it as more, rather than less, of an investment and as an awareness of our subject positions that creates a stronger, not a weaker, affect. We would like to put forth this book as a way in which the collective sum of the essays may permit an ephemeral, provisional, and contingent autoethnography. We do not try to make large-scale universal claims, nor can we provide a self-reflexive autoethnographic study, as Hills does, because this book is a collection of essays by different people and not a single-authored text that can make a claim about the self while it makes an argument. By remaining fan-scholars at the same time that we become scholar-fans,[4] we hope to shift the concerns from a dichotomy of academic and fannish identity to subject positions that are multiple and permit us to treat the academic and fannish parts as equally important. Our identities are neither separate nor separable. We rarely speak as fan or scholar; we rarely differentiate between an academic and fannish audience, except perhaps in formality of tone.

We return again to the theme of this introduction: the act of performing fandom parallels the act of performing academia. Both rely on dialogue, community, and intertextuality. All of us are academics who have spent years training in the particular discourses established by our disciplines. All of us have learned modes of interaction and mediation and specific forms of analysis in fandom. We'll continue to exist on the intersection of the two, trying not to aca-colonize fandom or lose our academic allegiance through our fannish one. But we also want to profit from this intersection and to use our academic and fannish tools and insights to give a more complex and multifaceted image of fandom and its communities. In fact, we contend that our self-definition as participants and observers does not hinder us from seeing but rather helps us to see a more comprehensive picture of fandom.

Many of us have tested our pronouncements against the responses of the community, which is varied and which debates many of the issues we address among ourselves; we thus hope that the ideas put forth in these essays approach the essence of what it means to be a part of the fan fiction community. Through this interaction, we simultaneously draw from and give back to the community. This collection speaks with a multiplicity of voices through which we attempt to recreate — albeit in a different venue — the very thing fandom itself does. None of our ideas, whether academic or fannish, is ever ours alone, and in choosing to offer a collection of fannish ideas rather than a singly authored volume, we hope to acknowledge our depth to the community at the same time that we present, if only metonymically, the complexity of thoughts that fandom itself generates.

This volume, then, presents a snapshot of fannish and academic interests at this point in time within the particular communities we inhabit. The essays speak to and with one another and represent a variety of methodologies, approaches, styles, and subject positions. If anything can begin to mirror the vitality, innovativeness, personal affect, and even contentiousness of fandom, it is their collective whole.

Overview of the Volume

PART I: DIFFERENT APPROACHES: FAN FICTION IN CONTEXT

One of the difficulties in defining fan fiction is the formulation of boundaries. Are media tie-in novels fan fiction? Is any derivative literature?

What about commercial fiction that is really fan fiction with the serial numbers filed off? Most definitions emphasize the amateur aspect, the community that surrounds the production, dissemination, and consumption of fan fiction. This aspect places fan production in a specific postmodern, post-capitalist moment with easy access to the source text — usually TV programs — and reproductive tools. As such, fan fiction is defined as much by its context as its content; its specificity is as much a function of its engagement with the source text as the way stories are disseminated and the communities that surround these fannish engagements. Part I of the volume analyzes these questions.

Abigail Derecho's "Archontic Literature: A Definition, a History, and Several Theories of Fan Fiction" expands the definition of fan fiction to include any writing she calls *archontic*. Her definition emphasizes the intertextuality and the repeated engagement with a source text in order to create an ever-expanding, collectively created archive. Unlike Jenkins, who considers any community storytelling as falling within the purview of fan fiction, Derecho clearly delimits fan fiction as a concept by placing it in relation to modern concepts of authorship, technologies of book production, and cultural availability of leisure time. She posits fan fiction as a practice that offers marginalized groups, especially women, a tool for social criticism in its opposition of hierarchical notions of ownership.

Catherine Driscoll's "One True Pairing: The Romance of Pornography and the Pornography of Romance" similarly returns to the eighteenth century to trace fan fiction's literary sources. Driscoll is less interested in fan fiction's derivative aspect. Rather, she focuses on its contentious generic fields of pornography and romance. By looking at fan fiction as indebted to both, yet unlike either, Driscoll contextualizes fan fiction in respect to both fields as she illuminates the generic definitions of both pornography and romance, as well as their traditional gendering, arguing that in fan fiction, the two genres are intimately connected, with each genre illuminating and altering the other.

Elizabeth Woledge, by looking at the generic conventions of slash in "Intimatopia: Genre Intersections Between Slash and the Mainstream," argues that rather than defining the field in terms of its amateur or professional status, a focus on narrative themes and styles indicates similarities that transcend the generic boundaries often used to identify slash. Woledge focuses on stories that thematically address homoerotic intimacy to define the concept of the *intimatopic* within and outside of fan fiction. Like Driscoll's essay, which refuses to position subversive potential in porn alone, Woledge argues that it is explicit intimacy rather than pornographic depictions that challenge the more traditional representations of interpersonal relationships. She thus emphasizes the similarities and ties between slash and mainstream forms of homoerotic writings outside the fan fiction community; as a result, she concludes that any definition of fan fiction must remain aware of the diverse generic possibilities within and the similarities outside of fan fiction.

The notions of context that are the focus of this section of the volume tacitly rely on the community that creates meaning. Derecho's notion of fan fiction as collectively created archive, with a canon that by its very nature can never be complete, calls into question any sense of individual ownership. Similarly, Driscoll, by refusing to pigeonhole fan fiction in either the realm of porn or that of romance (as so much previous research has done), recontextualizes the genre by refusing to fix the way it is situated or the way it is read by the community. Woledge applies methods of interpretation that transcend notions of an acceptability of genre, placing fan fiction within a community of readers who use the same strategies to read fan fiction as they use to read professionally published fiction. Working against community-created definitions, all three essays succeed in illuminating aspects of fan fiction by looking for similarities and differences with writings that must be excluded yet can help us understand the generic, social, and economic qualities that create the field of fan fiction.

PART II: CHARACTERS, STYLE, TEXT:
FAN FICTION AS LITERATURE

Even though close textual analysis has always been part of academic discussions of fan fiction, these readings often serve to establish larger cultural understandings of fans and fan culture rather than focusing on fan fiction as an object of study in its own right. The essays that comprise Part II highlight the literary aspects of fannish writings by concentrating on the texts themselves and using different modes of textual analysis.

Mafalda Stasi's essay, "The Toy Soldiers from Leeds: The Slash Palimpsest," foregrounds the intertextual aspect of fan fiction by using the model of the *palimpsest*. By reading slash through the lens of textual analysis, Stasi foregrounds how no story can ever fully have meaning on its own but must be read in conjunction with the source text's canon and the community at large. As such, individual authorship and the notion of discrete texts is problematic. Instead, it is replaced by a sense of collective authorship within a community.

Deborah Kaplan moves from the intertextual to the intratextual by focusing on character portrayal in "Construction of Fan Fiction Character Through Narrative," in which she compares the portrayal of characters within fan fiction to the creation of original characters in original fiction. Although fan fiction clearly facilitates the representation of characters that are already constructed within the source text, Kaplan emphasizes the ways in which any characterization is a complex negotiation among fan writer, source text, and context (be they other stories, fannish discussions, or non–fan fiction cultural artifacts). Any character portrayal is therefore in part a conversation between readers and writers. Even though the source text offers the broad framework, it is the fans who make often one-dimensional characters multifaceted and complexly intriguing.

The final essay in this section connects the text to its specific writer, particularly the emotional, intellectual, and political investment of the author in the fan fiction she creates. Ika Willis uses her own fan fiction in "Keeping Promises to Queer Children: Making Space (for Mary Sue) at Hogwarts" to reassert the subversive potential of fan fiction — not in the sense of subverting commercial productions, but in a more personal, intimate sense. By foregrounding the relationship between the writer's identity and self-positioning and her identificatory entry points into the text, Willis challenges neat conflations along lines of gender and sexual orientation and questions the all-too-easy dismissal of so-called Mary Sues in fan and academic discourses alike.

Even as this section ranges from the interrelationship of fan texts in their entirety to the highly personal relationship between author and text, all the essays concentrate on the text as literary artifact as well as fannish document. Be it their stylistic and compositional intertextuality, their meaning for fannish interpretation, or the very personal significance of particular plot events or characters, textual analysis deserves as central a place in our analysis of fan fiction and fan culture as it holds within fandom itself — after all, as an interpretive exercise, every piece of fan fiction is, in its own way, an analytic engagement with the source text.

PART III: READERS AND WRITERS: FAN FICTION AND COMMUNITY

The interaction between readers and writers — the dynamics of community itself — is one of the central differences between professional literature and fan fiction, and the study of this reader-writer dynamic is the focus of Part III. Not only are readers and writers emotionally invested in different ways, but their interaction is also always clearly visible and central — from the creating and editing of fan fiction to its reception and review and to the discourses surrounding fannish productions.

Angelina I. Karpovich's "The Audience as Editor: The Role of Beta

Readers in Online Fan Fiction Communities" studies the interaction between writers and their betas. Karpovich compares the role of betas with that of commercial editors, finding the former to be unique and community building. She thus positions beta reading practices clearly within the many interactive aspects of fan fiction communities interested in improving the literary qualities and entertainment values of a given fan fiction while, importantly, creating bonds and allowing conversation between fans.

Like Willis's essay in the previous section, Eden Lackner, Barbara Lynn Lucas, and Robin Anne Reid's "Cunning Linguists: The Bisexual Erotics of *Words/Silence/Flesh*" is self-reflexive insofar as it traces the reception of one particular fan work as seen by its authors and one reader. The authors closely study the eroticized (and often sexualized) discourse in feedback and discussions in order to complicate simplistic notions of gender and sexual orientation. As a result, they succeed in complicating the dichotomy that reads slash as either subversive or misogynist as they show the fan work and its surrounding discourses to be fundamentally queer in all its multiplicity.

This notion of fandom as a queer female space is continued in Kristina Busse's "My Life Is a WIP on My LJ: Slashing the Slasher and the Reality of Celebrity and Internet Performances," in which she focuses on the fannish community itself and its interaction. Busse extends the thread of fandom as inherently queer by reading online interactions as performative and not dissimilar to the fan genre of real person slash. By studying the often-repeated accusation of fan fiction's inherent dismissal of actual gay lives in its fetishization of virtual queerness, she addresses the homosocial component of online female friendships and the highly performative nature of all social interaction.

The dense interaction between the community of readers and writers that Karpovich covers in her analysis of betas and that Lackner and others' essay epitomizes complements the affective nature of fandom and the fannish community itself that is so central to Busse's essay. The last two essays, in particular, address the relationship between the fannish community and the individual fan's identity construction, especially in terms of the erotics of reading and writing; they thus hearken back to Driscoll's concern with the often pornographic content of the stories, as well as Willis's discussion of the relationship between story and writer in terms of (sexual) identity.

PART IV: MEDIUM AND MESSAGE: FAN FICTION AND BEYOND

All three essays in the previous section work around notions of performativity in the textual production and reception of fan fiction. Part IV,

"Medium and Message: Fan Fiction and Beyond," acknowledges and theorizes this performative aspect of fandom. It expands the field of study by considering both fan texts and performativity. Although most of this collection has focused on storytelling through literary forms—the artifact we call *fan fiction*—other creative artistic forms resonate in between the essays. As we mentioned earlier, the use of new media and new technologies not only eases access, but also directly affects form and even content. Starting with Francesca Coppa's provocative claim that what fans are really doing is manipulating bodies in space, the concluding essays exemplify how new media finally allow fans to further embody their creations. They do so, however, by moving beyond the use of words only as they hint toward the way fannish manipulation of source materials can take shapes other than simple (often linear) narratives and other than words on a page.

Coppa's "Writing Bodies in Space: Media Fan Fiction as Theatrical Performance" starts with the deceptively simple proposition of conceiving of fan fiction not as literature but as drama. She shifts the central fan studies discourse into the realm of performance theory, studying not only the fans but also their texts. She thus reorients the discussion of fan fiction's seemingly more problematic aspects, such as its focus on bodies and its repetitiveness, as a central function of the field rather than an artistic failure. Coppa argues that fan fiction creates a performance: text gets embodied in front of an interactive audience that shares extratextual knowledge.

If all fan fiction is a dramatic performance, none is so more clearly narrativized than role-playing games, one of the focuses of Louisa Ellen Stein's "'This Dratted Thing': Fannish Storytelling Through New Media." Stein uses new media theory and genre theory to illuminate novel ways of storytelling in online role-playing games and the computer game *The Sims*. Stein foregrounds the ways media shape stories as they simultaneously limit the narratives they bring into being. She thus suggests that a focus on the form and actual technological framework is paramount in understanding narrative productions and their similarities to more traditional forms of storytelling.

The final essay of this collection expands our notion of fannish creations by moving beyond the specific community of media fandom to look at an art form that derives from a different heritage yet uses similar poaching tendencies. Whereas the rest of the contributors are firmly steeped in what we have called *media fan culture*, the largely female, heavily text-oriented fan engagement, Robert Jones's "From Shooting Monsters to Shooting Movies: Machinima and the Transformative Play of Video Game Fan Culture" looks at the new art form of *machinima* in the light of fan theory that has developed around more female fannish cultures. Reading these (largely male) fan-created manipulations of video game images as transformative play, Jones connects this new art form to both game design theory and theories of media fandom, thus bridging those clearly gendered fields and indicating that new forms of fannish creations and producer/consumer relationships require us to draw from various fields to establish similarities and differences.

Whereas the media fan fiction community has developed its own tradition of visual filmic media with vidding, the setting of film clips to music, machinima must be traced to the different fannish heritage of gaming culture; nevertheless, its inclusion acknowledges the widening field of fannish creativity in terms of both the new media technologies and the recent mixing and merging of fandoms: fans with different genealogies, vocabularies, and values are beginning to engage with and influence one another. This cross-fertilization we see between media and other fandoms challenges some of the traditional notions of fans' identities, psychologies, and goals. As fannish engagements become ever more mainstream and as different forms of fans share similar spaces and engage in similar activities of understanding and cherishing their object of affection as they manipulate and alter it to create new works of art, the rigorous divisions that fan studies could draw a decade or two ago are more difficult to maintain.

Moreover, we end with a focus on new technologies because they continually interact with and alter the dynamic of the community itself: the software that permits the blog space is co-opted by fandom and used to generate new texts in new ways, and this in turn results in an expansion of fannish behavior, as Busse's essay in Part III exemplifies. Stein's description of the use of *The Sims* and Jones's description of the use of machinima show us that fans will willingly adopt tools to create new kinds of artwork, and we have no doubt that as new technology becomes available, fans will bend it to their own ends — repurposing it and playing with it — in ways perhaps never conceived of by the creator of the technology. We began with Barthes's notions of entering, interpreting, and expanding the text. We conclude with another Barthesian concept crucial to any understanding of fan culture: that of pleasure and play (1977). Although fandom continues to change with each new text added to the fantext (as Derecho's essay in Part I shows us and whose effects Stasi explores in Part II) and as new creative art forms join fan fiction as fannish artifacts, the community that interprets it remains just that: a community, one that continually shifts its boundaries and the roles assigned to reader, writer, and audience to permit, and even invite, play.

Notes

1. Full information on works cited here may be found in "Fan Fiction: A Bibliography of Critical Works," which follows this introduction.

2. For an example of the juxtaposition of contrary viewpoints, see Green et al. (1998); for a theoretical analysis of the contradictory positions held not only within fandom, but also within a given fan, see Stein (2005).

3. We have consciously left out academic studies of Japanese-centered media fiction, such as Sabucco (2000, 2003), McLelland (2000a, 2000b, 2001), and Chandler-Olcott and Mahar (2003), because we think that the historical context and cultural background of anime makes it different enough to not fall under the rubrics we outline here. In addition, the more ambiguous legal status of anime and manga separates them from the fiction, art, film, and vids of most western-based fan-created texts.

4. In his study of academics and fandom, Matt Hills (2002) distinguishes between the *academic-fan,* who co-opts fan cultures into his or her academic project, and the *fan-academic,* who is primarily a fan using academic strategies.

Fan Fiction: A Bibliography of Critical Works

Abbott, Stacey, ed. 2005. *Reading "Angel": The TV spin-off with a soul*. London: I. B. Tauris.

Abercrombie, Nicholas, and Brian Longhurst. 1998. *Audiences: A sociological theory of performance and imagination*. London: Sage.

Aden, Roger C. 1999. *Popular stories and promised lands: Fan cultures and symbolic pilgrimages*. Tuscaloosa: Univ. of Alabama Press.

Bacon-Smith, Camille. 1992. *Enterprising women: Television fandom and the creation of popular myth*. Philadelphia: Univ. of Pennsylvania Press.

_____. 2000. *Science fiction culture*. Philadelphia: Univ. of Pennsylvania Press.

Bargh, John A., and Katelyn Y. A. McKenna. 2004. The Internet and social life. *Annual Review of Psychology* 55:573–90.

Barthes, Roland. 1974. *S/Z*. Trans. Richard Miller. New York: Noonday Press.

_____. 1977. From work to text. In *Image-music-text*, trans. Stephen Heath, 155–64. New York: Hill and Wang.

Baym, Nancy K. 1993. Interpreting soap operas and creating community: Inside a computer-mediated fan culture. *Journal of Folklore Research* 30:143–76.

_____. 1998. Talking about soaps: Communicative practices in a computer-mediated fan culture. In *Theorizing fandom: Fans, subculture and identity*, ed. Cheryl Harris and Alison Alexander, 111–29. Cresskill, NJ: Hampton Press.

_____. 2000. *Tune in, log on: Soaps, fandom, and online community*. Thousand Oaks, CA: Sage.

Beirne, Rebecca. 2004. Queering the Slayer-text: Reading possibilities in *Buffy the Vampire Slayer*. *Refractory* 5. http://www.refractory.unimelb.edu.au/journalissues/vol5/beirne.html (accessed June 1, 2006).

Berg Nellis, Kelly Anne Colleen. 2002. Making sense of television: Interpretive community and *The X-Files* fan forum — An ethnographic study. PhD diss., Univ. of Missouri–Columbia.

Berry, Chris, Fran Martin, and Audrey Yue, eds. 2003. *Mobile cultures: New media in queer Asia*. Durham, NC: Duke Univ. Press.

Bick, Ilsa J. 1996. Boys in space: *Star Trek* latency and *The Never-Ending Story*. In *Enterprise zones: Critical responses to "Star Trek,"* ed. Taylor Harrison, Sarah Projansky, Kent A. Ono, and Elyce Rae Helford, 189–210. Boulder, CO: Westview Press.

Boese, Christine. 2003. The ballad of the Internet nutball: Chaining rhetorical visions from the margins of the margins to the mainstream in the Xenaverse. http://www.nutball.com (accessed June 1, 2006).

Braudy, Leo. 1982. Popular culture and personal time. *Yale Review* 71:481–98.

Brobeck, Kristi Lee. 2004. Under the waterfall: A fanfiction community's analysis of their self-representation and peer review. *Refractory* 5. http://www.refractory.unimelb.edu.au/journalissues/vol5/brobeck.html (accessed October 22, 2005).

Brooker, Will. 2003. *Using the Force: Creativity, community and "Star Wars" fans*, rev. ed. New York: Continuum International.

Brower, Sue. 1992. Fans as tastemakers: Viewers for quality television. In *The adoring audience*, ed. Lisa A. Lewis, 163–84. London: Routledge.

Bury, Rhiannon. 2003. Stories for ~~boys~~ girls: Female fans reading *The X-Files. Popular Communication* 1:217–42.

_____. 2004. Language on (the) line: Class, community and the David Duchovny Estrogen Brigades. *Communication Institute for Online Scholarship* 14.

_____. 2004. Of Mounties and gay marriage: Canadian television, American fans, and the virtual heterotopia. *Refractory* 6. http://www.refractory.unimelb.edu.au/journalissues/vol6/RBury.html (accessed June 1, 2006).

_____. 2005. *Cyberspaces of their own: Female fandoms online*. New York: Peter Lang.

Busse, Kristina. 2002. Crossing the final taboo: Family, sexuality, and incest in the Buffyverse. In *Fighting the forces: What's at stake in "Buffy the Vampire Slayer"?*, ed. Rhonda V. Wilcox and David Lavery, 207–17. Lanham, MD: Rowman & Littlefield.

_____. 2005. "Digital get down": Postmodern boy band slash and the queer female space. In *Eroticism in American culture*, ed. Cheryl Malcolm and Jopi Nyman, 103–25. Gdansk: Gdansk Univ. Press.

_____. 2006. "I'm jealous of the fake me": Postmodern subjectivity and identity construction in boy band fan fiction. In *Framing celebrity: New directions in celebrity culture*, ed. Su Holmes and Sean Redmond, 253–67. London: Routledge.

Butler, Judith. 1990. *Gender trouble*. New York: Routledge.

Cantwell, Marianne. 2004. Collapsing the extra/textual: Passions and intensities of knowledge in *Buffy*: The *Buffy the Vampire Slayer* online fan communities. *Refractory* 5. http://www.refractory.unimelb.edu.au/journalissues/vol5/cantwell.html (accessed June 1, 2006).

Carruthers, Fiona. 2004. Fanfic is good for two things: Greasing engines and killing brain cells. *Particip@tions* 1. http://www.participations.org/volume%20l/issue%202/1_02_carruthers_article.htm (accessed June 1, 2006).

Chandler-Olcott, Kelly, and Donna Mahar. 2003. Adolescents' anime-inspired "fan fictions": An exploration of multiliteracies. *Journal of Adolescent and Adult Literacy* 46:556–66.

Chaney, Keidra, and Raizel Liebler. 2006. Me, myself, and I: Fan fiction and the art of self-insertion. *Bitch* 31:53–57.

Chin, Bertha, and Jonathan Gray. 2001. "One ring to rule them all": Pre-viewers and pre-texts of the *Lord of the Rings* films. *Intensities* 2. http://www.cult-media.com/issue2/Achingray.htm (accessed October 22, 2005).

Cicione, Mirna. 1998. Male pair-bonds and female desire in fan slash writing. In *Theorizing fandom: Fans, subculture and identity*, ed. Cheryl Harris and Alison Alexander, 153–77. Cresskill, NJ: Hampton Press.

Clerc, Susan J. 1996a. DDEB, GATB, MPPB, and Ratboy: *The X-Files* media fandom, online and off. In *"Deny all knowledge": Reading "The X-Files,"* ed. David Lavery, Angela Hague, and Marla Cartwright, 36–51. Syracuse, NY: Syracuse Univ. Press.

_____. 1996b. Estrogen brigades and "big tits" threads: Media fandom online and off.

In *Wired women: Gender and new realities in cyberspace,* ed. Lynn Cherny and Elizabeth Reba Wise, 73–97. Seattle: Seal Press.

_____. 2002. Who owns our culture? The battle over the Internet, copyright, media fandom, and everyday uses of the cultural commons. PhD diss., Bowling Green State Univ.

Consalvo, Mia. 2003. Cyber-slaying media fans: Code, digital poaching, and corporate control of the Internet. *Journal of Communication Inquiry* 27:67–86.

Costello, Victor J. 1999. Interactivity and the "cyber-fan": An exploration of audience involvement within the electronic fan culture of the Internet. PhD diss., Univ. of Tennessee. http://oai.sunsite.utk.edu/links/CostelloVictor.pdf (accessed June 1, 2006).

Cumberland, Sharon. 2000. Private uses of cyberspace: Women, desire, and fan culture. *MIT Communications Forum.* January 25. http://web.mit.edu/comm-forum/papers/cumberland.html (June 1, 2006). Expanded and reprinted in 2003 in *Rethinking Media Change: The Aesthetics of Transition,* ed. David Thorburn and Henry Jenkins, 261–79. Cambridge, MA: MIT Press.

_____. 2002. The five wives of Ibn Fadlan: Women's collaborative fiction on Antonio Banderas Web sites. In *Reload: Rethinking women + cyberculture,* ed. Mary Flanagan and Austin Booth, 175–94. Cambridge, MA: MIT Press.

Cupitt, Cathy. 2003. A space for sex: Reproducing corporate product for the public domain. In *Liveable communities,* ed. Janice Haswell and Diana MacCallum, 117–29. Perth: Black Swan Press. http://www.geocities.com/ccupitt.geo/slash/spacesex.html (accessed October 22, 2005).

Darling-Wolf, Fabienne. 2003. Male bonding and female pleasure: Refining masculinity in Japanese popular cultural texts. *Popular Communication* 1:73–89.

De Certeau, Michel. 1984. *The practice of everyday life.* Berkeley: Univ. of California Press.

Dennis, Jeffrey P. 2003. Signifying same-sex desire in television cartoons. *Journal of Popular Film and Television* 31:132–41.

Doty, Alexander. 2000. *Flaming classics: Queering the film canon.* New York: Routledge.

Ehrenreich, Barbara, Elizabeth Hess, and Gloria Jacobs. 1992. Beatlemania: Girls just want to have fun. In *The adoring audience,* ed. Lisa A. Lewis, 84–106. London: Routledge.

Ferris, Kerry Orway. 1997. Star struck: The social worlds of serial television fans. PhD diss., Univ. of California, Los Angeles.

Fiedler, Leslie. 1960. *Love and death in the American novel.* New York: Criterion.

Fiske, John. 1989. *Reading the popular.* New York: Routledge.

_____. 1992. The cultural economy of fandom. In *The adoring audience,* ed. Lisa A. Lewis, 30–49. London: Routledge.

Foster, Derek. 1997. Community and identity in the electronic village. In *Internet culture,* ed. David Porter, 23–37. New York: Routledge.

Fraiberg, Allison. 1995. Electronic fans, interpretive flames: Performative sexualities and the Internet. *Works and Days* 13:196–207.

Ganz-Blättler, Ursula. 1999. Shareware or prestigious privilege? Television fans as knowledge brokers. *MIT Communications Forum.* http://web.mit.edu/comm-forum/papers/ganz-blattler.html (accessed June 1, 2006).

Geraghty, Lincoln. 2003. Homosocial desire on the final frontier: Kinship, the American romance, and *Deep Space Nine*'s "erotic triangles." *Journal of Popular Culture* 36:441–65.

_____. 2004. "Help when times are hard": Bereavement and *Star Trek* fan letters. *Refractory* 5. http://www.refractory.unimelb.edu.au/journalissues/vol5/geraghty.html (accessed June 1, 2006).

Gillilan, Cinda Lynn. 1999. Zine fans, zine fiction, zine fandom: Exchanging the mundane for a woman-centered world. PhD diss., Univ. of Colorado.

Glaubman, Jane, ed. Forthcoming. *Reconstructing Harry: "Harry Potter" fan fiction on the World Wide Web*. Durham, NC: Duke Univ. Press.

Green, Lelia, and Carmen Guinery. 2004. Harry Potter and the fan fiction phenomenon. *Media/Culture* 7. http://journal.media-culture.org.au/0411/14-green.php (accessed June 1, 2006).

Green, Shoshanna, Cynthia Jenkins, and Henry Jenkins. 1998. "Normal female interest in men bonking": Selections from the *Terra Nostra Underground* and *Strange Bedfellows*. In *Theorizing fandom: Fans, subculture, and identity,* ed. Cheryl Harris and Alison Alexander, 9–38. Cresskill, NJ: Hampton Press.

Grossberg, Lawrence. 1992. Is there a fan in the house? The affective sensibility of fandom. In *The adoring audience,* ed. Lisa A. Lewis, 50–68. London: Routledge.

Halberstam, Judith. 1998. *Female masculinity*. Durham, NC: Duke Univ. Press.

Hale, Laura M. 2005. A history of fan fic. Fanzine.

Hall, Stuart. 1991. Encoding/decoding. In *Culture, media, language: Working papers in cultural studies, 1972–79,* rev. ed., ed. Stuart Hall, Dorothy Hobson, Andrew Lowe, and Paul Willis, 128–38. London: Hutchinson.

Hamming, Jeannie. 2001. Whatever turns you on: Becoming-lesbian and the production of desire in the Xenaverse. *Genders* 34. http://www.genders.org/g34/g34_hamming.html (accessed June 1, 2006).

Harris, Cheryl D. 1992. Social identity, class and empowerment: Television fandom and advocacy. PhD diss., Univ. of Massachusetts.

Harris, Cheryl, and Alison Alexander, ed. 1998. *Theorizing fandom: Fans, subculture and identity*. Cresskill, NJ: Hampton Press.

Harrison, Taylor. 1996. Interview with Henry Jenkins. In *Enterprise zones: Critical positions on "Star Trek,"* ed. Taylor Harrison, Sarah Projansky, Kent A. Ono, and Elyce Rae Helford, 259–78. Boulder, CO: Westview Press.

Hellekson, Karen. 1997. *Doctor Who* fans rewrite their program: Mini-UNIT Minstrels as creative consumers of media. *Popular Culture Review* 8:97–108.

Herzing, Melissa Jean. 2005. The Internet world of fan fiction. MA thesis, Virginia Commonwealth Univ. http://etd.vcu.edu/theses/available/etd-05092005–125907/unrestricted/HerzingThesis.pdf (accessed June 1, 2006).

Hills, Matt. 2000a. Media fandom, neoreligiosity, and cult(ural) studies. *Velvet Light Trap* (Fall): 73–84.

_____. 2000b. To boldly go where others have gone before: *Star Trek* and (academic) narratives of progress [book review essay]. *Scope* (November). http://www.nottingham.ac.uk/film/journal/bookrev/star-trek.htm (accessed June 1, 2006).

_____. 2001. Interview with Henry Jenkins. *Intensities* 2. http://www.cult-media.com/issue2/CMRjenk.htm (accessed October 22, 2005).

_____. 2002. *Fan cultures*. London: Routledge.

_____. 2006. Not just another "powerless elite"? When media fans become subcultural celebrities. In *Framing Celebrity: New directions in celebrity culture,* ed. Su Holmes and Sean Redmond, 101–18. London: Routledge.

Hinderman, Stephen. 1992. "I'll be here with you": Fans, fantasy and the figure of Elvis. In *The adoring audience,* ed. Lisa A. Lewis, 107–34. London: Routledge.

Jenkins, Henry. 1990. If I could speak with your sound: Fan music, textual proximity and liminal identification. *Camera Obscura* 23:149–76.

_____. 1991. *Star Trek* rerun, reread, rewritten: Fan writing as textual poaching. In *Close encounters: Film, feminism and science fiction,* ed. Constance Penley, Elizabeth Lyons, Lynn Spigel, and Janet Bergstrom, 170–203. Minneapolis: Univ. of Minnesota Press.

_____. 1992a. Strangers no more, we sing: Filking and the social construction of the science fiction fan community. In *The adoring audience*, ed. Lisa A. Lewis, 207–36. London: Routledge.

_____. 1992b. *Textual poachers: Television fans and participatory culture.* New York: Routledge.

_____. 1998. The poachers and the stormtroopers: Popular culture in the digital age. *Red Rock Eater Digest.* Talk presented at the Univ. of Michigan, Spring 1998. http://commons.somewhere.com/rre/1998/The.Poachers.and.the.Sto.html (accessed May 14, 2000).

_____. 2000a. Digital land grab. *MIT Alumni Association Technology Review* 103:103–5. http://www.technologyreview.com/articles/00/03/viewpoint0300.asp (accessed October 22, 2005).

_____. 2000b. Reception theory and audience research: The mystery of the vampire's kiss. In *Reinventing film studies,* ed. C. Gledhill and L. Williams, 165–82. London: Arnold.

_____. 2001. Foreword to *Interacting with "Babylon 5": Fan performances in a media universe,* by Kurt Lancaster. Austin: Univ. of Texas Press.

_____. 2002. Interactive audiences: The "collective intelligence" of media fans. In *The new media book,* ed. Dan Harries, 157–70. London: British Film Institute.

_____. 2003. Quentin Tarantino's *Star Wars?* Digital cinema, media convergence, and participatory culture. In *Rethinking media change,* ed. David Thorburn and Henry Jenkins, 281–312. Cambridge, MA: MIT Press.

_____. 2004a. Game design as narrative architecture. In *First person: New media as story, performance, game,* ed. Noah Frup-Waldrop and Pat Harrington, 118–30. Cambridge, MA: MIT Press.

_____. 2004b. The cultural logic of media convergence. *International Journal of Cultural Studies* 7:33–43. http://ics.sagepub.com/cgi/reprint/7/1/33.pdf (accessed October 22, 2005).

_____. 2004c. Why Heather *can* write. *Technology Review* (February 6). http://www.technologyreview.com/articles/04/02/wo_jenkins020604.asp?p=1 (accessed October 22, 2005).

_____. 2006a. *Convergence culture.* New York: New York Univ. Press.

_____. 2006b. Fans, bloggers, and gamers. New York: New York University Press.

Jenson, Joli. 1992. Fandom as pathology: The consequence of characterization. In *The adoring audience,* ed. Lisa A. Lewis, 9–29. London: Routledge.

Jones, Sara Gwenllian. 2000. Starring Lucy Lawless? *Continuum* 14:9–22.

_____. 2002. The sex lives of cult television characters. *Screen* 43:79–90.

_____. 2003. Web wars: Resistance, online fandom and studio censorship. In *Quality popular television: Cult TV, the industry, and fans,* ed. Mark Jancovich and James Lyons, 163–77. London: British Film Institute.

Jung, Susanne. 2004. Queering popular culture: Female spectators and the appeal of writing slash fan fiction. *Gender Forum Gender Queeries* 8. http://www.genderforum.uni-koeln.de/queer/jung.html (accessed June 1, 2006).

Katz, Arnie. N.d. The philosophical theory of fan history. http://www.smithway.org/fstuff/theory/phil1.html (accessed June 1, 2006).

Kem, Jessica Freya. 2005. Cataloging the Whedonverse: Potential roles for librarians in online fanfiction. MS thesis, Univ. of North Carolina–Chapel Hill. http://etd.ils.unc.edu/dspace/bitstream/1901/137/1/jessicakem.pdf (accessed June 1, 2006).

Kozinets, Robert V. 1997. To boldly go: A hypermodern ethnography of *Star Trek* fans' culture and communities consumption. PhD diss., Queen's Univ., Ontario, Canada.

_____. 2001. Utopian enterprise: Articulating the meanings of *Star Trek*'s culture of consumption. *Journal of Consumer Research* 28:67–88.

Kustritz, Anne. 2003. Slashing the romance narrative. *Journal of American Culture* 26:371–84.

Lamb, Patricia Frazer, and Diane Veith. 1986. Romantic myth, transcendence, and *Star Trek* zines. In *Erotic universe: Sexuality and fantastic literature*, ed. Donald Palumbo, 236–55. Westport, CT: Greenwood Press.

Lancaster, Kurt. 2001. *Interacting with "Babylon 5": Fan performances in a media universe*. Austin: Univ. of Texas Press.

Laurel, B. 2004. Narrative construction as play. *Interactions* (September–October): 73–74.

Lee, Kylie. 2003. Confronting *Enterprise* slash fan fiction. *Extrapolation* 44:69–82.

Lefanu, Sarah. 1989. *Feminism and science fiction*. Bloomington: Indiana Univ. Press.

Lewis, Diane. 2004. Understanding the power of fan fiction for young authors. *Kliatt* 38, no. 2:4–7.

Lewis, Lisa A., ed. 1992a. *The adoring audience*. London: Routledge.

_____. 1992b. Something more than love: Fan stories on film. In *The adoring audience*, ed. Lisa A. Lewis, 135–62. London: Routledge.

Lichtenberg, Jacqueline, Sondra Marshak, and Joan Winston. 1975. Do-it-yourself *Star Trek*— The fan fiction. In *"Star Trek" lives!*, 221–74. New York: Corgi.

MacDonald, Andrea. 1998. Uncertain utopia: Science fiction media fandom and computer mediated communication. In *Theorizing fandom: Fans, subculture, and identity*, ed. Cheryl Harris and Alison Alexander, 131–52. Cresskill, NJ: Hampton Press.

MacDonald, Marianne. 2006. Harry Potter and the fan fiction phenom. *Gay and Lesbian Review Worldwide* 13:28–30.

Macor, Alison Grace. 2000. The visible audience: Participation, community, and media fandom. PhD diss., Univ. of Texas, Austin.

Mahiri, Jabari. 2000. Pop culture pedagogy and the end(s) of school. *Journal of Adolescent and Adult Literacy* 44:382–87.

McCardle, Meredith. 2003. Fan fiction, fandom, and fanfare: What's all the fuss? *Boston University Journal of Science and Technology Law* 9:434–68. http://www.bu.edu/law/scitech/volume9issue2/McCardleWebPDF.pdf (accessed June 1, 2006).

McLelland, Mark. 2000a. Male homosexuality and popular culture in modern Japan. *Intersections* 3. http://wwwsshe.murdoch.edu.au/intersections/issue3/mclelland2.html (accessed June 1, 2006).

_____. 2000b. No climax, no point, no meaning? Japanese women's boy love sites on the Internet. *Journal of Communication Inquiry* 24:274–91.

_____. 2001. Why are Japanese girls' comics full of men bonking? *Intensities* 1. http://www.cult-media.com/issue1/CMRmcle.htm (accessed October 22, 2005).

Merrick, Helen. 2004. "We was cross-dressing 'afore you were born!," or How sf fans invented virtual community. *Refractory* 6. http://www.refractory.unimelb.edu.au/journalissues/vol6/HMerrick.html (accessed June 1, 2006).

Murray, Simone. 2004. "Celebrating the story the way it is": Cultural studies, corporate media and the contested utility of fandom. *Continuum* 18:7–25.

Nellis Berg, Kelly Anne Colleen. 2002. Making sense of television: Interpretive community and *The X-Files* fan forum: An ethnographic study. PhD diss., Univ. of Missouri–Columbia.

Pearson, Roberta E. 2003. Kings of infinite space: Cult television characters and narrative possibilities. *Scope* (August). http://www.nottingham.ac.uk/film/journal/articles/kings-of-infinite-space.htm (accessed June 1, 2006).

Penley, Constance. 1991. Brownian motion: Women, tactics, and technology. In *Tech-*

noculture, ed. Contance Penley and Andrew Ross, 35–161. Minneapolis: Univ. of Minnesota Press.

———. 1992. Feminism, psychoanalysis, and the study of popular culture. In *Cultural studies,* ed. Lawrence Grossberg, Cary Nelson, and Paula A. Treichler, 479–500. New York: Routledge.

———. 1997. *NASA/Trek: Popular science and sex in America.* New York: Verso.

Pflieger, Pat. 1999, rev. 2001. Too good to be true: 150 years of Mary Sue. Presented at the Popular Culture Association, San Diego. http://www.merrycoz.org/papers/MARYSUE.HTM (accessed June 1, 2006).

Porter, David. 1997. *Internet culture.* New York: Routledge.

Pugh, Sheenagh. 2004. The democratic genre: Fan fiction in a literary context. *Refractory* 5. http://www.refractory.unimelb.edu.au/journalissues/vol5/pugh.html (accessed June 1, 2006).

———. 2005. *The democratic genre: Fan fiction in a literary context.* Bridgend, UK: Seren.

Radway, Janice. 1984. *Reading the romance: Women, patriarchy, and popular literature.* Chapel Hill: Univ. of North Carolina Press.

Russ, Joanna. 1985. Pornography by women, for women, with love. In *Magic mommas, trembling sisters, Puritans and perverts: Feminist essays,* 79–99. Trumansburg, NY: The Crossing Press.

Russo, Julie Levin. 2002. NEW VOY "cyborg sex" J/7 [NC-17] 1/1: New methodologies, new fantasies. http://j-l-r.org/asmic/fanfic/print/jlr-cyborgsex.pdf (accessed June 1, 2006).

Rust, Linda. 2004. Welcome to the house of fun: *Buffy* fanfiction as a hall of mirrors. *Refractory* 2. http://www.refractory.unimelb.edu.au/journalissues/vol2/lindarust.html (accessed June 1, 2006).

Sabal, Robert. 1992. Television executives speak about fan letters to the networks. In *The adoring audience,* ed. Lisa A. Lewis, 185–90. London: Routledge.

Sabucco, Veruska. 2003. Guided fan fiction: Western "readings" of Japanese homosexual-themed texts. In *Mobile cultures: New media in queer Asia,* ed. C. Berry, F. Martin, and A. Yue. Durham, NC: Duke Univ. Press.

Salmon, Catherine, and Don Symons. 2001. *Warrior lovers: Erotic fiction, evolution and female sexuality.* London: Orion.

———. 2004. Slash fiction and human mating psychology. *Journal of Sex Research* 41:94–100.

Sanders, Joseph L., ed. 1994. *Science fiction fandom.* Westport, CT: Greenwood Press.

Sandvoss, Cornel. 2005. *Fans: The mirror of consumption.* Cambridge, UK: Polity Press.

Saxey, Esther. 2001. Staking a claim: The series and its slash fan-fiction. In *Reading the Vampire Slayer: The unofficial critical companion to "Buffy" and "Angel,"* ed. Roz Kaveny, 187–210. New York: Tauris Park.

Scodari, Christine. 1998. "No politics here": Age and gender in soap opera "cyberfandom." *Women's Studies in Communication* 21:168–87.

———. 2003a. Resistance re-examined: Gender, fan practices, and science fiction television. *Popular Communication* 1:111–30.

———. 2003b. Review of Matt Hills, *Fan cultures. Popular Communication* 1:181–83.

Scodari, Christine, and Jenna L. Felder. 2000. Creating a pocket universe: "Shippers," fan fiction, and *The X-Files* online. *Communication Studies* 51:238–58.

Sedgwick, Eve Kosofsky. 1985. *Between men: English literature and male homosocial desire.* New York: Columbia Univ. Press.

Selley, April. 1987. "I have been, and ever shall be, your friend": *Star Trek, The Deerslayer,* and the American romance. *Journal of Popular Culture* 20:89–104.

Shave, Rachel. 2004. Slash fandom on the Internet, or Is the carnival over? *Refractory* 6. http://www.refractory.unimelb.edu.au/journalissues/vol6/RShave.html (accessed June 1, 2006).

Silvergleid, Robin. 2003. "The truth we both know": Readerly desire and heteronarrative in *The X-Files*. *Studies in Popular Culture* 25. http://pcasacas.org/SPC/spcissues/25.3/Silbergleid.htm (accessed June 1, 2006).

Smith, Eliot K. 1999. The romance of crossover: The cultural production of fandom in America. PhD diss., SUNY Buffalo.

Smol, Anna. 2004. "Oh ... oh ... Frodo!" Readings of male intimacy in *The Lord of the Rings*. *Modern Fiction Studies* 50:949–79.

Somogyi, Victoria. 2002. Complexity of desire: Janeway/Chakotay fan fiction. *Journal of American and Comparative Culture* 25:399–404.

Stein, Atara. 1998. Minding one's p's and q's: Homoeroticism in *Star Trek: The Next Generation*. *Genders* 27. http://www.genders.org/g27/g27_st.html (accessed June 1, 2006).

Stein, Louisa. 2002. Subject: "Off topic: Oh my god U.S. terrorism!" *Roswell* fans respond to 11 September. *European Journal of Cultural Studies* 5:471–91.

———. 2005. "They cavort, you decide": Fan discourses of intentionality, interpretation, and queerness in teen TV. *Spectator* 25:11–22.

Stilwell, Jessica. 2003. Fans without pity: Television, online communities, and popular criticism. MA thesis, Georgetown Univ. http://cct.georgetown.edu/thesis/JessicaStilwell.pdf (accessed October 22, 2005).

Suzuki, Kazuko. 1999. Pornography or therapy? Japanese girls creating the yaoi phenomenon. In *Millennium girls: Today's girls around the world,* ed. Sherrie A. Inness, 243–68. London: Rowman & Littlefield.

Tulloch, John, and Henry Jenkins. 1995. *Science fiction audiences: Watching "Doctor Who" and "Star Trek."* New York: Routledge.

Tushnet, Rebecca. 1997. Legal fictions: Copyright, fan fiction, and a new common law. *Loyola of Los Angeles Entertainment Law Journal* 17:641–86. http://homepages.nyu.edu/~rlt2/legalfictions.pdf (accessed June 1, 2006).

———. 2004. Copy this essay. *Yale Law Journal* 114:535–90. http://www.yalelawjournal.org/pdf/114–3/Tushnet.12.1.pdf (accessed June 1, 2006).

Verba, Joan Marie. 1996. *Boldly writing: A Trekker fan and zine history, 1967–1987.* 2nd ed. Minnesota: FTL Publications. http://www.ftlpublications.com/bw.htm (accessed June 1, 2006).

Vermorel, Fred, and Judy Vermorel. 1992. A glimpse of the fan factory. In *The adoring audience,* ed. Lisa A. Lewis, 191–207. London: Routledge.

Wakefield, Sarah. 2001. Your sister in St. Scully: An electronic community of female fans of *The X-Files*. *Journal of Popular Film and Television* 29, no. 3:130–37.

Walker, Cynthia W. Forthcoming. *A dialogic approach to creativity in mass communication.* Cresskill, NJ: Hampton Press.

Wexblatt, Alex. 2003. An auteur in the age of the Internet: JMS, *Babylon 5,* and the Net. In *Hop on pop: The politics and pleasures of popular culture,* ed. Henry Jenkins, Tara McPherson, and Jane Shattuc, 209–26. Durham, NC: Duke Univ. Press.

Williamson, Milly. 2005. Spike, sex, and subtext. *European Journal of Cultural Studies* 8:289–311.

Woledge, Elizabeth. 2005a. From slash to the mainstream: Female writers and gender blending men. *Extrapolation* 46:50–65.

———. 2005b. Decoding desire: From Kirk and Spock to K/S. *Social Semiotics* 15:235–50.

A Brief History
of Media Fandom
Francesca Coppa

Introduction

Not only has a comprehensive history of media fandom not been written, but there also have been very few histories of individual fandoms and the works of art they produced. Most academic studies take an ethnographic, not historical or literary, approach. But it's a different thing to write about fandom historically (which presupposes the relevance of specific fandom activities rather than seeing those activities as evidence in a case study that analyzes trends in communication or the rituals of a subculture) or from a literary perspective (which presupposes that the writing is actually worth reading, rather than evidence of a fan's behavior or ideology). Perhaps the only conventional published history is, fittingly, Joan Marie Verba's *Boldly Writing: A Trekker Fan and Zine History, 1967–1987* (1996), which chronicles the emergence of *Star Trek* fandom. Verba explains who the fan writers, zine editors, convention organizers, and various other historically important figures were. The reader learns the names of key movers and shakers like Devra Langsam, Sherna Comerford, and Paula Smith; she also describes the contents of *Star Trek* fanzines, year by year, describing significant stories as well as noting the emergence of writers and themes important to the fandom. But even as Verba embarks on this daunting task, she does so knowing that writing history isn't important to everyone, not even to fans themselves. As she poignantly notes in her preface:

> The incident that motivated me to finally sit down and write this book was an exchange of letters in June 1990. An editor had stated in her publication that *Universal Translator* had been the first regular publication to list fanzine

description. Checking my library, I found that *Scuttlebutt* had predated *Universal Translator*, so I wrote the editor, asking her to print a correction.

She replied, "...when I asked friends who have been in fandom longer than I (actually they've been in fandom since fandom came into being), the response was, "Who cares which was first?"

I care [viii].

Thus speaks a historian. This history, brief and incomplete as it is, is dedicated to her and follows her example. I briefly trace the emergence of U.S. media fandom (as something distinct from, but related to, science fiction, comics, anime/manga/yaoi, music, soap opera, and literary fandoms) and its development over the forty years of its existence, not year by year as Verba does, but half decade by half decade. The goal is to create a short, basic narrative of the development of specific media fandoms and the kind of art fans made in them. I am indebted to the work of the fans who came before me, and I hope that this essay is useful to those who will write the comprehensive histories we so badly need.

FIAWOL: Fandom Is a Way of Life

According to the *Oxford English Dictionary*, the word *fandom* was applied to sports and theatre before being adopted by science fiction literature enthusiasts, who developed much of the fannish infrastructure, jargon, and language still in use today. Science fiction fandom is commonly said to have developed on the letters page of Hugo Gernsback's magazine *Amazing Stories* (1926); as Arnie Katz notes in "The Philosophical Theory of Fanhistory," "The large letter column, copied by most of *Amazing*'s competitors, gave readers plenty of space to talk to the editor, and ultimately, to each other" (http://www.smithway.org/fstuff/theory/phil1.html, accessed June 1, 2006). It was this interactive element that allowed for the development of modern fandom; by publishing fans' addresses, *Amazing Stories* allowed science fiction fans to contact each other directly.

Perhaps unsurprisingly, these fans began to organize and produce art; the first science fiction fanzine, *The Comet*, was published in 1930 (Stephen Perkins, "Science Fiction Fanzines," http://www.zinebook.com/resource/perkins/perkins2.html, accessed June 1, 2006). According to Frederik Pohl (1974), "fans had begun to publish their own magazines to fill in the dry weeks between the times when the new issues of *Astounding, Amazing,* and *Wonder* came out" (23) because science fiction was published only irregularly in the depressed days of the 1930s; then, as now, fan art compensated for deficiencies and gaps in the marketplace. Fanzines, Pohl explains, "contained comments on the stories in the professional magazines, or news of fan activities, or gossip or debate" (23) as well as amateur stories and art. Pohl derides this art as "pretty poor stuff" before admitting that C. M. Kornbluth, Donald Wollheim, Ray Bradbury, and a hundred others, himself included, "got their start that way." APAs— or amateur press association zines— developed partly as a way to handle the sheer volume of correspondence this activity generated. In an APA, all correspondence would be sent to a central person, who would simply copy everything that was sent to him and send it out again. All of these zines, Stephen Perkins notes, take "advantage of the cheapest and most accessible technologies in any given period, i.e. mimeography, spirit duplicating (ditto) and xerography, as well as more traditional printing methods such as offset printing."

Pohl claims that the trip he and seven other New York–area fans took to meet a similar group of fans in Philadelphia in 1936 was the first science fiction convention; conversely, a group of British fans (including Arthur C. Clarke) had a more carefully planned public event on January 3, 1937. The first World Science Fiction Convention was held over the July 4, 1939, weekend in New York City, and aside from a few breaks during the war, that convention — now called Worldcon — has been held annually ever since.

In addition to the structure of zines, APAs, and fan convention, science fiction fandom also invented a fannish jargon that is still in wide use today, often by people who have no idea of its age or lineage. Words and acronyms like *BNF* (Big Name Fan) (antedating 1950), *con* (antedating 1942), *egoboo* (antedating 1947), *fanboy* (antedating 1919), *filk* (antedating 1955), *gafiate* (get away from it all) (antedating 1959), and *mundane* (as a noun; antedating 1955) have their roots in science fiction fandom, but they migrated first into media fandom, then onto the Internet, where they've been comfortably integrated with online fannish argot like *beta reader, flame,* and *listmom*.

Late 1960s: The Emergence of Science Fiction Media Fandoms

There's some debate as to what was actually the first media fandom, although there's no debate that media fandom emerged from within science fiction fandom around 1966. Conventional wisdom has it that many science fiction fans developed a particular enthusiasm for *Star Trek* (1966–1969), the groundbreaking science fiction series, which had been screened by Gene Roddenberry for fans at Worldcon in 1966. In particular, the show attracted the many female fans who, as Justine Larbalestier (2002, 23–27) has persuasively argued, have been present in science fiction fandom since the beginning but were underrepresented on the letter pages that were the public face of fandom. But as Cynthia Walker (2001) points out, many of the science fiction writers and fans who coalesced around *Star Trek* and turned it into a phenomenon had previously embraced another television series: *The Man from U.N.C.L.E.* (1964–1968). As Walker notes, "Whether it was the technology, the utopian politics, or something else again, *U.N.C.L.E.* attracted science and science fiction–minded audiences" (4). Walker points out a number of connections between *The Man from U.N.C.L.E.* and the science fiction fan community; not only did the show feature teleplays by known science fiction writers, but Harlan Ellison worked regularly on the series rewriting and polishing scripts, and Terry Carr hired a number of young science fiction novelists (such as Joan Hunter Holly, Robert "Buck" Coulson, and David McDaniel) to write a series of paperback tie-ins published by Ace. As Walker explains, "Ellison, Carr, and McDaniel were all originally SF fans who made the transition to pro writers, and all were well known in the SF community.... When Ellison, Carr, McDaniel and the others began to contribute to the shaping of *U.N.C.L.E.*, they brought these [science fiction] customs and practices with them" (4). Walker further cites Craig Henderson, editor and publisher of such fan newsletters as *File Forty* and *FYEO*, who asserts that "*U.N.C.L.E.* was very definitely the first television series to inspire a fandom-like reaction. *Star Trek* was the second, which is well worth remembering." During the height of its popularity,

> over half the television sets that were turned on Friday nights at 10 p.m. were tuned into *The Man From U.N.C.L.E. TV Guide* dubbed it "the mystic cult of millions." ... In a memo to programming vice president, Mort Werner, the NBC research department reported that viewers were watching U.N.C.L.E. " ... not just because they dislike other programs that are on ... [but] because they are fans, fanatics.... They talk about the program with other fans and go beyond that: they proselytize, they want to convert non-viewers!" [Walker, "The Gun as Star and the 'U.N.C.L.E. Special,'" http://www.manfromuncle.org/gun.htm, accessed June 1, 2006].

Unlike *The Man from U.N.C.L.E.*, *Star Trek* struggled for ratings the entire time it was on the air, and perhaps this pushed its fans to become more vocal and participatory. Walker, however, persuasively argues that the key players in both fandoms were drawn from the same pool; Juanita Coulson, a contributor to the very first *Star Trek* zine, *Spockanalia* (1967), and the editor of the second *Star Trek* zine, *ST-Phile* (1968), was married to Buck Coulson, the coauthor of two Ace *U.N.C.L.E.* paperbacks. Media fandom, now a gigantic international phenomenon, clearly began its life in a very small pool.

Whether the first media fandom was *U.N.C.L.E.* or *Star Trek,* the women who built those fandoms tended to fit the profile of science fiction fans: they were better educated than most, heavy readers, and scientifically literate. Verba herself has a bachelor's degree in physics, went to graduate school for astronomy, and worked as a computer programmer; Jacqueline Lichtenberg (professional novelist and creator of the Kraith universe, which explored the Vulcan cultures of *Star Trek*) was a chemist before becoming a writer; Judy Segal has a master's degree in botany. Perhaps their involvement in science or in science fiction partly explains some women's great and instant affection for the character of Mr. Spock; certainly a female engineer, botanist, or computer programmer in the late 1960s knew what it was like to be treated as an alien with an inappropriate and disconcerting emotional range.

From the start, *Star Trek* fans produced not simply the critical discussion typical of science fiction fandom but creative responses to their favorite show. From the first, *Star Trek* zines included fan art — poems, songs, stories, drawings, teleplays. As Walker observes, Gene Roddenberry's strategy of turning a blind eye to fan art and fiction was probably responsible for the flowering of media fandom. Indeed, a creative *Trek* culture rapidly developed through the proliferation of fanzines like *Spockanalia, ST-Phile, T-Negative,* and *Warp Nine: A Star Trek Chronicle.* Bjo Trimble produced the *Star Trek Concordance of People, Places, Things* as a fan production in 1969; it was published professionally in 1976. In 1969, science fiction writer Ruth Berman wrote "For the Good of the Service," a story that Verba lauds as good enough to have been an episode; that same year, Lelamarie S. Kreidler wrote "Time Enough," "a story about a woman who wins and beds Spock" (1996, 3) which was the first of many future relationship stories. The various genres of *Star Trek* fan fiction were developing apace.

But *Star Trek* would soon become a divisive issue within science fiction fandom; many traditional fans, whose culture continued to be centered around professional science fiction magazines, dismissed *Star Trek* as science fiction for nonreaders. This was an unfair slur against the (mainly) female fans who were helping to build *Star Trek* fandom and who were still active science fiction literature fans as well. The schism between science fiction and *Star Trek* fandom was exacerbated in 1974 when Jacqueline Lichtenberg and Laura Basta were nominated for the Hugo Award for best fan writer (the fan-awarded Hugo being the award given annually at Worldcon). As Verba (1996) notes,

> Both Jacqueline and Laura were nominated for the "best fanzine writer" solely on the basis of their *Star Trek* fanzine stories, and this created quite a furor in science fiction fandom. Some science fiction fans were aghast at the idea of fans writing stories for what they thought of as a second-rate

TV show. Some were afraid that *Star Trek* fans would distract the World Science Fiction convention from honoring those who wrote original science fiction novels. Other science fiction fans did not see what all the fuss was about. This began a debate about the relationship *of Star Trek* fans to the science fiction community which has continued, in some form or another, to this day [16].

Eventually *Star Trek* fans, feeling unwelcome at science fiction conventions, would start holding their own conventions. The first of these was held in New York in 1972, and this event really represented the beginning of the *Star Trek* fan phenomenon.

Early 1970s: Star Trek Lives!

Not only was a rift slowly developing between science fiction fans and *Star Trek* fans during the late 1960s and early 1970s, but there began to be a more nuanced rift within *Trek* fandom itself. The divide came, Verba (1996, 23) argues, between those fans who liked *Trek* primarily for the science fiction elements, and those who liked it for the characters, particularly the buddy dynamic between Kirk and Spock. Although I believe that this dichotomy is in many ways false (can *Star Trek* fans really have no interest in science fiction whatsoever?), the line she traces is one that arguably distinguishes media fandom from *Star Trek* fandom per se.

By 1975, *Star Trek* fandom was well established, as demonstrated by the publication of the seminal *"Star Trek" Lives!* (Lichtenberg et al., 1975) that same year. *"Star Trek" Lives!* is a fascinating history of the early years of *Trek* fandom, including the establishment of zine culture, the show's famous letter-writing campaign, and the phenomenon of the *Star Trek* convention. Even in 1975, the fandom was growing exponentially: as the authors note in their introduction, the 1972 convention drew over 3,000 people; the 1973 convention drew 6,000; and in 1974, 15,000 people attended and 6,000 more were turned away at the door (5). And yet it was the book's final chapter, "Do-It-Yourself *Star Trek*—The Fan Fiction," that influenced not only the extant *Star Trek* fandom but also the developing media fandom, with its celebration of *Star Trek* fan fiction as a literature written mainly by women.

Unlike Verba (1996), who professed herself surprised at the growing dominance of female-written "relationship" stories within *Star Trek* fandom, the authors of *"Star Trek" Lives!* believe that it is intrinsic to the material: *Star Trek*, they raved, "did not keep its distance from emotion; did not deny close, warm human relationships even among males; did not call for a stiff upper lip; did not deny the existence and importance of sex; did not ban psychological action as a plot-moving force; did not deny the possibility of women who might be more than damsels." They note that *Star Trek* was "startlingly sexy — sexy in theme, in attitude — not merely in gratuitous scenes of bodies," and that this made it particularly attractive to women writers, who have developed "a whole new genre of fan fiction and perhaps of science fiction generally. And suddenly," they add, not without a little bitterness, "the men have made themselves scarce" (225). Although there were and are many men in *Star Trek* fandom — making visual art, writing articles, organizing conventions—*Star Trek* stories are written almost entirely by women. In *The Best of TREK: From the Magazine for "Star Trek" Fans,* a compilation of articles from the magazine *TREK* published in 1978, men are responsible for at least half the entries, and yet fan historian Mary Ellen Curtin has calculated that 83 percent of *Star Trek* fan writers were women in 1970, and 90 percent in 1973. However else they were participating in the community, male *Star Trek* fans weren't writing fan fiction.

The rest of the "Do-It-Yourself" chapter is a serious literary examination of a number of stories the authors have determined to be important; many of the stories have strong female leads (although the prevalence of strong, perfect women in *Star Trek* fan fiction would lead Paula Smith to coin the term *Mary Sue* to describe them in 1973 [Verba 1996, 15]) or deal with unexplored aspects of alien (and particularly Vulcan) cultures. Specific stories discussed in the chapter include Laura Basta's novel *The Daneswoman,* about the first female starship commander; Judith Brownlee's stories about her original female Vulcan character, Captain T'Pelle; a trilogy of plays by Doris Beetem set on Vulcan in ancient times; Ruth Berman's story "It Seemed the Logical Thing," and Judith Brownlee's "Let Me Count the Ways," both about Sarak and Amanda's marriage; various stories of Spock's pon farr, mating, or marriage, including Catherine Blakey's "Encounter" and Diane Steiner's *Spock Enslaved;* "Mirror, Mirror" universe stories like Laura Basta's "Federation and Empire" and Juanita Coulson's "To Summon the Future"; and, almost as an afterthought, some Kirk-centric stories like "Joy in the Morning," by Claudine-Marie de Sisi and the *Alternate Universe #4* zine, in which "the heroism of Kirk is beginning to be better recognized." They also describe postscript or missing scene stories like Ruth Berman's "A Rose for Miranda" and a number of intense Kirk and Spock "bond" stories like Jennifer Guttridge's "Tower of Terror" and "The Winged Dreamers," Carolyn Meredith's "The Crossing Lords," and Clare Gabriel's "Ni Var." Last, they explain the genesis of Jacqueline Lichtenberg's own Kraith series.

I take the time to list these stories because the authors do; each story mentioned is discussed in detail, with excerpts and close readings, over the course of a couple of pages. The authors of *"Star Trek" Lives!* don't think these stories are important as examples of "fan communication" but for what they're saying in themselves, as stories in "a whole new genre of science fiction." This attention to detail and the tantalizing excerpts of individually named stories in particular fanzines was responsible for an explosive interest in fan fiction in the years after *"Star Trek" Lives!* was published. The book ended up publicizing the very phenomena it was celebrating. As Verba notes, "For thousands upon thousands of fans, this was when they became aware that such activity existed, and that they could join in" (1996, xviii).

The stories mentioned in "Do-It-Yourself" were only the tip of the iceberg; in addition to the "science fiction story" versus "relationship story" divide, there was also increasingly a divide in relationship stories between K&S (relationship) stories and K/S (homoerotic, otherwise known as *slash*) stories. The first of the latter is commonly thought to be Diane Marchant's "A Fragment Out of Time" (*Grup #3*, 1974) which depicted two nameless people (one male, one whose gender was not revealed) making love; Marchant acknowledged in the next issue of *Grup* that she intended these characters to be Kirk and Spock. Slash fiction took the buddy story to another level, sparking a series of arguments within *Star Trek* fandom as to precisely how close Kirk and Spock were. But as Verba notes, "One might argue that the 'relationship' (K&S) and the homoerotic (K/S) stories were merely two aspects of the same theme. Neither was concerned about science fiction. Both concentrated on the interactions between Kirk and Spock" (1996, 23). If relationship stories were the public face of *Star Trek* fan fiction and slash stories were kept relatively underground, it was the shared focus on relationships that led some Trek fans to become more broadly defined media fans in the second half of the 1970s.

Late 1970s: Buddy Shows and Blockbuster Sci-Fi

The mid to late 1970s were characterized by two phenomena that turned some *Star Trek* fans into self-defined media fans. The first of these was the appearance of the buddy cop show *Starsky and Hutch* (1975–1979) and its British counterpart, *The Professionals* (1977–1983). Although these mainstream shows might seem a far cry from *Star Trek*, stories about the importance of friendship and partnership were now prevalent, and fannish practices for creating and distributing those stories were easily adaptable to shows like *Starsky and Hutch*. As Lichtenberg et al. (1975) note in *"Star Trek" Lives!*, women "tended to identify more with the male heroes of the genre — the adventurers and problem solvers" (224). As police detectives working the mean streets of "Bay City" *(Starsky and Hutch)* or agents in CI5, a government organization dedicated to fighting crime and terrorism *(The Professionals)*, the protagonists of these shows were certainly adventurers and problem solvers; further, they were as isolated from mainstream society and dependent on each other as a result of their occupations as Kirk and Spock were — more so, in fact. The relative ease with which certain fans were able to apply their reading strategies and creative practices to these buddy shows gives additional credence to Cynthia Walker's theory that *The Man from U.N.C.L.E.*, and not the more famous *Star Trek*, was the prototype media fandom; *U.N.C.L.E.*, too, is a buddy fandom, with characters who have dangerous, problem-solving, socially isolating jobs as globe-trotting international spies (making it a much different thing than the story of that isolated loner, James Bond).

The same aspects that made buddy shows attractive to relationship-oriented fans also made them attractive to slashers; the fact that these shows were set in an era of tight jeans and unbuttoned shirts, and of the loosening of formerly strict standards of acceptable male behavior, only provided additional evidence for a homoerotic interpretation. As Camille Bacon-Smith notes in *Enterprising Women*, "When actors are shot in sufficient close up for the viewer to read facial expressions clearly, they cannot maneuver appropriate social distances and still look at each other while they are speaking ... so actors portraying friends consistently break into each other's spheres of intimate space" (1992, 233). This leads to what one of Smith's interviewees calls "Starsky and Hutch syndrome": the idea that the leads appear unable to stay apart or keep their hands off each other. Such body language encouraged homoerotic readings by many mainstream viewers as well. Slash was slowly coming out of the closet; a new 1978 *Star Trek* zine called *Naked Times* announced on the editorial page of its first issue that "While *Naked Times* did not start out as primarily a K/S zine, that's certainly the way this first issue has turned out, mainly due to the fact that that's the majority of material I received."

Buddy shows weren't the only things broadening the scope of media fandom beyond *Star Trek*: the debut of *Star Wars* (1977) triggered a science fiction blockbuster explosion in the late 1970s and early 1980s. Suddenly fans who'd been suffering from a dearth of science fiction stories were drowning in them. After the huge success of *Star Wars*, producers were quick to try to capitalize on the sci-fi craze, producing shows like *Battlestar Galactica* (1978), *Blake's 7* (1978–1981), and *Buck Rogers in the 25th Century* (1979), as well as films like *The Black Hole* (1979), *Battle Beyond the Stars* (1980), and *Flash Gordon* (1980). Perhaps most importantly, the popularity of *Star Wars* finally made possible the return of the *Star Trek* franchise so desperately desired; *Star Trek: The Motion Picture* debuted in theatres in 1979.

This is not to say that *Star Trek* fans and *Star Wars* fans happily shared space in the emerging subculture of media fandom; as one science fiction fan glumly noted, "As far as I'm concerned, SW was the great splintering of *my* fandom (Trek) as people zipped off into that new media trend (still bear a grudge) and stopped doing stuff for my Trek 'zine and started writing *shudder* Luke Skywalker fic" (Ithiliana, personal communication). Still, fans of *Star Trek, Star Wars,* buddy shows, and other kinds of mass media storytelling began to form their own distinct culture in the late 1970s. The first of the cons that would become MediaWest was held in 1978 and organized by Lori Chapek-Carleton and Gordon Carleton, founders of the T'Kuhtian Press, which put out such *Trek* zines as *Warped Space*. The con was called T'Con and held at the Lansing Hilton Inn. The MediaWest Web site describes the con's philosophy and lineage:

> When *Star Wars* began to generate a fandom of its own, some *Star Trek* fans felt threatened by this sudden upstart and began to treat *Star Wars* fans as badly as they had been treated. Others, however, thought there was room for a variety of interests, and Media Fandom was born....
>
> Under the tutelage of KWest*Con veterans Paula Smith and Sharon Ferraro, a format was conceived: an SF/Media convention run by fans, for fans, with no paid guests. It had been observed that at conventions with little or no Media programming, fans would gather in the halls, or wherever they could, and have their own discussions, workshops, etc., but it was anyone's guess if there would be enough interest to support an entire convention without the drawing power of professional authors, actors, etc.
>
> There was, and there is [http://members.aol.com/mdiawstCon/mwchist. htm, accessed June 1, 2006].

Smith and Ferraro also edited a number of important zines, most importantly the ongoing *Trek* zine *Menagerie* (1973). They also created the FanQ awards to honor *Star Trek* fan writers and artists. These midwives to the birth of media fandom brought the organizational structure and habits of *Star Trek* fandom with them; the conventions they helped to organize were formally reestablished in 1981 as MediaWest, which has been held annually ever since. Other media and media-friendly cons followed, including Creation Con and DragonCon.

Early 1980s: Good Television and Better Blockbusters

In the early 1980s, it seemed like every new issue of *Starlog* announced the coming of a new and exciting science fiction or fantasy-themed film;

some, like *Ice Pirates* (1984), were terrible, but most were of much higher quality than the films of the immediate post–*Star Wars* generation. Even the second *Star Trek* film was considered vastly superior to its 1979 predecessor, and within a few short years, films such as *The Empire Strikes Back* (1980), *Raiders of the Lost Ark* (1981), *Poltergeist* (1982), *Blade Runner* (1982), *Star Trek II: The Wrath of Khan* (1982), *Star Trek III: The Search for Spock* (1983), *Return of the Jedi* (1983), *Indiana Jones and the Temple of Doom* (1984), and *The Adventures of Buckaroo Banzai Across the 8th Dimension* (1984) flew across the screens. It was at this time that media fandom really grew and spread, not only because there were so many films to choose from, but also because the obsessively researching nature of most media fans meant that it was a rare fan who didn't see even the nongenre films that Harrison Ford starred in (such as *Force 10 from Navarone* [1978], *Hanover Street* [1979], and the few seconds of his turn as a bellboy in *Dead Heat on a Merry Go Round* [1966]). Being an informed media fan could be a full-time job.

On the small screen, two different kinds of television were having an impact on media fans. The first of these was British media, imported and made available to American viewers through their broadcast on PBS. For instance, the BBC had tried to sell the long-running British science fiction series *Doctor Who* to American television in 1975, but it failed to catch on. It was only in 1978 that the Tom Baker seasons were sold to PBS, where they attained a growing and fervent cult status through the 1980s (http://en. wikipedia.org/wiki/Doctor_Who_in_America, accessed June 1, 2006). Although *Monty Python's Flying Circus* had been broadcast on PBS since 1974, the early 1980s saw a rising interest in British media such as *Fawlty Towers* (1975), *Blackadder* (1983), and the various incarnations of Douglas Adams's comedy science fiction universe, *The Hitchhiker's Guide to the Galaxy* (radio series 1978, broadcast on NPR in March 1981; original trilogy of novels published in 1979, 1980, 1982; UK television series 1981, broadcast on PBS in 1982). Media fandom's affinity for the Doctor was only the most recent example of its growing BBC obsession; public television membership drives often featured scarf-wrapped media fen answering phones, and "British Media" became a catchall phrase indicating a love of a number of otherwise disparate British shows.

The other significant development in television was American. "Quality" television series like *Hill Street Blues* (1981–1987) and *Cagney and Lacey* (1982–1988) introduced more complex narrative arcs and characterization issues, changing the ways fan fiction writers thought about television, and leading to what longtime fan Jessica Ross calls "a non-genre fandom explosion — everything became zineable" (personal communication, June 21,

2005). Ross drew on her zine collection to make the point: a typical multimedia zine of the period, *Warped Space 50,* put out by T'Khutian Press in 1983, features the following list of fandoms: *Star Wars, Star Trek, Hill Street Blues, Remington Steele, Knight Rider,* and a comic based on *The Fantastic Four* crossed with *Star Wars. Cagney and Lacey,* it is worth noting, was the first show to actually be brought back from cancellation by a *Star Trek*–style letter-writing campaign to the network, and not only was it one of the first shows where women got to be adventurers and problem solvers, but it was also the first lesbian slash fandom.

Late 1980s: Crossovers

Crossovers were nothing new in fandom: there had been *Star Trek/Man from U.N.C.L.E.* crossovers, for instance, as early as 1979. But even a cursory examination of a typical zine blurb shows the creative lengths to which fans went in pursuing multimedia crossovers in the late 1980s. Here's an example.

> LIONS & TIGERS & ZINES, OH MY #1, Airwolf, Real Ghostbusters, MacGyver, Road Warrior, Buckaroo Banzai, SW, Land of Giants, Space Rangers, Equalizer, Kung Fu TLC, QL, Alf, B7, Are You Being Served/She Wolf of London, Fantasy Island, Moonlighting/Miami Vice, Miami Vice, 440p, $10.00.

Moonlighting (1985–1989) and *Miami Vice* (1984–1989) are both detective shows, so one can see the potential for crossover between their worlds. But *Are You Being Served/She Wolf of London?* Presumably even werewolves have to shop. Here we see fandoms mixed together with gleeful abandon.

Although the list of active fandoms during this period would be long and would include such strange bedfellows as *Space: 1999* (1975–1977), *Simon and Simon* (1981–1988), *The Greatest American Hero* (1981–1983), *Remington Steele* (1982–1987), *Tales of the Gold Monkey* (1982–1983), and *Robin of Sherwood* (1984–1986), the three largest and most important fandoms to emerge in the late 1980s were *Star Trek: The Next Generation* (1987–1994), *Beauty and the Beast* (1987–1990), and *Wiseguy* (1987–1990). Predictably enough, the relaunching of a televised *Star Trek* franchise attracted the attention of science fiction, *Star Trek,* and media fans alike. Henry Jenkins devotes a chapter of *Textual Poachers* (1992) to fannish engagements with the romantic *Beauty and the Beast. Wiseguy,* on the other hand, was an ongoing episodic drama about a federal agent undercover with the mob, but even the mainstream media noticed that the intense relationship between the agent and the mobster "verges on being homoerotic" (O'Connor 1987).

This colorful explosion of zines might well, in hindsight, have signaled the beginning of the decline of that culture; in the late 1980s, fannish interactions began to move away from the medium of print zines and onto what would come to be called the Internet. Fans began to move their communications onto Usenet and bulletin boards; in many ways, the Internet was the ideal medium for fannish interaction because, as Henry Edward Hardy noted in his "History of the Net" (1993), "The written culture of the Net is much like an oral culture in the immediacy of communication" (http://www.eff.org/Net_culture/net.history.txt, accessed June 1, 2006). Fans already had those written-oral cultures in their letter zines, APAs, and fanzines. Fans of every ilk began to colonize Usenet, creating space for their interests. A glance at just some of the group titles shows the diversity of groups who began to use the net: fans met in such communities as rec.arts.sf.fandom, rec.arts.startrek.fandom, and alt.drwho.creative.

Early to Mid 1990s: Developing an Internet Infrastructure

Many, if not most, of the new fandoms that developed in the early 1990s developed their culture in both the traditional ways—zines, letters, conventions—but also in new, online ways. Both new and established fandoms established Usenet groups for fannish discussion and the distribution of fan fiction —alt.tv.x-files.creative or alt.sex.fetish.startrek. Fans created centralized online, fandom-specific archives for their fan fiction, but these early archives were labor-intensive; by the end of the decade, fans would write software that would automatically format and store fiction in searchable databases.

The *Forever Knight* (1992–1996) fandom can claim the first online mailing list, ForKNI-L, started on December 9, 1992, by Jean Prior; other fandoms got e-mail lists if they had a member with access to the technology. In the early to mid–1990s, running a mailing list was a relatively restricted thing; it required Majordomo or ListServ software and was generally run off a university server by someone who worked or studied there. Home computers were generally not online; commercial Internet providers were only beginning to be popular. Fans, as a group, were technologically ahead of the curve; many worked from VT 100 terminals at university computer labs or were early adopters of home computing equipment. But the fannish list administrators, moderators, archivists, and Web hosts were drawn from the ranks of the most technologically savvy fans; if media fandom had expanded its traditional base in science fiction fandom, it still depended on a core group of highly educated, science-oriented women.

Important fandoms that emerged during this period include *Quantum Leap* (1989–1993), *Highlander* (1992–1998), *The X-Files* (1993–2002), *Lois and Clark* (1993–1997), *Babylon 5* (1994–1998), *Due South* (1994–1998), *Xena: Warrior Princess* (1995–2001), *Hercules: The Legendary Journeys* (1995–1999), and, of course, the nearly inevitable *Star Trek* franchises: *Deep Space Nine* (1993–1999) and *Voyager* (1995). In a way, the early 1990s can be regarded as a time of modernism for online fandom: a fandom was judged by the strength of its infrastructure; everyone knew you found *X-Files* fan fiction at the Gossamer archive, *Due South* fan fiction at Hexwood, *Star Trek* fan fiction at Trekiverse. A well-organized fandom might have two centralized mailing lists: one for distributing fiction, and one for hosting discussion, with fiction sometimes broken up into "gen" and "adult"; these lists had names like XFF, DSX, and ROG, which were a kind of code fans understood: *X-Files* fan fiction, *Due South* adult fiction (including slash), Really Old Guy (the 5,000-year-old Methos on *Highlander*). Eventually, as the Internet grew and the technology became more accessible, lists proliferated, with ever more specific mission statements; by the end of the decade, with the rise of OneList, eGroups, and Yahoo.com groups, anyone could create a splinter list or have her own fannish vanity list. From there, fandom arguably entered the postmodern era.

The movement of media fandom online, as well as an increasingly customizable fannish experience, moved slash fandom out into the mainstream. Whereas slash zines had often been sold at cons literally from a box under the table, the Internet allowed for slash-specific lists that fans who wanted to read homoerotic stories could join and that other fans could easily avoid. Similarly, slash-friendly discussion lists allowed these fans to consolidate and talk openly to each other; many began to articulate their reasons for slashing, reading strategies, and politics.

Late 1990s: When Fandoms Collide: Comics, Celebrities and Music, Anime

In the late 1990s, the mainstreaming of online technologies allowed ever more people to enter media fandom. Formerly, most fans had been mentored by older fans or had attended a convention in order to meet others who shared their particular obsession. Now people could just google their favorite show, join the available lists, or start reading fiction — even erotic fiction — on a public online archive.

Several new and important media fandoms emerged during this time, notably *Buffy the Vampire Slayer* (1997–2003), *The Sentinel* (1996–1999), *Stargate SG-1* (1997–present), and *Star Wars Episode I: The Phantom Menace* (1999). These fandoms all fit comfortably within the genres of shows typically attractive to media fans, but the late 1990s were distinguished by the crossover between traditional media fandoms and other kinds of fandoms, namely comics, celebrities, music, and anime. These intersections would quickly have a profound effect on traditional media fandom. None of these other fandoms was "new," and each of them has its own history distinct from the one I've attempted to narrate here.

Comics fandom has existed since the very emergence of comics in the 1930s and can be seen as another kind of offshoot of science fiction fandom. As Gerard Jones explains in *Men of Tomorrow: Geeks, Gangsters, and the Birth of the Comic Book* (2004), Superman creator Jerry Siegal was involved in early science fiction fandom and may have created the first science fiction fanzine, *Cosmic Stories,* at age fourteen. It was a compilation of stories he had written and was advertised through a classified ad at the back of *Science Wonder Stories.* Jones locates comics fandom as having emerged from science fiction fandom and argues that "every subsequent geek culture—comics, computers, video games, collectible figurines—has either grown directly or taken much of its form" (37).

Celebrity fandom is arguably the very earliest form of fandom; as Henry Jenkins notes in *Textual Poachers* (1992), one of the earliest uses of the word *fan* was to describe theatre goers who admired the actors rather than the play (12). The Nifty Archive, which provided a home for a number of erotic stories, many of them homoerotic, many about celebrities, was established online in 1993; as fan historian Laura M. Hale notes, "Historically, this archive is not viewed as a home to true fan fiction but rather celebrity based erotica which was absent the fannish fan fiction context" (Hale 2005, 34). Although not part of fandom per se, the Nifty Archive did provide a center around which people interested in celebrity fan fiction could congregate. Similarly, Barbara Ehrenreich, Elizabeth Hess, and Gloria Jacobs (1992) have described girls' fannish engagement with musicians like Frank Sinatra, the Beatles, Michael Jackson, and David Bowie. In the late 1970s, some media fen crossed over into music fandom, writing fan fiction about "Tris and Alex," who were thinly disguised versions of Led Zeppelin musicians Jimmy Page and Robert Plant, although this remained a relatively isolated phenomenon. According to Hale, Duran Duran slash and het fic was circulating in fanzines in 1991, but fans "did not seem to come from the same community as 'traditional fan fiction fans' were coming from. They did not have the idea the material they were creating was taboo.... until they started interacting with media based fen" (34). Ironically, the fact that celebrity and music fandoms are so mainstream and have so many commercial venues, such as *People* magazine and VH1's *Behind the Music,* meant that celebrity and music fandoms never had much of an organized subcultural presence. They were too close to mainstream culture, and although that mainstream culture has always looked askance at *Star Trek* fans or writers of *Buffy the Vampire Slayer* fan fiction, devotion to a band or a singer, or a public crush on a celebrity has always been considered relatively acceptable. Music fans don't generally need to attend conventions or to self-identify as "fannish" in order to explain their enthusiasm or defend their entertainment preferences.

Anime, manga, and yaoi have always had their fans in Japan; the problem for English-speaking fans has always been access, both to the materials themselves and to translations of them. Perhaps because of the access issue, anime fandoms were some of the earliest adopters of online communication. Hale (2005, 32) claims that anime fandom created their online fannish architecture as early as 1991, which was also the year of AnimeCon, one of the first conventions dedicated to anime and manga. The Internet has steadily increased the popularity of Japanese fan forms. Although western fans have always managed to find anime, manga, and yaoi, the rise of scanners, digital video, and file-sharing technology has made access infinitely easier.

When all of these fandoms — media, comics, celebrity, music, anime — moved onto the Internet, they gained a wider audience, and the most obvious audience for a "new" fandom was a person from what, for lack of a better word, we might call a neighboring fandom. So some media fans got interested in comics, some anime fans started writing about celebrities, and some celebrity fan writers began to model their work on that done in media fandom. This had several important repercussions, one of which was the rapid rise of the phenomenon known as *popslash* within media fandom. Fan fiction writer Helen, then a writer of *Sentinel* slash, currently a writer in the *Harry Potter* fandom, wrote the seminal popslash story "The Same Inside" (2001, http://www.helenish.net/samep.shtml, accessed June 1, 2006), whose premise is explained by its famous and endlessly replicated opening line, "Somehow, in the night, Chris had turned into a girl." Helen reimagined celebrity erotica through the conventions of speculative fiction, making boy band fiction explicitly about *gender* and about *genre.* Consequently, popslash grew popular among media fan writers, many of whom created similarly brilliant and science fiction–like premises to explore celebrity culture as a metaphor for gender identity and other performances of the self. Interestingly, however, the sudden surge in popslash connected media fans with entirely different groups of music fans who had never heard of *Star Trek* or MediaWest, and who may use fannish terms like *Mary Sue* or describe a story as being about Benji/Joel without having any connection between that joining slash and the slash that so famously joined K/S more than thirty years ago. If the expansion of the Internet allowed communication between fans in different worlds, the translation and adaptations of fannish terms, forms, and practices that has emerged from those communications is rapidly transforming the fannish landscape into something that older fans may barely recognize.

Early 2000s: The More Things Change, the More Things Are Totally Different

Media fandom may now be bigger, louder, less defined, and more exciting than it's ever been. Arguably, this is fandom's postmodern moment, when the rules are "there ain't no rules" and traditions are made to be broken. FanFiction.net, the largest multifandom archive, was founded in 1998; today, it contains literally hundreds of thousands of stories, with more than 200,000 of them from *Harry Potter* alone.

The infrastructure of fandom has changed yet again. Mailing lists are rapidly dying, abandoned in favor of personalized blogging technology. If mailing lists customized fandom by allowing fans to select from among their fannish interests, blogs such as LiveJournal.com allow them to select particular fans from among many. LiveJournal debuted in 1999 but began to be widely adopted across fandom around 2003, where it caused a wide-scale reorganization of fandom infrastructure. Fan fiction is now posted to one's individual LiveJournal, or to a LJ community devoted to a particular fandom, topic, or pairing. LJ comments are replacing letters of comment. People can move through fannish interests at an astonishing speed.

That being said, some things remain the same: major new fandoms include much in the way of tradition genre fare: *Smallville* (2001), *Harry Potter* (2001), *Lord of the Rings* (2001), *Stargate: Atlantis* (2004), the new incarnation of *Battlestar Galactica* (2004). And yet media fandom has also been visibly affected by the changes of the previous decade. For instance, there has recently been an explosion of fan fiction set in the DC universe of comics, films, and animated television, a trend that will no doubt be exacerbated by the release, as I write this, of *Batman Begins* (2005). Groups of female media fans now share space with groups of male comics fans, and they seem to be having productive exchanges, even if they do occasionally baffle each other. Similarly, the *Lord of the Rings* fandom has produced an offshoot fandom that, borrowing from the tradition of celebrity fandom, writes fan fiction not about the *Lord of the Rings* characters but about the actors who portray them in the Peter Jackson films. The practice of treating actors as characters was initially deemed more or less immoral by media fandom and was viciously debated during the emergence of popslash. Now the practice, although not universally accepted, is more or less condoned.

But media fans are making more kinds of art than ever before. Not only are they still writing fan fiction, but image manipulation software has also allowed for ever more sophisticated visual art. Digital editing software has taken the fannish art of creating music videos, or *vidding*— which began with slide shows over music in 1975, and was then developed into a high art by VCR vidders in the 1980s and 1990s— to a whole other level: the Vividcon convention, dedicated entirely to the art of vidding, was founded in 2002. Soon, media fans might simply be able to make movies on their home computers, as fans in the neighboring fandom of machinima are already doing (see Jones, this volume). And fans are continuing to create a rich critical literature about themselves and their art. Fans have always done a wonderful job of explaining themselves to themselves, and a tradition of fannish metadiscourse continues to flourish online at such places as the Fanfic Symposium Web site, the Glass Onion mailing list, and on LJ communities dedicated to self-reflexive fannish analysis. Panels on analytical and theoretical subjects continue to be held at fannish conventions. And critical books like this one are now being written by us, by the fans— smart women who no longer feel quite so much like aliens.

Note

I dedicate this essay to Joan Marie Verba. I am indebted to Jessica Ross, Laura M. Hale, Lucy Gillam of the Symposium, Margie Gillis, Shoshanna Green, elynross, Cynthia Walker, Gina Paterson, and the women of Eris. Thanks especially to Terri Oberkamper for her editing acumen. All remaining mistakes are my own.

References

Bacon-Smith, Camille. 1992. *Enterprising women: Television fandom and the creation of popular myth.* Philadelphia: Univ. of Pennsylvania Press.
Ehrenreich, Barbara, Elizabeth Hess, and Gloria Jacobs. 1992. Beatlemania: Girls just want to have fun. In *The adoring audience,* ed. Lisa A. Lewis, 84–106. London: Routledge.
Hale, Laura M. 2005. A history of fan fic. Fanzine.

Hardy, Henry Edward. 1993. The history of the Net. MA thesis, School of Communications, Grand Valley State Univ.

Jenkins, Henry. 1992. *Textual poachers: Television fans and participatory culture.* New York: Routledge.

Jones, Gerard. 2004. *Men of tomorrow: Geeks, gangsters, and the birth of the comic book.* New York: Basic Books.

Larbalestier, Justine. 2002. *The battle of the sexes in science fiction.* Middletown, CT: Wesleyan Univ. Press.

Lichtenberg, Jacqueline Sondra Marshak, and Joan Winston. 1975. *"Star Trek" lives!* New York: Bantam.

O'Connor, John J. 1987. TV reviews; Two crime series, on CBS. *New York Times,* September 16.

Pohl, Frederik. 1974. The publishing of science fiction. In *Science fiction, today and tomorrow,* ed. Reginald Bretnor. New York: Harper and Row.

Verba, Joan Marie. 1996. *Boldly writing: A Trekker fan and zine history, 1967–1987.* 2nd ed. Minnesota: FTL Publications. http://www.ftlpublications.com/bw.htm (accessed June 1, 2006).

Walker, Cynthia W. 2001. A dialogic approach to creativity in mass communication. PhD diss., Rutgers Univ.

1. Archontic Literature
A Definition, a History, and Several Theories of Fan Fiction
Abigail Derecho

ABSTRACT.— This essay offers an analysis of fan fiction not as a cultural phenomenon (as fan fiction has been studied by most fan-scholars to date), but as an artistic practice. What is fan fiction, where does it come from, and what does it mean, in a philosophical sense? These are questions that need to be addressed if we are to think critically and seriously about fan fiction as an art form. The first part of the essay defines fan fiction as a subgenre of a larger type of writing that is usually called "derivative" or "appropriative" literature, but which I choose to call *archontic*, a term borrowed from Jacques Derrida's definition of archives as ever expanding and never completely closed. The second part of the essay traces the history of archontic literature from the seventeenth century to the present day, with an emphasis on how archontic writing has been often used by minority groups and women as a technique for making social and cultural criticisms. The third part of the essay uses concepts from twentieth-century poststructuralists Gilles Deleuze and Edouard Glissant to argue that fan fiction and archontic literature are ethical projects that oppose outdated notions of hierarchy and property.

Introduction

On May 30, 2005, on the LiveJournal.com community called fan-tasm: Adventures in the Study of Fan Fiction (one of several communities dedicated to *meta*—that is, meaning and historical, theoretical, and conceptual issues of fandom), a poster named oblomskaya started a thread entitled "Pride and Promiscuity" asking whether a published book containing bawdy, sexually explicit parodies of Jane Austen's *Pride and Prejudice* can be called fan fiction or not. The post generated twenty-seven comments written by five posters. Of the five respondents, one lobbied for a broad definition of fan fiction, arguing that fan fiction has existed for thousands of years and includes, for example, ancient Greek and Roman literature, such as Homer's epic poems. Another poster argued that stories can only be defined as fan fiction if they originate in a self-identified fan culture, implying that the only fanfic is that body of work that explicitly labels itself "fanfic"—or at the least is composed by people who self-identify as fans. On the Fanfic Symposium, Laura Hale dates the origin of literary fan fiction to Jane Austen and Sherlock Holmes fan societies in the 1920s, and the origin of media fandom to *Star Trek* fans in 1967 (Hale 2005). Hale justified her preference for this narrower definition of fanfic by stating, "When anything becomes fan fiction, the distinction is meaningless and you might as well call it literature." Oblomskaya eventually took a middle position, asserting that "Of course, all literature IS one big Intertext where everybody is citing each other," but "Having established that all texts, including ff [fan fiction], have this same essence, one must make [*sic*] a step further and start looking for distinguishing particularities of each type of text inside of the 'field.'".

The posters in this fan-ta-sm thread articulated the three general lines of thinking on the origin and nature of fan fiction that I have seen and heard repeatedly proposed by fan-scholars,[1] not just on this site, but on other meta sites, in meta discussions on "ordinary" fan sites, and in conversations I have had. The three arguments typically made are as follows: (1) fan fiction originated several millennia ago, with myth stories, and continues today, encompassing works both by authors who identify themselves as fans and those who do not write from within fandoms (one commenter gave Tom Stoppard's 1967 *Rosencrantz and Guildenstern Are Dead*, a speculation on minor characters from *Hamlet*, as an example of the latter); (2) fan fiction should be understood as a product of fan cultures, which began either in the late 1960s, with *Star Trek* fanzines, or, at the earliest, in the 1920s, with Austen and Holmes societies; or (3) the first argument may be too broad, but the second line of thinking may be too narrow; some other identifying traits of fan fiction might be expressed that would more accurately situate the genre within the larger field of literature. I am of the opinion that the third option is the correct one; but where would this third path lead? If fan fiction is to be defined neither as encompassing most of literature (because not all works that refer to other works can be called "fanfic"—

it seems more specific than that) nor as the consequence of a relatively recent trend in audience response (because connections between fanfic and older forms of storytelling surely exist, and fanfic does not seem to be a completely new narrative approach that sprung up, without precedent, in the twentieth century), then how should we characterize it?

Once we have attempted to answer the questions "What is fan fiction?," "When did fan fiction come into being," and "Where does it come from?," we must also ask, "What does it mean?" These are the issues for which we must try to develop a theoretical vocabulary if we are to think seriously about fan fiction as art. In the pages that follow, I will attempt to expand on fan-scholars' work at greater length (most posts on meta sites are succinct opinion pieces) and in a slightly different register. I draw on poststructuralist and other critical discourses to piece together a definition, a history, and several theories of fan fiction. In so doing, I focus on a different set of issues than those that most professional scholars of fan cultures have given their attention to. Academics writing on fan communities have concentrated largely on fandoms as cultural phenomena to be approached and analyzed by means of various techniques of ethnography; in contrast, many of the fan-scholars I have read are interested primarily in investigating fan-authored narratives as a type of art. From the research carried out by academics, we have both data and analyses of what types of fan works are being made, by whom, and with what intention. What we lack — and what numerous fan-scholars are striving toward in their meta discussions — are concepts that would enable us to think more critically about how this enormous amount of artistic output called fan production works *as art,* and what they signify for broader culture — not just on a political level, in terms of whether they serve as adequate forms of resistance to the culture industries or are merely forms of cooperation with media corporations, but on a philosophical level.

What Is Fan Fiction? A Definition of "Archontic" Literature

Although the term *fan fiction* was not used until the 1960s, it must be acknowledged that fan fiction is a subgenre of a larger, older genre of literature that is generally called "derivative" or "appropriative." I wish to replace these terms with a new one: I choose to call this type of writing *archontic,* which I think better describes what fanfic is and how it operates as literature.

Archontic relates to the word *archive,* and I take it from Jacques Der-rida's 1995 work *Archive Fever,* in which Derrida claims that any and every archive remains forever open to new entries, new artifacts, new contents.[2] No archive is ever final, complete, closed: "By incorporating the knowledge deployed in reference to it, the archive augments itself, engrosses itself, it gains in *auctoritas.* But in the same stroke it loses the absolute and meta-textual authority it might claim to have. One will never be able to objec-tivize it with no remainder. The archivist produces more archive, and that is why the archive is never closed. It opens out of the future" (68). Derrida ascribes motivation and action to archives, as can be noted in the way he makes "the archive" the subject of sentences ("the archive augments itself, engrosses itself, it gains ... it loses ... it might claim ... it opens...."). Der-rida names the internal drive of an archive to continually expand: he calls it the "archontic principle." Without this principle or "function," or "power," as Derrida sometimes calls it, "no archive would ever come into play or appear as such." The archontic principle "gathers the functions of unification, of identification, of classification" and is "a principle of consignation, that is, of gathering together" (3). The archontic principle is that drive within an archive that seeks to always produce more archive, to enlarge itself. The archontic principle never allows the archive to remain stable or still, but wills it to add to its own stores.

The adjective *archontic* better describes the intertextual relationship at the core of the literature than the words *derivative* or *appropriative* do. Although *derivative* and *appropriative* both imply intertextuality, an inter-play between texts— one preceding and providing the basis for the other — these adjectives also announce property, ownership, and hierarchy. *Derivative,* when applied to artwork, has a negative connotation in every-day speech; it usually indicates a poor imitation or even a corruption of an original, pure work. Calling a text based on a prior text "derivative" thus signifies a ranking of the two texts according to quality and classifies the secondary text as the lesser one. Similarly, *appropriative* connotes "taking" and can easily be inflected to mean "thieving" or "stealing." To label the genre of fiction based on antecedent texts "derivative" or "appropriative," then, throws into question the originality, creativity, and legality of that genre. I prefer to call the genre "archontic" literature because the word *archontic* is not laden with references to property rights or judgments about the relative merits of the antecedent and descendant works. A literature that is archontic is a literature composed of texts that are archival in nature and that are impelled by the same archontic principle: that tendency toward enlargement and accretion that all archives possess. Archontic texts are not delimited properties with definite borders that can be transgressed. So all texts that build on a previously existing text are not lesser than the source text, and they do not violate the boundaries of the source text; rather, they only add to that text's archive, becoming a part of the archive and expanding it. An archontic text allows, or even invites, writers to enter it, select specific items they find useful, make new artifacts using those found objects, and deposit the newly made work back into the source text's archive.[3]

An archontic text's archive is not identical to the text but is a virtual construct surrounding the text, including it and all texts related to it. For example, we have Jane Austen's *Pride and Prejudice* (*P&P*) as a story that consists of several thousand specific words given in a specific order, and we also have a *P&P* archive, which contains such usable artifacts as Elizabeth Bennett, Fitzwilliam Darcy, the sprawling estate of Pemberly, and Austen's particular version of English manners and morals. Many writers, such as Linda Berdoll (author of *Mr. Darcy Takes a Wife,* published by Landmark in 2004) and Pamela Aidan (author of *Fitzwilliam Darcy, Gentleman,* published by Wytherngate Press in 2004) have made withdrawals from the *P&P* archive, used their selections to make new texts, and deposited their new creations back into the *P&P* archive. The *P&P* archive thus contains not only Austen's novel, but Berdoll's, Aidan's, and the hundreds of other stories based on Austen's novel that have appeared in print both officially (issued by publishing houses) and unofficially (issued in zines and Web sites).

Given that what I am calling archontic texts are always open and have the potential for infinite expansion, one might say that in a sense, all texts can be called "archontic." Julia Kristeva (1980) argues for the inherent intertextuality of all literary works: "any text is a mosaic of quotations; any text is the absorption and transformation of another" (66). Roland Barthes (1981) calls intertextuality "the condition of any text whatsoever," noting that intertextuality "cannot ... be reduced to a problem of sources or influences; the intertext is a general field of anonymous formulae whose origin can scarcely ever be located; of unconscious or automatic quotations, given without quotation marks" (39). However, it is the specific relation between new versions and the originary versions of texts, the fact that works enter the archive of other works by quoting them consciously, by pointedly locating themselves within the world of the archontic text, that makes the concept of archontic literature different from the concept of intertextuality. All texts may be intertextual — that is to say, it is possible to argue that all texts are archives that contain hundreds or thousands of other texts — but for the purposes of my discussion, "archontic" describes only those works that generate variations that explicitly announce themselves as variations (see Stasi, this volume). Archontic texts definitely "use quotation marks" by referencing characters and narratives in obvious ways. Fanfics tie themselves overtly to preexisting texts; this annunciation is a convention of the fan fiction genre, performed either in the identifying headers that precede and categorize individual fics, or by the location of each fanfic in fandom-specific zines or Web sites. Although no such convention exists for nonfan literary works—that is, readers do not expect a novel to state outright, in its first few sentences, that it is a revision of, a continuation of, or an insertion into, a prior narrative—nonfan works do explicitly mark themselves as revisions, continuations, and insertions through replicating titles (Isabel Allende's *Zorro*), using established characters (Rosencrantz and Guildenstern in Stoppard's play; Crusoe and Friday in J. M. Coetzee's *Foe*, Fitzwilliam and Elizabeth Darcy in Linda Berdoll's *Mr. Darcy Takes a Wife*), and/or using plots and dialogue recognizable from the source text (Jean Rhys's *Wide Sargasso Sea*).

Where and When Does Fan Fiction Come From? A History of Archontic Literature

Several fan-scholars have written histories of archontic literature. They call them histories of fan fiction, although what they have really produced are lists of the kinds of archontic writing that preceded fan fiction. Super-Cat's 1999 "A (Very) Brief History of Fanfic" (http://www.trickster.org/symposium/symp5.htm, accessed June 1, 2006) and Juice's 2004 "A History of Fan Fiction" (juice817, LiveJournal.com, August 6, 2004) summarize the best-known milestones in the evolution of archontic literature. Their examples of fan fiction that predate film and television include the Jewish exegetical tradition of midrash; John Lydgate's 1421 continuation of Chaucer's *Canterbury Tales*, called *The Siege of Thebes*; Milton's *Paradise Lost*; and the entire body of Shakespeare's plays. Sheenagh Pugh's 2004 essay "The Democratic Genre: Fan Fiction in a Literary Context" opens with a compressed history of archontic literature and cites examples ranging from Robert Henryson's fifteenth-century variation on Chaucer's *Troilus and Criseyde* (itself a variant of a Greek myth) to John Reed's 2001 *Snowball's Chance*, a reworking of George Orwell's *Animal Farm*.

Because the broad history of archontic writing has been covered by others, I present a slightly different, more limited history, one that emphasizes the way that archontic writing has often been used as a technique of social, political, or cultural critique in the hands of what John Fiske (1992), drawing on Pierre Bourdieu, calls "the culture of the subordinate" (32).

Although Bourdieu and Fiske use *subordinate* specifically to refer to the proletariat in the modern (twentieth century) era of the culture industries, I choose to apply the term to earlier periods as well, because many subordinate cultures throughout history, especially women and ethnic minorities, have chosen to record and/or publicize their opinions by writing archontic literature. As a genre, archontic literature has had lasting appeal for subordinated groups seeking adequate means of expression.

Although writers have used archontic literature to critique patriarchy, xenophobia, and racism at least since the fifth century BCE, when ancient Greeks produced politically motivated retellings of ancient myths like Euripides' *Medea*, I begin my history of archontic literature as a medium of political and social protest in the seventeenth century, when the first original prose fiction by a woman in the English language was published. That text was a work of archontic literature. The same was true of the first published sequel by a woman, and one of the only known printed novels from the early modern period to contain a woman's (the book's owner's) handwritten additions to the story. These works were all based on Sir Philip Sidney's *The Countess of Pembroke's Arcadia*, and they were, respectively, Lady Mary Wroth's 1621 *The Countess of Montgomery's Urania*, Anna Weamys's 1654 *Continuation of Sir Philip Sydney's "Arcadia,"* and the 1590 copy of Sidney's *Arcadia* owned by Lucy Hastings (Hastings wrote her insertions and continuation in the book between 1624 and 1664). The first published play by a woman in English was also a piece of archontic writing: Elizabeth Cary based her 1613 *The Tragedy of Mariam, the Fair Queen of Jewry*, on the midrashic scholar Josephus's story of King Herod's wife (Burow-Flak 2000), and also on a translation of Garnier's *Marc Antonie* by Mary Sidney (Philip Sidney's sister) (Weller and Ferguson 1994, 27–29). So archontic literature and women's writing, at least in the English language, have been linked for at least four hundred years, and from the first, the act of women entering the archives of male-authored texts and adding their own entries to those archives has generated conflict. Wroth, who was Sidney's niece, received sharp criticism for writing the *Urania* from fellow noble Sir Edward Denny, who lambasted her for producing a romance, a type of work unseemly for a woman — the only appropriate genres for women writers being, according to Denny, translations of scripture and other devotional material (Roberts 1983, 239). Wroth responded to Denny by parodying a poem that Denny had written to censure her. She adopted his rhyme scheme, including his exact rhyming words, and defended herself archly, demonstrating that a female writer could freely enter and add to any male-authored archive she wished, and that such archontic activity could be a successful technique for critiquing the style or message of the male writer's writing.

At the beginning of Weamys's *Continuation,* several prefatory poems by contemporary male poets and publishers give the reader to understand that Weamys was infused with the spirit of Philip Sidney, *Arcadia*'s author, downplaying Weamys's agency as an author by attributing her literary talent to spectral insemination by male genius. Ironically, the works of Wroth and especially of Cary are read today as examples of early modern feminism, because both works portray patriarchal aspects of English aristocratic society as ridiculous and unjust. Thus some of the earliest women authors who published in English chose to write within the genre of archontic literature, possibly sensing an opportunity to highlight the inequalities of women's and men's situations in their culture by creating new versions of earlier stories and producing a contrast between the old and new tales. Their efforts to add to male narratives were, for the most part, resented, minimalized, or ignored by their male contemporaries.

We do not have many instances of women's archontic writing published for more than a century after Weamys's continuation, although it seems unimaginable that women did not write their own versions of texts they read during this period. It is possible, even probable, that, like Lucy Hastings, women wrote their variations of stories as ephemera and marginalia in the pages of the books they read. In any case, the next instances I have found of women publishing archontic literature are Maria Romero's 1792 translation and augmentation of, and Madame Morel de Vindé's 1797 sequel to, Madame du Graffigny's *Lettres d'une peruvienne* (*Letters of a Peruvian Woman*). According to Theresa Ann Smith (2003), there are five known sequels to Graffigny's novel: two by anonymous authors who could have been either male or female, one by a man, and Vindé's and Romero's. There is also a copy of Romero's translation/augmentation of the Graffigny, which contains handwritten alterations/expansions of the text by an anonymous author whose gender is unknown. The markings are similar in style to Hastings's additions to the Sidney text. During this period of time in Europe, women sought publication in far greater numbers than in the time of Wroth and Weamys, but the path to public authorship was still difficult and dangerous. Smith writes, "'going public' could be a perilous prospect for female intellectuals in any nation during the early modern period, because publication involved a measure of transgression against social expectations of women's modesty, submission, and anonymity" (119). I am thus inclined to believe that the anonymous authors, including the author of the handwritten marginalia in the copy of Romero's book, were women.

Graffigny's novel, although popular, frustrated many readers by its ending, which does not unite the Peruvian heroine of the book's title, named Zilla, and her faithful French suitor, Déterville, in marriage, but has Zilla rejecting Déterville's proposal and deciding to live a life of reflection in relative isolation. All of the sequels to Graffigny's work, including the handwritten alteration of Romero's version, rewrite the ending and marry off Zilla and Déterville. These are readers who, we can infer by virtue of their not wishing to alter the main body of Graffigny's text, enjoyed most of *Lettres d'une peruvienne,* but found the absence of a wedding at the ending to be so unacceptable — despite Graffigny's goal being primarily to critique institutions that limit women's opportunities, including marriage — that they wrote conclusions that went against the spirit of most of the originary text, conclusions that reaffirmed the institution of marriage as the ultimate happiness for women. The Graffigny sequels are therefore an interesting example of how women have used archontic writing to express their dissatisfaction and to voice their own desires, but that in some cases, their desires coincide with the values of dominant, not subordinate, culture. In the case of the Graffigny sequels — and we see this trend in much of fan fiction today (as well as in romance novels, as Catherine Driscoll explains in greater detail in this volume, and in many so-called women's films) — archontic literature allowed women to publicize their narrative desires, but what they wanted was a narrative that concluded in an idealized marriage, a desire that the Graffigny text refused to satisfy.

The nineteenth century saw a wide array of continuations and sequels authored by women, including many versions of Lewis Carroll's *Alice in Wonderland* books (these are collected in Carolyn Sigler's 1999 *Alternative Alices*), and Mary Cowden Clark's *The Girlhood of Shakespeare's Heroines* (Garber 1999). However, as a tool of social criticism, archontic literature has reached its most productive period over the last eighty years, with the explosion of postcolonial and ethnic American literature.

There is a massive amount of archontic postcolonial literature. The archive of Shakespeare's *Tempest* has been enlarged by many postcolonial variations, beginning with Aimé Césaire's 1968 *Une Tempête* and more recent works like Dev Virahsawmy's 1995 *Toufann,* the later texts following the lead of Fernandez Retamar's 1971 and 1986 essays proclaiming Caliban to be the archetype of an indigenous person forced into colonial subjection. The *Jane Eyre (JE)* archive has been expanded by Jean Rhys's 1966 *Wide Sargasso Sea,* Jamaica Kincaid's 1990 *Lucy,* and Bharati Mukherjee's 1999 *Jasmine.* The *Robinson Crusoe* archive has been augmented by works such as Carlos Bulosan's 1946 *America Is in the Heart* and J. M. Coetzee's 1986 *Foe.* The last fifty years have also seen a tremendous growth in the amount of ethnic American archontic literature published. Some of the most notable of these are David Henry Hwang's 1988 *M. Butterfly,* based on Puccini's opera *Madama Butterfly* and on a newspaper account of a

French diplomat's unknowingly homosexual affair with a transvestite Chinese diva; Alice Randall's 2001 *The Wind Done Gone,* based on *Gone with the Wind,* narrated by Scarlett O'Hara's slave and half-sister; and Nancy Rawles's 2005 *My Jim,* based on Mark Twain's *The Adventures of Huckleberry Finn,* told from the points of view of the slave Jim and his wife. All of the works I have just listed are clearly intended to draw readers' attention to unjust power relations between dominant and subordinate subjects, to discriminatory policies, to psychological and institutionalized prejudices, and to the power of canonical texts to perpetuate stereotypes of race, gender, class, and nation. Although I lack the space here to adequately summarize all the scholarship issued by postcolonial and ethnic studies academics, I will try to indicate the high level of insight that this scholarship has brought to bear on archontic literature by quoting from one of the most prominent of this group of scholars, Gayatri Chakravorty Spivak. Spivak (1999) comments that what Rhys's *Wide Sargasso Sea* accomplishes is no less than a forced reevaluation, on the reader's part, of all that is taken for granted and blithely accepted as "necessary" in the *Jane Eyre* story:

> In this fictive England, she [Bertha, the "madwoman in the attic" of *JE,* daughter of Dominican plantation owners, and wife to Rochester] must play out her role, act out the transformation of her "self" into that fictive Other, set fire to the house and kill herself, so that Jane Eyre can become the feminist individualist heroine of British fiction. I must read this as an allegory of the general epistemic violence of imperialism, the construction of a self-immolating colonial subject for the glorification of the social mission of the colonizer. Rhys sees to it that the woman from the colonies is not sacrificed as an insane animal for her sister's consolidation [127].

Rhys' addition to the *JE* archive takes the older contents of the archive — Jane Eyre's goodness, innocence, and heroine status, Rochester's position as a tormented but deserving hero, and Bertha's role as the unreasoning animalistic shadow villainess — and changes them by refracting the *JE* elements through a mirror of her own design. By doing so, Spivak claims, Rhys critiques not just the fictive world of *JE,* but the project of British imperialism that gave rise to *JE* and other novels that depict the enslavement or dehumanization of colonial subjects, especially female ones, as necessary for the individual development of British subjects. To restate Spivak's point in the terms I've been using, every addition to an archive alters the entire archive.

　　Returning to the quantity of published archontic literature that serves as political, social, and cultural critique: So much archontic literature produced by postcolonial, feminist, and ethnic American writers has been issued recently that book critics at mainstream publications have begun to speak of it as a genre. Helen Schulman, in a January 2005 book review for the *New York Times,* called Rawles's *My Jim* part of "the fiction of reaction," along with Randall's *Wind* and Sena Jeter Naslund's 2000 "feminist response to Melville," *Ahab's Wife*. Barbara Lloyd McMichael wrote in the *Seattle Times* in February 2005, "In a fascinating development of the past decade or so, contemporary American writers have revisited some of the best-known works in America's literary canon and have engaged in some audacious revisionism. They're resurrecting characters that had been marginalized in the original stories and positing voices that had been muted." Although McMichael is wrong about this type of revisiting and revising being a recent development in literature, she is correct about the volume of production of ethnic American and feminist archontic literature trending upward.

Thus, since at least the early seventeenth century, archontic literature has been a compelling choice of genre for writers who belong to "cultures of the subordinate," including women, colonial subjects, and ethnic minorities. This body of work, this long tradition of archontic literature, is the heritage of contemporary zine and Internet fan fiction.

Fan fiction, too, is the literature of the subordinate, because most fanfic authors are women responding to media products that, for the most part, are characterized by an underrepresentation of women. The *Media Report to Women 2002* (Gibbons 2002) stated that although 51 percent of the U.S. population was female at the time of the report's writing, 37 percent of characters on prime time television shows were female, and 28 percent of characters of the 250 top-grossing domestic films were female. Only 17 percent of behind-the-scenes jobs in the motion picture industry were held by women. Over 20 percent of the highest grossing domestic films employed no women in top jobs (as director, executive producer, producer, writer, cinematographer, or editor). The same report predicted that by 2005, over 60 percent of Internet users would be women. Therefore, a disproportionately small percentage of women have positions of power and visibility in mass media organizations, and a disproportionately large percentage of women have (and use) access to the Internet. If, as Henry Jenkins (1992) claims, fans write fanfic out of a combination of fascination and frustration with their favorite media products, the *Media Report's* employment numbers indicate that women consumers are very likely frustrated and disappointed by mass media, perhaps feeling that media narratives to do not fulfill their desires or give them the programming that they want.

Even if a great deal of fan fiction, as I mentioned in the earlier discussion of the Graffigny sequels, tends to reinforce traditional gender roles and social norms, fan fiction on the whole qualifies as a resistant artistic practice because, if nothing else, it is the means by which women write *against* the media corporations whose products they consume by augmenting or sometimes replacing the canonical versions of media texts with their own texts. Fanfics that adhere to heteronormative ideals of social and sexual interaction, that privilege "romance" as an ideal narrative form, are also subversive of patriarchal culture in the same way that Janice Radway argues, in her 1984 *Reading the Romance*, that print romance novels are subversive. Radway, building on José Limon's analysis, claims that what patriarchal society does not give women "enough of," such as "emotional gratification," "attention" and "nurturance," women writers tend to supply for women readers, allowing readers to experience vicariously through narrative what they do not experience in sufficient quantities "in the round of day-to-day existence" (212). These female-constructed worlds, Radway states, often posit a value system, one privileging "love and personal interaction," that is significantly different, even opposite, from the value systems of male-dominated "reality."

Historically, writing archontic literature has been a risky undertaking for women, and this is as true of contemporary fanfic authors today as it was for the first published women authors. Today, women who write fan fiction write under threat of legal prosecution. Writing fan fiction is commonly regarded by copyright holders (the rights to films and television shows are held, in most cases, by large media corporations) as a violation of Title 17, and many moderators and administrators of fan fiction sites have received warnings or cease-and-desist letters from studio lawyers demanding that content be removed from the Internet. So even the most socially conventional fan fiction is an act of defiance of corporate control and a reclamation of women viewers' rights to experience the narratives they desire by creating them for themselves.

What Does Fan Fiction Mean? Theories of Archontic Literature

The reason I chose to focus, in the previous section, on archontic writing as the writing of subordinated groups was that I believe the larger philosophical import of this type of writing is that it undermines conventional notions of authority, boundaries, and property. In other words, archontic literature is inherently, structurally, a literature of the subordinate. I have pointed out that members of subordinate groups have gravitated toward this type of writing in different periods; now I will make the claim that the attraction that archontic writing holds for women and minorities may have something to do with the fact that the genre is intrinsically against "cultures of the dominant." I will explain this idea further by using concepts and terms from two twentieth-century poststructuralist thinkers to assist my explication.

ARCHONTIC LITERATURE "WORKS" BY REPEATING WITH A DIFFERENCE

Gilles Deleuze, in his 1968 *Difference and Repetition,* argues that "repetition" need not mean "physical, mechanical, or bare repetitions (repetition of the Same)," but can refer to "the more profound structures of a hidden repetition in which a 'differential' is disguised and displaced" (xx). In other words, repetition can be something other than a strict, exact replication — there can repetition with a difference, repetition that appears, at first glance, to be a repeating of the same, but in fact contains differences that make the second iteration to be completely new and distinct from the first. These repetitions, says Deleuze, "do not add a second and a third time to the first, but carry the first time to the 'nth' power" (1). Deleuze believes that this type of repetition could be found anywhere, and can certainly be found in texts. Although he speaks in this passage of scholarly commentary, consider how apt a description it is for the relationship between works of fan fiction and originary works: Commentaries, Deleuze states, should have "a double existence and a corresponding ideal: the pure repetition of the former text and the present text *in one another*" (xxii). When one reads a work of archontic writing, in other words, one is really reading two texts at once. The prior text is available and remains in the mind even as one reads the new version. The two texts resonate together in both the new text and the old one (with the old text, it is a retrospective resonance, in the way that *Wide Sargasso Sea* forces us to regard *Jane Eyre* with new eyes), and the reader thus notices the similarities and differences, however great or small, between them.

Deleuze's interest in making this argument, in redefining repetition and difference, is in part to enable us to rid ourselves of notions of hierarchy. "There is a hierarchy which measures beings ... according to their degree of proximity or distance from a principle" (37), Deleuze writes, and automatically I think of how narratives based on prior narratives are denigrated or dismissed as lesser because they are "unoriginal," they did not come "first," they are "derivative." "*The smallest becomes equivalent to the largest* once it is not separated from what it can do" (37) Deleuze continues, which leads me to think of how short works of fan fiction, or of any other kind of archontic writing — which can also mean short in stature in comparison to originary works, being written by unknown writers and lacking the cultural capital that has already accrued to the prior work —can have as much weight and affect as the originary texts, once preconceived ideas about what constitutes a complete, whole, or original work are forgotten. When we conceive of the "smallest" work as a repetition, with a difference, of an earlier work, we understand that the smaller work can have a great deal of resonance with the previously existing one. The resonance is what gives the smaller work meaning and significance, and no longer does its length or stature matter.

ARCHONTIC LITERATURE IS ABOUT THE REALITY OF VIRTUALITIES AND POTENTIALITIES

Another concept that Deleuze introduced was that of the "virtual" and "potential" being just as real as the "actual": "The virtual is opposed not to the real but to the actual. *The virtual is fully real in so far as it is virtual*" (208). Deleuze claims that there is a set of virtual realities, or possibilities, or potentialities, that exist at the same time that our actualities exist. The virtual is that which *could* happen, what we *could* become, at any given time; the actual is that which *is happening*, how we *are*, at any given time. Because both the virtual and actual exist, they are both real. The virtual realm, the realm of possibilities, is no less real than the realm of the actual. Fan fiction, and all archontic narrative, permits virtualities to become actualized. Archontic literature assumes that every text contains a wealth of potentialities that variations of the text can then make actual. Print culture allowed anywhere from a handful to a few hundred possibilities within texts to be actualized by fanfic writers; the Internet has enabled thousands of potentialities within single texts to be actualized and circulated (witness the number of *X-Files* or *Buffy* fanfics accessible on the Web). Alternate universe stories, stories that pair different characters than are paired in canonical texts, stories that posit interstitial material (that is, that fill in missing scenes— what takes place in the cut from one scene to another), stories that ignore large parts of the canon — all are examples of virtualities or potentialities within the originary texts becoming actualized thanks to fanfic authors.

ARCHONTIC LITERATURE IS CHARACTERIZED BY RELATION

I take the concept of "relation" from Edouard Glissant's 1990 *Poetics of Relation*. Glissant, a Caribbean intellectual, grounds his critical theory in the history of the Caribbean Islands, marked as it is by slavery, plantations, and creolization. For Glissant, the only viable ethics in a world traumatized by humanism that led to colonialism is to attempt to get rid of individualistic identities as such, and start defining ourselves and our world through relation. Relation can and should take place, Glissant claims, not only between people, but between nations, between objects, between ideas, between words. Relation gives equal privilege to parts and wholes; it never allows itself to be fixed into identity. Rather, changes and shifts are critical for relation; if relationship ever stabilizes into an "ideal relationship," a concept that stays permanently defined, the result can be totalitarian thought: "ghouls of totalitarian thinking might reemerge" (131). Relation thrives on chaos: "The way Chaos itself goes around is the opposite of what is ordinarily understood by 'chaotic' and ... it opens onto a new phenomenon: Relation, or totality in evolution, whose order is continually in flux and whose disorder one can imagine forever" (133). In chaos, the beings that have entered into relation never make a stable whole. They remain in constant flux with each other, as an "accumulation of examples" that "never complete[s] description of the processes of relation, not circumscribing them or giving legitimacy to some impossible global truth" (174). Archontic literature, with its parts and wholes that never stabilize into one definable text, with its texts in constant expansion and motion, its archives endlessly expanding, generating more texts that in turn generate more archives, exemplifies Glissant's theory of relation. Archontic literature, which does not privilege new variations over originary works and which does not aim to limit creative production to authoritative or canonical versions, enacts Glissant's ethical program at the level of literature.

This concept of relation is quite different from Kristeva's and Barthes's concept of intertextuality, although relation expands on the earlier idea. Intertextuality assumes a writer unconsciously under the sway of influences; it assumes texts have interplay without any conscious intervention on the part of the writer. Relation acknowledges this interplay to be possible, but it also requires that people be conscious of the play and remain vigilant, guarding against the possibility that the play will cease and become fixed and rigid. Relation requires humans to take responsibility for keeping objects in play, whether they be stories or racial categories or languages or geographical boundaries. The nature of fan fiction, the way that fan fiction operates, adheres to this requirement automatically. To write or read or study fanfic is to admit that the text is never stable, that virtualities inside source texts are perpetually in the process of becoming actualized, that between texts within a given archive there is repetition with a difference, and that the interplay between the texts can never be solidified and stilled, for fear of losing the difference, the spark, the chaos that is invention and innovation.

All three of the concepts just discussed — Deleuze's "repetition/differ-ence," his "virtual/actual," and Glissant's "relation"— are all attempts to initiate new ways of thinking ethically. They all seek to do away with out-moded perceptions and categorizations. Deleuze sought to overcome the notion that all repetition must be mechanical and identical, that virtuali-ties and potentialities do not count as real; Glissant aimed to discard the humanist project of defining identities and valuing totalizing systems and wholes. Both thinkers wanted to replace these older concepts with ones that allowed objects and beings without size or stature or conventionally defined identities to be regarded as powerful, creative, inventive, and worthy. This is why I stressed the fact that archontic literature and fan fiction are the cho-sen means of expression for so many subordinate groups over so many cen-turies: because archontic writing, the archontic principle, seeks to empower and elevate what is subordinate. The archontic genre suits the desires of cul-tures of the subordinate perfectly.

The larger import of fan fiction, then, is significant. Fan fiction is a genre that has a long history of appealing to women and minorities, indi-viduals on the cultural margins who used archontic writing as a means to express not only their narrative creativity, but their criticisms of social and political inequities as well. Fan fiction is not a genre of "pure" resistance; as Fiske (1992) and others have pointed out, there are elements of pacifi-cation by and cooperation with the dominant culture in fandom. But fan fiction and archontic literature open up possibilities — not just for opposi-tion to institutions and social systems, but also for a different perspective on the institutional and social. In the realm of the archontic, in the multi-verses of fan fiction, there is a recognition of the valuable innovations that occur in the process of repetition: one scene from a film or television show can be rewritten in fifty, or five hundred, different ways, with each repeti-tion elucidating some different aspect or dynamic of the scene (as Francesca Coppa also observes in "Writing Bodies in Space," this volume). In fan fic-tion, there is an acknowledgment that every text contains infinite poten-tialities, any of which could be actualized by any writer interested in doing the job: fic authors posit the question "what if" to every possible facet of a source text (asking "What if these two characters became romantically involved?" "What if this significant event had occurred earlier/later/never?" "What if this entire narrative arc took place in another era, in another coun-try, on another planet, in an alternate reality?") and explore situations that the makers of the source text simply cannot, because of the need for con-tinuity and chronological coherence in the source text's universe (and the lack of such a requirement in fan productions). In fan fiction, there is a con-stant state of flux, of shifting and chaotic relation, between new versions of stories and the originary texts: the fics written about a particular source text ensure the text is never solidified, calcified, or at rest, but is in continuous play, its characters, stories, and meanings all varying through the various fics written about it. Fan fiction is philosophically opposed to hierarchy, property, and the dominance of one variant of a series over another variant. Fan fiction is an ethical practice.

Notes

   1. I borrow the term "fan-scholars" from Hills (2002). Hills argued that "fan-scholars are typically viewed within fandom as 'pretentious' or not 'real fans,'" but currently, there are several sites dedicated to fan-scholars' theorizing, including the Fanfic Symposium (http://www.trickster.org/symposium, accessed June 1, 2006) and the Live-Journal.com communities fan-ta-sm, metafandom, and fanthropology.
   2. Archives often contain internal stratifications and divides. For example, both academic and fan discussions of fanfic often contain implicit assumptions about the "professionalism" or "canonicity" of source texts as opposed to the "amateurism" or "ephemeral" nature of fanfic texts. Thus, I do not claim that the work of "gathering together" performed by the archontic principle ever amounts to a utopian equalizing of the cultural status/hierarchy/capital of the works within an archive. The archontic principle's "consignation" does not do away with entrenched systems of qualitatively evaluating texts; it refers only to the quantity of texts generated. The archontic principle seeks to place many works under the sign of a single name (*con-sign* texts), such that, for instance, a multitude of texts (fan art, fan vids, fan slideshows, fanfics), not just a television show and movie and video games, exist under the one archival name, *The X-Files.*
   3. Some scholar-fans (in Hills's usage, these are academics who study fandoms) may object to my use of the term *archontic* as counter to the aims of fan criticism (Green, Jenkins, and Jenkins [1998], for instance, claim that fan criticism differs from academic criticism in its "rejection of specialized technical language and theoretical authority" [13]), and therefore potentially alienating to fan-scholars. However, as Hills states, many fan-scholars enjoy using "the theoretical approaches of academic media studies and literary criticism" to analyze fan activities (2002, 18). The term *archontic,* as well as the term *intimatopic* suggested by Elizabeth Woledge (this volume), are not words in common usage, but they are theoretically descriptive and useful.

References

Barthes, Roland. 1981. Theory of the text. In *Untying the text,* ed. Robert Young, 31–47. London: Routledge.

Burow-Flak, Elizabeth. 2000. Background, Cary, *The tragedy of Mariam.* http://faculty. valpo.edu/bflak/engl420/cary.html (accessed June 1, 2006).

Deleuze, Gilles. 1968/1994. *Difference and repetition.* Trans. Paul Patton. New York: Columbia Univ. Press.

Derrida, Jacques. 1995/1996. *Archive fever: A Freudian impression.* Trans. Eric Prenowitz. Chicago: Univ. of Chicago Press.

Fiske, John. 1992. The cultural economy of fandom. In *The adoring audience,* ed. Lisa A. Lewis, 30–49. London: Routledge.

Garber, Marjorie. 1999. "I'll be back": Review of *Part two: Reflections on the sequel,* ed. P. Budra and B. Schellenberg. *London Review of Books* 21, no. 16. http://www.lrb.co.uk/v21/n16/garb01_.html (accessed June 1, 2006).

Gibbons, Sheila, ed. 2002. *Media report to women 2002.* http://www.mediareportto women.com/statistics.htm (accessed June 1, 2006).

Glissant, Edouard. 1990/1997. *Poetics of relation.* Trans. Betsy Wing. Ann Arbor: Univ. of Michigan Press.

Green, Shoshanna, Cynthia Jenkins, and Henry Jenkins. 1998. "Normal female interest in men bonking": Selections from the *Terra Nostra Underground* and *Strange Bedfellows.* In *Theorizing fandom: Fans, subculture, and identity,* ed. Cheryl Harris and Alison Alexander, 9–38. Cresskill, NJ: Hampton Press.

Hale, Laura M. 2005. History of fan fiction. http://www.trickster.org/symposium/symp173.htm (accessed June 1, 2006).

Hills, Matt. 2002. *Fan cultures.* New York: Routledge.

Jenkins, Henry. 1992. *Textual poachers: Television fans and participatory culture.* New York: Routledge.

Kristeva, Julia. 1980. Word, dialogue, and novel. In *Desire and language,* ed. Leon S. Roudiez, trans. Thomas Gora et al., 64–91. New York: Columbia Univ. Press.

McMichael, Barbara Lloyd. 2005. Freeing the man inside Twain's *Jim.* Review of *My Jim,* by Nancy Rawles. *Seattle Times,* February 13.

Pugh, Sheenagh. 2004. The democratic genre: Fan fiction in a literary context. *Refractory* 5. http://www.refractory.unimelb.edu.au/journalissues/vol5/pugh.html (accessed June 1, 2006).

Radway, Janice A. 1984. *Reading the romance: Women, patriarchy, and popular literature.* Chapel Hill: Univ. of North Carolina Press.

Roberts, Josephine. 1983. Introduction to *The poems of Lady Mary Wroth,* by Mary Wroth. Baton Rouge: Louisiana State Univ. Press.

Schulman, Helen. 2005. Never the Twain. Review of *My Jim,* by Nancy Rawles. *New York Times,* January 30.

Smith, Theresa Ann. 2003. Writing out of the margins: Women, translation, and the Spanish Enlightenment. *Journal of Women's History* 15:116–43.

Spivak, Gayatri Chakravorty. 1999. *A critique of postcolonial reason: Toward a history of the vanishing present.* Cambridge, MA: Harvard Univ. Press.

United States Code, Title 17. N.d. Chapter 1: Subject matter and scope of copyright. Copyright Law of the United States.

Weller, Barry, and Margaret W. Ferguson. 1994. Introduction to *The tragedy of Mariam, the fair queen of Jewry,* by Elizabeth Cary. Berkeley: Univ. of California Press.

2. One True Pairing
The Romance of Pornography and the Pornography of Romance
Catherine Driscoll

ABSTRACT.— In this essay, I reconsider the relationship between romance and pornography in fan fiction, proposing that fan fiction allows us to think about them as genres that are not only compatible but intimately connected. Although romance and porn have been popularly associated with women and men, respectively, fan fiction intersects them and reflects on both. Fan fiction might be part of a recent commercial diversification of pornography into the sexual practices of women, but it is also a new mode of popular romance fiction. Considering what fan fiction can tell us about the intimacy of romance and pornography, I place fan fiction in a history of literacy, popular culture, and the private self, concluding that pornography is structured in relation to the conventions of romance, and romance fiction is sustained by porn's ecstatic relationship to exposure. Fan fiction, belonging to the categories of both porn and romance and yet to neither, allows us to rethink their form, content, and significance.

Out of the Closet: Reading and Fan Fiction

Despite apparently striking differences in content, style, and audience, the histories of romance and pornography often intersect. Both emerge in recognizable western forms in the eighteenth century as popular culture and as matters of social concern. Both were shaped by changed relations between the domestic and the personal and thus by the spread of literacy and the emergence of a public sphere (see Lacqueur 1995). The emergence of women's literacy in particular keeps pace with the emergence of the popular novel, of which women were the principal readers and, surprisingly often, early writers. Although the possibility of novels communicating moral lessons was sometimes discussed, the novel was more widely represented as a dubious practice, providing immoral and unhealthy stimulation and encouraging improper fantasies (see Derecho, this volume). Fan fiction has an as yet unacknowledged place in this history of women's literacy dominated by concern about what women and girls read.

Two major shifts shaped the appearance of genre romance fiction. The first was the Romantic movement, which detached the literary quest for the self as creator from sensational popular romances, and the second was the expansion and diversification of mass publication in the nineteenth century. The conventions of romance fiction began settling into a generic formula across this latter period, in both cheap novels and the newly popular ladies' lifestyle magazines, drawing in the process on the most popular examples of romance fiction by women. In contemporary pulp romance and TV soap operas, it is still easy to distinguish the "*Pride and Prejudice* plot" and the "*Jane Eyre* plot," and such familiar standards are equally influential in fan fiction. However, the romance genre is partly defined by content and mostly by the way it is distributed and consumed. The early novel and romance fiction are written and especially consumed by women. This consumption is framed as private and purely for pleasure, and thus as something like a guilty secret. Catherine Salmon and Don Symons note that "romance novels have been called, with some justification, 'women's pornography'" (2004, 96).

The same conditions that made the novel possible also enabled the reinvention of pornography as a discourse on illicit sex (Ferguson 2004; Hunt 2000; Jagodzinski 1999). Cecile Jagodzinski notes, "The novel began to reach maturity at about the same time as modern pornography became easily accessibly in print. Both genres had to be read in secret; both were regarded as especially harmful to the sensitive or naïve reader" (1999, 134). More particularly, these shifts locate the first signs of fan fiction itself. G. J. Barker-Benfield (1992) describes the eighteenth-century appearance of a domestic space in which a closet adjoined the bedroom, which held

> books and a writing desk. There, wrote Richardson, a young lady "makes her closet her paradise." ... Writing and reading letters could express appetite, "to discover, defend, assert and manufacture the self," in Spacks's phrase, echoing the notion of "self-fashioning." Readers wrote to each other with pseudonyms drawn from novels. The characters that readers met in real life they named for those they read about.... In short, readers and letter writers could add to the worlds they exchanged with each other by peopling them with alternative senses of selves [161–62].

Lynn Hunt suggests that this surreptitious pleasure of the novel in fact exacerbated the dubious reputation of pornography (2000, 371), and where romance and pornography meet in early novels, we can see the emphasis on discovery and exposure that is so pronounced in the pornography overwhelmingly associated with visual culture.

Historians have traced the influence of mass-produced postcards, photographs, magazines, and other visual media on changes to pornography, an influence that informs the currently clear distinctions between romance fiction and pornography. Contemporary spaces for porn are clearly far more specialized than those for romance narratives. Although there are dedicated TV channels for both, for example, porn genres are confined to those channels; romance genres are not. However, no development has bought pornography more publicly into the realm of the private than the Internet. There is far less Internet romance fiction than there is Internet porn, and Internet pornography is distributed as both emphatically anonymous/pseudonymous and intensely public and visible. It is hard to avoid porn on the Net, and yet it rarely involves particular individuals. This overexposure fits all too well into Linda Williams's (1989) reading of pornographic film as defined by a frenzy of the visible.

The privacy associated with the novel and pornography is emphasized in fan fiction and inseparable from its distribution on the Internet and thus from moral panics about pornography on the Internet. The Internet allows domestic spaces to contact a wider world, as the novel did, but its use by women has not inspired the same kind of consternation that novel reading once did. In fact, the Internet is often praised as providing opportunities for women's interaction and as a mode of communication particularly suited to women (see Turkle 1995). However, anxiety about exposure to inappropriate material does appear in discussion of how girls use the Internet. This anxiety exemplifies one of three important approaches to the relations between porn and romance in fan fiction to be considered here. Such public commentary routinely sees fan fiction as disseminating pornography under the cover of more acceptable genres, and especially romance. The fear that fan fiction might be appealing but dangerous for girls assumes they are interested in its romance and fantasy elements and will thus be, unwittingly or eagerly, exposed to pornography. Fanfic communities instead distinguish fan fiction from romance and porn as they are usually constructed outside fan fiction (although different communities have different concerns about being labeled one or both). Fan fiction scholarship, however, although also distinguishing fan fiction from both, tends to understand porn as injecting subversive potential into the field of romance.

Slashing the Romance: Studying Fan Fiction

Academic approaches to fan fiction often perceive it as exemplifying new, and preferably "subversive," developments in gender politics and the relation between media, identity, and desire. Sexually explicit and slash fan fiction seem especially useful to such discussion and romance fiction generally appears as the mute field on which it acts. Constance Penley typically dismisses reading slash stories as romance, claiming this "slights the pornographic force" of the genre (1997, 167). Penley, like Mirna Cicione (1998), Anne Kustritz (2003), and many other writers on slash, acknowledges the importance of romance to fan fiction (491), but this is not the subject of their analysis, and neither het fan fiction, which is closer to romance conventions, nor fan fiction without explicit sexual content is important in these analyses. Kustritz's title, "Slashing the Romance Narrative," can stand as a useful summary of this dominant form of analysis. Romance is posited as the traditional terrain on which women write, and in slash, porn uses that field and acts on that field. Penley acknowledges that romance is important to these writers, moving "imaginatively toward what *they* wanted: a better romance formula, and compelling pornography for women" (1997, 489). But porn is still the active force in this argument, transforming romance through a presumption that romance is not about women's desires, and that women writing romance merely repeat the formulaic.

In most fan fiction scholarship, romance is something against which slash appears and to which slash introduces significance, and the porn content of slash is separable from and acting upon its romance content. This claim takes the "gender switching" of slash as a pornographic move, as an exposure, as bringing to the surface the real force of desire. Although it uses a depth model — uncovering motives and ideologies — this argument insists that the meaning of slash is at the surface: it is porn. To actively resituate fan fiction in the category of romance for these writers would be to ignore the ways in which the stories attempt to escape the traditional narrative positions and styles of women. But not only is this a strange reading of pornography, in relation to which women's active desires are somehow more easily articulated, but it also ignores scholarship on romance fiction that recognizes the active interpretive skills of readers. Although Tania Modleski (1988) argues that the genre helps shape women's perspectives on the world, she does not reduce the reader to a passive receptor, and Janice Radway (1984) goes further, claiming that romance readers often read "against the grain" of the narrative. Fan fiction demonstrates the creative potential claimed by romance fans in these studies, where analysts were often skeptical that the genre encouraged women to write.

This prioritization of pornography over romance in studying fan fiction takes some of its force from the 1980s–1990s' feminist debates concerning pornography, and it provides a way of distinguishing fan fiction from the stultified image of romance fiction. There are, however, arguments that slash is a form of romance fiction, most influentially Lamb and Veith's early essay on *Star Trek* fanzines (1986). These usually conclude that "slash has turned out to be an exception that proves (tests) the rules" of the romance genre, "and the rules remain essentially intact" (94). This approach makes explicit one of the most standard presumptions of fan fiction studies: that whereas porn transforms romance, romance subverts pornography's abstraction from and depersonalization of sex/gender relationships, and that fan fiction recasts sex in terms of intimacy (see Woledge, this volume), producing a feminist reworking of porn. From this perspective, porn is to romance as male is to female, and slash cannot be porn. This argument must thus equally ignore fan fiction other than slash, simplify the generic variations of fan fiction, and dismiss romance as a more straightforwardly generic representation of women.

Like all of the above approaches to fan fiction, Lamb and Veith's analysis presumes and relies on a psychoanalytic understanding of the relationship between sex/gender, fantasy, and representation. Some fan fiction scholars are critical of the application of psychoanalysis to fans, although their understanding of how fan fiction is motivated remains indebted to psychoanalysis because of the dominant frame of "fantasy" for understanding how fan fiction works. But this neat template in which gender politics are overlaid onto a therapeutic, reparative, or cathartic model of representation of fantasy as wish fulfillment is not borne out by close generic analysis or ethnographic research in the field.[1] In this essay, I aim to reconsider, entirely without recourse to questions of motive, how the generic structures of fan fiction elucidate its significance to writers and readers.

Plot? What Plot? Genre in Fan Fiction

Certainly some fan fiction focuses on neither romance nor sex — although it is very rare for a story to exclude them entirely — and this is properly called *gen*. Gen is defined mainly by opposition. Horror, angst, darkfic, comedy, drabble, drama, and so on generally label the format or style of a narrative about romance and/or sex. Even comedy in fan fiction is generally romantic comedy or sex farce. Gen, however, is fan fiction that falls predominantly into no other available genre — or, more often, is fan fiction that is distributed in opposition to the categorization of stories by pairings. This is such a dramatic choice in the field of fan fiction that gen becomes something other than a genre. There is thus a layering effect to classification of fan fiction, where pairing and rating function as more important generic markers than terms like *comedy* or *angst,* and are more usual search categories for fan fiction archives. Restrictions on or preference concerning pairings and ratings span all the more recognizable genre labels, but above even these in the taxonomy of fan fiction are three broad fan fiction types: het, slash, and gen. The vast majority of fan fiction is het or slash, and these types are usually defined against each other as approaches to romance and porn, marginalizing gen as something outside of the dominant concerns of fan fiction.

More specific studies of fan fiction dissect it by using subgeneric themes such as first-time or hurt/comfort. I want to take a broader scope than this, acknowledging that the most consistent conventions of fan fiction remain those of formulaic romance. The conventions of romance encourage stories in which heroines are insufficiently aware of the world around them to negotiate it effectively, so that the story might trace their education. Heroes are obviously flawed, although those flaws usually conceal more valuable virtues; and the romance narrative culminates in heterosexual fulfillment. Narrative suspense depends on obstacles based on real or perceived distinctions of social status and on the theme of discovering love. Many of the motifs identified by Radway flesh out this discovery: heroines are often virginal or inexperienced, and for the teen romance form both are virgins, but if a character is promiscuous, they have usually never "known love" (1984, 130). Love and sex are thus closely aligned, but not exchangeable, and sex usually occurs offstage, or at the end and in veiled terms.

Most fan fiction invites identification with one or two protagonists, who can be understood as the heroine and/or the hero along these generic lines. This remains true when both are male or female, and many fanfic communities understand slash pairings as having a more or less feminized "bottom" and a more active "top." The same patterns of ignorance and revelation and obstacles arranged around status of different kinds are used to defer romantic fulfillment, which is the usual point of narrative closure. Many elements of the distribution of fan fiction draw out these generic conventions. The most spectacular is the way that fanfic communities are so often organized by pairings (couples), by the phenomenon of *shipping* (supporting certain pairings at the expense of others), and by distinctions between styles of romance narrative. Almost every fan fiction story is posted with a pairing label, or else a small number of complementary or consecutive pairings. Most stories also accommodate, if they do not advocate, one or more ships. Ships are forceful segmentations of a fandom or fan fiction community, and devoted followers of a ship will often be hostile to any other using one of their characters. Archives are usually structured to be searchable by pairings or are even confined to specific pairings, and most writers and subcommunities specialize in one or a small number of pairings. Beyond pairings and ships, the style of romance narrative in a story can determine where the story is read and by whom. Fluffy romance differs dramatically from angst romance; the latter, however, usually conforms to the rule against sad endings (Radway 1984, 73), or becomes darkfic rather than romance.

Fan fiction, like romance, is commonly represented outside its reading communities as immature because of its undiscriminating and excessive investment in popular culture. But fan fiction is also represented as a (usually secret) substitute for real romantic and sexual relationships—as a type of amateur porn. These representations can be tied together in characterizations of fanfic writers because the distinction between pornography and other representations of sex is not about content. Pornography is defined by being consumed for the explicit purpose of arousal (rather than merely arousing), or by being an illicit sexual representation.[2] Pornography does not inhere in accusations leveled at exhibitions or defendants; rather, these are side effects of pornography as something that should not be circulated. Although having an embarrassing romance addiction and consuming illicit pornography are far from the same thing, they are coterminous in the case of fan fiction. Even fan fiction stories that involve little or no sex are surrounded by the possibility of sexual representation. Discussions of this context in both fanfic communities and fan fiction studies frequently distinguish between porn and some other conception of sex. This other term is very often *erotica*, understood as sexually arousing representations which are neither visibly exploitative nor offensively explicit. Fandom terms like *pr0n* or *smut* also communicate something different from the mainstream image of pornography. Fanfic communities thus often reproduce the distinction between pornography for men and erotica for women by which women are assumed to have a qualitatively different relation to sex and sexual pleasure. This arbitrary distinction divides fan fiction into "sex of the self" and "sex of the 'other'" (Williams 1989, 6), unhelpfully confusing the way fan fiction is usually some version of *sex of the self as the other*.

In general, sex acts are depicted in fan fiction in one of two ways. In the first, which I will call *plot sex*, sexual contact between the central pairing or pairings marks out story development, usually in a sequence of escalating intimacy that maps onto the standard shape of the romance narrative.

In romantic fiction, the drama is usually how a given couple come together, not about whether they will, and in fan fiction, developing romance may be substituted or supplemented with sexualized encounters of building intimacy and explicitness, drawing on the pornographic convention of the delayed money shot and the teen romance conventions of bases and scoring. This is the dominant mode of the use of sex in fan fiction, where sexual intercourse usually closes the narrative to resolve plot and character, even if some other kind of sex had preceded it. The second way of using sex in fan fiction I will call *porn sex*, where sex is lingered over as a sex scene, a difference evident in the timing of the narration, where time is both condensed and extended to mimic the representative structures of pornography. At its most succinct, this is manifest in the PWP ("plot? what plot?") genre, where narrative context for a sex scene is minimal. Although this mimics the pornographic utility of an image of sex, getting to the arousing point of a story as efficiently as possible, PWP stories are never just any utilitarian sex scene because they must still be fan fiction. Porn and plot are thus not opposed in fan fiction, and a single story or scene often includes both plot sex and porn sex.

Realism/Fantasy

Both romance and pornography are commonly understood through discourses on fantasy as a distraction from or avoidance of reality. Whether under the label of fantasy or ideology, romance fiction in particular has seemed to exemplify the way fantasies of fulfillment in marriage are consumed by women in place of striving for more diversely fulfilling lives. As Louis Althusser insists, however, "ideology" has a "material existence," and, just as prayer instantiates belief (1972, 112, 114), the fantasies of gender mobility and sexual freedom apparently played out in fan fiction may be really manifest there. The field of fan studies has further complicated this recognition. As Jenkins (2000) writes,

> fans relate to favorite texts with a mixture of fascination and frustration, attracted to them because they offer the best resources for exploring certain issues, frustrated because these fictions never fully conform to audience desires. Some appropriations may reflect growing disenchantment with conventional constructions of gender and sexuality; others may be highly reactionary, preserving the status quo in the face of potential change [170].

Although fan fiction may challenge dominant ideologies or real limitations on the lives of participants, it is not even then necessarily understood as a critique.

Romance and porn remain firmly anchored in the "real world," not least in the way they strive to make desired objects visible and achievable. Pornography is obsessed with the real — with demonstrating the empirical reality of arousal and orgasm, even to the point of overdetermining these until they resemble no one's real life (see Williams 1989). Only the "realistic" portrayal of sexual display or sex acts can be pornographic (Hunt 2000, 363). In legal contexts, visual images are more liable to be found pornographic for this reason,[3] and antiporn activism is no more committed than porn itself to the idea that porn has real effects. For both, as Judith Butler notes on the side of the activists, "the real is positioned both before and after its representation: and representation becomes a moment of the reproduction and consolidation of the real" (2000, 488). The realism of pornography is, however, always under strain: "penises are always huge, vaginas multiply in number and sexual coupling takes place in a kind of frenzy that is hardly 'realistic'" (Hunt 2000, 372). In fact, despite this emphasis on the real, pornography tends "toward the elimination of external or social reality" (Marcus, quoted in Hunt 2000, 373), and pornographic representation is not a simple analogy between real and fictitious bodies (see Ferguson 2004, x). The real on which porn relies is a claim about bodily presence, but this realism is still evaluated by affect: does it get you off? do you believe in it?

Operating within the regime of fantasy, fan fiction always involves a doubling of the self as both inside and outside each story. As Butler notes, "the 'I' who fantasizes is displaced [in fantasy], for the 'I' occurs at least twice, as the one who 'has' the fantasy, and the 'I' who is *in* the fantasy, indeed, who is in a sense 'had' by that prior I" (2000, 491). Penley representatively applies this psychoanalytic model of fantasy to slash, arguing that the "subject participates in and restages a scenario in which crucial questions about desire, knowledge, and identity can be posed, and in which the subject can hold a number of identificatory positions" (1997, 480). But the doubling of identification in fantasy is also manifest in fanfic communities, where a fanfic reader reads herself reading pornography and writes herself writing/reading pornography. Fantasy demands that "identification is distributed among the various elements of the scene" (Butler 2000, 491), which in the case of fan fiction includes the circulation of stories. This is one way in which slash particularly exposes the dynamics of fan fiction, given the obvious effort required to place the (female) writer/reader in the scene.

This psychoanalytic model of fantasy is used to read fan fiction in ways that neglect its communal dimension. Jane Glaubman (forthcoming) distinguishes fan fiction from private fantasy by emphasizing,

On the one hand, it takes place within a scene of constant exchange—
including arguments about social issues and community norms—but, on
the other, fan fiction contains elements of fantasy that can make it seem
very private, and erotic writings designed to arouse are obviously aids to
masturbation. The use of pseudonyms to interact with strangers encapsulates this dichotomy.

The highest praise in feedback or recommendation is that the reader
was really moved, or the story was really convincing, and reading fan fiction
thus happens at the intersection of realism and fantasy. Community
members also often present fan fiction as a fantasy life with direct cathartic or exploratory benefits for their "real" lives. This does not mean
that fanfic communities should be reduced to a therapeutic narrative,
or that fan fiction is only significant in its external effects. Feminist readings of romance and pornography recognize that these genres are already
part of the real world in which we are constituted, and not just a commentary on it. However, these readings are most productive when they also consider the doubling of identification in fantasy. Radway, for example, notes
that "escapism" both references existing conditions and projects an alternative world (1984, 100). We learn from and negotiate with porn what
appears sexy as we learn from and negotiate with romance what it is to
appear "in love."

The web of canon drawn from a source text is the primary reality
against which fan fiction is written and read, and thus is the only way of
accounting for ideology. When reading *Buffy the Vampire Slayer* (BtVS)
(1997–2003) fan fiction, we cannot see ideological conformity in Buffy's
persistent femininity when that merely demonstrates appropriate canonicity. BtVS, like any other popular cultural text, is materially anchored to its
own conditions of production, but *canon* is the agreed framework through
which writers/readers' experiences are translated for other members of the
community. Canon, which connects the diverse backgrounds and locations
of community members, names a common ground, but every claim about
canon nevertheless raises the specter of its opposite. Fanon is a false image
of canon, a wish-fulfillment fantasy where, to quote Butler's analysis of
porn fantasies, "the wish and its fulfillment belong to the closed circuit of
a polymorphous auto-eroticism" (2000, 492). Fanon is not an inferior interpretation of canon in this light, but a fantasy based on the needs of individual writers rather than the reality established by shared source text. For
Harry Potter fan fiction, Fanon!Draco might be a boy wounded by his
father's neglect, concealing a needy heart of gold under his arrogance. Like
most fanon images, this replays a trope from popular romance fiction, and
the fanon label sets up within fanfic communities a category of immature

and unimaginative fiction based on stereotypes and clichés that mimics the way romance fiction is more widely denigrated.

This assessment of fan fiction in terms of realism — and the segmentation of fanfic communities that follows from this— are evident in, as one among many examples, the circulation of Buffy/Spike stories in the BtVS fandom. Stories about a vampire slayer and a vampire allow a great deal of freedom to manipulate or avoid any scripted reality. However, what is "realistic" is one of the key criteria by which Buffy/Spike stories are assessed in fan communities. Some Spike/Buffy stories were dismissively summarized as "Spuffy," combining the pairing as a homonym for *fluffy,* implying they were mere fantasies. These closed romance narratives about the (literally) undying love of Spike and Buffy, often complete with weddings and children filling in the traditionally omitted final movement of a romance, were particularly opposed by Buffy/Angel shippers on bulletin boards and in open archives as immature fantasy investments. The longer-suffering love of the canon Buffy/Angel story plays carefully with popular discourses on girlhood, where boys often turn into monsters who hatefully mock girls after sex. Precisely because this story is a staple of teen romance, Buffy/Angel laid a specific claim to be relevant to its audience's real world, however exotic the vampire love. The Spuffy label was later reclaimed by Spike/Buffy writers as the pairing moved onto the edges of canon and the pairing took on its own realistic narrative about power, sex, and loneliness.

The romance elements of BtVS canon are more consistently important to the canon on which BtVS fan fiction is based than fantasy details about vampires and slayers. Canon is required to enter a text into a fan fiction community — to provide a means of sharing the story — but fan fiction realism is not an agreed degree of accuracy in representation, but rather a registering of affective power. This is one of the most important ways in which fan fiction locates an intersection of pornography and romance. Nautibitz's multi-award-winning series "In Heat" (http://www.nautibitz.com/fic_sb.html, accessed June 1, 2006) provides an example of how both porn and romance conventions in fan fiction rely on this communal negotiation through what Kristina Busse and Susie Lute (2004) call "the fantext." The canon scenario of Spike watching Buffy's sister while Buffy rests is quickly diverted by porn's fast cut from realism to sex. "Don't worry baby, Daddy's got your cure" comes straight out of porn, heralding the story's escalation into pornographic fanon. The sexualization of vampire bites is canon, most famously in the controversial scene in "Graduation Day, Part 2" (aired July 13, 1999), where Buffy orgasms while Angel bites her, but Buffy's open pleasure in being bitten is as fanon as Spike's "pantheric growl." The scene is rescued from fanon by converting it into a sex dream that underscores the reality of Buffy/Spike's mutual attraction by expelling fanon into fantasy.

Most fanfic readers will admit to one or more favorite fanon tropes, like Gentleman!Spike or Prostitute!Harry, but hesitantly, because fanon connotes undiscerning identification with an unreal object. In fact, fanon is also associated with naive writing styles and is opposed to stylistic sophistication, demonstrating that fanon is less about strict lists of canonical content than about the specter of fantasy. Regardless of the gender or age of writers, fanon is particularly associated with girls. The association of girls with excessive attachment to commodities, romantic idealism, and sharing attachments as a group has a history entwined with the romance genre. In his *Group Psychology and the Analysis of the Ego,* Freud exemplifies immature identification by the contagious communication of enthusiasm among girls sharing a romantic ideal (1922, 64–65). This is the context in which Mary Sues should be understood. Although there have been attempts to coin terms like *Marty Stu* for an equivalent male character, the Mary Sue is generally associated with girl writers who have trouble distancing themselves from the source text enough to write about it rather than write themselves in it. Glaubman (forthcoming) also brings this figure back to the question of fantasy: "The presence of the self is the mark of fantasy, which is why Freud said that all fiction is an extension of daydreaming — a novel (or narrative poem or play), unlike real life, has a hero. But a literary work cuts itself off from readers when it becomes pure fantasy."

Romance/Porn

Porn and romance are often dramatically opposed in the internal discourse of fanfic communities, as if they were at opposite ends of a spectrum of choices. General-access archives like FanFiction.net exclude explicit sexual representations and are overwhelmingly dominated by romance, whereas communities centered on the production of self-designated porn rarely include extended romance narratives or the inflated romantic happiness sometimes called fluff. Given the dominance of pairings in fan fiction, this means the opposition between romance and sex can look like a sliding scale of visibility between G-rated stories, in which romance itself is only implied, and NC-17 stories, in which sex is explicitly represented. This emphasis on the visibility of sexual content through the use of the ratings system reveals the extent to which this assessment is drawn from the generic conventions of pornography. However, very explicit stories may also be very romantic, and the most popular romance stories may focus explicitly on sex. The genres are not poles at either end of a scale but axes between which every story can be plotted as more or less romance and more or less porn. Porn may be a slight or dominant element of a fluffy romance, and romantic completion can be used to ground PWPs as a rationale for the sex. Even this imaginary graph is a gross simplification, because porn and romance are not so separable in fan fiction and because they are not the only terms by which fan fiction is classified. Nevertheless, I would argue that while much fan fiction is explicitly romance and/or porn, all fan fiction is implicitly both.

The accusations leveled at Mary Sues would be entirely redundant for mainstream pornography. There is never a focusing protagonist in pornography, but rather an anonymous viewing position built into every scene. Not only is characterization not the point of most pornography, it is even an obstacle to the efficiency of pornography. This would be anathema to fan fiction because only by characterization, setting, and plot can a story enter the web of canon and become part of the community that will circulate it. Pornography appeals through a field of stereotypes and clichés, which function as the givens of a framing sex/gender regime and set out their feasible and permissible variations, like a vestigal canon. But comparison among fan fiction porn archives like eterniata.eros[unbound] (http://www.eterniata.com, accessed June 1, 2006) and online pornographic fiction archives like Literotica.com supports the claim that characterization is necessary to fan fiction in a way that is foreign to most porn. The character and plot inherent in the web of canon supplement every fan fiction story. Although it has often been claimed that women's erotica requires more "story," this evades some complex questions. Characterization and plot are less important to PWP stories, as the label indicates, and yet they are still produced and consumed by women in the same proportion as other fan fiction genres.

That fan fiction includes the only form of pornography mainly produced and consumed by women is important more for what it says about the gendering of pornography than for any question of motivation or effect. Williams dismisses the porn/erotica distinction precisely because of this blurring of the borders between "mass-market romance fiction for women" and pornography (1989, 6). If romance narratives always imply sex, there has been a recent shift in mainstream romance fiction to include more explicit sex, usually in segregated series like Mills & Boon's Sensual Romance, and the same is true of soap opera. Frances Ferguson argues that pornography's development of "a variety of genres with a variety of target audiences ... performs a major service by educating a self-selecting audience into the possibility of sexual self-realization. The meaning of the pornographic object, in other words, is its audience's self-image" (2004, 42–43). Although available sexual identities may be coded into porn as a dominant reading or packaged into its categorization, self-realization is a fantasy of pornography that does not necessarily either project or rely on "the audience's self-image." The element of fan fiction that most obviously contradicts this is not the diversity of sexual motifs and scenes but rather the communities that moderate all fan fiction, the shared reality demanded by canon, and the amalgamation of these in romance narratives.

The Pornography of Romance and the Romance of Pornography

Romance and pornography seem most easily distinguished by the fact that they are not consumed by the same sets of people or in the same ways. Having stressed the importance of thinking about fan fiction as inseparably community and text, I want to conclude by returning to the practices of writing, reading, and playing in the social contexts of porn and romance. Although fan practices cannot be reduced to questions of ideology and resistance, it is insufficient to displace this binary opposition with a model of fan consumption that focuses on their tactics for using the products of culture industries, a move that has become commonplace after Jenkins. Although fan fiction does involve such tactics—evading and manipulating the strategies of corporations that own source texts—this is only one set of structures it negotiates. Moreover, if strategies are, as De Certeau (1984) argues, the province of institutions and structures that provide authoritative places from which to define culture, then fanfic communities establish structures of their own that strategically generate and channel cultural forms—from public conventions to internal hierarchies of merit and fame.

Fan fiction always appears in a community in a qualitatively different way than romance or porn are determined by their "audience" or "market." Beyond market-framed generic conventions, romance consumers share, trade, and communicate through romance, and romance is often understood as representing that community's shared interests. Porn exaggerates the discreteness of its consumption, representing itself as producing highly specialized communities and solitary consumption. Fan fiction draws on the representation of community in romance — every heroine that centers romance fiction is in some sense continuous with very other heroine of romance fiction and exemplary of women as a genre — and the subcultural spaces for consuming pornography. These communities are both amorphous and mobile, but they nevertheless form structures and spaces that name and define fan fiction. Archives have not entirely displaced the older, more underground (because more transient and subcultural) spaces of zines and cons, but online mailing lists, discussion groups, and diary clusters with an endlessly shifting membership are now far more significant spaces from which to speak about fan fiction (see Busse and Hellekson, introduction to this volume).

Between these structures and spaces, names and stories make impermanent and unpredictable connections that, despite sometimes taxing systems of revision and review, are understood through the avowed amateurism of fan fiction as being entirely about pleasure. Yet there is no homogenous fan fiction community, and it is difficult to discern through the variety of groups, let alone the flames, kerfuffles, and wanks, anything like the coherence of an "interpretative community."[4] Every fandom is a web of communities distinguished by type, pairing, and/or genre, with varied degrees of overlapping or interlocking membership. In turn, every community is a field of subcommunities shaped by friendship groups, specific projects, geographic location, the contingencies of the Internet or other meeting places, and real-life conjunctions. Even this complicated assemblage is striated by internal hierarchies—by BNFs (Big Name Fans) and newbies, by networks of linked journals and other cliques. Remembering this is important because the most meticulous generic analysis of fan fiction will never explain why some themes emerge and others subside. With this qualification, fanfic communities are tethered in multiple ways to external debates.

Wendy Brown (2000) notes that for the MacKinnon-style critique of pornography women writing porn would be "thingified in the head," perpetuating a scene where "play conforms to scripted roles, fantasy expresses ideology" (MacKinnon, quoted in Brown 2000, 210) and where gender is "fully constituted by sexuality." This attitude, Brown says, is "historically produced by, on the one hand, the erosion of other sites of gender production and gender effects, and on the other, the profusion, proliferation, and radical deprivatization and diffusion of sexuality in the late twentieth century" (207). These comments are important for considering fan fiction today, because they encourage us to address changes to gender norms and ideals and also the incorporation of women into popular industries for representing sex. This "pornographic age," to use Brown's term, is a new approach to what analysts of pornography have drawn from Michel Foucault's work. Williams paraphrases Foucault's key points about "the modern compulsion to speak incessantly about sex," to "satisfy—but also, Foucault reminds us, to further incite—the desire not only for pleasure but also for the 'knowledge of pleasure,' the pleasure of knowing pleasure" (1989, 2, 3). But using Foucault's history of sexuality, Williams goes on to argue, would leave us with an aporia where women's pleasure in the arts and knowledges of sexuality might appear. Taking Foucault's argument seriously, however, means seeing how fields like romance fiction or fan fiction, associated with women, participate in this sexualization of the subject for women.

Fan fiction may not answer to Angela Carter's call for a "moral pornography" that would be the tool of historically situated women rather than a law under which they served (1979, 1), but it has certainly extended discussion of that question. Fan fiction provides us both with an example of porn by women and, I have argued, a commentary on the interpenetration of romance and porn. When Drucilla Cornell suggests that "the pornography debate portrays its contestants within sex and gender stereotypes, its contending figures drawn in the broad outlines of a Harlequin romance" (2000a, 551), she uncovers something crucial for understanding late modern pornography. Pornography has a glamorous certainty about sex and gender roles on the one hand and pulls them apart on the other, as this week's dominatrix becomes next week's blushing farmyard virgin. The romance of pornography promises to tell us the truth of sex by reducing the sex/gender system to a currency of exposure, but its closed fantasy system nevertheless aims to move us. Porn offers the seductive ambivalence of an image that excludes by its obvious subterfuges but includes with a promise of pleasure in any case.

It is easier to rethink romance when its similarities to pornography, understood as having a much more serious relation to the sex/gender system, are kept in view. The inseparability of sex and gender in practice is one of the things that romance genres make obsessively visible, and one of the ways in which romance is itself pornographic. Romance is always seeking to display the imperative bind between sex and gender without, perhaps, naming it as such. The imperative to visibility in porn is also embedded in the themes of revelation and discovery that shape a romance narrative, always exposing the truth of feelings, desires, and character, and always manipulating the audience's desire to know what they already know. Porn may rely on a far more efficient system of representation with, as Ferguson suggests, no hidden resources of meaning (2004, 11), but both romance and porn consume the question of sexed and gendered relationships more for its epistemological context than its content.

Pornography and romance share a number of common investments— in the power of a sex/gender system to determine practices (that is, both acts and identities), in moving a mass audience, and, although they approach them very differently, in interpersonal relationships. Fan fiction inherits the most criticized elements of both romance fiction and pornography as modes of popular culture, and where it does enter the public sphere, it is mostly seen as aesthetically inferior, morally dubious, or at best a curiosity. In different ways, romance fiction and pornography both emerged as genres that are in poor taste: as cheap literature/art, as predictable, as cultural forms that are presumed to have less value for being so predictably effective. Reading fan fiction might lead one to think that romance and pornography are not only historically contiguous and able to work together, but perhaps inseparable. Looking at the slip and fit of romance and pornography in fan fiction suggests that pornography is structured in relation to the conventions of romance, and romance fiction is sustained by porn's ecstatic relationship to exposure. In the field of fan fiction, porn and romance define one another, and fan fiction, belonging to both fields and yet to neither, thus allows us to rethink their form, content, and significance.

Notes

1. This research intersects textual analysis and ethnography and might be called, after Jenkins, "media ethnography" (2000, 180). My research has focused on the BtVS and *Angel* fandoms (2000–2002) and the *Harry Potter* fandom (2002–2005). Because every fan fiction community is composed of different subcommunities, my methodology has differed according to the kind and degree of my inclusion and participation, ranging from statistical and textual analysis, through interviews, to participant observation. No adequate genre study of fan fiction can proceed by textual analysis alone because of the inseparability of fan fiction texts and communities.

2. On the latter point, see Hunt (2000), 357. These definitions of pornography can be compatible in courts of law, in public commentary, and among consumers of popular pornography, but they are not necessarily so.

3. Recent Australian legislation specifies that there does not have to be any "real" effect in order for something to be deemed pornographic (Crimes Legislation Amendment, http://scaleplus.law.gov.au/html/bills/0/2004/0/2004080501.htm, accessed June 1, 2005).

4. In the terminology of online fandoms, a *flame* is an attack, a *kerfuffle* is a small scandal, and a *wank* is an extended public shaming of fan practice (usually for being too serious about fandom). Jenkins associates fan fiction with Stanley Fish's model of "interpretative community." See Busse's (forthcoming) revision of this concept for discussions of fan fiction as reading/writing practice.

References

Althusser, Louis. 1972. *Lenin and philosophy, and other essays*, trans. Ben Brewster. New York: Monthly Review Press.

Barker-Benfield, C. J. 1992. *The culture of sensibility: Sex and society in eighteenth-century Britain.* Chicago: Univ. of Chicago Press.

Brown, Wendy. 2000. The mirror of pornography. In Cornell, *Feminism and pornography*, 198–217.

Busse, Kristina. Forthcoming. Rowling's ghost effect: Reading and authority in *Harry Potter* fan fiction. In *Reconstructing Harry: "Harry Potter" fan fiction on the World Wide Web*, ed. Jane Glaubman. Durham, NC: Duke Univ. Press.

Busse, Kristina, and Susie Lute. 2004. "My slash is more canon than yours": Negotiating authority in Harry Potter fan fiction. Paper presented at the International Conference on the Fantastic in the Arts, March 24–28, Ft. Lauderdale, FL.

Butler, Judith. 2000. The force of fantasy: Feminism, Mapplethorpe, and discursive excess. In Cornell, *Feminism and pornography*, 487–508.

Carter, Angela. 1979. *The Sadeian woman: An exercise in cultural history*. London: Virago.

Cicione, Mirna. 1998. Male pair-bonds and female desire in fan slash writing. In *Theorizing fandom: Fans, subculture and identity*, ed. Cheryl Harris and Alison Alexander, 153–77. Cresskill, NJ: Hampton Press.

Cornell, Drucilla. 2000a. Pornography's temptation. In Cornell, *Feminism and pornography*, 551–68.

Cornell, Drucilla, ed. 2000b. *Feminism and pornography*. Oxford: Oxford Univ. Press.

De Certeau, Michel. 1984. *The practice of everyday life*. Berkeley: Univ. of California Press.

Ferguson, Frances. 2004. *Pornography, the theory: What utilitarianism did to action*. Chicago: Univ. of Chicago Press.

Freud, Sigmund. 1922. *Group psychology and the analysis of the ego*. Trans. James Strachey. London: Hogarth Press.

Glaubman, Jane. Forthcoming. Fans, fantasies, and the fantastic. In *Reconstructing Harry: "Harry Potter" fan fiction on the World Wide Web*, ed. Jane Glaubman. Durham, NC: Duke Univ. Press.

Hunt, Lynn. 2000. Obscenity and the origins of modernity, 1500–1800. In Cornell, *Feminism and pornography*, 355–80.

Jagodzinski, Cecile M. 1999. *Privacy and print: Reading and writing in seventeenth-century England*. Charlottesville: Univ. Press of Virginia.

Jenkins, Henry. 1992. *Textual poachers: Television fans and participatory culture*. New York: Routledge.

_____. 2000. Reception theory and audience research: The mystery of the vampire's kiss. In *Reinventing film studies*, ed. C. Gledhill and L. Williams, 165–82. London: Arnold.

Kustritz, Anne. 2003. Slashing the romance narrative. *Journal of American Culture* 26:371–84.

Lacqueur, Thomas. 1995. Credits, novels, masturbation. In *Choreographing history*, ed. Susan Leigh Foster, 119–28. Bloomington: Indiana Univ. Press.

Lamb, Patricia Frazer, and Diane Veith. 1986. Romantic myth, transcendence, and *Star Trek* zines. In *Erotic universe: Sexuality and fantastic literature*, ed. Donald Palumbo, 236–55. Westport, CT: Greenwood Press.

Modleski, Tania. 1988. *Loving with a vengeance: Mass-produced fantasies for women*. New York: Routledge.

Penley, Constance. 1997. *NASA/Trek: Popular science and sex in America*. New York: Verso.

Radway, Janice. 1984. *Reading the romance: Women, patriarchy, and popular literature*. Chapel Hill: Univ. of North Carolina Press.

Salmon, Catherine, and Don Symons. 2004. Slash fiction and human mating psychology. *Journal of Sex Research* 41:94–100.

Turkle, Sherry. 1995. The seductions of the interface. In *Life on the screen: Identity in the age of the Internet*, 9–76. New York: Simon & Schuster.

Williams, Linda. 1989. *Hard core: Power, pleasure, and the "frenzy of the visible."* Berkeley: Univ. of California Press.

3. Intimatopia
Genre Intersections Between Slash and the Mainstream
Elizabeth Woledge

ABSTRACT.— I challenge the assumption that slash fan fiction is unique, and I situate slash fiction within a wider literary context. Unlike others, who have linked slash fiction with the popular romance, I look elsewhere for mainstream literary equivalents. To avoid categorizing all types of slash fiction within the same rubric, I use a genre-based approach to isolate a subset of slash fiction that is centrally concerned with intimacy. I then trace the parallels between amateur and mainstream fictions, elucidating a hitherto uninvestigated genre of literature, which I term *intimatopic*. By analyzing intimatopic texts from both slash and mainstream communities, I investigate the features that link them. After considering how each structure is used to highlight intimacy, I trace these links across the representation of homosocial bonds, sexual interaction, equality, and hierarchies, as well as the pervasive structure of hurt/comfort. After exposing the core of intimacy that defines intimatopia, I discuss the subversive potential of slash and its mainstream equivalents, concluding that it is not erotics but intimacy that has the potential to subvert current assumptions about interpersonal relationships. Throughout, I consider intimatopic slash fiction to be part of a wider body of literature that is similarly concerned with representation of interpersonal intimacy and the ways it can be facilitated.

Introduction

To date, studies of slash fiction and fandom have tended to focus on the ways it is perceived to encapsulate the relationship between subgroups and the dominant hegemony. This approach, perhaps encouraged by the prevalence in media studies of what Nicholas Abercrombie and Brian Longhurst (1998) term the "incorporation/resistance paradigm," has led to the existing consensus that slash fiction is a unique genre of literature that subverts the dominant literary and cultural tropes through its use of appropriation and its explicitly sexual content. All the academics who investigated slash in the late 1980s and early 1990s commented on its perceived uniqueness: Henry Jenkins claimed that slash was the most "original contribution to popular literature" (1992); Constance Penley characterized slash as "a unique hybrid genre" (1992, 480); and Joanna Russ felt that slash was "the only sexual fantasy by women for women ... produced without the control ... of censorship" (1985, 95). Descriptions of slash fiction that characterize it as "guerrilla erotics" (Penley 1991, 136) have only added to the academic tradition of viewing slash fiction as both a unique and renegade form of literature.

Because my interest lies with the literature produced by certain slash fandoms, I do not presume to debate the claims of ethnographic studies that, like Camille Bacon-Smith's (1992), have found that fandom itself is unique. Although slash fandom can be considered unique, much of the literature it produces certainly cannot. Rather, as Abigail Derecho (this volume) notes, it is part of a literary tradition that has a long history. That fan fiction and professionally produced fiction cannot be separated has been already been recognized by at least one previous commentator, Jacqueline Lichtenberg, who draws parallels between fannish and professional writings that center around the dramatization of what she terms *intimate adventure*. This more recent trend toward viewing slash as less unique and esoteric can also be seen in work by Sara Gwenllian Jones, who asks whether slash is "really so oppositional" and suggests that slash stories "emulate" the style of mainstream popular romance novels (2002, 81). Catherine Salmon and Don Symons's evolutionary account of slash fiction at first appears to continue that trend: they claim that slash fiction is "so similar to mainstream genre romances that it could reasonably be classified as a species of that genre." However, Salmon and Symons are unwilling to completely reject the traditional paradigms segregating slash fiction from professionally produced literature, concluding that slash "*uniquely* fuses traditionally female romance with traditionally male camaraderie, adventure and risk taking" (2004, 97, 99, emphasis mine). It is interesting that both Jones and Salmon and Symons have suggested the popular romance novel, of the type produced by Harlequin and by Mills & Boon (Mills & Boon is the British equivalent of the Harlequin romances of the United States), as a mainstream parallel to slash fiction. However, I think that closer parallels can be found without the need to recast homoeroticism into heterosexuality.

Lichtenberg offers a different approach. She suggests her own genre, intimate adventure, as one that exists across both amateur and professional fields. This genre is, she claims, encapsulated by the "relationship driven story focusing on emotional heroism." Lichtenberg's approach of outlining a new genre is an appropriate one, and I agree that its central defining feature should be considered to be intimacy. However, Lichtenberg never really defines the characteristic features of intimate adventure, nor does she chart its landscape. Instead, she prefers to revel in its supposedly revolutionary potential to change "the world.... Fundamentally. Forever." What is needed is a new term, one that can be adequately defined and liberally illustrated with examples from both slash and professionally published literature. Salmon and Symons suggest that mainstream heterosexual romance novels exist in the fantasy world of "romantopia," a world in which sex becomes part of a larger plot where "the heroine overcomes obstacles to identity to win the heart of and marry the one man in the world who is right for her" (2004, 97). In contrast, the subset of slash fiction and its mainstream counterpart that I elucidate here takes place in a fantasy world I dub *intimatopia,* because its central defining feature is the exploration of intimacy.[1] Although Catherine Driscoll (this volume) shows how a proportion of fan fiction combines elements traditionally associated with romance with those traditionally associated with pornography, the fiction I wish to address requires a different approach. Although some intimatopic texts do indeed share stylistic features with both romantic and pornographic genres, in their most defining feature, they differ greatly from either of these two neighboring literatures. Romance novels and pornography, although in different ways, both work to separate sex and intimacy. Intimatopic texts, on the other hand, work to connect these two elements, and this is why they need a separate genre all to themselves. Since its origin in the print fanzines of Kirk/Spock (K/S) fandom, slash fiction has become such a wide-ranging phenomenon that it is reductive and unrealistic to consider it as a whole. I thus stress that the term *intimatopia* cannot account for all types of slash fiction (many of which will be better accounted for by other essays in this volume); however, exploring intimatopic texts will help me draw important parallels between a significant subset of slash fiction and professionally published literature, thereby highlighting the parallels I wish to draw between these two, traditionally separate, modes of fiction.

I do not intend to revisit the much-debated subject of whether slash is a legitimate decoding of its media source, as Jones (2002) suggests, or a misreading of media's generic codes, as Bacon-Smith (1992) suggests— indeed, both are probably correct within different subsets of slash fiction. Such questions become unimportant if we focus not on the interpretation of the source, but on the literature inspired by that interpretation. Intimatopia focuses on the product — slash fiction — rather than on the diverse communities that produce it. Although there is certainly interesting work to be done surrounding how slash communities differ from mainstream literary communities, such as the increasingly fluid movement between author and reader that exists online, it is also productive to consider how, despite these differences, intimatopic slash fiction is far from unique in literary terms and shares distinguishing features with intimatopic literature, some of which predates slash and which, like slash, is still being produced and consumed today.[2] The fact that these parallels exist between professional and amateur fields means that the literature of slash fiction (I make no claims about the community) cannot be considered to completely subvert cultural tropes. If it did, it would not have such visible parallels in more mainstream literary markets. Instead, intimatopic texts build on some of culture's less salient ideologies. Indeed, George E. Haggerty has suggested that "what culture finally represses" is "not sexual desire, but love" (1998, 15). Intimatopic texts may highlight images of love and intimacy that in our culture are not typically associated with interpersonal relationships between men. The following investigation of the features of intimatopia in both slash and professionally published literature illustrates the ways that the texts work to connect intimacy to male interaction.

The Landscape of Intimatopia

Intimatopia is a homosocial world in which the social closeness of the male characters engenders intimacy. Eve Kosofsky Sedgwick's work on male homosocial desire has highlighted how, "for different groups in different political circumstances, homosexual activity can be either supportive of or oppositional to homosocial bonding" (1985, 6). It is clear that in intimatopia, despite the diverse cultural and political backgrounds of individual writers, homosocial bonding is depicted as directly supportive of homosexual activity. In intimatopic slash fiction, it is not surprising to discover that it is always derived from a media source that already emphasizes homosocial bonds through the depiction of the loyalty between two men who live and work in a more or less homosocial community. Many of these media sources are themselves derivative of some nineteenth-century literature, the homosocial nature of which was explored by Leslie Fiedler (1960). In this literature, two close male friends share adventures in isolation from the wider heterosocial society. One of the most prominent antecedents of modern-day intimatopic fictions could be considered to be the male-authored American texts associated with writers such as Cooper, Melville, Twain, Whitman, and Hawthorne, rather than the twentieth-century heterosexual romances popularized in Harlequins and in Mills & Boon. Several commentators on *Star Trek* point to the centrality of its homosocial "kinship bonds" (Geraghty 2003, 447), which, as April Shelley suggests, echo the literary bonds of many nineteenth-century American texts that depicted the "fleshless," and hence "sacred," symbolic "marriage" between two men (1986, 96). In addition to the appropriation of homosocial narratives such as this, many slash stories enhance homosociality by isolating their characters alone on alien planets or in historical or futuristic eras, thus creating an intimate bond of two. Slash fiction uses this intense and homosocial background as a base and builds a homosexual relationship between its two protagonists atop it. This connection, in which homosocial and homosexual elements are supportive, is expressed by slash writer Janet Alex's Spock, who tries to explain just why people think he and Kirk are lovers: "since our work throws us so much together, it is only logical for the crew to assume that our professional relationship has led to a personal one" (1985, 7). In intimatopic slash fiction, the use of a homosocial backdrop is the "logical" way to explore a homosexual relationship.

Many professionally published intimatopias use homosocial backgrounds in similar ways. There are a vast number of professionally published intimatopias; however, for the sake of conciseness and clarity, I will refer to the mainstream work by Mary Renault, Mel Keegan (who also writes slash fiction), and Marion Zimmer Bradley.[3] Many mainstream intimatopias are, like slash, appropriative, and those that are choose to appropriate similarly homosocial settings. Mary Renault's Greek trilogy — *Fire from Heaven, The Persian Boy,* and *Funeral Games*— appropriates the homosocial worlds of ancient Greece and Persia in which Alexander and his friend/lover Hephaistion fight side by side, their love "as public as a marriage" (1972, 150). Intimatopic writers who make a less obvious appropriation from history nonetheless choose to make use of homosocial settings. Mel Keegan's *Fortunes of War* depicts her heroes Robin and Channon living and loving side by side on a Renaissance warship inhabited only by men. In such a homosocial environment, her male comrades can claim to one another that "no one would care if you kissed me in full daylight" (1995, 198). Mel Keegan's *An East Wind Blowing* also depicts a band of largely male warriors with whom her heroes Ronan and Bryn live at Eboracum. Within this homosocial community, homosexual activity is positively encouraged: "It's best for warriors to take warrior mates.... Some of us are friends, some are lovers, all are sword brothers" (1999, 113).

In these examples, the homosocial community supports homosexual activity by the creation of societies in which it is only "logical" for social intimacy to engender sexual ties. Even intimatopic writers who do not use any form of historical appropriation create their own esoteric homosocial worlds within which intimacy is easily developed. Marion Zimmer Bradley's *The Catch Trap* depicts two trapeze artists: Tommy and Mario, partners and lovers, live within a close-knit society where men and women are segregated and where Tommy feels "his whole life seemed to have been poured into a passion fiercer, purer and more intense than anything he had ever known" (1979, 135). The parallels between these homosocial worlds and the ones used in slash fiction are clear: they are all worlds in which the intimacy engendered by homosocial bonding can be used to facilitate the growing erotic relationship between the male protagonists.

Sedgwick's work on male homosocial desire is largely concerned with the way homophobia radically disrupts the continuum between the homosocial and the homosexual. However, most intimatopias present a world where the social and the erotic slip seamlessly into one another. Homophobia is conspicuous by its absence. This gap between what Sedgwick sees as a salient cultural feature and the fantasy world depicted by intimatopias raises the question of the relationship between intimatopia and queer politics. One professionally published text, *The Charioteer* (1953), by Mary Renault, which predates most intimatopic texts by fifteen years, deals with this issue explicitly in a way that helps to explain the attitude implicit in intimatopias from both the slash and mainstream worlds. Renault uses the homosocial elements of homosexual subcultures to throw her two protagonists, Ralph and Laurie, together. However, she makes it clear that they rise above the labels and queer identities that Laurie accuses of "shutting you away, somehow" (176). Renault's heroes forge their own way by following a Greek ideal that, in contrast to modern subcultures, they think allows them "a few standards and a bit of human dignity" (348). Renault's attitude toward, and distance from, the homosexual subculture she depicts has led some modern commentators to claim that she demonstrates "homophobia" and fails to represent "the real lives of gay people" (Summers 1990, 157). However, it is debatable whether Renault, or any writer of intimatopic texts, is in fact attempting to represent the real lives of gay people at all. Instead, these writers may be more interested in exploring intimacy between men who may be homosexual, but whose intimate relations are not defined by their sexual identities. Many writers of intimatopic fictions, although not explicitly distancing themselves from the subcultures as Renault does, use historical, futuristic, or fantasy plots to the same ends.

Much slash fiction has been criticized for its supposedly homophobic implication that its heroes are not gay but just two men who love each other — or as Penley puts it, its depictions of an intimacy in which "the two men are somehow meant for each other and homosexuality has nothing to do with it" (1992, 487). Homophobic or not, there are several reasons why writers of intimatopias may actively want to distance themselves from gay fictions and identities. First, many slash writers feel that existing self-consciously gay fiction does not represent intimacy at all; instead, it denies intimacy through its depiction of casual sex (opinions expressed by a group of K/S writers online at the Yahoo.com mailing list KirkSpockHeaven). This is similar to the attitude expressed by Renault's *The Charioteer*, in which one of the main objections to gay subcultures is that its members sleep together even though they personally dislike one another and share no real intimacy. Although the representation of casual sex can be seen in some subgenres of slash fiction, it is not a feature of intimatopia, in which even the short, sexually focused stories known as PWPs (which is said to stand for "plot? what plot?") are accompanied by carefully placed pointers to intimacy. Kira-Nerys's PWP "Nightly Revelations," for instance, is based around the existing intimacy between Kirk and Spock, which is highlighted in the first few lines of the story by the mention of "that small, almost tangible bond that existed between them." Second, many writers of intimatopic slash fiction share with professional intimatopic writers, such as Mel Keegan and Mary Renault, what Kevin Kopelson has described as the desire to "liberate sexual love from homosexual love" (1994, 104). Under this rubric, many writers do not want to confine their fictions to existing stereotypes by labeling their stories or characters as homosexual and thus sacrificing a universal view for the particular, and risking their texts' losing their polysemy and becoming "univocal" (Witting 1983, 65). Finally, intimatopia is simply not about modern homosexual identities, and thus, although it often depicts homosexual acts, it retains a distance from homosexual politics. Intimatopia is a world separate from our current realities, a world defined and shaped by its own rules and codes — a world of male intimacy, yes, but not the world of the modern homosexual. I question the accusation of homophobia leveled at a genre that makes so little use of modern homosexual politics. It is not homophobic so much as homoindifferent.

Sex in Intimatopia

Sex in intimatopia is used, not unlike the homosocial communities depicted, as a tool to enhance intimacy. Intimatopic slash fiction often borrows from sources such as *Star Trek*, *The Sentinel*, and *Highlander* where existing canonical material provides the possibility for psychic oneness.

Bacon-Smith points out that even "source products that do not offer a telepathic hero likewise receive the mind-meld treatment with references to
'almost telepathic rapport'" (1992, 231). For intimatopic K/S writers, the
image of the two men merging minds during sex is handily suggested by
the canonic Vulcan ability to meld mind, which allows for many descriptions of orgasm similar to that offered by Killashandra's *Surrender:* "He was
Kirk. He was Spock. They were one." In intimatopic K/S, even descriptions
that do not include the meld itself contain language that subtly evokes its
connotations: "there are no secrets between us, we are one, even here in the
physical universe outside the mind" (Sinclair 1998, 76). Descriptions of sex
in all intimatopic fictions are pervaded by these images of oneness, whether
derived from an appropriated source or not.

     Professionally published intimatopic fiction is also full of these images:
Alexander and his beloved eunuch slave Bagoas "seemed as one" (Renault
1972, 388); Mel Keegan's warriors Bryn and Ronan are "closer than brothers could ever be" (1999, 96); her Renaissance hero Channon feels that Robin
"seemed to read his thoughts" (1995, 339); and Zimmer Bradley's trapeze
artists "had only one heartbeat" (1979, 469). Sharon Cumberland (2000)
quotes a slash writer familiar with several fandoms whose opinion encapsulates the representation of sex in intimatopia: "I write erotic stories
because I like to explore themes of emotional intimacy." The sheer pervasiveness of images of oneness in both professional and amateur intimatopias
suggest that the view expressed here by a slash writer is not unique to amateur writers. Although amateur and professional writers may be working
in very different communities and may be accorded very different status
within our culture, the similarity between their products, at least in the
case of intimatopic fiction, suggests that their ideologies and perspectives
are not dissimilar.

     Across all intimatopic literature, sex is almost always embedded in a
plot, rather than included simply for its own sake. As one advertisement
for submissions to the intimatopic fanzine *Between Friends* makes clear,
this is an important element that writers must address: "quality and plot-
line are foremost, although raunchy is fine with us—if it includes a viable
plot" (seen in the fanzine *Way of the Warrior,* 1989, 188). As Cumberland
(2000) points out, this format is common to many slash fandoms where
sex scenes are frequently "embedded in a plausible and suspenseful plot."
Cumberland implies that this structure is unique to slash fiction and results
from the freedoms available to amateur women writers in cyberspace. However, in fact, this pattern of "embedded" sex scenes is a commonplace of
all intimatopic fictions, on the Internet, in fanzines, and in the world of
professional publishing. This weaving of the sexual plot into wider plots

allows sex to be used to enhance the intimacy that the story puts in place. In the case of slash fiction, this social backstory is often imported from the source material. The following extract from the K/S story "Lematya Lessons" by S. R. Benjamin is typical of the way intimatopic slash implicitly — and, here, explicitly — links the sexual to socially intimate bonds already established. Here is Spock's point of view as he and Kirk make love:

> He calls my name, breathlessly. I grasp his shoulders moving against him. This is the logical extension of everything we are. It is, on a deeper level, the same rhythm with which for years we have walked ships corridors at night. Or the way we moved, pacing each other, on Organia. And my hand against his elbow, urging him on, as we raced along the embankment on the shore leave planet, where a golden-haired girl and a white rabbit had become the least of our concerns [2002, 86].

As this quotation makes clear, the sexual relationship depicted is represented as an extension of the social relationship imported from the source material. The references to "Organia" and "a white rabbit," which inform Spock's erotic internalizations, are all canonical details lifted from *Star Trek* and used here to support the imaginative extrapolation that is K/S. The way that this passage integrates the source material from *Star Trek* and the interpretive norms of the fannish community is connected to the pleasure in interpretation so central to fandom and richly outlined by Deborah Kaplan (this volume).

In contrast to intimatopic texts that culminate in the joining of the social and the sexual, in intimatopic texts in which the heroes have sex early on in the plot, the sex itself is used to provide and increase social intimacy. An example of this is can be found in Mel Keegan's professionally published intimatopic text *An East Wind Blowing*, in which the two heroes, Ronan and Bryn, have flirted but "shared nothing" until, both separated from their real families, they form a band of two and become lovers. It is only through sexual interaction that they become as close as "kin" and Bryn is able to see "himself mirrored in Ronan" (1999, 96, 99).

Sex in intimatopia is often, as Patricia Frazer Lamb and Diana L. Veith point out with regard to K/S slash, "transcended by the psychic union it makes possible" (1986, 249). One of the many intimatopic slash fans that I have spoken to about their interests expressed this distinction very well: she claimed, in a comment that drew applause from her audience, that "K/S has not been, and never will be, about the sex. It is the *intimacy* of the sex they share that keeps us [fans] all together" (public interview conducted at KiS Con, Dallas, Texas, March 2004). Thus, contrary to popular belief, intimacy, not explicit sexual union, is the defining feature of at least one important subgenre of slash fiction. Often, as the stories progress, the characters come to realize, as Kirk does in Patricia Laurie Stephens's fanfic "That Darkness, That Light," "how little sex really had to do with the terms of a relationship" (1989, 160). This emphasis is as common in amateur intimatopic slash fiction as it is in mainstream intimatopias. In a similar moment of revelation to be found in the professionally published *The Catch Trap*, Zimmer Bradley's hero Tommy realizes that, "sex was only a part of it" (1979, 483). The pattern can be seen in Keegan's professionally published texts too, for as their relationship developed, "it was not Robin's body Channon wanted.... It was his heart" (1995, 71).

This is a distinctly different pattern to that found in many mainstream romances and explored in the fantasy world of romantopia, which Salmon and Symons use to describe slash fiction. In romantopia, although sex might provide a temporary oneness, it is a oneness enjoyed with reluctance, for the hero and/or heroine are generally ambivalent about the love they feel. It is also a temporary oneness that does not extend to other aspects of the relationship; indeed, in romantopia, the heroine may marry the hero still marveling at how little she knew him.[4] This is in stark contrast to the images of emotional sharing, mind linking, and psychic oneness that pervade sexual relationships in intimatopia. The crucial difference between romantopia and intimatopia is that in intimatopia, intimacy is normally established before sexual interaction and is always maintained after it, whereas in romantopia, it is only established by sexual interaction and is frequently transitory. Salmon and Symons mention this difference between slash and the romance novel, claiming that in slash, "the bond of friendship is firmly in place long before sex rears its head" (2001, 84). However, although they think that this is a minor difference, I believe it is a crucial one. Stories in romantopia are often structured around sexual misunderstandings that, Tania Modleski (1990) claims, function to explain a man's brutality as an expression of his love. In this way, the entire structure of romantopia is based on a hypothesis that would be impossible within intimatopia, for only in her ignorance of the hero's psychology can the heroine misinterpret violent behavior as brutal when in romantopia it is a manifestation of love. By contrast, in both amateur and professional intimatopic literature, the psychic oneness achieved by the protagonists prevents this kind of ongoing misunderstanding. Although there certainly are subsets of slash fiction that specialize in pairing characters who are apparently adversarial in the source material, these subsets are rarely intimatopic in nature. Perhaps this type of slash fiction has more in common with the romance novel than does the genre of intimatopia considered here.

Intimatopic slash stories often demonstrate an ambivalent relationship to sexual representation, and Andrew Ross's claim that slash is "always graphically sexual" (1989, 256) is in fact completely inaccurate, for many slash stories, for instance Carol Turner's "The Night Men" (1989), are hardly sexual at all, concluding simply with an admission of love. The supposed division between sexual "slash" and nonsexual "gen" fan fiction is, at least in *Star Trek* fandom, rather hazy. Gen zines like *Contact* often contain ambiguous descriptions that are not denoted as sexual but are nonetheless strikingly intimate: "They were close, so close, holding, clasping each other tight, their breath pounding in each others ears" (Bonds 1979, 25). Although debates in fandom often circulate around what is needed to make slash fiction qualify as slash, and although some fans do feel cheated if a slash story is barely erotic, on the whole, for most fans, the sex is not the primary motivation they offer for reading or writing slash.

During 2004, I conducted a survey of slash fans who had gathered at a K/S convention held in Texas. I asked them to rank sixteen elements for importance in slash fiction; "emotional sharing" came top of the list, with "at least one sex scene" ranking only fourteenth, well down the list of concerns. Although I suspect that sex is more important to the genre than these results suggest, partly because other sexual options, such as "sex that is tender," ranked higher, these results highlight the centrality of emotional intimacy to K/S readers. Sex is central only when it can be used as an extension of that intimacy. Although it may be suggested that emotional issues were ranked highly as a form of social conformity, this anonymous survey was conducted in the safe environment of a fannish convention and the results not advertised as being for public consumption. For these reasons, as well as because they reflect what the literature seems to suggest, I believe the results of this survey to be a relatively accurate representation of fannish concerns. Unsurprisingly, a similar ambivalence to the sexual can be found in professionally published intimatopic texts too, again suggesting common concerns and ideologies linking pro and fan writers. Renault's depiction of Alexander the Great in *Fire from Heaven* maintains that he "simply did not think [sex] very interesting" (1970, 259). However, this is no bar to the erotic and social intimacy he engages in with Hephaistion, to whom he was "everything" (219), and Bagoas. The point is that for Alexander, intimacy transcends sex. Although he does not quite enjoy sex, he does enjoy intimacy: from his point of view, "the true act of love was to lie together and talk" (259). This does not mean, however, that all intimatopic texts are as ambivalent toward the sexual as Renault's, nor does it mean that the sex depicted in intimatopia is always gentle and saccharine.

I have discussed how popular romances often depict scenes of sexual violence; so do intimatopic texts from both amateur and professional writers. However, whereas in romantopia sexual misunderstandings are caused by a lack of intimacy, in intimatopia, apparently similar scenes are based around intimacy and closeness. Even the violent sex that at times occurs between the heroes in intimatopic texts is used to engender intimacy. The amateur K/S novel *A Question of Balance* by Della Van Hise (1980) provides an excellent illustrative example of this use of violence, and a professionally published example may be found in Mel Keegan's *Fortunes of War*. In *A Question of Balance*, when Kirk and Spock are reunited after a lengthy adventure, their sexual passion spills over into aggression: "there was no gentleness in him as he thrust deep into Spock's body, burying himself to the hilt with the first brutal lunge" (1980, 56). The difference between this and the brutality that may be depicted in romantopia is that this sexual act, however aggressive, is encoded as one of intimacy. Van Hise tells us that Spock's motivation for enduring the pain was his desire to share Kirk's feelings: "He wanted to be hurt, wanted to feel the agony he knew Kirk had felt, both mental and physical" (57). Similarly, Kirk's motivation for hurting Spock enables unity: "He didn't want to hurt Spock; he wanted to be hurt himself. But it caused him pain to cause Spock pain. Endless circle" (57). Again and again, the accompanying descriptions offer the reader an act of violence encoded via images of intimacy, sharing, and unity. The aggressive sexual acts once completed are described as having led to an even greater intimacy: now "they could love together, laugh together, share losses together, cry together ... even die together when the time came. Totality. Union. Completion" (57). These scenes are not constructed to glorify or eroticize the violence but to use it just as all the structures are used: to engender intimacy. This intimacy, rather than the violence that provides it, may be read as erotic.

Hierarchy and Equality in Intimatopia

I have already briefly considered how many intimatopic texts, both amateur and professional, use homosocial structures, a parallel to which can be found in traditional nineteenth-century American literature. A further parallel between these two genres is what Frederick Zackel (2000) has called the "ethnic sidekick" paradigm. Within this structure, the hero and his partner are always separated by a more or less explicit hierarchy; in some cases, this is based on a racial difference, but it is also applicable to relationships where race is not an issue. This common feature of intimatopic literature has an interestingly ambivalent relationship to the egalitarian ideals implicit in many of the images of oneness already considered. Indeed, many of the classic descriptions of slash fiction offered by academics focus on its "egalitarian" structure (Kay 2002, 41), which depicts "co-warriors" (Salmon and Symons 2001, 89). In line with this perception, many fans of intimatopic slash speak of their attraction to the depiction of equality offered by two men. Gilda, for instance, claims that her preference for inti-matopic slash over heterosexual romance novels is accounted for by her ability to "see them [slash heroes] as equals, rather than as the hero–damsel in distress pairing of traditional romance novels" (personal communication, September 15, 2004). And yet equality in intimatopia is not straightfor-ward. Indeed, if equality is depicted, it is an equality based on difference, rather like that symbolized in the yin-yang symbol, and characterized by intimatopic slash fan Kathy as "equal but not identical" (personal commu-nication, September 9, 2004). However, it remains something of a puzzle as to why, if fans are drawn to intimatopic slash for its "equality," we see so many hierarchical structures. In the case of appropriative intimatopias, such as much K/S fan fiction, it may be because these structures are inher-ent in the source product: the hierarchy typical of the ethnic sidekick par-adigm has been noted by Leslie Fiedler (1982) between *Star Trek*'s Captain Kirk and his Vulcan first officer. But far from erasing the differences in hier-archy offered by the source product, fannish texts tend to highlight them.

Almost every intimatopic text I have read revels in the intimacy of hier-archized individuals, and the professionally published texts discussed here are no exception. Mary Renault's Bagoas is Alexander's slave; Alexander is Hephaistion's commander; and Marion Zimmer Bradley's trapeze artist Tommy will always be a "kid" to his partner and lover Mario (1979, 588). Mel Keegan too offers characters who struggle for dominance within their relationship, although in her texts, she uses homosocial societies as a way for the characters to partially transcend the ego games and dominance. Per-haps the heteronormative patterns typically associated with sexual intimacy in our culture are almost impossible to transcend; or, more in keeping with the theme of intimacy, perhaps hierarchies actually enhance intimacy. The greater the divide, the more intense the intimacy that must transcend it. Such a possibility is suggested by the slave stories of intimatopic slash fiction in which the slave is first trusted, then beloved, and finally given freedom, often at the risk of overturning the whole slave-based culture into which the heroes have been placed. A similar explanation is suggested by Mary Renault's fascination with the incident in which Alexander, on being mis-taken for Hephaistion, replies, much to the surprise of members of the court, who assume the king will be furious to be mistaken for his subordinate, "never mind.... He too is Alexander" (1972, 118). Without the underlying knowledge that Alexander is Hephaistion's commander, the reader might be less impressed by the intimacy suggested by Alexander's reply.

Suffering in Intimatopia

In intimatopic texts, the writer will do almost anything to engender intimacy, including depicting the extreme suffering of their heroes. This kind of pattern has a history as long as that of literature itself: David M. Halperin describes its most extreme manifestation in ancient Greek friendship stories as that in which "death is the climax of the friendship. The occasion of the most extreme expressions of tenderness on the part of the two friends" (1990, 79). The fan fiction genre of hurt/comfort, which tends to use suffering rather than death, is one manifestation of this classic pattern. Bacon-Smith (1992) suggests that hurt/comfort is used by writers who wish to explore intimacy but who do not feel able to describe that intimacy in sexual terms. Although at first it may seem that a sexual text would obviate the need for structures that legitimate intimacy, the appearance of hurt/comfort in the intimatopic and sexual texts of both mainstream and slash fiction suggests that it is of interest to the writer for more than its potential to depict physical interaction without direct sexual reference. In the sexually explicit text of *An East Wind Blowing*, published professionally by Mel Keegan, elements of hurt and comfort are often woven together throughout sexual passages. One sex scene begins like comfort, with Ronan "passive beneath ... gentle hands," yet images of hurt and injury are associated with penetration as Ronan is "pierced" like a "lance thrust into him" (1999, 197). Thinking of death, Ronan cries out, and Bryn stops, asking "Am I hurting you?" Upon finding Ronan's hurt is more mental than physical, sex is once again depicted as comfort: "He pressed closer, as if he could get into Bryn's skin and share it with him. 'Make love to me, Bryn,' 'shh, I will'" (197). The ensuing encounter appropriately combines images of wounded cries and comforting caresses, so interrelated are the complementary structures of hurt and comfort.

Mirna Cicione has claimed that hurt/comfort, as it manifests itself in slash fiction, represents the "eroticisation of nurturance" (1998, 163). However, in the case of all intimatopic texts, both slash and mainstream, it is used to enhance the eroticization of intimacy. Hurt/comfort provides a plausible way for any author to depict increasing closeness between two men, because when the hero is hurt, he is at his most vulnerable. The element of hurt permits him to share intimacies that would otherwise be kept private. Although hurt/comfort has only been labeled as an explicit genre within fannish literatures, it is yet another structure that connects amateur and professional texts. Its pervasiveness clearly demonstrates how similar concerns are being explored across literary fields that have traditionally been considered as vastly different. Hurt/comfort is often facilitated by the homosocial warlike settings that provide ample opportunity for injury, along with the subsequent comfort. In this way, although it is often tied up with sexual depictions, as in the example I gave above, hurt/comfort can also be used to create a world in which, in contrast to the typical heterosexual romance novel, sex is far from the only way of expressing intimacy. It therefore ties in with the way intimatopic texts from all fields value intimacy above and beyond sexual interaction and with the way these texts depict it in both sexual and social relationships.

Intimatopia's Wider Implications

In intimatopic fictions, both amateur and professional writers have created a world in which a variety of human interactions—even those that begin in injury, aggression, or violence — are mined for their potential for intimacy. Although slash fiction has often been represented as subversive, I maintain that its most subversive act is not the one readers will immediately suggest. The dissident or subversive texts of slash fiction have often been assumed to share their dissidence with other, superficially similar, literary and cultural forms such as pornography or queer literature. However, the true dissidence that intimatopic slash fiction showcases is almost the opposite. Mass media, much advertising, pornography and popular psychology, as well as a proportion of popular and literary texts on homosexual themes, work to foreground the centrality of sex within interpersonal relationships. In opposition to this, and striking a contrastingly subversive note, intimatopic texts insist that intimacy, not sex, drives human interaction. So pervasive is this assumption among intimatopic writers that it is completely normalized within their texts despite its dissident possibilities. Indeed, as Marie-Laure Ryan (1999) points out, what is subversive in one community may be completely normative within another. Thus in today's highly sexual culture, the *intimacy* of intimatopic slash fiction is most remarkable, although it is viewed as normative within its own community. Bacon-Smith implies that slash fiction's depiction of a world in which "sexuality is a function of love" (2000, 144) is both heterosexist and naive, but it would be equally plausible to conceive of this so-called naïveté as a reaction against the often pervasive ideological assumption that sex rather than intimacy is the driving force of interpersonal attraction. In this way, it can be seen that intimatopic slash fiction shares with professionally published intimatopic literature a desire to foreground an ideology that restores the links between love, friendship, and intimacy. The existence and popularity of intimatopic work across both amateur and professional markets suggests that this is currently a culturally important project that has gained momentum since its simultaneous emergence in both slash and mainstream fiction.

Notes

1. The slash fiction that I am familiar with is K/S fiction, predominantly as it is published in fanzines. Although much Internet-published K/S fiction is also an example of intimatopia, on the whole, the online fiction tends to be more varied. Although I'm most familiar with this fandom, of course the basic features of intimatopia are evident in others to some extent.

2. Most professionally published intimatopic texts are, like slash fiction, written by women. I don't have the scope here to deal with the implications of this for the question of "women's writing" and whether such a thing can be said to exist. However, I believe that many women share an ideology in which intimacy is of central importance. This draws them to reading and writing intimatopic texts across diverse markets.

3. Other professionally marketed texts that I define as intimatopias include the following: Pat Barker, *Regeneration* (London: Penguin, 1991); Susan Hill, *Strange Meeting* (London: Penguin, 1989); Susan Hill, *The Bird of Night* (London: Hamilton, 1973); Mel Keegan, *Aquamarine* (Brighton: The Gay Men's Press, 2000); Poppy Z. Brite, *Lost Souls* (London: Penguin, 1994); Diane Duane, *The Door into Fire* (London: Magnum, 1981); Mercedes Lackey, *Magic's Pawn* (New York: Daw Books, 1989); Patricia Nell Warren, *The Front Runner* (New York: Bantam Books, 1975); Patricia Nell Warren, *The Wild Man* (California: Wildcat Press, 2001); Anne Rice, *Cry to Heaven* (London: Penguin, 1991); and Marguerite Yourcenar, *Memoirs of Hadrian* (1951; reprint, London: Penguin). Several professionally published *Star Trek* novels are also intimatopic in nature, including: Della Van Hise, *Killing Time* (New York: Pocket Books, 1985); Sondra Marshak and Myrna Culbreath, *The Fate of the Phoenix* (New York: Bantam Books, 1979); and Sondra Marshak and Myrna Culbreath, *The Price of the Phoenix* (New York: Corgi, 1977). For a look at nonsexual intimatopic *Star Trek* fan fiction, I recommend Sondra Marshak and Myrna Culbreath, eds., *The New Voyages* (London: Titan Books, 1992), and Sondra Marshak and Myrna Culbreath, eds., *The New Voyages 2* (London: Titan Books, 1993).

4. These contrasting assumptions are extrapolated from Ferrarella (2000) and Browning (1994).

References

Abercrombie, Nicholas, and Brian Longhurst. 1998. *Audiences: A sociological theory of performance and imagination.* London: Sage.

Alex, Janet. 1985. The matchmaker. *Th'y'la* 5:3–42. Zine.

Bacon-Smith, Camille. 1992. *Enterprising women: Television fandom and the creation of popular myth.* Philadelphia: Univ. of Pennsylvania Press.

_____. 2000. *Science fiction culture.* Philadelphia: Univ. of Pennsylvania Press.

Benjamin, S. R. 2002. Lematya lessons. *Beyond Dreams* 4:80–87. Zine.

Bonds, Martha J. 1979. The miracle of Christmas past. In *A Contact Christmas,* 18–27. Zine.

Browning, Amanda. 1994. *Enemy Within.* Surrey: Mills & Boon.

Cicione, Mirna. 1998. Male pair-bonds and female desire in fan slash writing. In

Theorizing fandom: Fans, subculture and identity, ed. Cheryl Harris and Alison Alexander, 153–77. Cresskill, NJ: Hampton Press.

Cumberland, Sharon. 2000. Private uses of cyberspace: Women, desire, and fan culture. *MIT Communications Forum.* January 25. http://web.mit.edu/commforum/papers/cumberland.html (accessed October 22, 2005).

Ferrarella, Marie. 2000. *A hero for all seasons.* Surrey: Silhouette.

Fiedler, Leslie. 1960. *Love and death in the American novel.* New York: Criterion.

_____. 1982. *What was literature? Class culture and mass society.* New York: Simon and Schuster.

Geraghty, Lincoln. 2003. Homosocial desire on the final frontier: Kinship, the American romance, and *Deep Space Nine*'s "erotic triangles." *Journal of Popular Culture* 36:441–65.

Gwenllian Jones, Sara. 2002. The sex lives of cult television characters. *Screen* 43:79–90.

Haggerty, George E. 1998. Anne Rice and the queering of culture. *Novel* 32:5–18.

Halperin, David M. 1990. *One hundred years of homosexuality and other essays on Greek love.* New York: Routledge.

Jenkins, Henry. 1992. *Textual poachers: Television fans and participatory culture.* New York: Routledge.

Kay, Susan. 2002. The things women don't say. In *Science fiction, canonization, marginalization, and the academy,* ed. Gary Westfahl and George Slusser, 37–49. London: Greenwood Press.

Keegan, Mel. 1995. *Fortunes of war.* Brighton: The Gay Men's Press.

_____. 1999. *An east wind blowing.* Brighton: The Gay Men's Press.

Killashandra. N.d. *Surrender.* http://seacouver.slashcity.net/killa/surrend.html (accessed June 1, 2006).

Kira-Nerys. N.d. Nightly revelations. http://www.kardasi.com/bobw/index.htm (accessed October 22, 2005).

Kopelson, Kevin. 1994. *Love's litany: The writing of modern homoerotics.* Stanford, CA: Stanford Univ. Press.

Lamb, Patricia Frazer, and Diane Veith. 1986. Romantic myth, transcendence, and *Star Trek* zines. In *Erotic universe: Sexuality and fantastic literature,* ed. Donald Palumbo, 236–55. Westport, CT: Greenwood Press.

Lichtenberg, Jacqueline. N.d. The intimate adventure has just begun. http://simegen.com/school/workshop/IntimateAdventureFem.html (accessed June 1, 2006).

Modleski, Tania. 1990. *Loving with a vengeance: Mass produced fantasies for women.* New York: Routledge.

Penley, Constance. 1991. Brownian motion: Women, tactics, and technology. In *Technoculture,* ed. Contance Penley and Andrew Ross, 35–161. Minneapolis: Univ. of Minnesota Press.

_____. 1992. Feminism, psychoanalysis, and the study of popular culture. In *Cultural studies,* ed. Lawrence Grossberg, Cary Nelson, and Paula A. Treichler, 479–500. New York: Routledge.

Renault, Mary. 1953. *The charioteer.* London: Longman Green.

_____. 1970. *Fire from heaven.* London: Longman.

_____. 1972. *The Persian boy.* London: Penguin.

Ross, Andrew. 1989. *No respect: Intellectuals and popular culture.* New York: Routledge.

Russ, Joanna. 1985. Pornography by women, for women, with love. In *Magic mommas, trembling sisters, Puritans and perverts: Feminist essays,* 79–99. Trumansburg, NY: The Crossing Press.

Ryan, Marie-Laure. 1999. Cyberspace, virtuality and the text. In *Cyberspace textuality: Computer technology and literary theory,* ed. M. Ryan, 77–107. Bloomington: Indiana Univ. Press.

Salmon, Catherine, and Don Symons. 2001. *Warrior lovers: Erotic fiction, evolution and female sexuality*. London: Orion.

_____. 2004. Slash fiction and human mating psychology. *Journal of Sex Research* 41:94–100.

Sedgwick, Eve Kosofsky. 1985. *Between men: English literature and male homosocial desire*. New York: Columbia Univ. Press.

Shelley, April. 1986. "I have been and ever shall be your friend": *Star Trek, The Deerslayer* and the American romance. *Journal of Popular Culture* 20:84–104.

Sinclair, Jenna Hilary. 1998. From the heart. *First Time* 47:68–79. Zine.

Stephens, Patricia Laurie. 1989. That darkness, that light. *Way of the Warrior* 2:142–87. Zine.

Summers, Claude J. 1990. *Gay fictions Wilde to Stonewall: Studies in a male homosexual literary tradition*. New York: Continuum.

Turner, Carol. 1989. The night men. *Beside Myself* 1:4–9. Zine.

Van Hise, Della. 1980. *A question of balance*. Pon Farr Press. Zine.

Witting, Monique. 1983. The point of view: Universal or particular. *Feminist Issues* 3:63–69.

Zackel, Frederick. 2000. Robinson Crusoe and the ethnic sidekick. http://www.bright lightsfilm.com/30/crusoe1.html (accessed June 1, 2006).

Zimmer Bradley, Marion. 1979. *The catch trap*. New York: Ballantine.

4. The Toy Soldiers from Leeds
The Slash Palimpsest
Mafalda Stasi

ABSTRACT.— I examine slash fan fiction texts from a novel perspective by moving beyond the view of a static, uniform, and self-contained corpus. To this end, I propose a new metaphor for slash: that of a rich intertextual *palimpsest*. By viewing the vast slash corpus as a diverse and dynamic one, and considering each individual text in its own terms, a richer, more in-depth connection among genre and style is permitted. I examine how intertextual links between the slash text and its canon deeply influence the shape the text takes, allowing writers to use compression and allusion techniques reminiscent of medieval allegory; and I analyze how the collective, shared authorship of slash blurs the modernly established boundaries of individual author and discrete text, harkening back to classical mythological discourse. I then look at how intertextuality is even more pervasive in slash: most texts refer not only to their canonical source, but also to a variety of other texts. I conclude with an indication for possible further analysis into the material conditions of production of slash texts, and how these affect the text itself. As even the most cursory look to the history of literature shows, intertextuality is prevalent and pervasive, and slash is no exception: far from being a freakish oddity, slash is no different from any other literary text.

Introduction

Papa bought Branwell some wooden soldiers at Leeds ... I snatched up one and exclaimed: "This is the Duke of Wellington! This shall be the

115

*Duke!" When I had said this, Emily likewise took one up and said it should
be hers; when Anne came down, she said one should be hers.... Branwell
chose his, and called him "Buonaparte."*
                    —Charlotte Brontë, "History of the Year 1829"

In the last fifteen years or so, a number of scholarly texts studying slash fiction have appeared, but these texts, with very few exceptions, have dealt with it as a primarily sociological or anthropological phenomenon. Early critics such as Camille Bacon-Smith (1992) focus on the quirkiest facets of the fannish community, contributing the popular view of fans as freakish people devoted to weird activities disconnected from and unrelated to "real life." Similarly, Henry Jenkins's articulate and in-depth study *Textual Poachers* (1992) focuses mainly on the fan population and on reception issues: how fans see and interpret the original text they are interested in, how the fan community functions, and so forth. Most authors also classify and analyze the slash corpus according to narrow thematic criteria, often in view of extracting sociological or psychological meaning. Even when slash is being considered from the textual point of view, most analyses suffer both from oversimplification and from a judgmental approach, where the vast, diverse corpus of slash texts is lumped together as a monolithic and self-contained whole, usually to be dismissed summarily. As Green et al. (1998) note, "academic accounts of slash tend to deal with it in isolation from the larger framework of genres [and they] often consider slash to be a static genre, making generalizations that assume a consistent subject matter and thematics over time and across all slash stories" (11). Thus we have patronizing value judgments such as this remark about a literary corpus whose magnitude is probably in the order of millions of texts: "Considered strictly as fiction, I found [slash stories] pretty tedious (although some were very well written). Considered as clues to women's mating psychology, however, I found them riveting" (Salmon and Symons 2001, 3).

Slash texts are dismissed on the assumption that "they're just trashy romance novels." What is more, even when the critique is favorable, we do not really move away from a traditional, prescriptive classification of "good, literary" texts versus "bad, nonliterary" ones. Lamb and Veith (1986) pronounce slash texts "surprising[ly] ... of good literary quality" (237) and draw parallels with several canonical literary works. For example, they view the relationship between Kirk and Spock in *Star Trek* as representative of Leslie Fiedler's "mythic quality imbu[ing] the male-male bonding often found in American literature, especially between men of different races" (236). Ultimately, Lamb and Veith's (laudable) main concern with exploring the revolutionary and utopian dimension of slash's gender politics takes them back to the usual comparison between slash and romance novels (254). Although the parallels are undeniable, they can be restrictive and limiting: not only are the conditions of production of slash and romance fiction different, but slash texts encompass more than one genre and have a wide range of themes, voices, registers, and moods. As other essays in this volume show (Woledge; Driscoll), there are ways in which slash and romance can be profitably compared and contrasted. What I disagree with is the undiscerning and dismissive reduction operated by equating slash as a whole with romance (with the term often used to generically mean hackneyed, saccharine prose). The romance fiction genre should not be so easily dismissed, as Radway (1984) has shown us in her reevaluation and problematizing of the reception of romances. Driscoll (this volume) draws her parallels by going back to the origins of romance and by comparing its modes of consumption in relationship to slash; however, when it comes to conditions of production and distribution today, romance novels are a commercially lucrative business. Big publishing houses such as Harlequin or Mills & Boon adopt a mass-production approach, forcing authors into a template with stringent rules about what can and cannot be written. In contrast, the slash community does not have a single, centralized controlling and gatekeeping structure, and it is not run as a for-profit endeavor. This is not to say that there are no rules as to what is writeable and what is not, or that the slash community has no power structure or social rules, but simply that they are not structured the way those of a commercial enterprise are. Moreover, as Kustritz points out, the developmental history of fan fiction is "radically different from standard romance traditions" (2003, 371). This is why privileging and absolutizing the parallel between slash and romance can lead us down the wrong path; ultimately, most critics who introduce the "slash as romance" discourse tend to eventually move back toward a view of slash limited to the anthropological perspective, or confined to the reader's or writer's psychology.

In the last few years, scholarship has paid more attention to textual matters in fan fiction and has resolved to look "closely at the language" and at "the [fannish] group's linguistic play" (Wakefield 2001); yet even recent studies such as Smol's (2004) still echo Lamb and Veith's surprised attitude at finding "good" slash, with complex intertextuality and writerly authors masterfully manipulating literary language. Jenkins's continued contributions to fandom studies have pointed out how the impulse to write fan fiction is part of a basic drive toward storytelling as the preserve of a "shared cultural tradition" from Homer onward, and how this "process of circulation and retelling improved the fit between story and culture, making these stories central to the way a people thought of themselves... Contemporary web culture is the traditional folk process working at lightning speed on a global scale" (2000). However, this still takes a cultural studies perspective rather than a literary criticism one; textual considerations come after discussions of cultural reception, and production issues still focus on the "primary" media text.[1] For example, Scodari and Felder (2000) dismiss fannish text as secondary — as texts that even fans consider to be less important than the original ones. Hills (2002), who discusses fannish "texts" as diverse as costuming and cult geography, is still more interested in the larger cultural context and its relationship with the original text, rather than in specific instances of fan fiction. Essays such as Russo (2002) are almost alone in critiquing the standard reading where "fan fiction is always subordinate to its father text," and in stating that "it is equally possible to read the interpenetration of TV and fan texts as a sign that fans are appropriating the signifiers of mass culture in the service of their independent narrative and social needs — or to avoid rankings altogether, and begin by thinking of TV shows and fan writing as related manifestations of equally legitimate forms of desire" (12).

In short, slash has not been adequately studied as a textual artifact, with the possible exception of Pugh's (2004) essay, programmatically subtitled "Fan Fiction in a Literary Context," where she baldly states, "My primary interest in fan fiction is literary rather than sociological." So is mine — with the proviso that the narrow literary/textual dimension should not displace or eliminate the important larger cultural perspective: Driscoll (this volume) rightly points out that fanfic texts and communities are inseparable; performing textual analysis in isolation is impossible. Rather, what I am advocating here is a bracketing of textual/literary consideration to ensure that fan texts receive focused attention *as text,* thus balancing a field skewed to psychological and sociological analyses and contributing to a rich, multiperspective, and well-rounded analysis. Here, in addition to moving away from the psychological and sociological slant of so much published work on fan texts, I also strive to move away from a traditional, judgmental attitude whereby slash is substandard because it fails to measure up to some sort of literary standard. Such an attitude has been so largely discredited in contemporary textual studies that it is puzzling to find it still lingering around slash. What I aim to provide is a more in-depth study of the slash text as valuable, strong text by focusing on its intrinsic characteristics, which are related both to its conditions of production and its formal features: "'fanfiction' as a valid literacy practice" (Chandler-Olcott and Mahar 2003).[2] Once individual slash texts are analyzed on their own terms and merits, we can overcome aprioristic, limiting value judgments, and we can move beyond a binary, hierarchical view of texts toward a systemic, intertextual one.

To signify this reframing of slash, I would like to use a different metaphor from the one made famous by Jenkins: that of fan text as poaching. His use of De Certeau's metaphor of poaching is incomplete and misleading: poaching is an illegal appropriation, a theft — granted, in the case of slash, it is a Robin Hood type of theft, where fans are (at least potentially) countercultural activists, who problematize and turn on their heads the production and distribution system of mass culture, and then reappropriate some of those cultural messages and meanings through poaching. I am not denying the potentially oppositional nature and political relevance of slash, but I fear that the notion of theft may be misconstrued to indicate an inherent disparity between original text and slash rewriting — or at least to obscure the key point that there is no "legitimate" text (as opposed to "pirated" ones). De Certeau talks about writing in the margins, which implies a hierarchy where some texts are indeed "marginalized," and where fan writers are glossists rather than authors in their own right (see Derecho, this volume, for a discussion of literal marginalia). Moreover, the poaching metaphor focuses on the fans' actions rather than on the text, which is seen as object of an action, rather than the subject of a process. Poaching is only the beginning of what happens with a slash text. It's not just a question of "take the text and run": the initial text, once taken, is reworked in a postmodern, multivocal, and intertextual fashion. The movement away is followed by a complex shifting across different axes and dimensions, through genres, techniques, and writing conventions.

Like any other text, a slash text is a node in a web, a part of an often complex intertextual sequence, and it bears a close and running relationship with (at least) one other text. This is why I use the term *palimpsest* to indicate a nonhierarchical, rich layering of genres, more or less partially erased and resurfacing, and a rich and complex continuum of themes, techniques, voices, moods, and registers. With this new metaphor, I also want to emphasize the dynamic aspect of textual production in slash. The process of creating the slash palimpsest is no different from that through which any other branch of literature unfolds; it has a set of characteristics of its own, an internal variety and wealth beyond conventional formulas, and it also points back to other genres and traditions in the intricate, complex continuum that links all texts ever written. Far from being a monolithic, repetitive set of substandard texts created by a naive set of scribbling women whose bizarre hobby stands apart from any self-respecting body of literature, slash is a legitimate part of the literary discursive field. Equipped with the new perspective the palimpsest metaphor affords, it becomes possible to give due attention to the slash text itself, to look more closely at its complex relationship with other texts and genres. Thus, the bulk of this essay is dedicated to the discussion of various types of intertextuality in slash, and how they compare to other textual strategies in different genres, styles, and periods.[3]

Intertextuality and the Slash Canon

The constitutive characteristic of slash (indeed, any fan text), inherent in all its definitions, is that it is based on shared, preexisting characters and settings: each TV series, film, or book being slashed provides a base for authors to work with. Authors and readers have a thorough knowledge of the initial setting and characters, the *canon*. The use of such a word to signify the pervasively intertextual and self-referential nature of the slash text has some potentially unfortunate consequences: it can reinforce the superficial but still prevalent notion that slash is a second-rate, marginal product. The notion of both slash and the "canonical" source text as product, as static object, are particularly misleading because it can result in a narrow view of a binary set of the "good" (official and original) text and the "bad" (amateurish and derivative) one. It is much more productive to use the metaphor of the medieval palimpsest to illuminate the complex intertextual relation between the initial text and its slash retelling. A single sheet of vellum would be variously used for different texts: an early text would be more or less thoroughly erased to make space for a newer one, but more than one text could coexist in a close relationship on the page. Sometimes the older text was only partially erased, or a glossed commentary could expand to take most of the space available, or two or more different texts could end up bound and shuffled together.

This approach not only dispenses with the notion of an inbuilt and inherent hierarchy between different texts, but it also gives a more accurate and less reified view of the slash canon. Indeed, beyond the bare factual minimum, canon constitution and interpretation are a highly debated and controversial critical activity in the fannish milieu. Far from being a fixed and unproblematically shared set of references, the slash canon is based on a collective interpretive process. It is not monolithic, even within a given fandom. It is possible to outline a continuum going from quite basic, hard-to-dispute "facts" such as the occupations of the main characters, to highly debatable points of characterization.

For example, when it comes to the slash canon for the British TV series *The Professionals* (1977–1983), there is relatively little to discuss over main character Bodie's eye color, because the actor portraying him sports decidedly blue eyes; but fans manage to endlessly discuss the eye color of his coprotagonist Doyle: the actor's eyes are a less easily definable murky green. Even the apparently self-evident fact of Bodie's eyes being blue is not always to be taken for granted. When the TV series first aired in 1978, the quality of videotaped reproductions of the episodes was so poor that some early fans wrote stories featuring a brown-eyed Bodie. If eye color is already harder to determine than expected, it becomes impossible to agree with any finality whether Doyle is a sincere liberal trapped in a dirty but necessary job, or a hypocrite who moans about his violent job while enjoying the adrenaline rush. Between these two extremes, there is fanon: a series of details and characteristics that are shared by most slash stories, but that have no factual basis in the original media text.[4] Fanon is developed by the fan community as an integral part of the process of interpretation of the original text: as early or prominent slash authors start writing, they introduce their own perspective on the source text. The influence of these early authors leads to their choices being in turn appropriated by later writers, either because they share the interpretation or because they are not yet completely steeped in the original text and thus take the fanonical elements as canon. Again using *The Professionals* fandom as an example, in fanon, Ray Doyle is a vegetarian; he is sensual; and he is much smaller and younger than his partner Bodie — but all of this is contradicted or left unsaid by the original TV series.

If we look at other fandoms whose canon is less stable or simple to define, the situation becomes even more complicated. For example, fans of *The Lord of the Rings* have to somehow reconcile book and film canon, so that most stories are prefaced by an explanation of the choices the slash author made in matters ranging from important plot and ideology points to whether Boromir has blond or black hair, and which side one decides to be on has not unnegligible consequences for the social structure and dynamics of the fandom. A more extreme example of polarization could be found in the fandom for the TV show *Highlander* (1992–1998). This fandom developed well before the TV series was over, so that eventual developments in the series were either accepted or vehemently denied, sometimes creating very visible controversy, as in the case of character Richie's death. This process of negotiation of shared meaning via the molding of the original text into canon and fanon represents one of the main constitutive elements of the slash discursive field. The slash canon is constructed through a repeated collective fruition and interpretation of the initial text. Despite canon being a construct, it is regarded as normative by most authors and readers: even when it is turned on its head or flouted, it is hardly escapable.

It is thus not surprising that the strong frame of reference created by the intertextual relationship between the slash narrative and its canon heavily shapes the discourse at all levels, and it lends some peculiar characteristics to the slash text. All texts contain intertextual references, but some do so "more centrally than others.... As a form, fanfictions make intertextuality visible because they rely on readers' ability to see relationships between the fan-writer's stories and the original media sources" (Chandler-Olcott and Mahar 2003). Indeed, having much of the setting and basic characterization already filled in and an audience utterly familiar with them provides the author with a powerful shorthand device. For example, let us consider the following sentence, culled from a story first circulated on a fannish mailing list and then posted online: "Klaus opened his eyes and promptly closed them again. It didn't help. Even though he could no longer see the mane of golden curls on the pillow beside his, he could still smell the scent of roses" (Kadorienne, untitled short fanfic, http://belladonna.org/snippet01.html, accessed June 1, 2006). This sentence might not mean much to a nonslash reader, but a slash audience will gasp in horror and delight. This audience will have instantly gathered, by the name of the character and by the sketchy physical description of the other person in bed with him, a whole wealth of meaning. In fact, this is a sentence taken from a slash story in the *Eroica* Japanese manga fandom (Aoike 1978–ongoing), where Klaus is a violent, macho and homophobic character. He is vainly pursued by openly and flamboyantly gay Dorian (canon), who has blond curly hair, wears a rose scent (fanon), and bears Klaus a persistent and unrequited love. The reader is now holding her breath: how and why Klaus is in bed with Dorian? What happened? How will Klaus react?

The extreme compression that the tight intertextual coupling of slash text and canon allows is unparalleled in most modern prose genres, and it points back to techniques more commonly used in poetry, or in genres such as folktales or mythological cycles. Thrupkaew (2003) traces the connection between writing slash and writing poetry in the way constraints are reworked into affordances: writing slash "would be like crafting a sonnet, a villanelle, something with meter, method, and my own madness ... the room for both allegiance to and independence from the original material." Both Kaplan and Stein (this volume) similarly point out how constraints such as canon/fanon or genre discourse can paradoxically afford a richer freedom through rules.

Most poetry works through and with a series of formal constraints such as meter or rhyme, and it often uses a system of shared significants such as the classic symbolism of the rose, or the complex, precise medieval system of allegory. Such techniques help achieve economy the same way slash does with canon. Here is another example of how slash uses canonic symbolism to achieve economy and power of expression: "*Blue eyes* looked at the *scar on the other man's chest,* and clouded, briefly remembering how the whiteness of *milk mixed with swirls of red,* patterns and gradations of pink like an embroidered arabesque" ("Discovered in a Memory," 2005, circuit story [hard-copy fanfic in mail circulation]). This is another anonymously authored story, this time from *The Professionals* fandom. The phrases I have italicized are all canonical images pointing to precise events in the TV series: Bodie has blue eyes; he is remembering how his partner Doyle was shot in the chest and almost killed in the episode "Discovered in a Graveyard." Bodie found Doyle sprawled and unconscious in a puddle of blood and milk from spilled grocery bags, and he is now remembering the event by looking at the scar which resulted from the delicate operation to save Doyle's life after the shooting.

This strategy parallels the way poetry uses symbolism, relying on a set of known associations to maximize effect synthetically: thus, for example, the image of the rose typically stands for life and youth and love in medieval poems such as the *Roman de la rose*. If the reader is not aware of the associations between the flower and all those other concepts, she can only read those passages describing a rose garden at a superficial, factual level. Obviously, for the technique to work its full effect, it is necessary that all the readers of a given text have a good knowledge of its structure of symbolisms and of allegory, the way slash fans have of canon. Even the most cursory look at different literary schools through the ages easily shows the difference a shared canon (or the absence thereof) makes in the way the process of textual creation and elaboration is played out. In the Middle Ages, for example, cultured people were expected to have a knowledge of a shared allegorical code, which then allowed a compressed, multilayered reading, such as the four levels of textual fruition (literal, moral, allegoric, and anagogic) famously detailed by Dante in the second book of his *Convivio*.

Once such shared knowledge is lost, subsequent readers have to perform interpretive feats, and much scholarship has sought to clarify the lost layers of allegorical meanings. In later times, poets wishing to exploit this technique have had considerably more trouble than their medieval colleagues because they were confronted with the lack of a common cultural frame of reference that was congruent with their message. William Blake, for example, tried to recreate his own special system of symbols by making up a complex mythology inspired by the Bible, English folklore, and contemporary sociopolitics. The results were almost incomprehensible to the noninitiated: a fandom of one. W. B. Yeats similarly used the occultist tradition of mysticism and spiritism, mixed with Celtic mythology. These authors used these techniques to write poetry that was very thick with referential and symbolic elements; however, unlike slash fans, they could not be sure that their readers had enough knowledge of the symbolism to understand their meaning. T. S. Eliot, who did the same by referring to a plethora of other texts in *The Waste Land* (1922) tried to solve the problem by writing the footnotes to his own poem himself— footnotes that ended up being longer than the poem itself.[5]

This scenario of a pervasive and indeed constitutive intertextuality is not simply a bizarre literary quirk — on the contrary, it has a long and diverse list of antecedents not only at the level of textual techniques, but also at the level of entire genres. We can thus look at a parallel situation in mythological discourses and genres, such as the Homeric epics or the Arthurian legends.

In the case of Homer, the parallel is especially intriguing, as it is quite apparent at various levels. On one hand, slash canonical/fanonical elements sometimes assume the form of descriptive epithet: some authors are especially noted for this technique, and it is possible to think of it as a rough equivalent of the Homeric "fleet-footed Achilles" or "blue-eyed Athena." But whereas Homeric poetry used epithets as aids to compose, improvise, and remember metrical oral narrations, epithets in slash can be used as shortcuts to compress and layer meaning, even if sometimes they are regarded by the community as a sign of clichéd writing. As an example, here is an epithetic description by Jane of Australia's epic *The Hunting:* "Green, slanted eyes looked down at him out of a face that was beautiful in a savage way, fine-boned, cat-like, dangerous. A riot of copper curls haloed the warrior's head ... a beautiful, fey, little creature, ... whose thin body seemed to weigh like that of a child" (4). Here canon and fanon freely mesh: on the one hand, we have canonical elements such as "green, slanted eyes" and "thin body," and on the other, we have fanonical elements built on canonical ones, such as "fine-boned, cat-like," "beautiful, fey, little ... child."

But the most interesting similarities are at the level of collective authorship: the setting and the characters are shared by all authors, who thus collaborate in the creation of a large collective repository of interrelated stories, which together create a mythological discourse (see Derecho, this volume). This is the way in which mythology is formed: variant retellings of common legends accumulate to build a shared repertoire from which classical authors borrowed characters, events, and plots, each giving it his own twist, often while referring to each other. Myth making, or mythopoeia, is a way of making and transmitting meaning through collective narrative creation. Although this model of authorship and textual production was taken for granted in premodern times, the deep changes in the way individual authorship and "originality" are regarded in the modern age have by and large marginalized anonymous collective authorship, writing in a shared universe and using a common repository of legends and myths. The influence of modern conditions of textual production, and of Romantic (with a capital R) poetics stressing the primacy of individual author and original text have gone a long way toward influencing current thinking, which is why the first wave of academic studies of slash have seen it as an atypical, quasi-pathological phenomenon.[6] Pugh (2004) concisely describes such conceptual changes in authorship modes, authorial control/ownership of text, and their relationship to the rise of copyright legislations in the eighteenth century:

> the idea that there is some intrinsic virtue in using an "original" character or story would have puzzled most ancient or mediaeval writers ... they plundered the vast resources of myth and history just as happily... However

individualised by each successive poet who used them, they were still ... part of a resource that belonged to all.... But nowadays this form of dialogue attracts the notice of lawyers.

It's not that intertextuality went on a long holiday from the eighteenth century to today, of course, as a closer look reveals. Indeed, Harold Bloom's *Anxiety of Influence* (1973) showcases the power of the weight of tradition for Romantic poets—but the zeitgeist of the period tended to hide or condemn extensive intertextuality as "unoriginal" and "derivative." Not "content to play as passive a role" (Pugh 2004), readers would always play with the characters in the toy chest of literature the way the Brontë sisters did with their wooden soldiers: witness, for example, such diverse types of intertextuality as the massive corpus of Sherlock Holmes apocrypha pouring in almost since Conan Doyle started to write, or Charles and Mary Lamb's *Tales from Shakespeare* (1807), or Shelley's revisitations of the Prometheus myth. Even if the advent of postmodernism in literature has ushered a change back to a renewed appreciation of texts featuring strong intertextual characteristics and devices, the acceptance of writing in a shared universe is by no means smooth or taken for granted, however, especially when it comes to mainstream literature. Still, today, some books end up getting away with writing in a shared universe; others do not. Jean Rhys's 1966 *Wide Sargasso Sea*, which, as a prequel to *Jane Eyre,* can be legitimately called fan fiction, was published commercially as any other book and has received critical acclaim. However, Alice Randall's 2001 novel *The Wind Done Gone,* which retells the story of *Gone With The Wind* from the point of view of Scarlett's half-sister Cynara, was the object of a lawsuit that nearly prevented its publication. All the names in the book are allusively changed, and the book's perspective, ideology, and form (the text is a fictional first-person diary by Cynara) are vastly different from Margaret Mitchell's work; yet its publisher ended in court accused of infringing the Mitchell estate copyright. The dispute was eventually settled, and *The Wind Done Gone* is now in print; still, most of its reviews damn it for its derivativeness, accusing it of not standing on its own literary merit. Such reviews entirely miss the point that, as with slash, it is exactly the intertextual dialogue and commentary on another text that create the strength and powerful impact of *The Wind Done Gone.*

Intertextuality Extended

So far, I have shown how intertextuality is constitutive of slash, allowing authors to construct texts based on a shared universe; how this peculiarity shapes their writing at several levels; and how writing in a shared universe is by no means an atypical or marginal phenomenon in literature. I now extend my consideration of slash intertextuality to examine the relation of slash to other texts in addition to the canon/fanon of the original media source. If the relation between slash and its canon/fanon from the original media text can be called intertextuality in the first degree, intertextuality in the second degree is when the text refers not just to its canonical roots, but also to other texts.

"Simple" intertextuality most often follows the textual mechanism of the "what if?" Teresa De Lauretis (1987, 1994) has pointed out the intensity of the human urge to fill narrative blanks: we want to know what Medusa was thinking when she saw herself in Perseus' mirror, or what happened to Oedipus' sphinx. Slash is born from the same mechanism: fans watch the TV series and start wondering, "what if..." Derecho (this volume) quotes Deleuze's equating the reality of the potential and the actual: all possibilities exist at the same time, and archontic texts work toward actuating all possible variations. To paraphrase Todorov, if curiosity is wanting to find out about the past, the "what if" narrative impulse is wanting to find out about something never happened — in Hills's (2002) terms, the "endlessly deferred narrative." "What if" is a particularly common narrative impulse in fandoms based on shows that were canceled prematurely or ended with a cliffhanger: for example, much of *Blake's 7* (1978–1981) slash belongs to the PGP, or Post–Gauda Prime, category, named after the planet Gauda Prime, where the TV series tragically ended with the death — or apparent death — of all protagonists but one. The "what if" mechanism, however, can be used to different purposes and effects: from the creation of action-oriented stories that stay close to the original media text, to the referencing not only of the media text, but also of another genre or a specific text. For example, *Sand Castle* (1997), by Elizabeth Holden, stays close to the original media text. This novel is made up of three shorter sections, each retelling the events of *The Professionals* TV episode "Wild Justice" from the point of view of the three main characters. The shifting of point of view from the omniscient TV camera to the intimate first person helps the author comment on and interpret a controversial episode in the series, and of course there are many other examples of stories that tell events directly taken from the episodes — using snippets of dialogue, extending scenes, and so on. This type of extremely close intertextual relationships has a strong component of textual playfulness and craftsmanship, a desire to work in pastiche mode. To put it again in classical terms, it is worth referring to the Latin concept of *imitatio* ("imitation"). A popular way of creating poetic anthologies or collections of verses was to gather together in one volume a series of poets who retell a similar story or vignette, or who use a similar theme. For example, a volume might be a gathering of poems describing a rose garden, or a retelling the story of Achilles and Patroclos.

If many slash texts stay relatively close to the original media text, others deviate more sharply from the fandom canon, to the point that they are specifically labeled as AU (alternate universe) stories. In AUs, the characters are taken out of their original setting and put into another one, be it specifically made up by the author or drawn from some other source. Some AUs thus effect a generic change of setting. For example, it is possible to find *Lord of the Rings* Web sites where hobbits are vampires (Anklebiters, http://www.rosiesamfrodo.com/~anklebiters/fiction.html, accessed October 22, 2005). In *The Professionals,* we find the example of *The Hunting,* a long and complicated adventure tale by Jane of Australia, where CI5's tough guys Bodie and Doyle find themselves in a sword-and-sorcery universe, where Doyle is an elf. The AU may also be crossover — that is, elements from two or more different fandoms may be brought together: Madelein Lee's 1995 novel *Revolution* manages to put together four different fandoms — *The Professionals, Starsky and Hutch, Star Trek,* and *Tris/Alex* — in a dystopian science fictional setting. An author can also refer more or less explicitly to a specific text, be it slash or nonslash, in addition to the original one. Sequels, prequels, and alternative versions of slash stories abound, especially for stories that are deemed controversial or outstanding by the community. For example, the controversial and anonymously authored *The Professionals* story *Consequences* (n.d.; an early story, perhaps the very first, it is circulated in the circuit library), where Bodie rapes his mate Doyle, has spawned dozens of alternate versions, sequels, and prequels, which variously attempt to explain, justify, or negate the perceived problematic nature of *Consequences* itself. In *Lord of the Rings,* Mary Borsellino's sequence of AU stories *Pretty Good Year* (http://muse.inkstigmata.net/pgy. html, accessed June 1, 2006) has become the hub of a whole subset of the fandom, complete with its own canon, art, songs, and AUs.

All the examples I have made are of course instances of squared intertextuality. A particularly interesting example of this category in view of my discussion of romance novels is Meg Lewtan's undated *The Luck of the Draw.* The author prefaces her novel with a "Health Warning," saying, "be sure you have replenished your supply of brown paper bags" and "checked your box of Kleenex." This is because "the plot has again been cheerfully purloined from the assembly line of Barbara Cartland. The author apologises for not being able to properly acknowledge her source but, quite frankly she can't remember the name of the particular dose of Cartland syrup ... which inspired her to write it" (1). In this case, the ties between slash and romance, so often taken very seriously by critics, who mistake the part for the whole, is actually ironic, tongue in cheek, and postmodernly playful: Lewtan's text is a shameless, energetic romp in and out of the loops of romance novel clichés.

Sometimes the "squared" referentiality is to a well-known nonslash text: in Jane Mailander's 1998 "I Never Met a Morphosis I Didn't Like," Doyle from *The Professionals* stars as a tragic Gregor Samsa — Mailander's story follows the plot of Kafka's "The Metamorphosis," and the story ends equally (and *crushingly*) badly. Other authors have borrowed fairy-tale themes. In some cases the reference is subtle and used to great effect: classically knowledgeable author Sebastian often uses classical Latin quotes and references this way. She writes in her short story "Vivamus, Amemus":

> There was a scraggy sparrow darting across the grey slate roof. Probably nesting in the eaves. Bodie watched it duck beneath them, twig in beak. Yeah, nesting all right. Making a nice cosy bed for a mate. There was no mate yet, but mate there would surely be: written in its blueprint, that was. Eggs in the spring. Greedy squawking open-beaked kids to feed for a brief furious summer. And then it would probably die in the winter freeze [1].

The title of the story comes from Catullus' verse "let's live and love, my Lesbia, and let's not care about the malevolence of evil people" (my translation). The reference in the title, and the favorite Catullian image of the sparrow, resonate with the theme of Sebastian's story: here, Bodie is suffering unrequited love for a capricious, cruel Doyle, who either obliviously or maliciously taunts and teases him without, of course, ever delivering what he promises.

I will use one last example to illustrate the complex and intriguing ways in which intertextuality is squared and cubed in slash. "Brother's Keeper" is an anonymous short story in *The Professionals* fandom: its intertextuality is already squared because it takes the main characters and puts them in a sort of Lawrence of Arabia setting. Policeman Doyle is kidnapped by a slave trader in Africa, and undercover CI5 agent Bodie rescues him; they have many adventures in the desert, they fall in love, and they return to England. "Brother's Keeper" is in turn the referent for *Heat-Trace*, a strongly and skillfully written novel: the author of *Heat-Trace* refers explicitly to "Brother's Keeper," continuing the tale where "Brother's Keeper" left off. However, *Heat-Trace* is not a straightforward sequel, because it purposefully and forcefully changes the setting and situation in important ways. In *Heat-Trace*, Bodie and Doyle are back in England, and their escapist affair in Africa is now confronted with the grim reality of the country and of their own dysfunctional personalities. Both grapple with issues stemming from child abuse, and have to fight internalized and cultural homophobia. Bodie has a complete psychotic episode, and Doyle attempts suicide. They are broken men in a broken society, in the background of an incisive and critical representation of the Brixton Riots of the early 1980s.

Several more changes occur in the transition from one text to the other. Table 4.1 provides a synoptic comparison of interrelated slash texts that hints at the dense intertextuality and play of these texts. Although *The Professionals* can be termed semirealistic (on one hand, it presents gritty settings and current-affairs situations; on the other, it showcases a power fantasy of machismo), "Brother's Keeper" swings to the extreme escapist and romantic setting of the desert, complete with tents, Bedouins, and white slavery; *Heat-Trace* brings back realism with a vengeance. The London setting is meticulously researched and represented, and social issues and current affairs are enlarged from the simplistic fight against crime of the TV series to encompass a variety of complex and fascinating issues. This move makes for a text that is definitely ex-centric in the etymological sense: although both the TV series and "Brother's Keeper" are fairly typical examples of their respective genres, *Heat-Trace* stands apart for its explicit political views, its strong writing, and its psychological depth.

Table 4.1. Synoptic Comparison of Interrelated Slash Texts

The Professionals	"*Brother's Keeper*"	*Heat-Trace*
semirealistic	escapist	realistic
mainstream	mainstream	ex-centric
popular	popular	controversial
formulaic (canon)	formulaic (fanon)	nonformulaic
action adventure series	fantasy/fable	psychological novel
dominant ideology	ambivalent	antidominant ideology
indifferent writing (but strong cinematic pace)	indifferent writing/craft	strong writing/craft

Conclusions

Slash is not just an anthropological or sociological phenomenon whose main interest lies in the fannish community, and whose textual output is a simple, formulaic, and naive bunch of scribblings. On the contrary, slash fan texts present us with a rich and varied corpus of literature, many of which warrant an in-depth textual and critical analysis. The slash text's intricate and complex game of references and pastiches, and the presence of peculiarities such as shared authorship, *imitatio*, symbolism, and multiple intertextuality, signals how slash is canny, sophisticated, and resonant with contemporary postmodern textuality. Moreover, slash's noncommercial conditions of production and distribution make it an intensely innovative, potentially oppositional phenomenon that deserves to be treated like any other literary corpus. Unfortunately, the pressing need to reframe the critical discourse around slash fan fiction left space for only brief glimpses of in-depth textual analysis; I could only work toward close reading, and simply mention in passing many other potential topics for discussion (see Kaplan, this volume, for close readings of fan texts).

Intertextuality makes for a varied and rich meeting point of genres and texts. Concepts such as intellectual property, originality, and individual genius are relative newcomers in literature: they started to develop after the eighteenth and nineteenth centuries as a result of a precise and specific set of historical, social, and cultural circumstances, just as circumstances are now changing, requiring a reassessment of these terms. Yet if we look beyond the Romantic grand narrative praising originality and individual genius, we can see how intertextuality has always been an important part of literature: even at the apex of the Romantic period — albeit in a less overt way and more often in marginal spaces — we can find a great deal of inter-textuality. A case in point is the epigraph to this essay, which is taken from Charlotte Brontë's autobiographical account in "History of the Year 1829." The passage could be used to describe the way a fandom is born and develops.[7] Someone sees interesting and topical characters (the Napoleonic Wars had raged only about fifteen years before the events retold by Charlotte and were a topic of debate in the Brontë household), so she snatches up a favorite character and starts playing with it, together with like-minded friends. The four Brontë children soon started to write stories and poems about their toy soldiers, and they filled a huge quantity of tiny notebooks with stories upon stories, often written together, Charlotte and Branwell on one side, Emily and Anne on the other. This literary play went on for many years, when the sisters were well into their twenties. Their little fandom of four developed a progressively stronger and larger fanon: the siblings created a rich, complex universe around the original characters.[8] Fan fiction and the fan community (including this essay, and the book it appears in) do the same thing, but in a public, shared space rather than a constrained, private one.

Notes

I acknowledge the help of Tonya Browning, who as far back as 1996 was intriguing me with her work on interfaces as virtual palimpsests. This essay also owes substantially to all the thought provoked by discussions with fan friends on a myriad of mailing lists, cons, chats, and mad house parties.

1. Throughout this essay, I liberally use quotation marks to problematize widely used terms whose connotations run counter to my argument. So, for example, I put Fiske's terminology of primary, secondary, and tertiary texts in quotes because the terms imply a hierarchy I want to do away with. I introduce my own terminology (intertextuality squared, cubed) to obviate the problem. I am not alone in my concerns: as Derecho (this volume) explains, there is a pressing need to create a terminology for fan fiction without negative connotations, and hence her selection of the term *archontic* over words like *derivative* or *appropriative*.

2. Even if Chandler-Olcott and Mahar's (2003) essay is firm in its definition of fan fiction as a legitimate text spanning diverse styles and genres, I find it problematic in its reduction of fan writing to adolescent practice instrumental to gaining literacy skills.

3. Many contributors to this volume are equally working toward a reframing of fan fiction, some of them in palimpsestual terms: Derecho makes a comparable claim in her designation of fan fiction as an archontic literature that is characterized by a consciously and openly referential intertextuality; Willis points out how fan fiction makes space in the original media text, creating gaps where the fan writer can inscribe their new, reoriented intertext; and the entire final section of this volume goes even further by pointing out the performative nature of fan fiction.

4. I second Kaplan's (this volume) positive acceptance of the term *fanon* as the main affordance of Bakhtinian polyglossia.

5. When it comes to modernism, my analogy is only partially accurate, because modernist poetics were not primarily concerned with a clear understanding of a univocal meaning, but rather aimed at an almost mystical and subconscious resonance and ambiguity. I am indebted to Michel Hockx for pointing out the limits of my parallel.

6. See Jenson (1992). For a reaction against the reductionistic view of fan fiction, see Coppa, "Writing Bodies in Space" (this volume). My relativization of romantic, authorial high literature in favor of mythopoietic, nonmodern text is comparable to the shift Coppa makes from literary (in the narrow, Ruskinian sense) to performative text, if we consider how semioral, mythopoietic storytelling is indeed a performative textuality.

7. In this light, see Hills's discussion of fandom as Winnicottian play (2002, 104–12).

8. Although I have not discussed them in my essay, there are important performative implications in describing fan fiction as playing with toy soldiers. For an even more performative example of doll play as fan fiction, I point out Todd Haynes's *Superstar: The Karen Carpenter Story*, a 1987 movie "acted" entirely by Barbie dolls representing the singer and her family. For a discussion of fan fiction as performance, see Coppa ("Writing Bodies in Space," this volume), Busse (this volume), and Lackner et al. (this volume).

References

Aoike, Yasuko. 1978–ongoing. *From Eroica with love.* Tokyo: Akita.

Bacon-Smith, Camille. 1992. *Enterprising women: Television fandom and the creation of popular myth.* Philadelphia: Univ. of Pennsylvania Press.

Bloom, Harold. 1973. *The anxiety of influence: A theory of poetry.* New York: Oxford Univ. Press.

Brontë, Charlotte. 1857. History of the year 1829. In *The life of Charlotte Brontë,* by Elizabeth Gaskell. http://www.lang.nagoya-u.ac.jp/~matsuoka/EG-Charlotte-11.html#V (accessed June 1, 2006).

Brother's keeper. N.d. http://www.kelper.co.uk/trace/keeper.htm (accessed June 1, 2006).

Chandler-Olcott, Kelly, and Donna Mahar. 2003. Adolescents' anime-inspired "fanfictions": An exploration of multiliteracies. *Journal of Adolescent and Adult Literacy* 46:556–66.

De Lauretis, Teresa. 1987. *Technologies of gender: Essays on theory, film, and fiction,* Bloomington: Indiana Univ. Press.

_____. 1994. *The practice of love: Lesbian sexuality and perverse desire.* Bloomington: Indiana Univ. Press.

Green, Shoshanna, Cynthia Jenkins, and Henry Jenkins. 1998. "Normal female interest in men bonking": Selections from the *Terra Nostra Underground* and *Strange Bedfellows.* In *Theorizing fandom: Fans, subculture, and identity,* ed. Cheryl Harris and Alison Alexander, 9–38. Cresskill, NJ: Hampton Press.

Hills, Matt. 2002. *Fan cultures.* London: Routledge.

Holden, Elizabeth. 1997. *Sand castle.* Minneapolis, MN: Allamagoosa.

Jane of Australia. N.d. *The hunting.* http://www.thecircuitarchive.net/tca/archive/4/the-hunting.html (accessed October 22, 2005).

Jenkins, Henry. 1992. *Textual poachers: Television fans and participatory culture.* New York: Routledge.

_____. 2000. Digital land grab. *MIT Alumni Association Technology Review* 103:103–5. http://www.technologyreview.com/articles/00/03/viewpoint0300.asp (accessed June 1, 2006).

Jenson, Joli. 1992. Fandom as pathology: The consequence of characterization. In *The adoring audience,* ed. Lisa A. Lewis, 9–29. London: Routledge.

Kustritz, Anne. 2003. Slashing the romance narrative. *Journal of American Culture* 26:371–84.

Lamb, Patricia Frazer, and Diane Veith. 1986. Romantic myth, transcendence, and *Star Trek* zines. In *Erotic universe: Sexuality and fantastic literature,* ed. Donald Palumbo, 236–55. Westport, CT: Greenwood Press.

Lee, Madelein. 1995. *Revolution.* Zine.

Lewtan, Meg. N.d. *The luck of the draw.* Circuit story [hard-copy fanfic in mail circulation].

Mailander, Jane. 1998. I never met a morphosis I didn't like. In *B&D's excellent adventures.* Whatever You Do, Don't Press. Zine.

Pugh, Sheenagh. 2004. The democratic genre: Fan fiction in a literary context. *Refractory* 5. http://www.refractory.unimelb.edu.au/journalissues/vol5/pugh.html (accessed June 1, 2006).

Radway, Janice. 1984. *Reading the romance: Women, patriarchy, and popular literature.* Chapel Hill: Univ. of North Carolina Press.

Raven, Helen. 1992. *Heat-trace.* Pear Tree Press. Includes the anonymously authored "Brother's Keeper." http://www.kelper.co.uk/helenraven/trace.html (accessed June 1, 2006).

Russo, Julie Levin. 2002. NEW VOY "cyborg sex" J/7 [NC-17] 1/1: New methodologies, new fantasies. http://j-l-r.org/asmic/fanfic/print/jlr-cyborgsex.pdf (accessed June 1, 2006).

Salmon, Catherine, and Don Symons. 2001. *Warrior lovers: Erotic fiction, evolution and female sexuality.* London: Orion.

Scodari, Christine, and Jenna L. Felder. 2000. Creating a pocket universe: "Shippers," fan fiction, and *The X-Files* online. *Communication Studies* 51:238–58.

Sebastian. N.d. Vivamus, amemus. http://www.thecircuitarchive.net/tca/archive/8/viva
  musamenus.html (accessed October 22, 2005).
Smol, Anna. 2004. Oh ... oh ... Frodo! Readings of male intimacy in *The Lord of the Rings.*
  Modern Fiction Studies 50:949–79.
Thrupkaew, Noy. 2003. Fan/tastic voyage: A journey into the wide, wild world of slash
  fiction. *Bitch* 20 (May). http://www.bitchmagazine.com/archives/04_03slash/slash.
  shtml (accessed June 1, 2006).
Wakefield, Sarah. 2001. Your sister in St. Scully: An electronic community of female
  fans of *The X-Files. Journal of Popular Film and Television* 29, no. 3:130–37.

5. Construction of Fan Fiction Character Through Narrative

Deborah Kaplan

ABSTRACT.—I analyze the narrative techniques used to develop character in a small cross section of novel-length fan fiction stories. I examine
the development of character at the level of both discourse and story,
and follow the creation of character as original but sourced in canon
and fanon characterization. Narrative conventions work at the discourse
level to develop character. These characterizations play into and grow
out of the source text. Because both the producers and consumers of the
fan works are aware of the source materials as well as of sources that are
extratextual to the fan productions, a rich interpretive space is created
in which fan fictions participate actively through narrative tools with
their source materials. Characters that exist outside the fan fiction texts
therefore become available for complex play and re-creation.

Introduction

Literary analysis of fan fiction texts for its own sake is still mostly
unexplored territory; literary theorists have left the field clear for the social
and cultural theorists. Traditionally, analysis of fan fiction is sociological,
focusing on the desires that might drive writers to create fan fiction and the
effects on community of the written works. The produced works themselves, however, are usually valued only as windows onto the producers.
Most treatment of fan fiction as a literary form comes in the form of defen-
sive statements of quality, and nearly exclusively from within the fan community (O'Shea n.d.; Mortimer 1997). In this volume, Mafalda Stasi

(specifically investigating slash, although I believe her analysis holds true for fan fiction in general) offers a review of the critical literature and concludes that the majority of academic studies are rooted in a cultural studies perspective. Fan fiction texts themselves, then, are ignored except inasmuch as they shed light on a cultural studies perspective.

Fan fiction has not been much studied *as fiction,* as texts that, under a literary criticism lens, can be fascinating as nonfan-produced work. The cultural studies lens on fan fiction may analyze text, as literary theory would, but it does so in order to shed light on the peculiarities of fandom. For example, Victoria Somogyi's (2002) analysis of *Star Trek: Voyager* fan fiction uses close reading to speculate on the motivations and sexualities of the authors. Literary analysis, on the other hand, can invert this analytical mode, using the mores and standards of fandom to provide exciting insights into the construction of fan texts as texts. As fandom itself — a community that contains many academics, well schooled in formal modes of thinking about text — can be passionately interested in analyzing texts, it seems ironic that academia elides the texts in favor of the community. Whatever their modes of production, fan-produced texts can be works wholly open to close readings and textual analysis. Although amateur fiction lacks commercial editing controls, the corpus as a whole contains many works that reveal fascinating layers when examined under an analytical lens.[1] Fan works can be analyzed as individual works of literature, or collectively, for genre-specific analysis. I focus on some genre-specific traits, examining how characters are developed by using narrative techniques, given that these characters are already complex creations complete with physical descriptions, histories, personalities, and rich fan interpretations.

Fan Interpretation: Symposia, Manifestoes, and Fiction as Interpretive Acts

A *Saturday Night Live* sketch about Trekkies, Henry Jenkins explains, clarifies negative stereotypes about fans as being, among other things, "brainless consumers ... intellectually immature" (1992, 10). In reality, fans are members of an active interpretive community. A large part of the fannish experience lies in analyzing the source texts of fandom. Fans interpret these texts through discussion and formal analysis, but also through the creative act of writing fan fiction. Manifestoes on characterization, reactions to individual moments in the source text, community in-jokes rooted in the source text and the community's reactions to it, and creative fan works such as fan fiction, artwork, and vids all contribute to a shared understanding of the source text. In the interpretive community of fandom, one individual's interpretation in a work of fan fiction can inform another fan's reaction to a later moment in the source text. Fans in a given community may accept as fact some of these shared interpretations and analyses. Thus *fanon,* the noncanonical knowledge about a source text, is the sum of the community's shared interpretive acts (see also Driscoll, this volume).

Rewriting characters for a work of fan fiction is an interpretive act along these lines, in which the text offers one possible understanding of characterization. The work both contributes to and draws from the community's collective understanding of character. The roots of fan fiction's characterization lie both in this interpretive community and in an individual interpretation of the source text's characters. Although a work of fan fiction might otherwise follow the conventions of original fiction character development, it must also be in constant dialogue with the source text's characters, already fully realized and well known to the story's reader. The reader, before ever beginning a specific work of fan fiction, already knows the physical appearances of the primary characters, as well as their backstories, their reactions to certain life events, their voices, their base characterizations, and fanon constructions of character.

Although fan authors need not create original characters from scratch, they produce complex texts that take advantage of the multiplicity of fanon and canon characterizations available. Fan writers create texts that rely on the interplay between knowledge of the source text and knowledge of the fanon. Between canon knowledge and agreed-upon fan conventions, the readers know quite a bit about a source text's characters before the fan work is ever created, and that knowledge plays into the fiction as part of the transaction between text and reader.

The community that produces and consumes fan fiction is virtually the same as the community of fan critics; most fan fiction readers and authors critique and analyze source text. Although not all fan authors are producers of formalized nonfiction character analyses, many are members of communities where such analyses are produced and consumed. Analysis ranges from the casual reaction at a convention, messages exchanged on a mailing list, or an item posted in a blog, to a more formal statement at a convention panel or in a critique community. Web sites and online communities exist to archive formalized essays on plotting, characterization, "shipping" (justification of the romantic pairing between two characters), and other analyses of the source text. The essay collection at the Fanfic Symposium, for example, has seventeen articles dedicated to "Characters and Characterization" (http://www.trickster.org/symposium, accessed June 1, 2006).

E-mail lists are created for the purpose of discussing the source text's characters. The advent of blogging has made it even easier for individual fans to share both informal and formal analyses in informal forums. An individual fan can now make interpretive statements about characterization in a personal blog in a fan-saturated community such as LiveJournal.com or Journalfen.net, and the statements can become part of fandom's collective interpretation even if the individual makes no attempt to publicize them in a formal fan forum. Cumulatively, these formal and informal analyses come together to inform a community understanding of character in the source text.

For example, fans who search for the potential of a romantic relationship between the characters Angel and Spike from *Buffy the Vampire Slayer* and *Angel* can look in the LiveJournal community Ship_Manifesto, where fan critics from a multitude of fandoms explain the canon support for various romantic pairings. Here, in "A Century of Slash: Angel & Spike," fan Kita (2004) examines extratextual elements (statements of the show's actors and writers), provides textual subjective analysis of characters (the interaction between the characters in the *Buffy* episode "School Hard" read as sexual tension), assesses the textual objective of the characters (Angel's flashback statement, "I've been wondering what it'd be like to share the slaughter of innocents with another man"), and invokes theoretical support (citing Eve Kosofsky Sedgwick). Kita's analysis therefore draws on the text, on fandom's interpretive community, and on extratextual materials; her interpretation then informs other fans' interpretations in their own fan fiction. Likewise, in her "Manifesto (Let the Fun Begin)" analyzing the arc of the first season of *Veronica Mars,* fan Fox1013 breaks down the actions of the character Lianne Mars into extratextual (interviews with the show's creators; an economic understanding of the production of the television series; a critical understanding of twenty-two-episode story arcs), textual subjective analysis of character ("It is Veronica's curse to find out that she is both right and wrong"), and textual objective analysis of known events (certain characters have alibis) (Fox1013, LJ, May 3, 2005). Again, the fan analysis draws on textual, fannish, and extratextual interpretation, and contributes to the community's understanding of character. These rich analyses are merely examples of the more formal kinds of fan interpretation that happen constantly in the fan community. To be a member of fandom is to be a member of this interpretive community, because regardless of whether or not an individual fan produces or consumes analysis, the environment of fandom is richly interpretive. The analyses thus produced form a dynamic interpretive space in which a multitude of understandings of the source text's characters can form, grow, and change.

Character in Fiction

Fan writers write in a wide range of narrative styles and genres, and fan works can range from the drabble (a piece exactly one hundred words long) to a series of novel-length works. Character development requirements will be substantially different for a drabble than for a more lengthy work. Here, I concentrate on relatively lengthy complete works; the individual stories I examine range from under 10,000 words to nearly 100,000 words. Each of these falls into one of the three most frequently used subcategories of fan fiction: gen (general audience — not focused around romance); het (focused around opposite-sex erotic or romantic partnerships); and slash (focused around same-sex erotic or romantic partnerships). As with story length, the varied focuses require different forms of character creation, as the different genres may use characterizations that diverge in varying extremes from the easiest and most conventional readings of the source text. Yet although the methods differ, some of the tools used are the same for all these stories. For example, as will be discussed in more detail below, all three texts play games with focalization, the discursive method by which events are narrated from a character's point of view (Jahn 2003; McCallum 1999, 30–31) in order to influence reader identification with character.

The stories examined incorporate traits from each of these structures. Torch's 1997 *Ghosts* is a 96,000-word *X-Files* novel that pairs Fox Mulder with Alex Krycek. Peg Robinson and Macedon's *Talking Stick/Circle* is a 350,000-word *Star Trek: Voyager* romance between Captain Kathryn Janeway and Commander Chakotay that comprises eight short stories and novellas; I concentrate on the first two (which are 7,800 and 10,000 words). Sylvia Volk's *She, or The Slave Girl* is an 11,000-word *Highlander* short story about the character Methos in a series of seventeen short stories that includes a number of recurring original characters, and that, as the title implies, also brings in characters and themes from the works of H. Rider Haggard, increasing its metafictional complexity. These pieces constitute a selection across fan fiction genre and fandom. They share some traits (each is relatively lengthy; the source text for each is an episodic science fiction or fantasy television series; and each has a reputation within its own fandom for being representative of some of the best the fandom has to offer), and these similarities clearly limit the ability to generalize findings to fan fiction as a whole. But in other ways, these stories are substantially different. One examines emotional and romantic entanglement between enemies, whereas another develops romantic entanglement between two characters who are close. Two of the stories explore rich and complete personalities for characters who in the source text are only occasionally recurring characters who act as foils for the main character's development and storylines. One story is focused entirely through the eyes of fully realized original character, whereas another is focused through two of the most important characters in the source text. Yet all three of the stories, with their vastly different directions and characterization needs, use narrative tools in similar ways in order to develop character.

Ghosts: *Mixed First-Person and Third-Person Narratives*

Both pairing-based stories I examine, Torch's *Ghosts* and Peg Robinson and Macedon's *Talking Stick/Circle* sequence, have two explicit narrators: one for each member of the romantic pairing. This is common in fan fiction relationship-based stories, specifically those involving slash or other noncanon pairings (Jenkins 1992, 199). As stories explore the explosive emotional potential of relationships between characters that are minimized or denied in the source text (Saxey 2001, 187–210), close character focalization allows fan fiction authors to explain the underlying reasons these noncanon relationships might be happening despite the text as seen on screen. *Ghosts* and *Talking Stick/Circle* are therefore explicitly polyphonic texts (McCallum 1999).

Ghosts builds its character identification and emotional power through mixed first- and third-person narration. The *X-Files* characters Alex Krycek and Fox Mulder participate in the telling of their developing emotional attachment through interweaving threads of story. Intriguingly, Krycek's narrative thread is told in the first person; Mulder's is a narrowly focused third-person limited narration. The result of this unusual structure is to encourage reader identification with Krycek, who is a villain in the source text.

Before reading *Ghosts,* the reader familiar with *X-Files* canon has preconceived notions of the characters. Although Krycek only occasionally appears in *X-Files* canon, he is a multivoiced character. The program, which revels in aliens and secret government conspiracies, has an excessively convoluted story arc (known as *mytharc* to the show's fandom). Although Alex Krycek is a minimally drawn secondary character, he appears first as a suit-clad young naif of a federal agent and Agent Fox Mulder's protege, only to reveal that he is a double-crossing double or triple agent, wickedly clever, and a killer in a dashing leather jacket. Krycek, who works for the Cigarette Smoking Man, the show's prime villain, may have killed Mulder's father. On the other hand, Krycek has also performed a number of actions that seem slated to help agents Mulder and Scully, not harm them.[2] In the story's first-person narrative, he is still recognizably a murderer and a trickster, but he is also made appealing. His obsession with Mulder, swiftly revealed to be physical and probably romantic in nature, gives him an immediate point in common with readers who are likely to share a sense of Mulder's appeal (Scodari and Felder 2000).

Krycek begins his narration suffering, provoking potential reader sympathy — but this is not unequivocally good: Krycek clearly feels no compulsion about killing at the appropriate time except where it might affect him personally, as when he speculates about allowing Scully's death. In the source text's canon, Krycek is a villain (if a complicated villain with unclear motivations). Because the novel begins with Krycek confused and in pain, the scene is set from the beginning that this will be a story that portrays that villainous character sympathetically. Yet even in this sympathetic first-person focalization, he is cavalier about murder and fraud. The story does not deny the less savory aspects of it protagonist. After a scene in which his weakness and lust for Mulder are apparent, maximizing the possibility of reader sympathy, Krycek thinks, "Come to think of it, he hasn't even checked if I have a weapon. I do, of course. I may be insane, but I'm not stupid."

Krycek is aware of his multiple portrayed personalities and how they are in dialogue with each other: "It's protective coloring, I become whoever I have to be, the name on the passport, this non-existent person... I'm cute, I'm fluffy, I'm harmless." Mulder later asks the question that is fundamental to the text's characterization of Krycek: "You're like one of those dolls, secrets inside secrets, made to be picked apart. I guess it's useless to wonder what you're like deep down when there probably isn't anything there." Through this deeply personal and sympathetic first-person portrayal, which does not sidestep any of the murders or betrayals that Krycek has committed as a character, the text asks, but never answers, the question of who Alex Krycek is. Later in the story, Mulder attempts to interpret some (noncanonical, original to this text) information Dana Scully has discovered about Krycek's childhood to understand him better, and he rejects the attempts: "You're going to believe that this is a solution, you're going to think that this explains me, and it doesn't. Don't sit there looking like someone handed you a puzzle piece you actually know what to do with."

Krycek's narration serves not just to introduce himself as a canon character only slightly divergent from the canon text yet created for the novel, but to introduce his view of Mulder. Krycek thinks Mulder has bad taste in ties. He has attempted to serve Mulder in some way but acknowledges that he should never have expected gratitude, and his feelings for Mulder include lust or at least physical obsession ("a certain FBI agent's pouty lower lip"). He acknowledges that Mulder hates him and is physically violent toward him, and he "might let him" be violent. He portrays Mulder as completely loyal to Scully. All of this construction of Mulder comes through before Mulder has ever entered the scene, while the narrative is ostensibly focused on Krycek committing another murder and leaving Russia.

When Mulder enters the picture, still seen through Krycek's first-person narrative focus, he is portrayed as suspicious, violent, and the object of Krycek's obsessive desire. Canon knowledge of Fox Mulder offers a brilliant FBI agent who is driven and maybe a little bit crazy. Nothing in Krycek's view of him contradicts that knowledge (except inasmuch as it portrays him as somewhat dimmer about human interaction), but it redirects the focus, so Mulder is formally seen as an object of desire. When Mulder knocks the one-armed Krycek down, Krycek thinks, "It's adorable when he tries to sound tough, like a pitbull puppy dreaming of greater things." In Krycek's eyes, he's a contradiction of gentleness and violence: "Those terribly, terribly gentle eyes.... And then he's off the couch and right in front of me in one smooth movement, grabbing me by the collar of my shirt and dragging me up into a standing position." Mulder is specifically described: "They said he was moody, mildly crazy, emotionally unbalanced, neurotic, obsessive, highly intelligent. They never mentioned his sense of humor though, or his beautiful eyes."

Because Krycek's view of Mulder in the text does not diverge substantially from canon, his descriptions serve not just to introduce Mulder and to reassure knowledgeable readers of the source text that this Fox Mulder will be a character they recognize, but also to identify this Alex Krycek as somebody who finds Mulder's humor appealing, who is physically attracted to him. Spoken in immediate engaging first-person narration that is designed to draw readers into the character (Wylie 1999, 185–201), overwhelmingly concerned with physical and emotional attraction to Mulder, Krycek operates on two levels: first as an object of attraction himself, and second as a reader stand-in, a character through which a reader's attraction to Mulder can be realized.

The Mulder-focused sections, on the other hand, retain a step of distance from the reader. In these sections, despite third-person narration, all events are colored by Mulder's perspective (Jahn 2003). The third-person narration moves between direct and indirect narration, between the narrator's and Mulder's point of view:

> He jerked upright out of uncertain sleep, wondering about whiplash damage. It wasn't the first time he'd nodded off in front of the computer; one time he'd woken up with his forehead pressed against the screen and a closer

view of the "Bill Gates does Windows" screen saver than anyone should have to endure. When he blinked the sand out of his eyes and pushed the sliding glasses back up again, he found that he was staring at a web page about Leyden Creek, California. Well, that was definitely the wrong place; no help there. And all he knew about the Virginia Leyden Creek was where it was.

"A closer view ... than anyone should have to endure" and "Well, that was definitely the wrong place" both slip into direct narration, focalized directly on Mulder's thoughts, not the narrator's. But for the most part, Mulder's sections of the text retain the step of distance given by third-person narration.

In Mulder's narration, the narrative view of Krycek switches back toward the canon portrayal: "He wasn't just a villain, he was a lying, two-faced, cowardly, betraying, amoral little —" Unlike Krycek, Mulder has no hidden agendas, no secret lust. It's information and the X-Files that arouse Mulder: "the thought of the information that might, with patience, coaxing and a spot of torture, be extracted from Krycek made his heart beat faster." Although later slippages between Mulder's explicit thoughts and the incongruity of his reactions reveal sublimated desires, he's certainly unaware of them on a conscious level.

The arrival of Dana Scully cements the portrayal of Mulder. By her excessive skepticism —far less prone than Mulder to fall into comfortable conversation with Krycek—she highlights his tendency to trust and casual behavior. Yet unlike Mulder, she has sympathy for Krycek. Mulder offers Krycek the constant threat of physical violence; but Scully is nonviolent except as much as is required to contain Krycek and protect herself and Mulder. She offers professional concern with his amputated arm and expresses concern with Mulder's violence toward him. When she discovers his family history, she offers unrequested pity and understanding. Her professional behavior and appropriate caution put Mulder's too violent anger and too trusting reciprocation of affection in sharp relief.

The scene where Scully discovers Krycek's missing arm highlights the characterizations of all three characters:

> Recovering from her shock, Scully probed the scar tissue, then held Krycek's shoulder and rolled it this way and that.... "For approximately how long were you in pain after the anesthetic wore off?"
> Krycek made a sound that no one would have taken for a laugh. "Anesthetic? ... I passed out from the pain, I don't know if that counts." When he'd finished buttoning the shirt he tucked the loose sleeve into the waist of his jeans, and faced both of them, chin ever so slightly lifted.
> Before Scully could ask yet another medically related question, Mulder

decided he'd better take charge of the situation. Standing here discussing Krycek's missing arm wouldn't get them anywhere, he thought. "Let's go," he said. "We have a long drive ahead of us. And Krycek, I'm sure we can find something to cuff you to."

As he passed them both to go get his luggage, he thought he heard the faintest of whispers, "You and your bondage fetish."

Scully shows very human shock, but reverts immediately to professional detachment. Krycek's reaction is calculated to provoke sympathy for the character known to canon viewers as a villain. He makes "a sound that no one would have taken for a laugh" and turns back to Mulder and Scully with his chin "slightly lifted," a signifier of stubborn pride. More than simply eliciting a sympathetic response from the readers, this presentation of Krycek clarifies the characterization of Mulder in a section of the text that is focused on Mulder's perspective. This sympathetic portrayal thus also provides an illustration of Mulder as somebody capable of seeing Krycek's pain. Yet immediately afterward, Mulder takes over the conversation and responds with the callousness toward Krycek that he has been exhibiting since the beginning of this scene. What a polyphonic moment this is—where Mulder's explicit thoughts are at odds with the implicit sympathy visible in his portrayal of Krycek. Krycek, as usual, gets the last word, in "the faintest of whispers," which is therefore inaudible to Scully, turning the sympathetic moment to sexualized humor at Mulder's expense.

Throughout *Ghosts,* characters are in constant dialogue with each other, with the source text, and with the fan community's interpretation of source. *Ghosts*'s reading of Krycek may not be at odds with the interpretation insisted upon by the source text: it does not contradict the character's less savory aspects. Nevertheless, it is certainly at odds with a common fan interpretation of Krycek as despicable—a character referred to in the fandom as "Ratboy." Yet *Ghosts*'s interpretation of both Krycek and the Krycek/Mulder relationship strongly informed a fandom that otherwise held a strong dislike for Krycek and focused on the romantic pairing between Mulder and Scully (Scodari and Felder 2000). Had the characters and their emotional ties not been so carefully drawn, both entirely within the context of *Ghosts* itself and in the metatextual conversation between *Ghosts* and the *X-Files* canon and fanon, the story's character interpretation could not have taken such strong hold. But this Krycek—self-consciously multivoiced, focalizing as a fan reader through his obsession with Mulder, Ratboy yet sympathetically damaged—is carefully constructed as a recognizable source character interpreted in a new light.

Talking Stick/Circle:
Intertwined First-Person Narratives

Star Trek: Voyager is the fourth television series in a franchise that, at the time the television show was created, contained television, movies, and novelizations. The characters Captain Kathryn Janeway and Commander Chakotay were in an unusual state of emotional tension from the series' first episode. In the series premiere, a Federation starship (commanded by Janeway) and a Maquis vessel in rebellion against the Federation (commanded by Chakotay) are thrown into a distant region of the galaxy, where they must band together to survive. From the series' beginning, then, the two characters are in constant conflict—and in the opinion of some fans, their relationship is rife with unresolved sexual tension. Two characters who are inclined to be at odds—politically, racially, militarily, sexually—are forced to work together.

The opposite-sex romantic relationship in Robinson and Macedon's *Voyager* story *Talking Stick/Circle* provides a study in contrasts: contrast between Indian and white, between Starfleet and Maquis, between past and present, and most importantly, between the source text's understanding of character and the authors' understanding of character. The relationship is developed, like the relationship in *Ghosts,* through a dually focalized series of narratives. There are hidden focalizers as well, such as the didactic voice that speaks through the character Magda D'Esperance (McCallum 1999). These multiple focuses in the narrative all contribute to the conversation among the varied perspectives under consideration in the text. The dialogue between canon and fan fiction characterization begins in the romance between two characters, who in the source text shared emotional tension but never consummated a love relationship. Additionally, the structure of this story—the authors call it a "braided novel"—leads to an interesting dialogue between focalizers, between fan fiction and canon. Macedon's author's note for *Talking Stick* reads, "The above story was conceived in something of a pique after watching 'Initiations.' I get tired of the Hollywood Plastic Medicine Man. I thought it time a native voice was heard, speaking for a native character." So *Talking Stick,* although paying explicit homage to the source material, also refocuses and recontextualizes what the author considers to be a racist character portrayal, thus creating dialogue with the source in standard fan fiction fashion (Jenkins 1992; Grossberg 1992). *Talking Stick,* Macedon writes, "generated a 'sequel' of sorts, or perhaps an answer, written by Peg Robinson, telling Janeway's side of the story." So the two stories are in dialogue with one another as well as with *Voyager,* and the two characters remain in dialogue, with no unified author's voice privleging one or the other. McCallum (1999, 33) proposes certain methods by which polyphony appears in first-person narrative, but it works most simply here because there are two separate threads of first-person narrative. Because neither narrator has access to the narration of the other but the readers do, each narrative thread is colored by the different perspective of the same events as seen in the other narrative thread.

The fan fiction's perception of Indian and the source text's perception of Indian stay in conversation through the narrative voice of Commander Chakotay. Chakotay's voice is more explicitally polyglottic, more multi-voiced, than is usual for a single character, with his an explicitly dialogic voice in which conventional language and tribal language are at odds (Bakhtin 1996; McCallum 1999). As Robyn McCallum would have it, Chakotay exhibits multiple language worldviews (1999, 31). He begins his tale using the self-conscious voice of native storytelling, yet within that introduction lies the seeds of the dual-voicedness that will color the text.

> He-d'ho!
> I want to call here the ancestors.... I think of them often, here, where the only soil from the land of my birth is that held in a bag which Starfleet regulation does not permit me to carry.
> ... My father was a meda, medicine man, among Potawatomi, first in Oklahoma and later on a colony world which lies now in the de-militarized zone between Federation space and the Cardassian Empire.

Even in this tribal storytelling introduction, the dialogue between (potentially romanticized) native history and current circumstances is made explicit. The soil that Chakotay ties to his ancestors is forbidden him by Starfleet regulation. His father is identified by tribe, then by geographic location (given the English name of the American state), and then by final galactic location of a colony world far from original tribal lands.

Soon enough, Chakotay's discursive style switches to conventional idiomatic English. It is still touched by storytelling tone — "I felt the hands of my ancestors on my back" — but overall retains a casual style, even when Chakotay is telling a story within the overall narrative. Yet the effect of the polyglottic introduction remains. Chakotay has been established as a character who lives in two worlds with two distinct methods of communication. One of those discursive methods is also explicitly associated with the past: "the land of my birth," "the ancestors," and the traversal of heritage from tribe to state to colony world to demilitarized zone. This traversal of voices over time initializes the conflict that will run throughout this text with the conflict between romanticized past (Maquis) and practical present (Starfleet).

Captain Janeway's narrative thread is much more subtly dual voiced. Her first chapter, "Circle," opens, "Captain's personal log, stardate 2785.9." The formal introduction, reminiscent of hundreds of episodes of *Star Trek* and its various spinoffs, sets up a formal narrative. But the prologue is immediately followed by a casual, idiomatic voice: "Hell. I hate this log." By placing the angry curse and statement of distaste immediately after the formulaic opening, Janeway, like Chakotay, is introduced as a character with voices in conflict. Her conflicts develop accordingly — her desire to keep Starfleet regulations in the depths of the Delta Quadrant clashes with her desire to have a personal and romantic life on the ship where she is likely to spend the next several decades.

The two conflicts internal to Chakotay and Janeway also play out in the intertwined threads of narrative. The characters must not just mediate the conflicts internally and between one another, but they must mediate the conflict for the entire ship. The crew of *Voyager* comprises an unlikely amalgam of Starfleet, Maquis, and Delta Quadrant natives. Chakotay sees a mode of speech that is true to his ancestors and appropriate for dealing with the Maquis. Janeway, on the other hand, perceives Chakotay's style as harkening back to a romanticized metaphysical past that is inappropriate for maintaining discipline on a Starfleet vessel. By the same token, the language of regulation, which Janeway believes is necessary to control the crew in a fair and appropriate manner, Chakotay and the Maquis believe to be an unnecessary imposition on the realities of their histories. The negotiation of this dialogue, introduced narratively in the opening passages of the first two stories, is the primary concern of the entire text.

Combined with these negotiations of past and present, culture and discipline, is the dialogue between canon portrayal of Chakotay as romanticized and unrealistic Native American with the explicitly stated desire of Macedon to create a genuine and fully realized character. To a lesser extent, there is also the dialogue between Janeway as a rule-bound captain who has explicitly stated that she will not be involved in shipboard romance and who has a fiancé waiting at home, and the text's portrayal of her as willing to lessen the strictness of rules and become romantically involved with her first officer. The canon portrayal of Chakotay as romantic Indian, seen by the text's creator as inherently invalid, can be completely ignored and replaced with the storytelling Chakotay of the text. But the canon portrayal of Janeway is not completely ignored. Rather, as the narrative constructs the dialectic through its own structure, the Janeway of *Circles* negotiates the morphing of her own character from canon portrayal to fan fiction characterization, from hidebound character ostensibly concerned with practical regulations in the present to eroticized figure capable of seeing the power of romanticism and the past. As with *Ghosts,* the source characters Janeway and Chakotay are reframed in such a way that, although they remain recognizable, their focus and characterization are original. The complex interpretation that Janeway and Chakotay engage in, their constant negotiation of past and present, is made possible by the fan fiction's negotiation of source material and fan interpretation.

She, or The Slave Girl: *Original Character to Recontextualize Canon Character*

Gen stories, which lack the focus on specifically romantic social tensions, approach character through a number of different angles. One common style of long gen story, not discussed in detail here, is the episodic story, which tells of original events in the source text's characters, expanding the series timeline (Jenkins 1992, 163). Although a romantic story focuses on the perspectives of the romantic leads, a television series is shot to include the perspectives of multiple characters, although it may have one primary focus. *Angel,* for example, contains flickering, kinetic sequences from multiple perspectives, with both visions and densely image-packed transitions providing an opportunity to show brief narrative moments from a multitude of points of view (Kinsey, 2005). Yahtzee's *Angel* story "A Stitch in Time" relates an episode in the life of the Angel Investigations crew through a multitude of narrator focalizers, paralleling the switching perspective of the television series. The close focus of Yahtzee's characterization, unlike that on the television series, allows access to the thoughts and feelings of the focus characters. The result is an episode-like structure that provides a more personal experience of the events, Jenkins's "emotional intensification" (1992, 174). "A Stitch in Time" doesn't work to create original characters or original worlds; nor does it develop new perspectives on existing characters.

Sylvia Volk's *Highlander* fan fiction *She, or The Slave Girl* (1998) approaches its nonromantic storyline entirely differently and produces character analysis as a side effect of story. Although "A Stitch in Time" is structured something like an episode of television, *She* is a simpler tale. Fascinatingly, *She* can be read either as a coming-of-age story for the original character Peach or as a character study of the canon character Methos, an immortal warrior, occasionally recurring character, and fan favorite in a series focused around immortal Duncan MacLeod. The narrative is implicitly polyphonic, as it offers the narrowly focused narrator Peach (also known as Second Mooi-jai) as well as the more knowledgeable Methos as seen uncomprehendingly through Peach's eyes (McCallum 1999, 25). This implicit polyphony is common in fan fiction. An original character acts as a sole explicit focal point, and with very little slippage from this narrow focus, the perspective is solely hers. Nevertheless, the readers of the piece of fan fiction can be assumed to be familiar with the source text and can therefore have knowledge about the nonoriginal characters and metaphysics of the world that need never be explicitly stated in the fan fiction.

The character study of Peach requires some knowledge of the *Highlander* canon for comprehension of plot events, but not for understanding Peach's character. Absent any *Highlander* references, Peach's character is established simply in the text's opening:

> When she was very young, the first tale that struck her heart was that of the female warrior Mu-lan, the brave and dutiful daughter who saved her family's honor, who won victory in battle on behalf of her aged father. Many stories related the exploits of Mu-lan, and one could buy pictures of her: the heroine in armor, sword uplifted. Second Mooi-jai had no money to buy such a picture, but to herself she imagined that she was Mu-lan, the good daughter. In a time of trouble she had begged her aged father to let her save him.... And so, giving in to her pleas, her father (weeping bitterly) had sold her to a retired amah: Choo Kwai, the procuress.
>
> Of course none of this was true. When Choo Kwai bought her, the girl later called Second Mooi-jai was a laughing infant; she remembered no house save that of Choo Kwai, and Choo Kwai told her that she was sold to pay for her father's opium debts.

The text's inversion (Todorov 1977, 80–88) immediately establishes Peach as a character who tells stories. There is a tight congruence between story (Peach has an imaginary backstory that she tells to herself), internal discursive style (Peach's internal narrative follows a narrative structure that implies surprise and therefore storytelling), and extratextual discursive style (focused on the story in that inversion creates surprise). From this point, Peach is consistently developed as a character with a poetic style of speech in the model of Chinese prose ("While her heart fluttered and danced and played like a butterfly in her breast") who nevertheless has the yearnings and concerns typical of the twenty-first-century coming-of-age story. When she is being prepared for her eventual sale as a concubine, the narrative focuses in nonjudgmental terms on the obscenities she will be subject to and only allows her perspective to appear indirectly. "Mu-lan; she must be Mu-lan. Think only of that," she thinks, after detailing the procedure her sale will take.

Although the story is ostensibly about Peach, her perception of Methos draws him as a character to readers who are more knowledgeable about his history that she is. Peach's Chinese, provincial eyes do not provide enough information about the physical appearance of the male lead to distinguish among the two most likely choices—extratextual knowledge of the fandom implies strongly that the story will be about either Duncan MacLeod or Methos, and the physical description, "Homely as a he-goat. Round eyes. Highly expensive clothes," hardly distinguishes which. Instead, the male lead is introduced as "Methos her master" by the narrator at the closing of the first section, in a rare slippage of the narrative voice from Peach, in the story's present, as focalizer. Once the reader, aware of the source text of the television series *Highlander,* knows that the character is Methos, much more information about the situation is accessible to the reader than to Peach the narrator. This disjoint between focalizing narrator knowledge and reader comprehension is not uncommon in fiction. What makes this situation unique to fan fiction is that the disjoint comes not from the reader's better interpretive ability than the narrator's, but explicitly from an unwritten knowledge that the author can assume is possessed by the readers. Knowledgeable readers know that Methos is immortal and can therefore interpret from Methos's actions (training Peach in languages and martial arts) that she is likely to become immortal, and in that light, readers have a far different understanding of the interactions between Methos and Peach. Seen in this light, *She,* although it is the only one of the works I analyze that has only one explicit narrator, is in some sense the most polyphonic of all of them.

Methos is a minor character who only appears in a few *Highlander* episodes, and therefore the character provides substantial free rein for fan fiction character creation. Compared with how much is known about Duncan MacLeod's four-hundred-year lifespan, almost nothing is known about Methos's five thousand years. Canon knows remarkably little about him, except that he spent a good long time as a warlord and mass murderer during the Bronze Age, that he no longer fights indiscriminately, and that his sense of morality, although not reprehensible to modern viewers, is flexible and self-centered. His construction as an independent character through fan fiction has been significant. In *She,* although the text never enters his perspective, his persona is presented as affectionate, moral, and flawed—consistent with canon portrayal, but defined entirely by this text. He repeatedly names Peach his "child," he insists on taking her in because he doesn't trust the uses to which another immortal would put her, and he teaches her what she will need to know to be an immortal. With such background, this portrayal seems to be affectionate and moral. But combined with structural elements of character construction, this Methos is given some of the self-centered nature consistent with his canon construction. His interactions with Peach are entirely mentoring: spare, undecorated moments of dialogue in which he teaches her about jewels and martial arts. Were the story from Methos's perspective, these educational scenes might seem wholesome. But the text is told through the prism of Peach's perspective, and she is wholly focused on her master, Methos. In that context, the sparse educational dialogue, lacking in the interaction Peach longs for, reveals his blindness to her need — a blindness that eventually proves fatal.

She can be read, without any knowledge of the source text, as a character study for the focalizing character. It is the source text, unwritten in this story, that allows it to be read instead as a character study of Methos. The story, which can stand alone, has the potential to become something entirely different when read in the context of its source material, merely because of the disjoint between reader and the knowledge of the focal narrator. Whereas *Talking Stick/Circle* generates new characterizations out of existing characters, *She* instead creates a new understanding of existing characters by showing them through the lens of original characters. In that light, the story is in dialogue not only with the source text and fandom's community, but with itself. This multivoiced tale will likely gain readership because of its status as fan fiction in a fan community. But its fully realized original protagonist exists in a community that can be quite condemning of original characters in general as mere author inserts. *She* informs not just the community's understanding of *Highlander* and Methos, but of narrative, of story, of original characters, and of the strengths of alternative methods of focalization.

"Causing Reactions Wherever I Go": Interpretive Play and Narrative Games

The stories analyzed here do not represent a wide range of the possibilities of fan fiction character creation. Nevertheless, they all encourage interpretive play between the fan fiction texts and their source texts. They use narrative techniques in manners that are common to many forms of fiction, but they also play on the disjoint between canon and fan. Necessarily, because of this dialectic, fan fiction stories are polyphonic. McCallum argues that having multiple focalizing perspectives "enables the representation of a plurality of narrative voices, social and cultural discourses, and the construction of a range of perceptual, attitudinal and ideological viewpoints" (1999, 36). The fan fictions discussed here all use their multitude of voices to encourage constant conversation between the simplistic interpretation of the source text (Krycek is a villain; Chakotay is a romanticized Indian; Methos exists only to be a foil for MacLeod) and the more complex interpretations spoken for in fan fiction.

The interpretive community of fans has been widely discussed as a dynamic critical space where multiple interpretive activities can take place. The same fans who analyze character in the source text so closely will be writing fan fiction that plays into that interpretive and critical activity. Character analyses, rather than being constructed in a nonfiction essay, are constructed in a fictional environment in which one interpretation of character can be maintained. In a community populated by competing and often contradictory understandings of characterization, a fan fiction work's interpretation of character can only carry substantial weight if the characters are well-rounded and carefully drawn.

Narrative techniques allow the fan fiction to develop an interpretation of character both wholly within its own text and in dialogue with the extratextual knowledge of the source text and the fanon accessible to the reader. Because both the producers and consumers of the fan works are aware of the source materials that are extratextual to the fan productions, a rich interpretive space is created in which fan fictions actively participate through narrative tools with their source materials. Characters who were created and who exist outside the fan fiction texts therefore become available for complex play and re-creation. Fan fiction can be considered a limited genre, restricted in its possibilities by the need to work with already existing characters and settings. But by taking advantage of the narrative games inherent in the interplay between reader knowledge and fan fiction creation, fan authors find the potential for empowering dialogue in what initially seems to be a restricted form of creation.

Notes

1. There is also the question, which I will not attempt to resolve here, whether only literature of a certain quality rewards literary analysis. Regardless, there exists plenty of fan fiction available that meets the criteria of quality usually desired by literary critics.

2. Krycek's motivations become even more questionable later on in the program's mytharc, when he does a number of acts that seem designed to help Mulder and hurt the Cigarette Smoking Man. *Ghosts* spins off after the *X-Files* episodes "Tunguska" and "Terma," at which point Krycek's motivations are not nearly so twisted as they will later appear.

References

Bakhtin, M. M. 1996. Epic and novel: Toward a methodology for the study of the novel. In *Essentials of the theory of fiction,* ed. Michael J. Hoffman and Patrick T. Murphy, 43–62. Durham, NC: Duke Univ. Press.

Grossberg, Lawrence. 1992. Is there a fan in the house? The affective sensibility of fandom. In *The adoring audience,* ed. Lisa A. Lewis, 50–68. London: Routledge.

Jahn, Manfred. 2003. Narratology: A guide to the theory of narrative. May 28. http://www.uni-koeln.de/~ame02/pppn.htm (accessed June 1, 2006).

Jenkins, Henry. 1992. *Textual poachers: Television fans and participatory culture.* New York: Routledge.

Kinsey, Tammy A. 2005. Transitions and time: The cinematic language of *Angel.* In *Reading "Angel": The TV spin-off with a soul,* ed. Stacey Abbott, 44–56. London: I. B. Tauris.

Kita. 2004. A century of slash: Angel & Spike. August 23. http://www.livejournal.com/community/ship_manifesto/3515.html (accessed June 1, 2006).

Macedon. 1996. *Talking stick.* http://members.aol.com/diavolessa/talking.txt (accessed June 1, 2006).

McCallum, Robyn. 1999. *Ideologies of identity in adolescent fiction: The dialogic construction of subjectivity.* New York: Garland.

Mortimer, Jane. 1997. The advantages of fan fiction as an art form: A shameless essay. September 20. http://members.aol.com/janemort/fanfic.html (accessed June 1, 2006).

O'Shea, Tara LJC. N.d. Profic vs. fanfic. http://ljconstantine.com/column1.htm (accessed June 1, 2006).

Robinson, Peg. 1996. *Circle.* http://members.aol.com/diavolessa/circle.txt (accessed June 1, 2006).

Saxey, Esther. 2001. Staking a claim: The series and its slash fan-fiction. In *Reading the Vampire Slayer: The unofficial critical companion to "Buffy" and "Angel,"* ed. Roz Kaveny, 187–210. New York: Tauris Park.

Scodari, Christine, and Jenna L. Felder. 2000. Creating a pocket universe: "Shippers," fan fiction, and *The X-Files* online. *Communication Studies* 51:238–58.

Somogyi, Victoria. 2002. Complexity of desire: Janeway/Chakotay fan fiction. *Journal of American and Comparative Culture* 25:399–404.

Todorov, Tzvetan. 1977. *The poetics of prose.* Trans. Richard Howard. Ithaca, NY: Cornell Univ. Press.

Torch. 1997. *Ghosts.* http://strangeplaces.net/torch/ghosts1.html (accessed June 1, 2006).

Volk, Sylvia. 1998. *She, or The slave girl.* http://www.iras.ucalgary.ca/~volk/sylvia/She.htm (accessed June 1, 2006).

Yahtzee. N.d. A stitch in time. http://www.thechicagoloop.net/yahtzee/chivalry/chivfic/StitchIntro.htm (accessed June 1, 2006).

Wylie, Andrea Schwenke. 1999. Expanding the view of first person narration. *Children's Literature in Education* 30, no.3: 185–202.

how—by what cultural or subjective logics, by what (written) practices of reading—a "surface" of meaning is produced in the first place. Along what paths of association—personal and idiosyncratic, cultural and hegemonic—does a fan reader/writer come to an interpretation of canon?

Queerness (as a special case of "resistance" in general), then, is not an inherent property of a text—but neither is it an inherent property of a reader. "Slash featuring women and penned by lesbians ... is transparently resistive," writes Christine Scodari (2003, 114), in an article rightly aiming to undo the assumption that male/male slash by straight women is necessarily resistive (or even antihomophobic): where, then, does this self-evidence of resistance come from in the case of lesbian-authored female/female slash?[2] Scodari does not mention m/m slash written by queer women, so it cannot simply be lesbian or queer *authorship* which guarantees the resistiveness of a story. Rather, it seems to be the coincidence of gender and sexuality between author and characters that guarantees a line of straightforward continuity between the author's self-positioning in her own "world" and the subject positions staked out, through fan fiction, in the fictional "world" of canon. Circumscribing queer readings and writings in this way—accounting for identification mainly along the axis of gender, and assuming that it means the same thing for an author to be a woman in her own world and for a character to be female in a fictional world—seems to me inadequate to account for the complex circulation of desire and gender in texts and subjectivities, or for the way in which an author's self-positioning corresponds to her identification with characters in canon.[3] A fan/reader's extratextual self-identification does not slot neatly into a marked space in a text: as I will argue, reading involves the negotiation of painful gaps between the desiring subjectivity of the reader and the ability of the text to sustain that subjectivity and those desires.

Fan fiction, then, is generated first of all by a practice of reading which, rather than expressing its latent meanings, *reorients* a canonical text, opening its fictional world onto a set of demands determined by the individual reader and her knowledge of the (fictional and nonfictional) world(s). It thus occupies a charged crossing point between a reading organized around the desiring subjectivity of the reader and a reading organized around the reader's knowledge of what is possible in the world she lives in (in dialogue with her knowledge of what is possible in the fictional world of the text she is reading). It is through writing fan fiction that a fan can, firstly, make space for her own desires in a text which may not at first sight provide the resources to sustain them; and, secondly, recirculate the reoriented text among other fans without attempting to close the text on the "truth" of her reading: but these desires and these demands circulate unpredictably, in ways conditioned by the discontinuities between the author's world and the fictional world, or by (for example) cross-gendered or multiply gendered identifications.

Doxa

The work of fan fiction (especially slash) can be experienced as *both* a hedonistic, erotic practice which could even be opposed to a thoughtful or critical relation to a text, *and*, on the other hand, a deliberate, politically loaded, practice of recontextualization that reorients a text in order to demonstrate that it bears the trace of a desiring structure not wholly congruent with the most literal (which is to say, the most ideologically obedient) reading. Fan fiction thus seems to me to intertwine the pleasure of queer[4] textuality with a deeply political project of resistance and *in*-sistence that people must have the right to make and circulate meanings outside the circuit of ideologically or institutionally guaranteed transparency, provability, and, ultimately, enforceability. In this intertwining, fan fiction is best accounted for in the work of two writers who do not mention it by name but who seem to me to describe its structure and its practice very closely: Roland Barthes and Eve Kosofsky Sedgwick. In turning to these theorists of textuality, I signal my agreement with Stasi (this volume) that fan fiction should be read with all the rigor and complexity of which poststructuralist and queer literary/textual criticism is capable.

In his work from the 1960s and 1970s, Barthes articulates a theory of textuality opposed to the *concatenated*, the *continuous*, and the *thick*. In "Change the Object Itself," he writes, "Languages are more or less *thick*: certain amongst them, the most social, the most mythical, present an unshakeable homogeneity ... woven with habits and repetitions, with stereotypes, obligatory final clauses and key-words, each constitutes an *idiolect*" (1977, 168). Of all the "languages" which participate in a text — all the sets of knowledges and references that bring a text to legibility — the "thick" languages, or idiolects, are those which depend for their legibility on the reader's familiarity with certain "stereotypes, obligatory final clauses and key-words." "Thickness" therefore refers to the density of the weaving which binds these languages into "habits and repetitions"— into culturally overcoded readings. In his essay "Brecht and Discourse," Barthes links the "abusive" "false logic" of the "cultural code" with continuity (1986, 217). For Barthes, therefore, continuity is not inherent in a text. Rather, continuity is an *effect* produced by a practice of reading according to the idiolect. A stereotype, an obligatory final clause, or a keyword (what Barthes [1986] calls a "maxim"), serves as "the outset of a continuity surreptitiously developing in the docile inter-text which inhabits the reader" (217). A text gains the effect of continuity, then, when it is interpreted according to the *docile* intertexts—that is, according to the idiolect, the "habits and repetitions" which weave the work's "unshakeable homogeneity."

As Barthes argues in "Writing Reading," "'only the text' does not exist," since the logic of reading "is not deductive but associative: it associates with the material text ... *other* ideas, *other* images, *other* significations" (1986, 31). To read a text, therefore, is to produce, out of the totality of significations and associations available to each reader, a docile or a resistive intertext within which a text makes sense. A reading which attempts to follow a deductive, rather than an associative, logic — one concerned to eliminate "impossible" readings and to attain the final remaining truth (however improbable) of a text — is only a special ("thick") case of associative reading, one which obediently selects the associations by which the text will be rendered legible according to "obvious" and transparent codes smuggled in by the culture's abusive logic of continuity. The thicker a language is, then, the more it approaches the limit-case, in which it is *only* legible in the terms of the cultural code (what Barthes elsewhere calls the *doxa*).

All texts, of course, depend for their legibility on intertextual and extratextual knowledges: literacy in a given script; shared knowledge about, say, the physical behavior of objects (a writer need not chart the trajectory of a dropped cup, since we know it will fall and smash on the floor); social and cultural representational conventions and codes (fictional characters are presumed to be heterosexual unless they conform to certain stereotyped "habits" of representation). The question of reading is the question of the "docility" of the intertext, the question of *which* extratextual/intertextual knowledges and codes a reader uses to orient a text, and, crucially, whether these are prescribed in advance by ideology. Outside this docility, reading becomes associative rather than deductive: rather than subscribing to the "surreptitious continuity" for which the *doxa* seeks to make the text the point of departure, the reader breaks open the concatenation of discourse, opening the text onto other outsides and other knowledges about the world.

This Barthesian resistance to concatenation is strongly resonant with Eve Kosofsky Sedgwick's characterization of queer readings in her essay "Queer and Now" as those where meanings don't "line up tidily"—that is, where meaning isn't fully determined by the *doxa*. Sedgwick, writing about the intense childhood attachment of "many of us" to "cultural objects ... whose meaning seemed mysterious, excessive or oblique in relation to the codes most readily available to us," insists that "we *needed* there to be sites where the meanings didn't line up tidily with each other" (3, my italics).

This passage makes explicit much of the political moment of Barthes's formulations. The refusal to subject a text to an organization consonant with and guaranteed by bourgeois (homophobic, racist, sexist) ideology, is *necessary*, Sedgwick insists: these sites of oblique meaning are "a prime resource for survival" (3).

In "Brecht and Discourse," Barthes gives an account of a Brechtian strategy for reorienting a "mendacious" text (a speech by Hess) away from the surreptitious continuity which would line its meanings up tidily. He writes:

> [Brecht's] exercise consists in saturating the mendacious text by intercalating between its sentences the critical complement which demystifies each one of them: "Legitimately proud of the spirit of sacrifice..." Hess pompously began, in the name of "Germany;" and Brecht softly completes: "Proud of the generosity of those possessors who have sacrificed a little of what the non-possessors had sacrificed to them..."—and so forth. Each sentence is reversed because it is supplemented: the critique does not diminish, does not suppress, it adds [1986, 215].

This exercise of "intercalation," of reversal-through-supplementation, is a reorientation of the text around an axis that is "oblique in relation to the codes most readily available to us." This exercise of supplementation breaks open the continuity of the text as read in the terms of its thick concatenation; intercalation opens the text onto an intertext, a set of associations, formed by the reader's knowledge of the world.

It is only through this idea of *supplementation,* I would argue, that fan fiction can be understood (as it often is, both by academics and by fans) as "filling in the gaps" in canon. For these gaps may only become visible—may only, indeed, *be* gaps—when the text is read from a position that refuses the illusion of continuity; and textual gaps are filled in according to an associative, not a deductive, logic. Writing fan fiction is not simply adding the final piece of a jigsaw—completing a text with a known unknown, whose correct shape and dimensions can be deduced: rather, writing fan fiction first of all *makes* gaps in a text that the cultural code attempts to render continuous, and then, rather than filling them in, *supplements* these gaps with intertexts which are not docile but which—like both Sedgwick's promise to her younger self (cited in the epigraph to this essay) and Barthes's Brecht intercalation—"make the tacit things explicit."

But what drives and shapes this practice of supplementation? How, in the interaction between the fan/reader and the canonical text, does it come about that certain associations are brought into play rather than others? I want to show, through a consideration of my own fan writing practice in the universe of J. K. Rowling's *Harry Potter* books, one possible way that this comes about: in Sedgwick's terms, this is a practice of writing/reading as keeping promises to queer children — of making a text keep the promises *it* (almost) makes to its queer child readers (or at least to its readers as [if they were] queer children). I don't claim that my practice is typical (I don't think it, or any fan writer's, is). I hope, though, that from a consideration of this pattern of reading/writing will emerge a preliminary map of the interaction between *doxa,* desiring subjectivity, and knowledge-about-the-world, which enables the production of fan fictions in their particularity and multiplicity.

Harry Potter *and the Effacement of Queer*

In the *Harry Potter* books,[5] a specific pattern of readerly engagement is provoked by each individual book's being structured as a mystery, so that clues planted throughout the text are to be reread in the light of the information revealed at the solution of the mystery. Furthermore, the series as a whole (unfinished at the time of this writing) is structured similarly, with each book revealing more information about the events of the past, and therefore more about the probable resolution of the narrative arc of the whole series. The reader is thus encouraged to be open to the possible resignification of events and characters in the books, while reserving to canon the final rights of such a resignification. The mystery structure of the books organizes the pattern of readerly activity and passivity around the term *suspense:* readers are to *actively* search out the books' ambiguous signs and *passively* await the resolution which will retroactively determine how they will have had to be read.

Some readings, however, cannot be resolved through the idea of "suspense," since certain resolutions are delegitimated by the terms of the fictional universe, or by the thickness of the books' relation to the "docile intertext," the "most available formulae for reading." For example, Harry himself, up to the age of fifteen,[6] has experienced (what is named, or almost named, as) heterosexual desire only faintly and fitfully and only for one girl, Cho Chang; this desire appears to die as soon as he has physical contact with her. Harry describes his first kiss with Cho simply as "wet" (Rowling 2003, 405), saying, "She was the one who started it... I wouldn't've — she just sort of came at me... I didn't know what to do" (406). Hermione's suggestion that Harry might see Cho again "opened up a whole new vista of frightening possibilities. He tried to imagine ... being alone with her for hours at a time ... the thought made his stomach clench painfully" (406). As a portrait of teenage (hetero)sexuality, this is at odds with my knowledge of the world.

By contrast, Harry's very intense, physicalized reactions to, interactions with, and fantasies about, other *male* characters—especially, in my reading, his Potions teacher, Severus Snape—are never named in the text as sexual. The vocabulary and imagery of these interactions potentially open them onto a set of sexual associations: Snape's "fathomless black eyes bor[e] into Harry's," for example (*Azkaban* 448); or he "eyed Harry, tracing his mouth with one long, thin finger as he did so" (*Phoenix* 469). In all his interactions with Harry, Snape's villainy is conveyed in a way that recalls the romanticized conventions of the Gothic novel: after almost every line of dialogue, delivered "silkily" or "sleekly," Snape's eyes glitter, or his lips curl into a sinister smile or sneer, and Harry reacts with emotions—fear, anger, wounded pride—which romantic conventions readily sexualize.

It is, however, (almost) certain that Harry is not going to come out in the last book[7]: in this case, therefore, the pattern of activity/passivity in reading cannot be organized pleasurably through "suspense." Rather, the active engagement of my desiring subjectivity through the recognition of queer desire in canon is cut off by the lack of a sustaining fictional world within which queer desire can be recognized and read by the characters themselves. This painfully (for me, educated mainly in Britain under Section 28) echoes the homophobic tactic of, precisely, cutting queer children off from information about the possibility, the validity, and the livability of queer desires and lives.

The possibility of homosexual desire is absent from the conceptual organization of the *Harry Potter* books. There is exactly one moment in the books where the existence of homosexuality is referred to: this is in *Harry Potter and the Order of the Phoenix,* when Harry's cousin, Dudley Dursley, having overheard Harry mention the name Cedric in his sleep, mocks him: "Who's Cedric—your boyfriend?" (19). Implying that only the crass, bullying Dudley would ever suggest that Harry's feelings for boys were sexual, and that such a suggestion could only ever be an insult, the book eradicates the possibility of homosexuality even as it designates it—and effaces precisely the dimension of readerly subjectivity through which I am engaged with the books. "Filling in the gaps" here becomes a question of opening the world of the novels onto a wider world that *can* sustain my engagement with the characters' desires; that can force the text to keep, rather than to disavow, the promise of queerness it makes insofar as it engages me as a reading/desiring subject.

For instance, in my Harry/Snape story "Crucius," one of Harry's canonical fantasies about Snape is revisited and recontextualized as sexual (this is the point in the story when Harry begins to realize that he fancies Snape):

Harry ... stared angrily at Snape.... His old fourth-year fantasy, the day he'd seen Crouch/Moody performing Cruciatus for the first time and been fascinated and sickened, swam back into his head: Snape flat on his back, jerking and twitching: Harry standing over him and...
Jesus. That's revolting.
Harry flushed and hurriedly tried to think about herbs or anything that would make his sudden erection go away [Crane 2003].

The reference is to a moment in *Harry Potter and the Prisoner of Azkaban* where Harry is "picturing horrific things happening to [Snape] ... if only he knew how to do the Cruciatus curse ... he'd have Snape flat on his back like that spider, jerking and twitching" (1999, 263–64). The passage from "Crucius" quoted above thus performs in miniature the larger recontextualization performed by the story: that is, by suggesting that the intensity and physicality of Harry's relationship with Snape has been *misrecognized* and misnamed (by Harry) as anger, it opens up the possibility of reading that canonical intensity and physicality according to a set of sexual associations, informed by the readerly knowledge that homosexual desire *does* exist in the wider world.

Thus, writing slash (whose fundamental intervention into canon is often to assert the existence of same-sex desire) chimes with the Sedgwick epigraph after which this essay is titled: by challenging the queer-eradicating impulses of the *Harry Potter* books' thick languages, by refusing to submit to their effacement of homosexuality, I resolve the painful double bind I find myself caught in, and I refuse to repeat the prohibition against knowledge-of-homosexuality that was inflicted on me and that is still inflicted on queer children.

For it is not just as a queer person, but specifically as a *young* queer person, that Harry lacks a sustaining world. The contradictions of Harry's fictional situation as a child caught up in the continuing life-or-death conflicts of his parents' generation are painful and claustrophobic. He frequently has to take on adult responsibilities: in all five books, it is Harry, in a situation set up by adults yet isolated from adult help, who ends up in life-or-death conflict with Voldemort. Despite the fact that it is in part through Harry's intervention that Voldemort has been thwarted in each of the five books, he is not yet allowed to have full information about the situation nor to have any say in the adult decision-making processes which structure the conflicts, on the grounds that he is still a child and should be "protected." Harry, that is, has neither the protection to which he is said to be entitled as a child (since the adults' problems are regularly resolved at the risk of his life), nor the autonomy to which his status as a combatant should perhaps entitle him.

This is another fiction-generating contradiction for me: it requires me to open the text onto a world in which relationships between adults and young people[8] can be organized differently, and in which Harry would have access to the resources he needs, both to make decisions about his own life and to continue the conflict with Voldemort. It was through exploring, in writing "Crucius," the conditions which would make it possible for Harry to have a relationship with Snape on equal terms that I was able to negotiate the contradictions of Harry's canonical position — and, as an important part of that negotiation, to "make the tacit things explicit:" that is, in reorienting the text, to give a critical account of the structures that disempower Harry in the first place.

"Crucius" is therefore oriented around the point where Harry's position as a quasi-adult fighter against Voldemort intersects with his position as a quasi-child in the care of Dumbledore. In the story, when Dumbledore and Sirius become aware that Harry is attracted to Snape, they deny the reality of his feelings— Sirius insisting that Harry has been bewitched by Snape, Dumbledore asserting that "It's just a crush... Harry's just practising for falling in love... If [he was] really ready ... [he]'d fall for someone who was *possible*. But Snape's *so* impossible, it's safe." Harry's insistence on the reality of his attraction to Snape thus becomes an insistence that he is capable of being the subject, as well as just the object, of sexual desire, and that his youth does not keep him "safe" from love — or war. As Harry tells Snape:

> Albus and Sirius don't listen to a word I say, you know. They want — I mean, I *can't* keep relying on being able to muddle through all innocent and brave. Like I'd win because my heart is pure, even if I'm stupid and ignorant and childish.... I want to make a move. I want to get Voldemort out in the open, I want to face him, I want to get it over with, but they say wait. I can't do it any more, Severus, I *can't* wait, it's killing me.

Dumbledore and Sirius's attempts to protect Harry are here constructed, like their denial of the reality of Harry's sexual and romantic feelings, as attempts to keep him passive — "stupid and ignorant and childish"— and as withholding the information he needs to survive. Harry's position vis-à-vis Dumbledore and Sirius thus has strong resonances with the subject position of the queer child: the reality of his feelings is denied, and he is not given the resources he needs for his own survival: moreover, these abuses are inflicted on him in the name of his "protection," his "innocence," and his "safety." These two strands of the story (love and war) come together in Harry's relationship to Snape, since Snape is the only character in the books who represents an "outside" to Hogwarts— he does not share the values that "line up tidily" with opposition to Voldemort — but who is not entirely characterized as evil (that is, as siding with Voldemort). Harry's violently experienced and expressed anger toward Snape is recontextualized in "Crucius" not only as sexual, but also as designating Snape as the only character to whom Harry is able to express the anger and frustration of his doubly disempowered position, thus making Snape the only character with whom Harry is able to operate from a position of relative autonomy.

Dumbledore and Sirius in "Crucius" figure the queer-denying and child-disempowering impulses in the *Harry Potter* books (or in the *doxa* which governs their legibility), and Harry's struggle to forge a relationship with Snape on equal terms opens the world of Hogwarts onto a place where young people have access to queer desire and queer individuals as well as having the resources and the autonomy to live the life they want (in "Crucius," this is demonstrated in part by the fact that Snape begins to fall for Harry only when he sees him in the flat he has rented in London — that is, only in a space outside both the system of the wizard world and Harry's abusive family home). "Crucius," then, is an attempt to keep promises to *queer children.* In "Queer and Now," Sedgwick asks, "How to tell kids who are supposed never to learn this that, farther along, the road widens and the air brightens; that in the big world there are worlds where it's plausible, our demand to *get used to it?*" (2). Writing fan fiction that makes room for queerness is making a textual world wider, brighter, bigger, in a way that has particular resonance with the predicament of young people.

Mary Sue

The narrative of "Crucius" dramatizes the supplementation of canon which is required by my engagement with canon. Making space for Harry in "Crucius" is thus a way for making space in canon for my own subjectivity insofar as it is invested in and partially constituted by my investment, not only in the *Harry Potter* books, but in the *doxa* within which they are brought to legibility. Fan fiction — for me — thus comes out of the conjunction between my desiring subjectivity, the *doxa* which tries to orient a text around the cultural code, and my knowledge of the world as it contradicts that *doxa*. Fan fiction, as I have argued, brings a text to a legibility formed out of a set of associations "chosen" on the basis of the demands made by a reader's desiring subjectivity: one of those demands might be precisely that the fictional universe should have space for the reader herself, for her desires, her demands, her politics. It is for this reason that work on queer reading practices provides some of the best theoretical models for fan fiction, since queer readings insist on the text's recognizing the possibility of the queer desires invested in the text by its reader, and on the text's providing a context which can sustain those desires.

Fan readings of the sort I am describing need not always be oriented specifically around making space for queer sexualities, however. In my story "In Loco Parentis," I attempt to make visible a dimension of Hermione's experience which is effaced in the novels: this is her growing estrangement from her parents and from Muggle (nonwizard) culture in general. Although we are told very little about Hermione's relationship with her parents, we do know that they "don't read the *Daily Prophet*" (the wizarding paper, which Hermione reads even in her holidays [*Goblet* 392]); that by the time Hermione is thirteen they are giving her money, a month in advance of her birthday, to buy her own birthday present in the wizarding world (*Azkaban* 47); and that Hermione runs away from them at Christmas to help Harry (*Phoenix* 440). Again, this is not resolved within the books—it isn't even explicitly designated as a problem — but, from these scattered hints, a painful and growing cultural and emotional gap between Hermione and her parents can be brought to visibility. This is where "In Loco Parentis" begins:

> It wasn't until she got the letter from her parents asking, tentatively enough, when they should meet her train that Hermione realized she'd forgotten to sort out a place to stay over the summer.
> *Shit.*
> No exams.... No friend with a dangerously ill father. Nothing that had any equivalent in the few shreds of language she still shared with her parents. Nothing left but: *I don't want to. I don't want to come home* [Crane 2005].

The population of the school mainly consists of the children of wizarding parents, but a few children, including Hermione, are "Muggle-born" (or, to use the derogatory term, "Mudbloods"). Muggle-born children with magical ability receive a letter inviting them to Hogwarts when they turn eleven: this is a family's first introduction to the wizarding world, whose existence is hidden from Muggles.

Despite the fact that in every generation a significant minority of wizards are thus "recruited" from the nonwizard population (two out of ten children in Harry's year and house at Hogwarts are Muggle-born, and Harry is wizard-born but Muggle-raised), the wizarding world is culturally entirely separate from the Muggle world. Wizards dress differently, follow different sports, read different newspapers, listen to different pop music, and so on. Assimilation of Muggle-born wizards into this absolutely foreign cultural milieu seems to be complete: there are no adult wizard characters whose Muggle origins are visible. Even the government employee charged with preventing the misuse of "Muggle Artefacts" is so ignorant of Muggle culture that he cannot even pronounce the word *electricity* (*Goblet* 45). My reading of the few hints about Hermione's increasing estrangement from the culture of her birth and from her parents suggests that this situation must involve painful contradictions and complex cultural negotiations for her: this reading is backed up by my awareness of a world in which the assimilation of second-generation immigrants is not achieved completely, silently, or without violence.

The fictional world of the *Harry Potter* books seems to me, then, simultaneously to require and to make impossible the subject position of the incompletely assimilated Muggle-born wizard — and, as the "sustaining world" for this subject position, also to require and to make invisible the politicization of Muggle-wizard relations, and a form of resistance against assimilation and segregation on the part of Muggle-born wizards. In "In Loco Parentis," this subject position is occupied by a Mary Sue character, Hestia Jones.[9] She is clearly marked as nonassimilated from the beginning by her clothes and her use of a Walkman. This is the conversation which introduces a politicized Muggle-born vocabulary:

> "You talk like a Muggle," said Hermione.
> "I am a Muggle," said Hestia immediately.
> Hermione frowned. "But..."
> "Oh," said Hestia. She put her cup down and flapped her hands. "Muggle-*born*. But that sounds so... Oh, I don't know. So *grudging*... You know? I was *born* a Muggle but *now* I *am* a witch. I usually call myself a Mud, actually. I've got a badge which... Oh, it's on this t-shirt." She plucked at her vest to show Hermione the MUD PRIDE badge.
> "Like in Mudblood," she added. "But also, like, *my name is mud*, and like *muddying the waters*— you know, like it's not so simple — and also like *earth*."

It is through her friendship with Hestia and her involvement in Mud politics that Hermione begins to come to terms with the contradictions of her own position, to achieve some sort of autonomy, and to mend her relationship with her parents.

The two characters, Hestia and Hermione, thus correspond to the two sides of my readerly subjectivity. Hestia brings Hermione out into the "wider world" where "it is plausible, our demand to *get used to it*"— our demand to be able to refuse assimilation — just as this story makes space in the *Harry Potter* universe for those elements of my readerly subjectivity which are effaced by the books' suppression of any discourse around assimilation and resistance.[10]

The adult-child relationship in "In Loco Parentis" dramatizes the split in my readerly subjectivity between the passive reader, constrained by *doxa* (the child disempowered by the lack of resources in the fictional universe), and the active reader who brings her own knowledges about the world to the text (the adult who provides information and opens up a new subject position within the fictional universe). Again, there is an isomorphism between my experience of reading *Harry Potter* and my experience of writing fan fiction (it may be, in fact, that it is writing fan fiction which has made the complexities of my subject position as a reader visible to me). And again, it is in Sedgwick's work — this time in her essay "Tales of the Avunculate," which cites the "uncle" as the adult figure who can represent queer sexualities to the child — that I find a theorization of this experience.

Multiple Desires

As a reader of *Harry Potter,* "disempowered" by the suspense structure of the books, I still have some degree of choice over *whose* desire — which pattern or structure of desire, out of all the possible sets of associations (structured as desiring subjectivities) that bring a text to legibility — I internalize. Sedgwick writes:

> Suppose we assume ... the near-inevitability of the child's being "seduced" in the sense of being inducted into, and more or less implanted with, one or more adult sexualities whose congruence with the child's felt desires will necessarily leave at least many painful gaps.... A child, objectively very disempowered, might yet be seen as being sometimes in a position to influence — obviously to radically varying degrees—*by whom s/he may be seduced;* as having some possible degree of choice, that is to say, about *whose* desire, what conscious and unconscious needs, what ruptures of self and what flawed resources of remediation, are henceforth to become part of her or his internalized sexual law [1994, 64].

The child's near-inevitable seduction by an adult becomes a useful metaphor for the fan's negotiation of the multiple possible organizations of the canonical text. The child's position of objective disempowerment corresponds to the fan writer's always being a *reader* first of all: canon precedes the fan, and fan fiction cannot change canon (or can it? It can change canon for the reader/writer, as I've suggested, and perhaps for other readers of the fan story).

Here fan fiction becomes a way not so much of "filling in the gaps" with a known unknown, but rather a way of negotiating the "painful gaps" left in the encounter between a reader's "felt desires" and the read text, which is itself structured by the conscious and unconscious desires of another subjectivity — or more than one other subjectivity. For fan fiction is a way of alerting other fans to other potentially choosable structures of desire in the text. To illustrate this, here is the story of how I started to write Harry/Snape slash.

I had decided, consciously, that I would never be able to write *Harry Potter* fan fiction because in order to do so, I would have to slash Harry, the point-of-view character and hence the densest crossing point for all the thick languages of the *doxa* with readerly/desiring subjectivity, with Snape, its "outsider" character and hence the point of densest possibility for opening the fictional world onto its outside(s). However, I was unable to imagine a way in which Harry and Snape could form an equal sexual relationship within the terms of the books, and so there was no story I could write —

Until, at the Red Rose slash convention in 2002, I saw X's stunning Harry/Snape picture, "Disarmed." The picture shows Harry and Snape facing each other, in profile, about to kiss. Harry's eyes are closed, his hand is clenched in the fabric at the shoulder of Snape's robe, and he is lifting his face toward Snape. Snape, looking at Harry with a mixture of irony and tenderness, is taking Harry's glasses off. The picture is clearly about the age gap between the two of them, but the composition and coloring of the picture balances them against each other so that the difference in their ages becomes just one of a number of contrasts between them: Harry impulsive, Snape cautious; Harry light — his hair is paler brown than usual in this picture — Snape dark. The picture also makes the point that the age gap between Harry and Snape in the books is about twenty years — much less than the difference between Daniel Radcliffe and Alan Rickman, who play Harry and Snape, respectively, in the films — and therefore allowed me to revisualize the characters. This portrait of their relationship — in particular, Snape's hesitation, Harry's confidence, and the sense that they complement one another — has been the model of the resolution for which all my Harry/Snape narratives have aimed, the axis around which I was finally able to reorient canon, finding a way out of the contradictions and effacements in which it caught me.

So fan fiction, as a *sharing*, as a *making legible* of these difficult negotiations between subjectivity and textuality, these complicated subject/text/world relations, is a way of reassuring each other that we have what Barthes calls the "immoral right" to make and circulate meanings. And, crucially, fan fiction allows us to *take pleasure* in that immoral right, to negotiate from a position of taking and giving pleasure: while academic discourse can also attempt to reorient texts, to open them onto knowledges of wider, brighter, queerer worlds, it always runs the risk of seeming to speak from a position of authority, of attempting to *prove* its reading of a text, rather than attempting simply to circulate it as one among many readings, taking pleasure in multiplicity itself.

Fan fiction, then, can be a site of resistance not only to the *doxa* which tries to govern the reading of a text, but also to the "vengeful rigor" of academic discourse. Once again, Barthes's description of "intercalation" in "Brecht and Discourse" also describes fan fiction. He writes that "the destruction of monstrous discourse is here conducted according to an erotic technique;" not according to "the vengeful rigor of Marxist discourse (the science which knows the reality of fascist speeches), ... but rather as if it were natural *to take pleasure in the truth*, as if one had the simple right, the *immoral* right to submit the bourgeois text to a critique itself formed by the reading techniques of a certain bourgeois past" (1986, 216). This passage speaks to me, in the paradox of the "immoral right" and of "pleasure/truth," of Sedgwick's work: for Sedgwick, too, reading is a matter of "fascination and love"—not so much for particular texts, but for "sites where the meanings didn't line up tidily with each other" (1994, 3): that is, for readings which resist the docile intertext, the continuity which would *keep meanings in line*. It speaks to me, too, of the hard-to-articulate way in which I, as a fan fiction writer, feel I have (despite copyright law, despite being aware that there are writers who experience fan fiction written about their work as a painful effacement of *their* investment in the text) a *right* to the stories I tell, a right which is granted in part by my *readerly* implication in a text, a right which has something to do with pleasure. Fan fiction, for me, is a way of taking pleasure in the truth — in the reorientation of a text away from the abusive false logic of the cultural code; a way, moreover, of taking pleasure in scandalously acting *as if* it were natural to do so, *as if* all readings (or at least all readings that can themselves become legible for other fans) were equally possible — as if there were not strong cultural prohibitions against (for example) recognizing queerness in children's fiction.

Notes

1. See Alexander Doty (1993): "conventional heterosexist paradigms ... always already have decided that expressions of queerness are *sub*-textual, *sub*-cultural, *alternative* readings.... I've got news for straight culture: your readings of texts are usually 'alternative' ones for me, and they often seem like desperate attempts to deny the queerness that is so clearly a part of mass culture" (xii).

2. This argument is particularly odd because Scodari (2003) specifically cites Xena/Gabrielle "slash" as resistive; however, the relationship between Xena and Gabrielle was deliberately coded as lesbian by the show's creators and arguably became canonical by the end of the series (see Angie B, 2003). In what sense is it "resistive" to acknowledge a canonical gay relationship?

3. Lackner et al., in their essay in this volume, present an important challenge to the assumption (which underestimates both the complexity of gender identity/identification and the difference between fictional and nonfictional people) that gender difference constitutes an absolute break between (male) characters and (female) authors/readers in slash.

4. As Sedgwick points out in the foreword to *Tendencies,* "the word 'queer' itself means *across*"; it comes from the same root as "German *quer* (transverse), Latin *torquere* (twist), English *athwart*" (xii). Queer readings are thus transverse, oblique readings. In this case, all fan fiction is a kind of queer textuality.

5. I discuss *Harry Potter* here as if the books were the only canonical texts, in order to avoid the complex questions of the relation between books and films, which are not relevant to my arguments here.

6. That is, up to the end of *Harry Potter and the Order of the Phoenix* (2003). *Harry Potter and the Half-Blood Prince* (2005) was published after this chapter was in its near-final form; since I had not read it when I wrote "Crucius" and "In Loco Parentis," I do not take it into consideration here.

7. The fact that I am sure that Harry won't come out, but that I am unable to account in detail for *why* I am so sure about it, suggests that this is an instance of ideology which "goes without saying" (Barthes 2000, 11).

8. I avoid the word *child* here because of its quasi-legal connotations—a child is unable to give legal consent to sex or to make decisions about where and with whom to live.

9. Hestia Jones is actually a canonical character — she appears in *Order of the Phoenix*—but, apart from using her name and hair color, I made her up from scratch. I consciously intended her to be a Mary Sue.

10. Here I challenge Scodari's (2003, 5) assertion that "Mary Sue ... fan fiction ... can seek to construct a subject position within which the writer-reader projects herself as the focus of attention for idolized and idealized male heroes." Of course Mary Sue stories *can* do this, but Scodari does not even mention the possibility that they may seek to construct a nonheterocentric subject position (my Hestia Jones is gay). Less explicitly, Scodari's characterization of Mary Sue as "autobiographical" (Jenkins) and as "re-creating the adolescent self" (Bacon-Smith) denigrates any consciously autobiographical investment in fan fiction, especially one which constructs a subject position for the reader/writer's "adolescent self" (3).

References

Abercrombie, Nicholas, and Brian Longhurst. 1998. *Audiences: A sociological theory of performance and imagination.* London: Sage.
B, Angie. 2003. Xena and Gabrielle: Lesbian icons. http://www.afterellen.com/TV/xena.html (accessed October 22, 2005).
_____. 1971/1977. *Image-music-text.* Trans. Stephen Heath, 165–69. London: Fontana.
_____. 1975/1986. *The rustle of language.* Trans. Richard Howard. Berkeley: Univ. of California Press.
_____. 1957/2000. *Mythologies.* Trans. Annette Lavers. London: Vintage.
Crane, Dolores. 2003. Crucius. http://www.restrictedsection.org/story.php?story=173 (accessed June 1, 2006).
_____. Forthcoming. In loco parentis.
Doty, Alexander. 1993. *Making things perfectly queer.* Minneapolis: Univ. of Minnesota Press.

Jones, Sara Gwenllian. 2002. The sex lives of cult television characters. *Screen* 43:79–90.

Rowling, J. K. 1999. *Harry Potter and the prisoner of Azkaban.* London: Bloomsbury.

_____. 2000. *Harry Potter and the goblet of fire.* London: Bloomsbury.

_____. 2003. *Harry Potter and the Order of the Phoenix.* London: Bloomsbury.

_____. 2005. *Harry Potter and the Half-Blood Prince.* London: Bloomsbury.

Scodari, Christine. 2003. Resistance re-examined: Gender, fan practices, and science fiction television. *Popular Communication* 1:111–30.

Sedgwick, Eve Kosofsky. 1993/1994. *Tendencies.* London: Routledge.

7. The Audience as Editor
The Role of Beta Readers in Online Fan Fiction Communities
Angelina I. Karpovich

ABSTRACT.— I examine the role that beta reading plays in fan fiction communities by tracing the evolution of this practice in the context of technological and demographic changes throughout the recent history of fan fiction communities. I then examine a number of online resources specifically dedicated to beta reading in order to test the validity of the structuralist approach to online fandom. A variety of modes of address present in the Web sites under consideration points to differing assumptions about the potential readers' status within the fan fiction community; thus, an analysis of basic guides to beta reading reveals which social norms the community emphasizes most. The evolution of beta reading and the variety of online resources dedicated to its practice are discussed as examples of the general technological sophistication of the online fan community and are presented as an example of medium-enabled convergence of the technological knowledges and social practices of a variety of subcultures. The role of beta readers in fan fiction communities is examined in relation to the superficially similar roles performed by commercial literary editors and test audiences for prerelease films. This comparison reveals that the relationship between beta readers and fan texts is unique. Beta reading is also discussed in the light of the ever-increasing volume of metafandom discourses, which serve to augment both the social networks and textual productivity within fan communities while simultaneously challenging the previous Cartesian definitions of fan communities and highlighting the intrinsically problematic nature of defining fan communities.

Introduction

Beta reading, the practice of releasing a story to a selected (and trusted) fellow writer or other member of the fan fiction community before making it available to a general readership through a fiction archive, a newsgroup, or additional avenues such as LiveJournal.com, is arguably a phenomenon that came about as a result of the move from paper-based to Internet-based fan fiction. It has proved difficult to find examples of this practice in pre-Internet days, when the underground nature of published fanzines made their readership circles smaller and more intimately connected. In print zines, the person who beta read the story was probably also the editor of the zine. Although some fanzine editors performed a wider range of editorial functions than simply collating fan fiction stories for publication, "editing" was not necessarily seen as a general fandom-wide prerequisite for publication in fanzines. The terms *beta* and *beta reader,* or indeed any reference to a universally structured practice of editing individual fan fiction stories, do not appear in glossaries of fandom terminology published before the Internet became widely available, such as Bruce Southard's "The Language of Science-Fiction Fan Magazines" (1982) or Joseph L. Sanders and Rich Brown's "Glossary of Fanspeak" (1994). There is no mention of the term or even of the practice that we now know as beta reading in Joan Marie Verba's (1996) history of the development of fan fiction in *Star Trek* fanzines, *Boldly Writing: A Trekker Fan and Zine History, 1967–1987.* Nor does the term appear in the early academic studies of the largely pre–Internet fan fiction communities (Bacon-Smith 1992; Jenkins 1992).

This lack leads me to conclude that although some paper fanzine editors did indeed shoulder traditional editorial functions, the very term *beta reader* is intimately connected with the Internet age, deriving from the so-called beta testers of computer software:

> Beta, in strict software parlance, referred to the antepenultimate release of the software product, and its function was to discover coding errors known charitably as "bugs." The beta release followed the *alpha* release, in which the software functioned enough for basic testing but in which could be found bugs galore and missing major features. After the beta version had gone through its testing paces, it was released in a *gamma* version for final testing, and gamma was followed by the official release. In practice, however, the gamma version was frequently skipped, so the beta release became the last version before shipping. Throughout the history of software, beta versions were released only to registered beta testers, who included selected information managers at corporations who were continuing customers of that product, to single users who had contributed extensively to the

> development team by submitting comments and suggestions about the product, and to computer magazines who needed an early version ... on which to base reviews and evaluations.... Of course, *all* software is released in a somewhat unfinished state ... but beta releases are *intended* to be unfinished [Randall 1997, 317–18].

A search for the earliest mentions of "beta reading" on Usenet finds messages that date back to late 1999 and appear, perhaps unsurprisingly, in alt.startrek.creative and alt.tv.x-files.creative. Some of the earliest appearances of the term on Yahoo.com mailing lists date back to May 1998 and appear on the UnConventional Shippers List (ucshippers), the *Space: Above and Beyond* FanFic Flightdeck (saabfanfic), and a dedicated multifandom group, Beta_Unlimited (Beta_Unlimited). The diversity of fandom sources indicated here suggests that beta reading was adopted as a cross-fandom fan fiction practice from its inception. The fact that the tone and content of all these messages assume that their readers will be already familiar with the term suggests that it had probably become fairly widely accepted within the context of fan fiction even earlier. However, although the exact point at which the term *beta reader* became a part of the shared language of online fandom is still unclear, its roots in software development terminology, as well as the way in which the functions performed by beta readers so closely follow the functions performed by the original beta testers of software, all imply that the online fan community is literate in media and technology.

This singular instance of the adoption of a term from the lexicon of software development into the social practice of the online fan community is an early example of the medium-enabled convergence between the linguistic and social practices of seemingly entirely diverse online communities. The Internet has facilitated such instances of convergence through the combination of the easy-to-navigate nature of hypertext (and the consequent ease of retrieving and understanding information previously considered "specialist") and the literal overlap in the range of expertise and interests between the members of fandom and members of other subcultures. In practice, membership of online fandom does not preclude the individual fans' continuing membership and expertise within other online subcultures. Indeed, Henry Jenkins, in "Quentin Tarantino's *Star Wars*" (2003), describes fans as "early adopters" of a range of new media technologies and argues that the aesthetics and cultural politics of fandom have had an impact on the wider public understanding of new media. Participation in online fandom frequently entails drawing on a range of different kinds of expertise and technological skills, and consequently, different vocabularies. Contemporary online fandom frequently calls for a degree of practical competence in, or at the very least familiarity with, Web design, archive maintenance, a variety of online chat and message board formats, blogs, graphic design, and digital video editing, as Busse and Hellekson's introduction to this volume notes.

Any consideration of the social practices of online fandom reveals the complexity of the engagement between the social and textual norms of the community and the technological competences that enable the community's existence and development. However, it would be fallacious to try to present an unreservedly utopian view of the impact of technology on online fandom, because technological factors determine not only the kinds of interaction available to members of the community, but also the individual fans' level of access to community practices. Although the Internet has largely negated the two previous biggest obstacles to communication among fans—time and distance—participation is now largely precluded by access to the Internet. The new medium theoretically allows for immediate communication around the clock, but in practice, a gap exists in the availability and quality of Internet access between North America and the rest of the world.[1]

Nevertheless, the proliferation and variety of online resources for fan fiction writers is one of the symptoms of the general technological sophistication of the community, as well as an example of the way in which the community attempts to share its members' individual knowledges in order to sustain itself. The practice of releasing a story to beta readers has become a convention within the fan fiction community, and even at a micro level, there is an aspect of community maintenance to this convention, as the continuing dialogues between the fan writers and their betas help to maintain personal links within the community. In practice, the beta process can be viewed as a series of distinct stages. The process is almost always initiated by the fan writer, who, upon completing a draft that she is happy to make available to a beta reader, either makes contact with an existing beta reader or seeks one by searching in online forums, posting public requests for beta readers, or approaching other fan writers. A beta reader will read the story as a draft and will offer feedback and suggestions for improvement on all aspects of the story, from narrative structure and characterization to grammar and spelling. It is not unusual for an author to use more than one beta reader, perhaps with different betas specializing in different aspects of writing. Beta readers themselves often specify their particular strengths and weaknesses before they begin beta reading a story for a new author, thus allowing the author to seek additional critical input elsewhere.

At this stage, the story remains a draft; it is customary for authors not to make the story available to the general readership while it is in the process of being beta read. Beta readers tend to maintain some contact with the authors during this process, in order to keep the writers up to date with their progress with the story. Obviously, such dialogues have been enabled by and benefited from the medium of the Internet, which offers the fan fiction community an unprecedented and uniquely suitable combination of communicational immediacy and level of detail. Although the fan author is under no obligation to use any of the beta reader's suggestions, the community does expect the beta readers' efforts to be acknowledged. It is customary for authors to include the name of the beta readers in the header information that precedes the actual text of the story. This informal convention extends to not merely listing the beta reader, but thanking her; the combination of the thanks and the usual spatial proximity of the beta reader's name to the title of the story is a subtle indicator of the prominence that the community invests in the role of the beta readers within the overall process of creating fan fiction.

Although the variety of ancillary online fan fiction resources, such as the writing guides, fandom-specific and subject-specific reference sites, and the ever-increasing volume of so-called meta (that is, the critical and often introspective discussions of aspects of fandom by the fans themselves), facilitates the development of the community, it simultaneously adds new layers of complexity to any consideration of what elements might actually constitute such a community. Jenkins, for example, emphasized the Cartesian qualities of fandom, in which the "products" of fandom become its own artifacts: the solid proof, or reminder, that the community exists (or, at the very least, has existed at some point) even while its members are not in direct communication with each other — in effect, using the production of creative materials such as fiction, filk, art, videos, and costumes as the defining aspect of the distinct practice of fandom: "Many fans are regular and enthusiastic viewers of programs that never motivate them to write stories, share letters, join clubs, or attend conventions" (1992, 90). Thus, explicitly or otherwise, Jenkins and most subsequent academic writers on fandom (for example, Bacon-Smith 1992; Abercrombie and Longhurst 1998; Hills 2002) see the production of artifacts as the main feature that distinguishes fans from mere regular and enthusiastic viewers. While the traditionally creative aspects of fandom remain its most visible aspects, the development of metafandom resources and discussions, which are focused on and around the fan community itself, rather than the original source material, is, like the practice of beta reading, closely linked with fandom's adoption of and adaptation to the medium of the Internet. Although fan meta discussions have existed for almost as long as fandom itself, the Internet has been crucial in making most these discussions accessible (at least in theory) to a much wider audience of fans and neofans.

In a discussion of fan-produced films, Jenkins describes this particular example of fan productivity as an instance of intersection between "the corporate movement towards media convergence and the unleashing of significant new tools which enable the grassroots archiving, annotation, appropriation, and recirculation of media content. These fan films build on long-standing practices of the fan community but they also reflect the influence of this changed technological environment" (2003, 281). Beta reading may not be an immediately obvious parallel example of convergence (because it does not use as wide a range of the possibilities offered by new technologies as the production of fan films), but it introduces an even greater degree of complexity to our conceptualizing of the relationships among writers, readers, and texts.

Beta readers, by being routinely and directly involved, and indeed sought after, as active commentators on works in progress, do more than simply enhance the practices of fannish textual productivity. If fan fiction is an avenue for the reinterpretation and reappropriation of media texts, if one of its functions lies in disrupting the hierarchies established by media conglomerates by transforming media consumers into producers, then the practice of beta reading represents a further refutation of the idea that individuals or groups can claim sole intellectual ownership over the texts and images that combine to form a shared frame of reference for a diverse and international community. Moreover, beta reading has influenced the way fan fiction is conceived of and presented within the community itself: the social expectation that a piece of fan fiction ought to be submitted for peer criticism before it is published online represents a distinct move toward the adoption of professional-level standards and an appreciation of fan fiction as not only a tribute to the original source material but also as readable, grammatically correct, edited prose. Authors and beta readers make no profit from their work, but they share a common aim of improving the writing before it is to be presented to a wider readership. Although the beta reader's specific suggestions are usually not identified within the final published version of the story, her investment in the text is normally explicitly acknowledged by the author. This relationship between fan fiction beta readers and the text combines elements of the traditionally distinct roles of the reader (who is the target audience of the text, but whose engagement with it, although potentially interpretive, does not allow for a *direct* intervention), the commentator or critic (who judges the text) and the editor (who ensures that the text fulfills its requirements and who, in contrast with the reader and the commentator-critic, is entitled to stipulate alterations in the text).

The position of beta reader is unlike that of the professional copy editor because the beta reader performs her function on a voluntary basis, and more importantly, because the beta reader is a priori understood to be approaching the text as somebody who is entitled to be just as invested in the characters and their story as the author. Similarly, beta readers are distinct from another group with broadly similar aims: the test audiences for prerelease films. Whereas test audiences do generally participate on a voluntary basis, and have even been known to affect the narrative elements of films before their release, their participation in the creative process is still very far from a regular convention of filmmaking: their suggestions tend to be taken up only in the most drastic of circumstances, and, perhaps most crucially, their contribution is never directly acknowledged, leaving the authorship of the finished film solely in the hands of its original creators.[2] Thus, the practice of beta reading fan fiction represents a unique form of audience engagement with the text, enabled by but more conceptually complex than fan fiction itself, because it allows some members of an audience to significantly affect a text addressed directly to them in ways that greatly exceed the possibilities afforded to the audiences of any commercially produced texts.

The practice of beta reading can be seen as building on an earlier creative fan practice of "talking story,"[3] which involved fans discussing potential story ideas and incomplete stories, either in the context of fan conventions or an even less formal gathering of fan writers, as described by Jenkins in *Textual Poachers* (1992, 161). Although both practices aim to improve individual works of fan fiction through collaborative discussion, talking story differs from beta reading both in its principal mode of interaction (primarily, although not exclusively, verbal rather than written), and consequently in its relatively greater degree of performativity, which, particularly in the context of official and semiofficial fan gatherings, closely aligns it with the more public and performative forms of fandom, such as filking and role playing. In other words, I would argue that despite the similarity of purpose between the practices of talking story and beta reading, the difference between the modes in which they are performed and the consequently diverging range of associated practices ensures that they remain distinct from each other. This distinction simultaneously underlines both the diversity and the interconnectedness of fan practices.

Of all types of fannish productivity, fan fiction seemingly offers the least potential for convergence in terms of the technology involved in the process; unlike fan vid making or filmmaking or fan art, the production of fan fiction demands only a word processing program and basic Internet access. Nevertheless, the range of social processes that has evolved around the production of fan fiction, as exemplified here by beta reading, offers the most sophisticated example of medium-enabled convergence between grassroots technical knowledge and the reappropriation and reinterpretation of not only media texts, but more crucially, the very means by which they are produced.

Beta Reading and Levels of Knowledge

Unsurprisingly, in a group as diverse as the online fan fiction community, a neophyte fan may potentially encounter more than one vision of what beta reading means to the community. In fact, there are at least three distinct categories of online fan resources that offer detailed considerations of the subject of beta reading. Although imposing any kind of distinction runs the risk of appearing arbitrary, I believe that in this case, the vocabulary and style used by the various fan-ran Web sites are sufficiently different to be considered distinct, and that these differences are conscious and purposeful, indicating what kinds of readerships the Web sites are aimed at. In *Enterprising Women* (1991), Camille Bacon-Smith's structuralist approach to fan fiction communities posits that intimate knowledge of fannish practices can only acquired by a progression through a series of "circles," with movement forward assured only by mastering the current level of knowledge and therefore acquiring the trust of the community. Although Bacon-Smith's eventual conclusions appear to be, at least with the benefit of hindsight, problematic, I intend to test the extent to which her structuralist model can be applied to considerations of online beta reading resources.

In the case of online guides to beta reading, the first level of knowledge is the most general, and arguably neutral, introduction to the subject, which usually presents links to further resources for those interested. Writers University,[4] one of the most comprehensive online support resources for fan fiction authors, began its guide with a definition of a beta reader: "A person who critiques a story for an author. The critique normally examines the following parts of a piece: grammar, spelling, characterizations, plot, similarities to canon, and language" (http://www.writersu.s5.com/english/beta.html). From this deliberately brief and general introduction, the main page of the beta-reading section of Writers University offered links to more detailed essays on the various aspects of the beta reading process and on the author-beta relationship. Each of these essays, in addition to providing their own definitions, offers some more practical tips on beta reading and on maintaining the relationship between the writer and beta. Each of the essays is also general enough not to be considered contradictory to the other essays in the section, although slight contradictions do appear, even they are expressed as neutrally as possible. For example, although for one essay author "a beta reader should be someone with a strong grasp of the mechanics of writing, but need not be a writer" (Tara, 2001, http://www.writersu.s5.com/english/betaessay07.html), another essay author on the same site asserted that "many of the best beta readers are also the best writers, though this is not always strictly true" (Elizabeth Durack, 2000, http://www.writersu.s5.com/english/betaessay02.html). Most of the articles at Writers University present the author-beta relationship as a form of contract, with both sides having responsibilities to each other as well as to the story itself. Consciously or otherwise, most of Elizabeth Durack's essay on beta reading is actually laid out in a form that closely approximates that of a contract, and it is worth quoting both parts of this "contract" in their entirety. Durack characterizes a "good beta reader" as someone who

- admits to the author what his or her own strengths and weaknesses are — i.e. "I'm great at beta reading for plot, but not spelling!"
- reads critically to analyze stylistic problems, consistency, plot holes, unclarity, smoothness of flow and action, diction (choice of words), realism and appropriateness of dialog, and so forth. Does it get bogged down in unnecessary description or back-story? Do the characters "sound" like they're supposed to? Is the plot logical and do the characters all have motives for the things they do?

- suggests rather than edits. In most cases a beta reader shouldn't re-write or merely correct problems. Calling the author's attention to problems helps the author be aware of them and thereby improve.

- points out the things he or she likes about a story. Even if it was the worst story you ever read, say something positive! Say multiple somethings positive! See the potential in every story.

- beta reads stories she is genuinely interested in. We all do better work when we're interested.

- gives detailed advice about specific ways the author can make her story better.

- lets the author know how long it will take to get the story beta'ed, and tries to be timely about it.

- is tactful, even with things she considers major flaws — but honest as well.

- improves her skills. If you are serious about wanting to help authors, consider reading some of the writing resources linked at the bottom of the page, which will give you some great perspective on common mistakes fanfic writers make, in addition to basic tips about what makes for good writing.

The parallel qualities of what constitutes a "good author" (purely in terms of the author's relationship with the beta reader) directly correspond with the above characteristic of a "good beta reader," which underscores the quasi-contractual nature of the relationship between the two. According to Durack, a "good author"

- is clear when asking around for a beta reader what she thinks her own strengths and weaknesses are. If she needs a lot of work on her characters she should say so, and if she needs a lot of help with basic spelling, grammar, and punctuation, she should ask specifically for someone who is strong in those areas.

- does not rely on the beta reader to re-write the story for her, but rather accepts the reader's suggestions and re-writes or edits it herself based on them.

- pays attention to the beta reader's performance. If one beta reader is weak in an area that the author needs help in, she may consider having a second or even third one look at it specifically for that.

- doesn't have TOO many beta readers. Beta'ing is time-consuming, so asking a whole lot of people to give you a detailed analysis isn't the most polite thing to do. Have only as many as you need.

- does not take offense at the beta reader's criticisms, which are intended to help and not to hurt.

- [is] understanding about the time it takes to get something beta read.

- takes the beta reader's advice. It is frustrating for a beta reader to make a lot of suggestions for specific things she knows will improve the story, and then have the author ignore them. Yes, the author must use her own judgment, but if you do not trust your beta reader enough to take their advice, you need to reconsider or find a different beta reader whose advice you *do* respect.

- thanks the beta reader for all her hard work — a thorough beta read can be VERY time-consuming, and a good beta reader is worth her weight in gold!

- improves her skills by paying attention to the beta reader's corrections and suggestions and tries not to repeat mistakes over and over. You may also want to check out some of the good advice at the links below.

As the last paragraphs of both quotations indicate, this outline of beta reading was aimed at relatively new writers and beta readers, and it serves as a general and neutral introduction to some of the accepted practices of the community. The neutrality of this introduction to the process and purpose of beta reading is most evident in the fact that it does not locate the authorship of the final story entirely with the writer. Instead, Durack chooses to approach the beta reading process from the perspectives of both the writer and the beta reader. Although Durack acknowledges that the writer is the person ultimately responsible for the story, because she is the person whose name will be most directly associated with the story once it is made publicly available online, this account of the writer-beta relationship does not overlook the fact that any beta readers involved with a given story are conventionally also named by the story's writer, and thus are also seen by the rest of the community as in some way accountable for the quality of the finished story.

Beta readers, like the fan writers themselves, also acquire reputations within the fan fiction community. For fan writers who also beta read, their reputation as a writer may become intertwined with their reputation as a beta reader, especially in the case of well-known fan writers, whose participation as beta readers may be actively sought after by less established fan writers. In addition to improving the quality of the story, a well-known writer who beta reads may be seen as in some ways providing a seal of approval for a less well-known fan author. With such considerations of status in mind, it is not surprising that although the usual practice of beta reading a story does not involve actual contracts between the writer and the beta, there may exist a tacit understanding that what is ultimately at stake in the beta editing process is not just the improvement of the quality of an individual story, but also the enhancement, or at the very least maintenance, of the combined and individual public reputations of both the writer and the beta reader.

Unlike the deliberately general advice offered by Writers University, the specialist beta reading Web sites for particular fandoms (for example, *The X-Files* Beta Readers Circle [http://panthermoon.com/brc/index.html, accessed October 19, 2004], the *Battle of the Planets* Beta Reading Group [http://www.geocities.com/betareadg, accessed June 1, 2006], and the *Star Trek* Beta Reader Index [http://members.tripod.com/~DarrelB/ BRI.html, accessed June 1, 2006]) tend to begin with much shorter definitions of beta reading, or they forgo a definition altogether. The *Star*

Trek Beta Reader Index, for example, offers the most basic factual introduction to the topic:

> We can thank the Information Age for lending to the etymology of this description for who is essentially an editor of fan fiction. I don't know where or how the terms originated, but many technology-centered businesses can be said to use two strategies for testing software products. In the first method, called *alpha testing*, occurs before the product is released commercially to the public (in other words, the testing occurs by an internal component of the company). The second method, *beta testing*, usually occurs just prior to a commercial release and depends on external sources. This is done mainly to catch unanticipated errors and to field suggestions for improvements that can be developed in a future product release. The World Wide Web became a natural venue for software companies to employ this strain of testing: it was only a matter of downloading the software from a web page or FTP site, and the beta tester could send their comments back immediately via e-mail.
>
> I suppose you can see how the term beta reader came to be used in fan fiction circles [Darrel Beach, n.d., http://members.tripod.com/~DarrelB/BRI.html, accessed June 1, 2006].

In addition to providing specialized writing and fandom-focused advice, sites like these may also offer to match writers with beta readers registered on the Web site. The first two Web sites listed above include advice on what information the writer ought to include in the outline of their story when they request a beta reader. This is the most concise way of categorizing a story and also pinpoints which aspects of the story are considered to have the potential to cause concern to a reader. The *X-Files* Beta Readers Circle (http://panthermoon.com/brc/request.html, accessed October 19, 2004) lists the following categories of information: genre, length, violence content (scale of 0–4, with explanations and examples for each category), rating (decided by language, sex, and violence, with the additional advice of, "If you're not sure, err on the side of caution and overrate your story"), plot summary, and special considerations ("Be sure to mention if there's rape or character death. These topics can be upsetting to some readers"). Similarly, the *Battle of the Planets* Beta Reading Group lists the information that the writer "might consider including": which series, length of story, characters featured in the story, timeline, mood (examples given include "romance," "action," and "angst," making this category similar to the "genre" category in the *X-Files* group), and mature subjects ("violence, sex, rape, abuse"). If the categories listed by the two Web sites appear similar, this is largely because they constitute the metainformation that is expected to precede any publicly available piece of fan fiction. Requesting this information at the beta stage serves the dual purpose of inducting new authors into the behavioral norms of the community and of reminding the established authors that their beta readers, aside from performing the beta function, have the same concerns as the "ordinary" readership.

In contrast, the *Star Trek* Beta Reader index asks the beta readers themselves to categorize in detail what kinds of stories they are prepared to beta read, leaving the fan writers to choose which of the beta readers listed in the index they wish to approach for assistance with particular stories. At the same time, the categories listed for the beta readers in the *Star Trek* index closely correspond with the information requested from the fan writers in the *X-Files* Beta Readers Circle and the *Battle of the Planets* Beta Reading Group. The categories here include not just beta reader specialties (areas where the beta reader feels most able to help the author, such as proofreading, sentence structure, grammar, characterization, plot, setting, writing style, and general *Star Trek* knowledge), but also detailed information on which genres of story a beta reader will read, which particular characters and series of *Star Trek* the beta reader is most familiar with, and any additional information the beta reader feels necessary to include in order to improve communication with the fan writers.

Initiation into Fan Practice

Although the tone, vocabularies, and the choice of which information to include in the specialist fandom-specific beta reading resources such as the ones discussed above make it clear that they are aimed at those fan writers and beta readers who already have some degree of familiarity with fandom, the very fact that they seem to largely address those fan writers who do not yet have sufficient experience or connections to have found a beta reader elsewhere points to a conclusion that their primary readership is assumed to be enthusiastic but perhaps still relatively new to the social practices of online fandom. However, this assumption is by no means explicit; the explanation of the role of beta readers is deliberately short in all three Web sites, which suggests that the creators of such resources expect the fan writers to already know the purpose of beta reading. In contrast to the essays at Writers University, the focus here is not on a theoretical introduction to the vocabulary and social norms of fandom, but rather on the practical task of improving the quality of individual stories that develop the cultural capital of the community.

For a comparatively more "experienced," or at the very least more involved, fan, there are the more detailed — and also far more subjective — views on beta reading from those actively engaged in the process: the fan writers themselves. Working Stiffs, the *X-Files* Fan Fiction Resource (http:

//www.geocities.com/workingstiffsfanfic, accessed June 1, 2006), is a comprehensive collection of a multitude of useful articles on all aspects of *X-Files* fan writing. It combines the more general essays on beta reading, which are often similar in tone to the advice found on the pages of Writers University, with interviews with noted writers within the community, and asks them, among other things, about their views on and experiences of beta reading. Although a range of experiences is presented, perhaps the key point here is the level of detail the writers go into in their responses.

The general guides to beta reading discussed above are precisely that — general (even an outline of the author-reader relationship as a form of contract is presented as an ideal-type recommendation, rather than a concrete example to be followed). In contrast, the personal testimonials of the authors on Working Stiffs present their own examples and use those to discuss the value of beta reading in general. This is the case with both positive and negative experiences of beta reading. The author Narida Law states that she has "never, ever regretted submitting something for beta. Without fail, my beta readers have made every story I've written, better" (http://www.geocities. com/workingstiffsfanfic/interviews/NaridaLawintpt3.html, accessed June 1, 2006). Law goes on to describe in detail how she looks to each of her four regular beta readers to provide comments on a certain aspect of the story, as well as its overall quality. The role of beta readers in Law's writing process is evidenced by an example of a beta reader wanting to change the ending to one of Law's stories: "At the time of course, it was a difficult decision to make — anyone who's written something they particularly liked and then had to change/cut it should know — but in retrospect I'm glad [my beta reader] Trixie made me do it. There's nothing more valuable than a beta who will toss your ego under a moving truck and be honest with you."

In contrast, the fan author Sheryl Nantus, in an interview on the same Web site, states that she has

> great fears of working with beta readers. My concern (and it's MINE, so don't state this as a fact for the majority of writers) is that beta readers aren't really qualified to tell you how to rewrite your story.... Maybe it's just the stories I've seen, but I've seen a lot of "beta read" stuff that is truly horrible. Bad grammar, bad spelling... I don't/can't use one for two reasons, mainly. First, when I was in my heyday I didn't have the time to send stuff off to a reader who might get it back to me in a month or so—I wanted it to be posted now or ASAP.... Second, and it's my ego talking here, so bear with me — I went to college for two years to learn how to write. I spent thousands of dollars learning how to construct stuff. Excuse me for not wanting to hand it over to anyone under an assistant editor to trash it. [http://www.geocities.com/workingstiffsfanfic/interviews/Sherylintpt2.htm l, accessed June 1, 2006].

If this seems a negative, or even hostile, view of beta readers, it should be noted that Nantus goes on to suggest, albeit in harsh terms, the ways in which people can train themselves to be good beta readers.

A university degree in a writing-related subject also appears to be one of the most frequently cited reasons for not using beta readers by the authors on the *Star Trek*–focused Writers and Writing Web site (http://users.iafrica.com/x/xk/xkhoi/question6.htm, accessed March 6, 2003). NovaD writes,

> I've had many offers for beta readers over the years.... I suppose the typos can be annoying.... Some who offered to beta took issue with some of my English usage. Since I have a Masters in English and a BA in Journalism, I explained that I was fully aware of what I was doing. Usually, any grammar quirks were a function of experiments in voice.... The main reason I don't have an independent beta reader is because this is the only bit of writing that I do that does not get edited and altered by a second party.

Gamin Davis writes, "I've read stories using them, and I'm convinced — based solely on observation of the stories, not as a statement of ego on my part — that I have a better grasp of writing, composition, grammar and spelling than many of those currently doing the beta reading simply because... I've been trained to be pickier." And Lori writes, "After a few decades of reading and writing, and majoring in English Communications a long time ago, and seriously working on writing skills, I'm confident enough to know that I can turn out a story that needs minimal attention so far as grammar and such goes.... I have beta'd other people's work, and operate a non–*[Star Trek]* writer's group, so I'm well-versed enough in being objective to manage being my own beta."

However, even those who do not use beta readers in their own work recognize their potential value. Gamin Davis, quoted above, ends with, "Without comments of some kind, I really have no reason to post stories at all." Of those who do use betas, comments range from "Beta readers can be a very big help, especially when you're just starting to write in a genre. I have had readers point out cannon errors and logical flaw, as well as suggest possible changes in the storyline" (DebbieB) through "The only story I've ever posted that wasn't beta read was the first. It had spelling errors, grammatical errors, the punctuation was wrong, and needed more action.... Now, I wouldn't post a story without several beta reads. I've learned that while I know the plot, the reader may or may not get the idea" (Nightbird), to "I have changed stories based on [the beta reader's] comments. At the very least, thinking about what the beta reader has said forces me to consider why I don't want to change something. That's of great value in and of itself" (J. A. Toner).

The tacit acceptance of beta reading even from those writers who do not use it themselves, as well as some of the more enthusiastic evidence from those writers who do, is, I would suggest, another result of the evolution of fan fiction on the Internet. The move from closely knit underground communities to online communities accessible (in theory) by anyone from anywhere, has resulted in a shift in the demographics of fandom. A significant proportion of today's online fans may be, by and large, younger than the fans described by Jenkins and Bacon-Smith, and for a number of them, English is not their first language. Reactions to this demographic shift within fandom itself have not been uniformly positive; notably, some of the most popular themes in criticisms of fan fiction, both from within and from outside the fan community, have been poor formatting and the associated use of Netspeak or textspeak in fan fiction, both of which are popularly associated with the younger generation of fans, as well as the apparently notable lack of beta reading in a significant proportion of stories recently published in some of the largest online fan fiction archives. The connection between these criticisms is not coincidental. The practice of beta reading has developed if not as a response to then certainly in parallel with the community's acceptance of a huge, ever-growing number of new and diverse members, and part of becoming a fully fledged member of the community involves learning about and participating in the community practice of beta reading.

The writers' testaments, such as those quoted above, form arguably the most "specialist" circle of knowledge about the process and purpose of beta reading. Here, no attempt is made to clarify the terminology for the uninitiated, and the discourse is both far more personal and frank than in the beginners' guides of, for example, Writers University. There is of course a counterpoint to the writers' views in the form of the beta readers' own testaments of their experiences and practices. Although I have not included them here because, unlike the writers, the beta readers are fairly unanimous about their own value to the community, the fact that they too have an arena to describe and discuss their contributions to the community is worth noting. The beta readers' testaments, just as those of the writers, are detailed, personal, and located firmly within the community's own frame of reference.

However, although the circles of knowledge within pre-Internet-era fandom described by Bacon-Smith appeared to invite a neat linear progression, the online process of gaining knowledge is deliberately nonlinear, and any attempt to present it as such would be fallacious. The very nature of hypertext makes it impossible to assume that a novice will always have a first encounter with the community at the most "general" level, or that having entered the community, its new member will progress in a set, predefined direction. In fact, a neophyte fan fiction writer may not become aware that the community expects any fan writer to use a beta reader unless she or he moves beyond the production of the more traditional textual artifacts of fandom and becomes actively involved in the wider and increasingly more important social practices of fandom, such as the online and real-life meta discussions about fan fiction writing. Moreover, the inherent instability of the Internet further precludes any attempt at linearity; for example, some of the Web sites I have discussed in this chapter are currently offline, and no doubt there are other, equally relevant, online resources that I have failed to include. Although I acknowledge these limitations, they serve to underline the fact that online fandom, through its vast diversity and medium-specific temporality, tends to resist easy classification. The analysis of the history and current attitudes to widespread community practices, such as beta reading, may offer a way of approaching wider community considerations and be a starting point for comparative studies of the social and textual practices of individual fandoms.

Notes

1. At the time of writing, 67.4 percent of the population of North America were classified as Internet users, in comparison with 12 percent of the population of the rest of the world (http://www.internetworldstats.com/stats2.htm, accessed October 22, 2005).

2. Radway documents a less well known but similar process of "pretesting" commercial texts implemented by the romance publishers Simon and Schuster "whereby all books were to be pretested before publication by two hundred readers from a preselected group. Those readers were queried about plot and character and asked to answer open-ended questions about the 'overall quality of the book'" (1984, 43).

3. I am indebted to Henry Jenkins for this observation.

4. References here are to the October 2003 version of the Writers University Web site (http://www.writersu.s5.com). The site changed its address and began undergoing reorganization soon thereafter, although all Web pages quoted further in the essay are still available via Archive.org's Wayback Machine. The current version (http://www. writersu.net) was still in an incomplete beta stage at the time of writing.

References

Abercrombie, Nicholas, and Brian Longhurst. 1998. *Audiences: A sociological theory of performance and imagination.* London: Sage.

Bacon-Smith, Camille. 1992. *Enterprising women: Television fandom and the creation of popular myth.* Philadelphia: Univ. of Pennsylvania Press.

Hills, Matt. 2002. *Fan cultures.* London: Routledge.

Jenkins, Henry. 1992. *Textual poachers: Television fans and participatory culture.* New York: Routledge.

_____. 2003. Quentin Tarantino's *Star Wars?* Digital cinema, media convergence, and participatory culture. In *Rethinking media change,* ed. David Thorburn and Henry Jenkins, 281–312. Cambridge, MA: MIT Press.

Radway, Janice. 1984. *Reading the romance: Women, patriarchy, and popular literature.* Chapel Hill: Univ. of North Carolina Press.

Randall, Neil. 1997. *The soul of the Internet: Net gods, netizens and the wiring of the world.* London: Thomson.

Sanders, Joseph L., and Rich Brown. 1994. Glossary of fanspeak. In *Science fiction fandom,* ed. Joseph L. Sanders, 265–69. Westport, CT: Greenwood Press.

Southard, Bruce. 1982. The language of science-fiction fan magazines. *American Speech* 57:19–31.

Verba, Joan Marie. 1996. *Boldly writing: A Trekker fan and zine history, 1967–1987.* Minnesota: FTL Publications. http://www.ftlpublications.com/bw.htm (accessed June 1, 2006).

8. Cunning Linguists
The Bisexual Erotics
of *Words/Silence/Flesh*

Eden Lackner, Barbara Lynn Lucas,
and Robin Anne Reid

ABSTRACT.—We focus on a dual-authored single work of real person slash fiction in *The Lord of the Rings* fandom and readers' response to it in the two writers' blogs at LiveJournal.com in order to complicate the extent to which the concept of "women" writing slash in earlier decades of fandom risks being ahistorically universalized. Drawing on recent work by Judith Halberstam and Alexander Doty, we ask how differences among women in fandom (of age, regional and national cultures, class, ethnicity, sexual identity) can be read within the complex matrix of queer theory. We analyze the queer erotic relationships between the two writers of the story, their readers, and the three authors of the essay that question the binary of straight/gay in fan scholarship, problematizing the stereotype that slash is written by straight women about gay men. We acknowledge the contemporary culture in which the straight/gay construct has been challenged by bisexual, transsexual, and transgender activists. By analyzing collaboration, queerness, and boundaries, we conclude that the range of sexualities it is possible to construct through slash is greater than has been previously realized. On one end of the spectrum is the notion that women writing erotic fiction in a patriarchal society should be celebrated as subversive. On the other is the notion that women writing homoerotic fanfic should be denigrated as misogynistic for the absence of women characters. We complicate this binary position by hypothesizing the existence of a nuanced spectrum that has yet to be explored or analyzed.

Introduction

"Talk is foreplay," writes the real person slash (RPS) character Harry Sinclair[1] in *Words/Silence/Flesh* (Galadriel and Savageseraph 2003–2005). Later, the RPS character Viggo Mortensen remembers late-night phone calls with his absent lover Sean Bean while writing in his journal, describing "all those nights we fucked each other with words alone, because they could reach farther than lips and fingers, tongues and cock." These quotations bring together the spoken (words) in the silent (form of the written language) by creating an analogy between language and sex. The two characters are separated and are communicating by means of modern technologies and, in many ways, their situation in this work of *The Lord of the Rings* slash fiction reflects that of the writers of their story, one of whom lives in Calgary, Alberta, Canada, and the other in Cleveland, Ohio, USA.

The writers of this essay, ranging in age from twenty-nine to forty-nine as of May 2005, are citizens of two countries. Our academic degrees include four Master of Arts degrees in English with specializations in British literature (various periods) and creative writing, and a doctorate in English with specialization in marginalized twentieth-century American literatures. We have been fans of *The Lord of the Rings* for decades, but our other fandoms have included anime, *Star Wars, Star Trek,* and *Harry Potter.* We all read and write *LotR* fictional person slash and RPS, maintaining personal sites as well as moderating communities on LiveJournal.com (LJ). We are working at different stages—graduate student to professor—of our shared profession. We are engaged not only in the unusual process of producing scholarship on fan fiction, a genre that has not even reached the status of marginalization within the academy, but also in an unusual collaborative process growing out of fandom and professional relationships primarily conducted by means of the Internet, which has offered more women more options for participation in fan communities. Our engagement has led us to speculate not only that there are more women participating in fandom activities today (including women as writers of fanfic) but that, because of historical, technological, and social changes during the past decades, different nationalities and generations of fans of many different sexual identities are visibly interacting in ways that were impossible to see even a decade ago, let alone in 1976, when one of us joined a *Star Trek* Outpost and published mimeographed fanzines.

Aspects of the historical context we consider possible causes for the differences in fandom and fan fiction include: the history of women as science fiction and fantasy fans; the history of feminism and identity politics; the development of sexual civil rights movements by gays, lesbians, bisexuals, and transgendered people; cultural debates over pornography and sex; and cultural debates over changing gender roles. We see our work as moving away from constructing fandom as a homogenous (one gender, one nationality, one sexuality) culture or subculture to question the extent to which the concept of "women" writing slash in earlier decades of fandom risks being ahistorically universalized. We argue that the construction of those fans (even if it was once accurate) may not apply to later generations.[2] The standard assumption that "fan" denotes "adolescent" has been challenged by the extent to which women in their thirties and older have taken advantage of the Internet. We situate our discussion within the context of earlier scholarship not to contradict it, but to expand the field of fan studies. Our analysis of a collaborative story published in LJ, the authors' writing process, and the interaction among the writers and readers will show multiple sites of identity for contemporary women and a greater diversity within the subcultures of fandoms.[3]

Our work is influenced by recent work in the field of queer theory that builds on and expands earlier work by such founding scholars as Eve Kosofsky Sedgwick (1985). Alexander Doty (2000) provides a model for moving away from a normative approach in which "straight readings" are universal and inherent and "queer readings" are stigmatized as being "imposed" from outside the text; he also avoids the homonormative stance of claiming a singular queer reading. Instead, his usage of queer is open and multiple, arguing for the need for a specific descriptions of a variety of queer "readings and pleasures," including bisexual readings. One definition of *bisexual* that Doty (2000) provides is useful for our work: "having desires for both the same sex and the opposite sex within bisexual identities that don't reference straight or lesbian or gay ones, but may reference less binarily defined queer or non-straight identities" (131). Similarly, although Judith Halberstam (1998, 2005) does not directly consider the Internet or fan texts, she too provides a useful framework. She makes a strong case for not excluding any texts from scholarly consideration, for careful consideration of historical contexts as well as awareness of the lived experience of people within a queer methodology that "refuses the academic compulsion toward disciplinary coherence" (1998, 13). The ahistorical approach risks the danger of "rendering historical sexual forms as either universal or completely bound by and to their historical moment. The challenge for new queer history has been, and remains, to produce methodologies sensitive to historical change but influenced by current theoretical preoccupations" (1998, 46).

Halberstam's work, which focuses on the complex project of separating gender from the body to understand many possible identities, including a range of same-sex desires in the past and in the present, has led us to focus on one postmodern space, the Internet, at a specific historical moment. Our preliminary analysis examines the erotics of a queer female space constructed in LJ in which a variety of queer identities and practices—including heterosexual, homosexual, and bisexual partnerships and group relationships—exists in an elaborate spectrum created by two authors and their readers. The analysis is presented in a collaborative academic essay between the two authors and one of their readers. The complex erotics of the relationships developed in the story and between the fan writers and readers allows us to suggest some productive avenues for further work. We suggest that it may no longer be useful or appropriate to maintain the straight/gay binary assumption in discussions of fandom and fan fiction, at least in part because of the extent to which the postmodern nature of the Internet acts as a space for production of what Halberstam calls *counterpublics*, thus permitting more complex and multiple constructions of queer female spaces in an easily accessible public venue. Part of the spectrum of this queer female space is the erotics of collaborative writing and the interaction that exists between female readers and writers in fandom, which have been overlooked by previous scholarship in fan culture.

Words/Silence/Flesh

The collaborative story *Words/Silence/Flesh* was begun in June 2003 and, as of this writing — spring 2005 — is not complete. The completion of any creative work is a complicated question; crucially, our analysis does not depend on the work being finished. A long multipart work in progress is representative of much of fan writing. This story was 130,000 words long in spring 2005. It consists of a group of texts created around a narrative core. The texts comprise narratives generated by a number of characters based on the cast and crew of *The Lord of the Rings* film. It began as a series of letters (some mailed, some unmailed) that soon expanded to include a series of journal entries, e-mails, transcripts of voice mail messages, tape recordings, chat sessions, reproductions of official forms, order forms, and newspaper gossip columns. The narrative center is a traditional slash one involving a plot to break up a romance between the two main characters, Viggo Mortensen and Sean Bean. Other pairings in the story include a past affair between Karl Urban and Harry Sinclair, the breakup of which is part of Harry's motive for trying to force a divide between Viggo and Sean, a budding affair between David Wenham and Miranda Otto, and the beginnings of an involvement between Harry and Andy Serkis. Some installments involve some cross-pairing sexual activity between the two main partners: Viggo and Sean, and David and Miranda.

Words/Silence/Flesh originated with a planned collaboration between the writers on what was going to be a set of fairly traditional narratives told in third person, with Sean on break from filming in England and Viggo in New Zealand, dealing with the sudden interest and advances of Harry. A lag in story development led Savageseraph to post a letter in her LJ. The letter, written from the perspective of her character, Harry, to Sean, taunts him for his slowness and threatens to "molest Viggo without [Sean's] assistance." Seeing the letter, Galadriel responded in kind, in a letter from her character Sean to Harry, admonishing him to hold off or suffer the consequences. This metatextual taunting of writer through character continued for several exchanges in the writers' personal journals, but then the writers' friends (people who read their journals regularly) became involved: that is, they began posting comments and feedback to the letters, which were originally intended only for the other collaborator. The first comment was made to the fourth installment and was posted by the friend who is the coauthor of this essay, illustrating the extent to which the three authors' fan and academic lives overlap: "Didn't know you were going the epistolatory route.... could this be considered postmodern (ducks and runs away)" (Ithiliana, personal communication, LJ, July 7, 2003). Over the course of several weeks, the letters started developing into their own storyline. By the ninth installment, the writers began collaborating on a new piece, plotting future letters and narrative threads.

Although the reader/writer relationship is important in fan fiction, the extent to which it plays a part in the development of this story seems notable. The writers say that they did not take the "letters" seriously as a potential story until feedback from readers appeared, demanding more. The more they posted, the more readers provided feedback and recommended the story to others, thus drawing in a larger audience, and the more the story grew. The story's content is not only erotic and sexual, but the structure also creates sexual tension in readers in at least two ways we consider specific to fan fiction. The first is the extent to which the story's form — postmodern and heteroglossic —caters to fans' voyeuristic impulse to eavesdrop on the objects of their worship (in this case, the actors). The second is the extent to which the story embodies metacommentary on the source texts of the fandom and on the important aspects of fan culture, such as references to earlier films and projects the actors have participated in and as the use of a manipulated photograph as a key plot point.

Blurring the Straight/Gay Binary

If, in earlier years of fandom and fan studies scholarship, a heteronormative identity was assumed, then part of the change in recent years has been simply to add the singular counterpoint of a homonormative identity, an assumed single and stable lesbian or gay identity. The term *queer* has been at times defined as a singular identity (gay, lesbian, or bisexual); our usage follows Doty's and Halberstam's more multiple and open-spectrum definition. The straight/gay binary, even if connected to positive social changes, still excludes many people's expression of selves and desires that are marginalized and perceived as deviant or wrong. Our focus is on slash fiction, but we believe that the default binary can be productively questioned in all areas of fan studies, as it is being questioned in many cultures. Earlier scholarship on fan culture draws from a range of theories for vocabulary to identify the sexual identities of the female fans writing slash: *androgyny, masculinity, homosocial continuum, homosexual desire, repressed homosocial desire, femininity* (Bacon-Smith 1992; Jenkins 1992; Penley 1997; Russ 1985).[4] Although some of the vocabulary comes from early academic work in gender and queer theory, language from 1970s and 1980s North American feminist discourse and the discipline of psychology also appears. Disagreement exists over whether or not the male characters in slash are women disguised as men, androgynous men, (straight) men the way (straight) women want them or want them to behave, or gay men. We identify the problem as trying to fit all slash characters into one theoretical box instead of acknowledging that a number of categories might be needed to analyze a range of diverse stories.

Additionally, the scholarly critical vocabulary, viewed through a contemporary theoretical lens, tends to be associated with identity politics. Although identity politics is a valuable consciousness-raising tool for activists and scholars, it can fall into the trap of freezing identity in terms of one aspect—gender or sexual identity—so that, for example, two of Bacon-Smith's (2000) chapter titles have "women" in them, and a separate one includes "lesbians."[5] Henry Jenkins, arguing for the subversive nature of slash writing by "women," postulates a range of reading responses among women in a way that limits the category to mostly straight women who do not enjoy "boy's" stuff (a description that does not fit many female fans of the fantastic who enthusiastically enjoyed reading books that were said to be for boys only): "The school girl required to read a boy's book, the teenager dragged to see her date's favorite slasher film, the housewife forced to watch her husband's cop show rather than her soap, nevertheless, may find ways to remake those narratives, at least imaginatively" (1992, 114). The assumed heteronormativity of fan writers and readers that exists in fandom and scholarship accompanies a certain ongoing categorization that has become part of the common wisdom regarding the slash genre: *slash is straight women writing gay men.* This commonsense definition is repeated in the media, among (mostly straight) fans, and must be deconstructed in scholarship as it is often deconstructed in fandom, primarily by queer fans. The extent to which queerness in fan readings/writings extends across fandom is shown by Ika Willis's analysis in this volume of the interaction between canon and ideologies of reading in the *Harry Potter* fandom. Arguably, all women — asexual, heterosexual, lesbian, bisexual, transsexual, transgendered — are born into and raised in the dominant patriarchal culture. The extent to which they are forced to read from that perspective is a complex one, allowing for a range of readings from accepting to resisting, complicated by the extent to which "masculinity" may be claimed and constructed by both men and women.

Recent scholarship on fan culture reflects the influence of a new generation of queer theorists and broadens the discussion to include earlier forms of Internet fandom. Susanne Jung (2004) and Sharon Cumberland (2000) both focus on Internet fandoms and incorporate the concept of queerness in its later theoretical sense, as encompassing multiple alternate forms of sexuality and not simply gay or lesbian, but although both do important work, they assume the relationship between the women readers and writers of the queer material is solely one of nonerotic friendship.[6]

Queerness in a Counterpublic Space

Our argument widens the range of sexualities it is possible to construct through slash and emphasizes the extent to which parts of Internet fandom communities could be read as what Kristina Busse has described as a queer female space (2005). The two extremes of the spectrum of arguments regarding slash fiction are that, on the one end, the writing of erotic fiction by women in a patriarchal society should be celebrated as subversive, and on the other, that women writing slash fiction should be denigrated as misogynistic for the absence of women characters. Our purpose is neither to confirm nor deny either of these extremes, but rather to complicate the position by advancing the hypothesis that a spectrum exists between these two end points, with many shadings that have yet to be explored. Either evaluation may be true for some stories and some writers and readers at some times, but neither can be true for all slash fiction by all writers in all fandoms at all times.

In either case, one claim continually made in scholarship and fandom is the "absence" of women from slash fiction. Our response to that question is to point out that women have always been present in slash. The writers and readers *are* the women, and as our cultures and fandoms change, it becomes possible to write more women like us into slash. The assumption that women were not present in fandom has been questioned and problematized throughout decades of feminist scholarship.[7] In the pre-Internet days, women were active in fandom, as Francesca Coppa points out in "A Brief History of Media Fandom" (this volume), although historiographic problems of representing the "history of fandom" mask the presence of women, many of whom report attending fan conventions and reading laboriously produced, hand-circulated texts. Today, on the Internet, especially with the growth of personal blogs, people do not need to be computer experts to post their work. We see fans working in a virtual queer space that allows the integration of fictions with other markers of our lives. Although people talk casually about the Internet as if it were one space (as they speak of fandom as one culture), one mode of thinking is that the Internet contains many spaces. As Kristina Busse and Karen Hellekson point out in their introduction to this volume, paper and APA (amateur press association) zines still exist, just as group lists and Web archives still operate, and blogs have added another dimension that some (but not all) fans find enjoyable. The results can include a greater awareness of the presence of femaleness and women's lives as reported in their own words woven in and around fan fiction. Only in a modernist structuralist approach — which posits that a text exists as an artifact separate from the artist, the culture, and the human body and is analyzed only in terms of its formal elements— does the claim of "no women characters" support the argument that no women are present. Such theories assume the default male author and completely fail to address the readership. Perhaps the postmodern slogan of the death of the author or the general cultural disdain for "amateur" (as opposed to professionally produced) texts leads to the inability to see the contradictions in the claims that first, (mostly or primarily) women write, produce, read, and interact around these stories, and, second, that women are absent.

We argue that the relationship between writers and readers of the story, between the two writers of this story, and the three authors of this essay suggests one way the Internet can serve as a postmodern geography, a queer time and space, which, as Halberstam argues, allows for "the place-making practices within postmodernism in which queer people engage" and "describes the new understandings in space enabled by the production of queer counterpublics" (2005, 6). Halberstam does not include the Internet in her discussion of queer spaces and counterpublics, but her arguments concerning "postmodern geographies" apply to the Internet, especially with regard to the extent to which it can break down some barriers to communication. For example, the three authors of this essay meet in person only once a year, at the scholarly conference where we first met. However, we communicate daily through chat — a medium more immediate than e-mail — and through blogs.

The collaborative aspects of *Words/Silence/Flesh* were initially loose. Savageseraph would post a "letter" (usually in the evening) and Galadriel would post a response (usually during the early hours of the morning). This format was an accident of time zones. However, the effect was that when either writer logged on the evening after her post, she did so without being aware of what the other may have written the night before. Their collaboration was a sort of improvisation, with each responding to a prompt that the other provided while at the same time making sure to leave her partner enough room to keep advancing the story. Being positioned as both writer and reader of the text that is *Words/Silence/Flesh* initiated a sort of erotic textual play between the writers not unlike the one that formed between the readers and the writers.

It is perhaps not coincidental that during this same period, the characters in *Words/Silence/Flesh* were not interacting directly. Sean was in England and the rest of the cast was in New Zealand; the bulk of the exchanges were messages crossing that great geographical divide. However, when Sean returned to New Zealand in the story, the characters had to interact more closely. Although they still might exchange e-mails, chat online, call one another, or leave one another phone messages, their geographical proximity made direct interaction necessary. As a result, both the format of the "letters" and the shape of the collaboration had to evolve. The bulk of the posts became a series of personal journal entries kept by the main characters. Although this format lacks the immediacy of the trigger/response exchanges, it compensates by providing a series of different perspectives on the events of the story as each character records and ruminates over them in his or her journal. The writers then began producing the text of the story collaboratively in role-playing chats, with the writers interacting as their characters. The chats themselves do not consist of finished text ready for posting, but rather dialogue and physical actions, responses, and cues. Description and characters' thoughts and interpretations of events are added later, when each writer works alone on the collaboratively produced "raw chat."

One characteristic this new structure allows to carry over from the earlier letters is its ability to allow the writers to also be readers. Although both writers are aware of how events will unfold in the scenes they collaborate on through chat, they do not know the individual spin each character will put on events. For example, in an entry posted by Savageseraph, Miranda recounts the aftermath of an argument that followed a bit of erotic play she had with Sean in his car:

> I drew a deep breath and smelled him, his scent rising from his body, from his come in my hair. There was a certain intimacy in standing in someone's bathroom, both of you half-dressed, with your hands on him. I became aware of the heat of his body against mine. I wanted to press my lips against his skin, tease the tension out of him with my mouth.... I allowed myself to slide one hand up his chest, cup his chin, and tilt his head back so he had to meet my eyes in the mirror.

Not long after this entry was posted, Galadriel voiced surprise at Miranda's response to the scene, a scene that she (as Sean's writer) knew that Sean did not find erotic in the slightest. Each writer knows how situations will play out, but not what they mean to the other writer's characters. That is something each discovers along with other readers when an individual entry is posted.

Although the sort of writer/reader blur detailed above is not unlike that which occurred in the earlier letters, the effect becomes more pronounced as the process of initial composition moves into the medium of instant messaging, where the cycling between the roles of reader and writer becomes so instantaneous, so seamless, that each writer exists in both spaces while new scenes are being composed. This effect is further enhanced by the fact that many scenes have little more than a time prompt ("Let's move to the next evening") to start the narrative, so neither writer knows in advance where the scene is heading. The direction is determined solely on the basis of characters' responses and on events that the writers will toss in as prompts. For instance, in a chat session from January 4, 2004, Savageseraph introduces a new character into a scene between Miranda and Dave that has ended as Miranda walks away:

> *Savageseraph:* From behind Dave: "Looks like trouble in paradise."
> *Galadriel:*   (Oooh, you ARE evil.)
> *Savageseraph:* (Why thank you very much. :-))
> *Galadriel:*   (Let's see if I can call it... ;-))
> Dave turns around. "Harry."
> *Savageseraph:* (How'd you guess?)
> *Galadriel:*   (No idea. Totally pulled out of the air.)

During any single chat session, the *Words/Silence/Flesh* characters and the writers can be having conversations with each other at the same time. The remarks in parentheses are writer-to-writer ones, with the convention of placing them in parentheses the only thing that distinguishes them from character chat. Although the writer-to-writer commentary may focus on the story (for example, one writer asking the other for clarification about the tone of voice) or may provide one writer's response to something the other had a character do or say, it often wanders to personal conversation about a range of different topics, so that in the midst of creating the raw chat of a sex scene between Harry and Andy, Savageseraph is talking in parenthetical comments to Galadriel about the week's episode of *American Idol*, which she is listening to while they are chatting.

Although this blurring of writer/reader roles occurs more dramatically in the later letters, which are perhaps not coincidentally the ones that are increasingly erotic in content, the earliest letters also suggest it. After all, Harry's first letter to Sean was, in essence, Savageseraph reaching through the fictional character of Harry and then Sean to talk to Galadriel, with the discourse between the characters running on the surface of and parallel to the submerged discourse between the writers. One particularly vivid example of this occurs in one of the earlier letters written by Galadriel where Sean says to Harry:

> If it wasn't for the fact that my ~~writer~~ children are dragging me out and forcing me to eat mini doughnuts and fudge today, you can bet my arse would be firmly planted on a plane *shudder* winging its way back to Wellington so I can teach you some manners.

The strikethrough of the word "writer," something that Sean would have no reason to say, as well a hyperlink to a Web site for the Calgary Stampede (http://cs.calgarystampede.com/, accessed June 1, 2006) in the phrase "forcing me to eat mini doughnuts and fudge today," position the text of the letters somewhere between the fictional and the real. When fans discuss blurring the boundaries between writers and characters, it is often in the context of critiquing the Mary Sue. Readers are hyperaware of this device, and they respond with everything from amusement to mockery when they see the writer hijacking a character or text for her own wish-fulfillment fantasy.

However, the criticism of Mary Sue has never been leveled against *Words/Silence/Flesh*, perhaps because the writer/character blurring does not result in idealized versions of the writers being expressed through the characters. Characters make good decisions that bring about moments of pleasure and joy, but they also make bad decisions that hurt themselves and others. The story may also escape the traditional Mary Sue label because the characters in *Words/Silence/Flesh* remain characters — fictional constructs with personas that exist apart from the writers' own. Yet the writers — their words, their responses — are undeniably a part of the characters. As such, the subtextual interaction between the writers through the medium of character does not hijack the story. In many ways, it *is* the story.

As a result, just as the relationship between writers and readers exists in a queer female space, so too does the writer/writer collaboration. Three longtime readers, Aprilkat, Ithiliana, and Gotham Syren, describe the early sections of *Words/Silence/Flesh* as "love letters" between Savageseraph and Galadriel (conversation with *W/S/F* writers, March 2004). These early segments, Aprilkat, Ithiliana, and Gotham Syren agree, extend beyond affection among characters to encompass the fondness the writers display for one another in other entries in their separate blogs and in face-to-face encounters. In an e-mail message to Galadriel on May 17, 2005, Aprilkat expands on this observation, explaining that the writers interact "the same way in real life as [the] characters [do] in the story. It was quite amusing, especially as you both [Savageseraph and Galadriel] seemed startled the first time I pointed it out." This blurring between writer and character roles becomes even more pronounced as the collaborative format moves into the realm of instant messaging. Where the earlier segments of the story reach through character and across distance (both between the characters and that between the writers), the later sections remove the distance entirely. The writer/character drift is more compartmentalized by virtue of the dramatic situation in the earliest portions of the text, but as the characters converge on the same fictional locale, the shift to role-playing scenes through messaging systems removes all distance. Although Savageseraph and Galadriel remain in separate physical locales, this electronic method of instant communication allows for an immediacy of shared space. Within that space, both writers are able to compress the distance further by performing actions and emotions (through asterisks that set apart virtual movement and emoticons that imply tone). This conscious performance of physical reality allows for a literal slide between general conversations into writer/character space. This movement is especially notable in the following excerpt from a chat log between Galadriel and Savageseraph on May 3, 2005, which directly precedes the beginning of a role-playing session:

> *Galadriel:*   So... Other than food, whatcha up to? *wink*
>
> *Savageseraph:* Ummm, writing a post griping about losing an hour. Staring at Miranda/Sean file and novel file, but not working on either. Why? *looks curious and innocent*
>
> *Galadriel:*   (*snicker* Did I mention that part of the reason I was asking about writerly relations was because I was discussing how you seem to enjoy being "seduced" into writing w/Robin? ^_~) Oh, no reason. Just ... *shrug* have Sean sitting here, wondering if Viggo's around to play... Should I tell him to find another playmate for the afternoon? ^_~
>
> *Savageseraph:* Heh. I suppose I could scare him up. *looks around* Seduced into writing, eh? *chuckles* All writing is about seduction.

Galadriel: *G* That might be nice. Oh? Is it? Do tell. *G*
Savageseraph: Of course it is. It's a writer giving you a wink and calling you
over and saying, "Hey, if you spend some time with me, I'll
make it worth your while."
Galadriel: Ah, I see. ^_^ Makes sense. So, you think I can make it worth
your while? ^_~ *beckons*
Savageseraph: I suppose we'll have to see. *grins*

Although the slide into writer/character space is made explicit in this example, it is a pattern repeated over and over again as the writers continue to
collaborate on *Words/Silence/Flesh*. In addition, the writers perform a type
of gentle coercion, one seducing the other with the promise of the erotics
of the written word. This pattern of eroticism between the two writers of
the collaborative story works to shape the interaction between the characters and to seduce the readers of the story. All these factors combine to
make this story stand out as unusually queer, even within the cultural and
genre conventions of slash fiction.

Exploding Fangirls

The sexual pleasure caused by language is part of what slash is all
about. However, the too-easy identification of slash as *straight women writing gay men* has served to mask the extent to which the sexual pleasure is
created by women (of all genders/sexual identities) for women (of all gen-
ders/sexual identities). The general perception today is that a larger proportion of lesbian, bisexual, and other queer women are writing in many
of the fandoms than was the case in earlier years, but, as Busse (this volume) argues, even the "straight" women are doing something that can
arguably be seen as pretty "queer" (producing writing designed to give sexual pleasure to other women, whether the texts are called erotica, pornography, slash, or smut, whether the texts are defined as het or queer or bi)
and interacting with each other through and by means of writing. As Jenkins notes, "the meaning of slash resides as much in the social ties created
by the exchange of narratives, the sharing of gossip, and the play with identity as it does with the words on the page" (1992, 222). These social ties
include erotic elements— an element that remains unacknowledged in most
of the existing scholarship, although fans are well aware of it — and are well
aware of how much of it is performative and playful.

The erotic discourse between readers/writers of *Words/Silence/Flesh* is
made explicit in feedback that acknowledges the content and mimics inter-

course. The posts include textual representations of nonverbal response such as Ribby's: "Am now having steam coming out of my ears from the thought of these four.... *guh* Just ... *guh* Oh, and *meep* too" (personal communication, LJ, May 10, 2004). Kirby Crow writes: "*incoherency* *runs into walls banging head against stuff* *whacks off furiously* GUH" (personal communication, LJ, July 29, 2003). This comment is followed by another reader writing "ditto" (Ithiliana, personal communication, LJ, July 29, 2003). A third reader writes: "This post — and yesterday's? Just. Wow. Hot. 'Scuse me, think I need to, um... Ahem. ::runs away, blushing::" (Gotham Syren, personal communication, LJ, July 31, 2003). Throughout the story, readers claim to be "dying" as an expression of their great pleasure, accusing the writers of the fic of "killing" them, but saying they will die "a kinky, happy death" (Cinzia, personal communication, LJ, August 3, 2003). Dying in the comments is clearly analogous to the Elizabethan meaning of orgasm as the final culmination of a long, complex, happy, sexually discursive relationship between readers and writers. Few would debate the notion that slash fangirls define themselves in sexual terms in relation to their objects of adoration, which can include the source text and actors as well as favorite fan fiction writers. Readers of *Words/Silence/Flesh* announce themselves as fangirls in various ways: Kirby Crow notes that "if you were any more competent at ratcheting up sexual tension in text, you would be knee-deep in exploding fangirls. *dies of heat stroke*" (personal communication, LJ, September 23, 2003). Although such responses and fangirling are given to many a slash story on the Internet, one element that sets this story off is how the self-identified fans of male/male fic are surprised at their response over time to the presence of more fully realized female characters, especially Miranda Otto, who interacts not only with the men, but also with other women who were involved in the film without the fic becoming femmeslash or traditional het. Klimop notes this difference: "I think what I like best about the correspondence between Cate and Miranda is that it so must have been like that, in many ways, for them on a testosterone laden set. This was very much a guys' set, and the two of them must have felt that acutely" (personal communication, LJ, July 18, 2003).

As Klimop's comment shows, Miranda and Cate are perceived to occupy the stereotypical position of women on this set and in fandom at large. The women exist as a minority in the "guys' world" even while ostensibly being equals (in the sense of being actors among a group of actors, not just occupying the position of girlfriend or wife). Rather than lament the gender imbalance, both women are constructed as powerful, claiming their own sense of the erotic and sexual while commenting freely on their male costars' bodies, beauty, and sex appeal. Their discourse reproduces fans' responses without raising the specter of Mary Sue. Indeed, responses show that one element of perversity in the interactions around this text is the extent to which the readers begin to realize they want something they do not normally desire:

> You're making me want to see hetsmut between these two. Damn you! [Kirby Crow, personal communication, LJ, July 17, 2003].
>
> To be honest, had there been hetsmut to go with the gaysmut when I turned on my computer this morning, I never would have made it to work [Bexone, personal communication, LJ, July 30, 2003].
>
> I'm pleasantly surprised by how much I liked that scene between them. It really avoided all the scary clichés that can ruin a perfectly good het scene, although frankly, I'm still not sure I'd call it entirely het. There's something pretty bent about it, and I mean that in a good way [Klimop, personal communication, LJ, July 23, 2003].

The use of the term *het* to reflect what primarily slash readers are desiring/ seeing in this story reflects the prevalence of the straight/gay binary in the het/slash terms used in fandom. Yet the writers and readers also struggle to create a different terminology. They can agree that clichéd, vanilla het is not what they want or are usually interested in. In a response to one of the comments, however, Galadriel notes that *The Lord of the Rings* slash fandom "seems a bit more open to [het] than others, and there are so many, many chances for a shot at good slash, femmeslash, and het in LotRPS that it seems worthwhile looking into it" (personal communication, LJ, July 21, 2003). Even more openly, Ithiliana questions the terminology: "Het smut my ass. It's bi smut. And I will damn well prove it. In a paper" (personal communication, LJ, August 3, 2003). Responding, Savageseraph foregrounds the contested definition of *het* when she notes that "if het is just boy/girl, then it's het. But if het presupposes a set of stereotypical attitudes toward gender roles and sexual expression, then it's not het. But it is. Sort of" (personal communication, LJ, August 3, 2003).

The debate among the writers and readers over whether the story is gaysmut or hetsmut shows the extent to which the straight/gay binary is assumed. The responses to this story are no different than responses to many slash fics in many fandoms, but we argue that any situation in which two women create a space where a number of other women experience sustained sexual pleasure around and through a text consisting of narratives by and about women and men, whether or not that pleasure involves actual sex, has to be read as more complicated erotically and discursively than "straight women" and "gay men." The multiple kinds of queerness in this story and the relationships (both in the story and between the readers and writers) are complex. None of the characters identifies as gay or lesbian;

David Wenham's installments especially support a reading that his character at least may identify as bisexual. Such complex relationships in the story and between the writers and their readers undercut the notion of slash as binary (hetsmut and gaysmut) by introducing what we might call bismut, especially with regards to the relationship between the characters of David Wenham and Miranda Otto, and Sean Bean and Viggo Mortensen. These four characters seem particularly prone to blurring the boundaries between binaries.

The possible questioning of boundaries raised by this story and the readers' responses requires much more development. Part of what makes the David Wenham/Mirando Otto pairing in this story work is the queerness of characters who only appear to be het, especially Miranda. Kirby Crow notes, "I loved how we got to hear what Miranda was saying. Oh she's naughty. I like her." Klimop expands on that notion: "I love the picture of Miranda as not just your typical female lie back and think of England type. Too often women get written that way in het. You've made her into very much a complex, adult women with needs for which she feels no compulsion whatsoever to apologize. It's very nice to see that" (personal communication, LJ, August 7, 2003). Adding female characters to slash fiction does not necessarily change the genre, as the legions of Mary Sue stories show, but adding "a complex, adult woman with needs for which she feels no compulsion whatsoever to apologize" may change a great deal. So why do certain readers so love Miranda? Perhaps because we feel that in a very direct way, she is us, and we are, like her, "complex adult women with needs," which we are meeting in part through the queer female space of Internet slash fiction about male and female characters in a book and film that we also love.

Conclusion

Our discussion of a single story and the interactions between its writers and readers has allowed us to open a space to consider how the differences among/between women and men (complex differences in age, regional cultures, national cultures, class standing, ethnicity, racial identification, sexual identities) can be read against and within the complex matrix of queer theory. Splitting socially constructed or even essentialist notions of gender from the individual body allows a development of ways to analyze some of what goes on in Internet fandoms that foreground the performative aspect of gender through text in a virtual environment that shifts from the extent to which gender performance is read as attached to individual bodies in face-to-face interactions. In the future, it will be possible to consider the extent to which a wider range of selves will be presented as the norm within postmodern geographies and subcultures. A number of activist movements are based on the need to move away from such hierarchical evaluations, and although none of us would claim that fanfic alone can replace activism, it's worth considering the extent to which this story blurs boundaries, sexual and otherwise: between the two writers, among characters, among readers and writers. The story does not privilege a single/stable identity and presents as the norm/default a range of queer characters, reflecting changes in the cultures and cultural constructions of fandoms, of academia, and of Canada and the United States.

Notes

1. Each of the characters referred to in *Words/Silence/Flesh* is based on an actor from Peter Jackson's *The Lord of the Rings* films. Harry Sinclair played Isildur, Viggo Mortensen played Aragorn, Sean Bean played Boromir, Miranda Otto was Éowyn, David Wenham was Faramir, Andy Serkis was Gollum, Cate Blanchett was Galadriel, and Karl Urban was Éomer.

2. The question of how many women in a stigmatized area of fandom (itself a marginalized subculture in the 1960s and 1970s) would have identified themselves as lesbian or bisexual raises questions that we cannot answer at this time other than to note that today, after decades of activism, a larger percentage of any sexual minority may be more out than in the past.

3. Hills (2002) presents a persuasive argument about the extent to which academics engaged in fan studies have ignored disagreements and diversity among fans as well as being unconscious of the extent to which their disciplinary training shapes their assumptions and methods.

4. We do not know of similar attempts to categorize gender/sexual identities of male fans—which, although outside the scope of this project, raises interesting questions about that gap in scholarship.

5. Bacon-Smith (2000), chapter 5, "The Women Were Always Here," and chapter 6, "Women in Science Fiction," are followed by chapter 7, "Gay and Lesbian Presence in Science Fiction."

6. Jung (2004) notes that readers can choose to identify with either the dominant or the submissive partner (both men), can switch between the two perspectives, or can occupy the position of voyeur. Her awareness of the multiple subject positions fans as readers (and arguably, as writers) can take reflects the growing layers of analysis possible, although the erotic focus is still primarily on female readers' arousal by male characters. Cumberland (2000) analyzes how the Internet may have allowed (more) women (more) freedoms and thus more encouragement to participate actively in fandom and, in the case of slash writing, gain the freedoms that have been in the past only for men, but she still sees friendship as the primary relationship between women.

7. Larbalestier (2002) melds historiographic and linguistic methods to analyze how both male and female fans debated issues of gender in science fiction from the 1920s forward.

References

Bacon-Smith, Camille. 1992. *Enterprising women: Television fandom and the creation of popular myth*. Philadelphia: Univ. of Pennsylvania Press.
_____. 2000. *Science fiction culture*. Philadelphia: Univ. of Pennsylvania Press.
Busse, Kristina. 2005. "Digital get down": Postmodern boy band slash and the queer female space. In *Eroticism in American culture*, ed. Cheryl Malcolm and Jopi Nyman, 103–25. Gdansk: Gdansk Univ. Press.
Cumberland, Sharon. 2000. Private uses of cyberspace: Women, desire, and fan culture. *MIT Communications Forum*. January 25. http://web.mit.edu/comm-forum/papers/cumberland.html (accessed October 22, 2005).
Doty, Alexander. 2000. *Flaming classics: Queering the film canon*. New York: Routledge.
Galadriel and Savageseraph. 2003–2005. *Words/silence/flesh: The Harry/Vig/Sean letters to date, in order*. http://caras_galadhon.livejournal.com/29873.html (accessed June 1, 2006).
Halberstam, Judith. 1998. *Female masculinity*. Durham, NC: Duke Univ. Press.
_____. 2005. *In a queer time and place: Transgender bodies, subcultural lives*. New York: New York Univ. Press.
Hills, Matt. 2002. *Fan cultures*. London: Routledge.
Jenkins, Henry. 1992. *Textual poachers: Television fans and participatory culture*. New York: Routledge.
Jung, Susanne. 2004. Queering popular culture: Female spectators and the appeal of writing slash fan fiction. *Gender Forum Gender Queeries* 8. http://www.genderforum.uni-koeln.de/queer/jung.html (accessed June 1, 2006).
Larbalestier, Justine. 2002. *The battle of the sexes*. Middletown, CT: Wesleyan Univ. Press.
Penley, Constance. 1997. *NASA/Trek: Popular science and sex in America*. New York: Verso.
Russ, Joanna. 1985. Pornography by women, for women, with love. In *Magic mommas, trembling sisters, Puritans and perverts: Feminist essays*, 79–99. Trumansburg, NY: The Crossing Press.
Sedgwick, Eve Kosofsky. 1985. *Between men: English literature and male homosocial desire*. New York: Columbia Univ. Press.

9. My Life Is a WIP on My LJ

Slashing the Slasher
and the Reality of Celebrity
and Internet Performances

Kristina Busse

ABSTRACT.—I connect the performance of queerness with a general reading of real person slash (RPS), focusing on LiveJournal.com (LJ)'s often highly sexualized interactions and the way identity is performed in this medium. This performance brings together the fannish, political, and personal in ways previously separated. By looking at the way fans perform their online identities and enact certain roles with and for one another, I suggest that much of fannish interaction contains its own version of RPS. I use discussions centered around fannish displays of affection, mock queerness, and concerns about the political implications of such behavior. LJ users relate to each other through adopted personas and avatars, tending to view one another as extrapolations of these highly performative roles. In so doing, our fannish daily interaction on LJ and off may not be that dissimilar from the RPS that LJ users read and write. Discourses about fans—where real-life identity is partially hidden and where online identities are partially performed—allow fans to engage with one another's personas, which are understood to not fully coincide with the actual person. In both RPS and LJ discourses, there is a certain awareness of its simultaneous reality and performativity. Rather than dismissing LJ and other fannish roles as false, we must acknowledge the similarities of online social networks to face-to-face ones. These roles may tell us more about our actual identities than any attempt to separate real from false, real from virtual, or real from fictional ever could.

Fandom as Queer Female Space

Although fan fiction may always have had its share of lesbian, bisexual, and even gay male writers, their greater visibility among both fans and academics is more recent. As late as 2004, academics still claimed that the majority of fan writers were straight women (Smol 2004). However, anecdotal evidence and informal polls suggest that the number of self-identified not-straight women is proportionally greater in fandom than in the population at large. Part of the recent greater visibility is obviously a reflection of changes in culture, so that there are both more young women who are out as well as women who may not have been comfortable declaring their sexuality in surveys in the 1980s but who can do so now that there are more inclusive understandings of queerness.

Within slash fandom in particular, issues of homosexuality are central, and fandom, with its greater tolerance, has often been a place for women to explore and negotiate issues of sexuality by reading and writing their desires, by acknowledging and sharing sexual preferences. Validating various desires in media fandom dates at least to *Star Trek*'s IDIC ("infinite diversity in infinite combinations"), but slash in particular raises particular issues of identity and sexualities: women writing fantasies with and for one another projected through and by same-sex desires suggests that fandom may be a queer female space — if not at the level of the text and the writers, then at least at the level of their interaction. I have previously inverted Sedgwick's (1985) argument and described this phenomenon as "a homosocial — even homoerotic — bond 'between women' where reader and author are making love over the naked bodies of attractive men" (Busse 2005, 121). Furthermore, within the often disembodied culture of the Internet, physical gestures of interaction, such as *hugs*, *pets*, or even *smooches*, are common. In the absence of real physicality, the virtual one is exaggerated and often sexualized (Lackner et al., this volume). Emotional intimacy frequently gets translated into images of physical intimacy so that close fannish ties become verbalized in sexual language. After all, slashers are trained to tease out homoerotic subtext in the texts they encounter, which applies to their own interaction as well. Also, the vocabulary of slashers tends to be sexual, so it does not seem far-fetched to use similar images and terms in other areas of discourse: slashed objects and other slashers alike get appraised with a *lick*. Random *snogs* and *humps* get distributed as general tokens of friendship in the same way porn gets written as metaphoric interaction: gratitude, comfort, or even apology.

These modes of discourse create an ambiguous space in which sexuality has shifted almost completely into the realm of fantasy: slashers can present themselves as any chosen gender or none at all, with any degree of sexual orientation and preferences they want to project. We don't live in the virtual world alone, however, so embodied reality and virtual fantasies can clash. Moreover, the virtual exhibitionist demonstrations of this sexual behavior often seem strange, even sometimes offensive, to those who live with discrimination on a daily basis, rather than those who simply playfully engage with their sexualities in a safe, queer-friendly space. Although statements about sexual identity are hard to substantiate, many women acknowledge that their queerness often is restricted to the virtual realm as they live their "real" heteronormative lives. Fans for whom there are less clearly defined boundaries between their "real" and online queerness often resent behavior that restricts itself to the safety of the online community. But sexualities are just one aspect of fannish identity: slashers perform their identities in many ways, and the concept of queerness itself is clearly complex and not wholly containable in a straight/gay binary, or even a continuum including a variety of sexualities and expressions thereof (see Halperin 1990; Doty 1995).

Here, I want to connect the performance of queerness with a general reading of real person slash (RPS). In particular, I focus on LiveJournal.com's often highly sexualized interactions and how LJ users (and I am one myself, so I say "we" and "our") perform identity in this medium that brings together the fannish, political, and personal in ways previously separated in fannish discourses. By looking at the way fans perform their online identities and enact certain roles with and for one another, I suggest that much of fannish interaction contains its own version of RPS. LJ fan discourses at times read like slash narratives; this is especially the case for cowritten erotic stories and role-playing games, which present more formalized and performed instantiations of such erotic interactions. There is an awareness in both RPS and LJ discourses of their simultaneous reality and performativity. RPS discussions address the fact that for most fans, celebrities are simultaneously real and fictional, and that fans can talk about their fantasies as if they were real while being aware that this "reality" merely constitutes a fandomwide conceit. Fans engage with one another's personas, all the while knowing that they may not fully coincide with the actual person offline. In fact, within fannish spaces, it is not altogether clear whether one persona is any more "real" than another; after all, the extreme intimacies shared among fans may reveal more of a person than most offline interactions can.

I begin this essay with a review of some of the arguments about what one fan has termed the "queer minstrel show" (Jenny, LJ, January 1, 2005) by using a particular incident that spawned debate within the LJ fan community. These discussions centered around fannish displays of affection and concerns about the political implications of such behavior. In order to find one possible explanation of such sexual LJ performances, I turn toward RPS, its relationship to reality, and its particular canon construction. From this perspective, I analyze Isilya's 2004 fan fiction "Not Based on a True Story," which connects fannish friendships and RPS concerns. Much of our fannish interaction and behavior must be read as partially performative. Although I don't want to dismiss the real friendships and romantic relationships that evolve around online fandom, I want to foreground the ways in which many of us do interact through various personas and avatars, and how easily we view one another as extrapolations of the performative role enacted within fannish spaces. In so doing, I suggest that our fannish daily interaction, both on and off LJ, may not be that dissimilar from the RPS we read and write insofar as both draw from the contradictory information presented by a consciously constructed public persona. These imagined and imaginative roles may tell us more about who we are than any facile attempt to separate real from false, virtual, or fictional ever could.

Lust Memes and Sexualized Discourses

This essay was inspired by debates sparked by a late 2004 "lust meme," which introduced me to the term "queer mistrel show." The lust meme asked respondents to anonymously name a person on LJ with whom they wanted to have sex. The question this immediately raises, of course, is whether any these posters actually experience real lust for their chosen LJ user, or whether such an articulation of appreciating someone's thoughts, writing, or friendship ought to be articulated in terms of sexual desire. The responses on the issue range from seeing such sexualized discourse as innocent play to finding these highly charged same-sex interactions offensive. Much of the debates ultimately depend on how closely one connects online fannish with real-life identities. As such, many want to distinguish between women who come to terms with their own sexualities in safe fannish spaces and those who use fandom to play at a queerness that they would refuse to acknowledge in real life. Whereas the former constructs the fannish fantasy space as a place where women can experiment and explore, the latter uses the fantasy as a self-contained space where queerness is played out in lieu of any potential effects on real lives. In other words, if the fannish space is seen by most sides as a safe place to explore one's sexualities and sexual fantasies, the question remains whether and how these insights connect to nonfannish areas of the fans' lives.

Some fans see this playful exploration of queerness and sexualities without consequences as exploitative and offensive. Not being able to distinguish between actual flirting and its safe, straight mimicry, not being able to separate potential partners from women who simply like to draw attention, some lesbian and bi fans feel marginalized by a culture that permits a masquerade of queer discourse and thereby trivializes queer identities and experiences. The following description is fairly representative of a particular response on the part of some fans to the sexualization of fan space that threatens to exclude gays and bisexuals in its very appropriation of discourses of queerness and in its simultaneous seeming dismissal of their sexual desires:

> That discourse makes me cranky. The gay-for-LJ stuff as a whole makes me cranky — not just the *licks* and *I love yous*, but the *oh, look, we're so *cool* because we're straight chicks turning on other straight chicks!* stuff, too. 'cause, hey, we're not all straight chicks. And we're not all always about the pseudo-porn, either. The discourse, both the performative stuff and the meta *about* the sexualization, usually ends up estranging me even farther, because at my crankiest, it feels like offensive, demeaning play of the over-privileged [Glossing, LJ, January 1, 2005].

Beyond such a sense of exclusion, many gay, lesbian, and bisexual writers indicate that they perceive homophobia within slash writing and its surrounding discourses, most importantly in the fetishization of gay sex and the lack of a clear sociocultural and historicopolitical context. These objections are important, if only to sustain a debate about the difference between fan fiction and political activism. Simply reading and writing gay sex and enjoying the depiction of gay characters is not necessarily an act of subversion; in fact, it may become its opposite when such an engagement occurs completely divorced from any realistic context and in the absence of awareness of sexual politics in general and gay rights in particular.

Given postmodern gender theory's propensity for performativity and ludic experimentation, it would be easy to simply write off fannish queer gender performance as a positive and useful fantasy; in fact, it would be easy to subsume it under the larger categories of all identity construction and the way we enact multiple roles online and off (Schechner 1988; Butler 1990; Haraway 1991; Balsamo 1997). Then again, for many slashers, their hobby may ultimately be a highly personal exploration of desires. Although they may be politically aware and working in varying degrees to fight homophobia, they do not necessarily do so through their fan fiction. Their writings, and the discourses surrounding them, are as varied as they are. Often the particular genre or even the fandom makes it difficult to foreground political statements: for example, many science fiction–based fandoms have difficulties addressing contemporary sociohistorical issues such as gay marriage or AIDS; they may be mapped onto other concerns, such as xenophobia. Moreover, much slash writing focuses on the lives *not* seen on screen. Where most series focus on the protagonists' jobs or callings, often showing them encountering (and fighting) crime, evil, or aliens, many slash stories skew towards the personal. Slash fic is thus often more concerned with the characters' feelings than the political climate surrounding them.

This phenomenon of sexualized online interaction can possibly be explained by regarding these discourses as an extended metaphor for a variety of relationships along a continuum of friendship and intimacy that can — but need not — be sexual. In effect, this recalls discourses on nineteenth-century female friendship that foreground the range from friendship and emotional intimacy to desire and sexual relationships (Smith-Rosenberg 1985; Faderman 1981). Fabu, for example, suggests that the sexualized discourse in fandom may be a signifier for levels of intimacy and friendship:

> But I wonder if, for those who are "performing," if what they're acting out isn't sexual identity but friendship; if the credibility that people gain from those interactions is not "queer street cred" but a more general kind of status.... If nothing else, that sort of flirty talk makes it very clear to everyone else in the conversation that these two posters are friendly with one another. So do all the ::squishes your boobies:: and ::dipsnog::s function as a kind of advertisement of how close we are? [LJ, May 11, 2005].

Only close friends can comfortably address one another in such a manner, so that communicating in such a suggestively sexual way, especially in a semipublic forum, in effect clearly indicates one's friendship. Explicit forms of affection become a code used by the participants to signify their relationships, and the terms of affection also function as a form of symbolic currency to signify these friendships to others. This evidence of friendship is especially important in an environment like LJ, where one's social capital often is measured in length of "friends-of" lists (an indication of readership), numbers of comments received, and acknowledgments in other journals.

This interpretation of the sexualized discourse among fans interestingly mirrors one of the earliest explanations of slash: Patricia Frazer Lamb and Diane Veith suggest that slash should not be understood as pornography but rather in terms of "true love and authentic intimacy" (1986, 238). In other words, explicit sexual descriptions in slash resonate on some level as metaphors for close friendship and intimacy between the slashed protagonists. The relationship between slashers thus parallels the relationship between the men that they write about: both for descriptions of their own relationships and in their slash narratives, women use sexual metaphors that stand in for, or stand instead of, emotional intimacy and friendship love. Returning to Fabu's argument, slashers are women who write sexually explicit fiction with and for one another at the same time as they often use similar explicitness in their actual interaction. Although one purpose of these sexualized discourses within and outside the fiction is certainly sexual, another aspect testifies to close friendship and intimacy that may be eroticized, but not necessarily sexual.

Many women describe fandom as the first place where they truly created friendship ties with other women and found levels of intimacy otherwise foreclosed to them. These friendships may include or may be played out in physical closeness—for example, some women meet partners or lovers through slashdom. Others simply enjoy the comfort they feel around other slashers and can show that through physical affection. Michelle, for example, describes how "physical affection as an expression of respect is something I've rarely seen outside of feminist and fandom circles" (personal communication, May 21, 2005). The sexualized discourse then becomes as much a testament to these friendships as it celebrates women taking control of their own sexuality, if only in their minds and virtual bodies. Far from arguing that online friendships are less real than ones initiated offline, I'd suggest that the lines often blur: many slashers who are close will get to know one another offline and thus add another level of meaning to their online relationship. Moreover, these friendships can be often more intense (both in terms of frequency of contact and levels of intimacy) as a result of a different level of anonymity that invites opening up quickly (Turkle 1995; Rheingold 2000; Donath 2003; Henderson and Gilding 2004).

How Real Is Reality?

This metaphoric reading of online sexualized LJ discourses suggests that there exists a strong performative aspect of demonstrating one's relationship to other fans (Hills 2002). I therefore want to put forth a related yet slightly different reading of the lust meme, one that connects it to its medium, LJ. The move to LJ as the primary mode of fannish interaction in many fandoms has created a plethora of discussions and self-analysis among fans. One of the central differences between mailing lists and LJ is the personalization of interaction, as noted in Busse and Hellekson's introduction to this volume. On LJ, all levels of discourse — personal, public, fannish — exist on the same level: a reader must read what is posted, whether it is an update on someone's personal life or her latest story update. Fannish discourse is thus often merged with the personal, and someone's stories may become inextricably linked with the way she performs her identity on LJ. People as well as stories become central to fannish interaction because the fan follows an individual's LJ, where before she would have joined a fandom- or pairing-specific mailing list. This growing emphasis on personality partly explains the lust meme and its underlying motivations.

I want to consider the lust meme and the sexualized LJ discourse as an engagement between the personalities constructed for the specific LJ interaction. Much of the sexualized LJ discourse between slash fans can instead be understood as a performance played out between the slashers' LJ personas. In RPS, fans purposefully use real-life information to create fictional worlds inhabited by fictional protagonists. Likewise, the process of creating LJ personas is not unlike RPS character construction: in both cases, "real people" get transformed into characters, and factual information becomes the canon on which to base fan fiction. Understanding the way fan writers create RPS canon and conceive of their creations as ultimately fictional and constructed — and yet with a basis in a certain mediated reality — allows us to reconsider online fannish interactions as similarly constructed, yet tied to reality. The lust meme, read in relation to a close study of RPS, can be understood as another version of RPS, with fandom itself as the playing field; or rather, fannish engagement among fans within the LJ space encompasses some of the same concerns with identity, reality, and performance as RPS.

One of the central concerns of RPS is the question of reality, both in the sense of how real events enter and shape the stories, and the impact these stories can have on the real lives of fans. Unlike much of the tabloid press, which purports to tell the truth, RPS writers consciously declare their writing to be fictional and clearly separate their stories from rumors. But they simultaneously refuse to follow the cliché of declaring the stars' public performances a fiction and the celebrities fake and fabricated. Instead, RPS narratives present celebrities as fully formed, intricate, and interesting characters, in opposition to their often one-dimensional media portrayals. This humanizing process allows the RPS authors to create the celebrity as she wishes: as an object of desire, as someone to identify with, or as a re-creation of the celebrity's supposedly "real" self.

Canon formation in RPS is more complicated than in most media- and book-based fandoms— or rather, its complications are more clearly visible. Canon is a constructed narrative created by selecting and juxtaposing "official" and "personal" material. Official material may be as varied as magazine, TV, and radio interviews, commercially released DVDs and CDs, or even more or less supported rumors. Personal material includes accounts of celebrity encounters by fans, shared through a fannish online network. Because there doesn't exist any true author(ity) or true owner of the source text, no single canon source can be claimed; as a result, the canon is created simultaneously by the celebrities, the media, and the fans. As RPS writers try to establish what exactly constitutes canon, they constantly determine the authenticity and truth status of any given footage, debating whether seemingly candid moments are really premeditated or rehearsed. Given that most RPS is written in a "collaborative fantasy space" (Mary, LJ, November 23, 2002), the authenticity of any canon fact is ultimately irrelevant. If the fans agree to treat given information as fact, if they collectively include it in their canon, it has become truth within the fannish universe, regardless of its objective truth status.

As I've argued elsewhere (Busse 2006), RPS lends itself to investigating issues of identity: it imagines the real life of a celebrity, someone whose life is forever in the public eye, whose every action and feeling is put on display for the world to see. The relationship between the media image and the actual person is a constant topic for celebrities because the discrepancy between the public and the "real" self is significant at that level of public exposure. RPS stories thus often tease out the relationship between private and public self as they imagine a reality behind the celebrity persona; these inquiries also allow readers and writers to contemplate their own identity construction and performative roles. At the center of most RPS lies the complicated negotiation between the actual public performances and the author-imagined fantasies of the celebrity's reality.

The anxieties among RPS writers about their ability to separate public and private became clear in the aftermath of the October 2004 discovery of personal photos of the *Lord of the Rings* cast. After pictures from a private party were leaked online, the fan community passionately debated the appropriateness of seeing these photos, which were clearly not meant for public consumption. One *LotR* RPS fan pinpoints the discomfort as being situated within fans' desire for observing the celebrity privately as well as in their guilt in so doing:

> there probably isn't any direct effect on the guys of having a bunch of fans see their personal photos. i think people chose to see it as that, though, because of the way it made *them* feel to see them —I know that when i was looking at them i was like "hee, these are great!" but the more i looked the more i could see they were personal, and that made me uncomfortable [Hope, LJ, October 15, 2004].

Rather than agreeing with the consensus that viewing these personal photos offends the actors because their privacy is violated, Hope suggests that the pictures and their seeming intimacy and private nature make fans uncomfortable because they collapse an imagined and fictionalized private life onto actual personal images. She argues that fans' own anxieties about RPS get projected onto the celebrities so that the fans' own sense of intrusion becomes a protective gesture for the stars' privacies. One of the reasons fans may be so protective of the celebrity's privacy is an underlying discomfort with slashing actual people. This concern is controlled by maintaining a clear dichotomy between the public and the private, a dichotomy that collapsed with the publication of these clearly private shots. Moreover, aware of the fact that any celebrity's public face is necessarily a well-constructed performance, fans often fetishize a conceived reality behind the media facade, and fans identify with these fetishized, protected, private aspects of the stars, even as the fans' very observation destroys its private quality.

RPS writers use media images to create their own versions of the celebrity to interrogate the relationship between these various constructions and, self-consciously aware of how any social interaction shapes and constructs identity, thematize the difficulties in negotiating public and private self. They repeatedly confront the issue of reality and performativity, both in regard to the celebrities and in their perceptions of their own experiences as author-fans. RPS then is both about a collectively created fan space and about a desire to reach the private persona behind the public one; it functions in the constant paradox of being simultaneously real and constructed, of reveling in its own constructedness at the same time as it purports a clear connection to reality. RPS is both more fictional and more real than its media-based counterparts, and possibly because of this, its writers are often more self-conscious of their role and the various functions that RPS serves.

Not Based on a True Story

Celebrity studies, following Richard Dyer's groundbreaking *Stars* (1998), has often focused on the ways in which fans interact with celebrities, and, most importantly, how they use celebrities as objects of identification (Stacey 1991; Rojek 2001; Turner 2004). However, it is also important to note that fans relate to celebrities in any number of identificatory patterns, and that slash fans in particular often control and manipulate these identifications. Slash fans write their RPS characters as addressing issues of identity construction and performativity, and in so doing, they deal with their own identities, relationships, and desires (Busse 2006). Isilya's popslash story "Not Based on a True Story" (2004) is an unsettlingly familiar account of fannish anxieties and hopes, dreams, and fears that casts *NSYNC's band members as boy band slashers and describes in great detail the writing of a popslash story and the emotions that accompany such a process. Isilya creates characters that readers recognize: they are simultaneously the celebrities they actually are and representations of slashers. In so doing, this self-recursive story recounts not only the act of fannish writing, but also the complicated, often homoerotic, ties it creates between slash readers and writers.

"Not Based on a True Story" begins with an excerpt from "This Must Be Pop," an RPS story written by the central character, Justin. The creation of this fanfic constitutes the essential part of the plot: "Nick is not a snob, but AJ is a fanboi with an i. It's maybe something to do with the endless song lyrics AJ posts in his journal, the quizzes, the anime smilies." The title evokes a line from *NSYNC's "Pop" and thus clearly situates the story within a fannish alternate universe where Justin doesn't pen song lyrics but fan fiction instead.

The story's central characters, *NSYNC band members Justin and JC, are cast as slashers, who in turn slash the pop stars of their own reality. Justin's fan fiction, "This Must Be Pop," is in itself a slasher AU in which its protagonists, Backstreet Boys band members Nick and Howie, have themselves become authors of popslash. In other words, the story operates on three levels of reality: Isilya's (and our own) reality with her as a pop-slasher and Justin, JC, Nick, and Howie as pop stars; the reality of "Not Based on a True Story," with Justin and JC as popslashers and Nick and Howie as pop stars; and the reality of "This Must Be Pop," with Nick and Howie as popslashers. By placing boy band celebrities in the role of "us," the story evokes several analogies: the use of well-known song lyrics in place of a fanfic title suggest similarities between various creative writing impulses, and the relationship between *NSYNC's band members (which popslashers obviously have already accepted as homoerotic) is sketched onto the relationship of the slashers within the story and — by extension — onto the readers.

Like most recursive fiction, "Not Based on a True Story" invites the reader to move in both directions. Although every story becomes an indistinct replica of the reality of its writing, the reverse is also true: as Justin writes his life onto the character of Nick, Nick's story offers insight into Justin. The various excerpts from "This Must Be Pop," which track the meeting, instant connection, and subsequent friendship between Nick and Howie, are interspersed with Justin's thoughts about himself, the story, fandom, and his aborted friendship with former friend and cowriter JC. Justin and JC's relationship is thus mirrored in Nick and Howie's, and the happy ending between the latter two becomes a means to invite the same for the former. The conclusion finds Justin using his writing to approach JC anew, so that the story within the story becomes a means to create a potentially happy ending.

This invites the reader to create a second mirroring of realities and wonder whether "Not Based on a True Story" might have a purpose within real life fannish interaction as well. In other words, by realizing how much of Nick is in Justin, and how much of Nick's reality mirrors Justin's, the reader is encouraged to question how similar Justin and JC's world is to our own. In fact, although "Not Based on a True Story" itself denounces its basis in reality in its title, the similarities between the two levels of narrative within the text are obvious. Readers are invited to move beyond the boundaries of the fictional text by seeing the fictional interactions mirrored in actual fannish ones. With Justin autobiographically writing Nick's anxieties about self-insertion and other fannish concerns, Isilya succeeds in distancing these issues while simultaneously bringing them to the fore. By making all characters male, she allows readers a certain level of detachment (Lamb and Veith 1986; Penley 1992; Jenkins 1992). By displacing our neuroses onto these celebrities, who in turn write them into their own stories, she forces us to confront some of our more embarrassing behavior while making it more attractive in the familiar characters of Justin and Nick. The story displaces onto fictionalized celebrities "unpopular fannish truths," as in this moment of fannish fatigue where Justin fantasizes about leaving fandom:

> You brush your teeth, staring at yourself in the mirror, thinking about how you came to be in fandom, who you've loved, who you've lost and all the reasons for you now to leave. You spit and rinse and pull out a length of floss, counting wanks and wars and flames ... you have stored in copy-pasted emails and chat logs. Kind of a litany of unpopular fannish truths, if you like. Bizarre and slightly sickening sex triangles. Cat chemotherapy. Authors flaming their own stories under religious sockpuppets to rally support. Betrayal, backstabbing and the IP addresses of all 567 comments in the Anonymous Hate meme.

Isilya's story creates a certain level of discomfort in many of its readers. By casting the pop stars as slashers, she makes them more like fans and thus not protected by their celebrity otherness; and by revealing aspects of fandom that fans do not often talk about in public, she holds up a disconcerting mirror to fandom. Trobadora describes, "In a way it hits just a bit too close to home, doesn't it? It feels like publicly psychoanalysing your own family, and part of it is not that you don't want to, but that you don't want to expose yourself in that way to outsiders" (LJ, December 28, 2004).

And Betty Plotnick writes, "I very much enjoyed it, and at the same time it made me extremely uncomfortable and I wondered if I should maybe be telling a trusted adult about it" (LJ, December 28, 2004). Part of the discomfort, of course, is how much of the Nick to Justin analogy can be read as Justin to author, and how intimately the story explores the homosocial and homoerotic space of fandom, with all its positive and negative characteristics.

The slash community has extensively discussed this issue of slashdom as a homoerotic space. A panel at Escapade (an annual slash convention) in 2004 was entitled "Slashing the Slasher: Slash as Not So Virtual Circle Jerk." Many slashers agree that the writing and reading as well as the inter-action surrounding the fiction is erotically charged and that this may or may not extend into real life and actual relations. Elizabeth Guzick calls this the "erotics of talk" and notes, "No matter what identity of behaviors many women readers and writers of slash claim, there is an unmistakable erotics between and among them, often taking a triangular form like Justin's new song or Chris's script being the point of contact between the two mutual readers" (personal communication, 2004). Guzick's description of the erotics of reading and writing with and for one another, triangulated through the erotic slash text, is exemplified both in the way Justin describes his slow courtship with JC and in the way he finally uses his story as an offer of reconciliation.

In a way, then, Isilya's story strongly resonates with many readers because she captures both the psychological dimension of many fan experiences and the complicated dynamic of many fannish relations. The story is clearly set in a version of our own fannish space of LJ. Current fan vocabulary is used and specific fan events are referenced — wank, hate threads, Escapade, sock puppets. Moreover, the relationship between Justin and JC, written into an alternate universe in which their avatars, Nick and Howie, are popslashers, is perhaps uncomfortably familiar to many slashers. Justin's memories of his and JC's relationship resonate with the way most slash fans interact online, growing closer through intense LJ debates, extensive e-mail exchange, instant message conversations, phone calls, and personal meetings. As such, Justin and JC stand in for slashers, and the homoerotic relationships explored within the stories facilitate and mirror the ones between the fans.

LJ, Slashing the Slasher, and Performing Identities

In order to slash Justin, the writer must imagine what the "true" version underneath could look like; in other words, RPS creates a fictional "real" self, extrapolated from the public persona. As a result, RPS deals with at least three different versions of the celebrity: the real star whom we can never know, the public performance of the star, and the extrapolated star where the writer fictionalizes a supposed private life. Similarly, slashers themselves exist in these various roles where the "real" person is not necessarily much like her LJ persona. After all, RPS fictionalizes a reality out of clues gathered from public discourse — in this context, LJ. Such a "real" persona might be extrapolated by readers from the information, tone, and ethos they have picked up in LJ, but it can never be more than an approximation of the actual person.

One of the repeated objections most RPS writers encounter is the question of how they themselves would feel if someone used them as raw material for writing fan fiction, which most RPS writers refute by emphasizing the split between public and private individuals. After all, although all of us create various identities to present to the world, celebrities display them publicly, as part of their celebrity text, and as a result, "celebrity status always implies a split between a private and a public self" (Rojek 2001, 11). Such a clearly pronounced public persona makes celebrities particularly apt for fanfic writers who manipulate the celebrity text to imagine a more private alternative identity. Nevertheless, the often-voiced objection invites the comparison of how similar slashers' online personas may be to those of public celebrities: both pop star and slasher exist on the same ontological status of textual artifact, neither being real but only referencing the real person and body. The fall 2002 "Slashing the Slasher" challenge exemplified the awareness that there often is little difference in what kind of source text produces the slash stories' canon. The challenge, which asked writers to slash an assigned slasher with other characters (other slashers, celebrities, fictional characters), places all three on a level and reveals all of them to be textual creations. Louisa Ellen Stein (this volume) describes how role-playing games often create a similar situation: RPG character journals coexist with "real" journals, and the characters communicate with regular LJ users.

In many cases, then, the lust meme did not actually make any statements about real sexual desire, but rather performed a sexualized discourse by taking personas and expanding a fictional universe for them. In fact, given the often elusive nature of Internet identities in general, readers have to rely on the information that is revealed by the Internet persona. Often, we share aspects of our "real" lives on LJ, but rarely can others determine whether they are truthful or not. At the same time, especially on LJ, there are all kinds of overlaps between these various selves. There is no clear separation between the various roles any subject performs. Even though LJ is indeed a performance, this performance is often supplemented by other forms of interaction that may contradict or enhance the information provided on LJ. Just like RPS canon construction, with its contradictory and complicated sources, extrapolating any real person from the various information we are given is complicated and likely impossible.

LJ as Postmodern Space

All subjects perform a variety of roles when interacting, and any real person one might meet is similarly an extrapolation of the information she discloses, a creation of their (fictionally "real") persona. We all play roles; we all interact with versions of our interlocutors that often depend on the context of these interactions. Online discourses, however, which lack all but the purely textual levels of interaction, allow for a greater variety of role playing, and at times a greater ability for a subject to control her performance of varying roles. After all, online interaction allows people to meet, talk, and interact without the restraints of knowing one another's physical status, whether it be gender, age, color, or any other qualifying characteristics. In fact, much of the research in the area of Internet identity construction has focused on the fact that identity claims are generally not verifiable, so one can enact different identities (Haraway 1991; Balsamo 1997; Turkle 1995; Donath 2003). Interestingly, fandom on the whole rarely seems to engage in such blatant role playing; although some fans choose to not reveal central identifying characteristics, in my experience and that of most people I have talked to, how fans present themselves online is often very similar to the way they present themselves in real life. Yet it would be wrong to simply assume that our fannish online personas are identical to our real life ones — if only in the most basic sense that it is impossible to determine one's real identity.

LJ, in particular, as a result of its rhizomatic and multipurpose quality, provides a complex and challenging medium in which to construct a textual identity. Not only do we get the serial narrative of a poster's life in her own journal, we may also see her name referenced, or come across comments she has written in other places. LJ users constantly interlink and reference each other, so that one can easily have a sense of another user solely from encounters in other journals. Of course, even an LJ persona is not necessarily consistent. Just like in offline interaction, context affects behavior. One LJ user says of personas,

> I'm beginning to think there are two aspects to the LJ persona: there's the more ornate "performance" of the personal blog and commenting within that (decorating your house just the way you want, and then inviting the neighbourhood); and most LJs have a definite, individual mood to them;

and then there is the commenting persona, running off to chat and argue, and in so doing performing the dialogue and creating the mood on yet another LJ [Parthenia, LJ, May 26, 2005].

Parthenia perceives her identity as constructed in different ways, depending on the context and environment in which she writes. Any factual evidence about a given LJ user that contributes to her LJ identity — her canon, so to speak — may be contradictory or false. And as noted above, LJ interaction is often supplemented with other forms of communication, including e-mail and face-to-face encounters. The LJ persona is actually a complex and complicated construction, drawn from various sources. Like with celebrity constructions, there is a shared understanding, yet each observer has her own idiosyncratic reading. In other words, although fandom may interpret a celebrity/LJ user in a certain way, any individual fan's personal interpretation and/or experience may subtly change this common reading.

As the last few years have experienced the shift from a more formalized mailing list culture to LJ as the primary mode of interaction, issues of popularity and fame have become more pertinent and visible. The very nature of Big Name Fan as something to be aspired to (or derided), the repeated discussions on how to become "someone" in fandom, all suggest that online persona is indeed an important aspect of many fans' identity and affects their self-worth in a supposedly separate "real life" as well. What is interesting in terms of our discussion here is the way we have become accustomed to the various manipulations of reality and the way reality is always already narrativized and packaged to entertain. Pop stars may be more obvious instantiations of this trend, with Jessica Simpson and Britney Spears performing even their most intimate private moments, but these are just examples of a more general interest in stars' supposedly private lives that in turn become public.

Similarly, LJ has effectively placed public and private personas next to each other, allowing them to intersect, mix, and merge. Where before we had a seeming distinction between an author persona and a more focused and thematically contained discussion of shows and stories on mailing lists, LJ places all information on an equal level, whether it be an intensely personal revelation, a random show discussion, a generic quiz, or a political call for action. As a result, the LJ poster becomes a performer of her own life, sharing private details next to fannish ones, switching between her various roles and between a variety of discourses. In effect, this is what Swmbo alludes to when she says, "my life is a WIP on LJ" (LJ, January 6, 2005): she narrates her life in installments — serially, a work in progress, just like many of the stories we follow; and the character she plays may be as constructed as the protagonist of that story.

When looking at LJ identities in such a way, it becomes obvious how slashers who already are used to sexualizing interaction between the characters they fictionalize may indeed do the same to their own LJ personas, that the lust meme is indeed another RPS in which the anonymous commenter imagines her LJ identity having sex with the admired, fangirled, maybe even fantasized about and desired LJ user persona. One of the things RPS can teach us, then — especially RPS, which blurs the lines between authors and celebrities and imagines authors as fictional personas— is that any belief in clear separation of the real and fictional are illusory. Rather than use that awareness to vilify RPS as more real than we'd like it to be, I think we need to look at interactions fans perceive as "real" and observe their performative components. This may be particularly apparent in the online world, but performative behavior is clearly not restricted to online interaction; it affects every aspect of our "real" lives.

Rather than dismissing LJ and other fannish roles as false or using them to imply that the fannish online community is, at best, an illusory space and, at worst, dangerous in its mimicry of personal intimacy (Ludlow 1996), we must acknowledge the similarities of online social networks to other, face-to-face, ones (Henderson and Gilding 2004). On a practical level, many fans don't rely solely on online contact, so the dichotomy becomes ineffectual; on a theoretical level, real-life encounters enact similar but different modes of performances. Critics of queer online performativity are correct in assessing a danger that such engagement may try to function as a sole substitute for political action. However, with the ever-widening reach of fanfic and slash, not only do its uses and abuses increase, so do the debates surrounding it. It is these ongoing and important discussion about homophobic slash and slashers— it is the dialogue, however aggressive or confrontational at times, that make this fannish space not a utopian community but a real one.

References

Balsamo, Anne. 1997. *Technologies of the gendered body: Reading cyborg women.* Durham, NC: Duke Univ. Press.
Busse, Kristina. 2005. "Digital get down": Postmodern boy band slash and the queer female space. In *Eroticism in American culture,* ed. Cheryl Malcolm and Jopi Nyman, 103–25. Gdansk: Gdansk Univ. Press.
_____. 2006. "I'm jealous of the fake me": Postmodern subjectivity and identity construction in boy band fan fiction. In *Framing celebrity: New directions in celebrity culture,* ed. Su Holmes and Sean Redmond, 253–67. London: Routledge.
Butler, Judith. 1990. *Gender trouble.* New York: Routledge.
Donath, Judith S. 2003. Identity and deception in the virtual community: Communities

in cyberspace. In *Communities in cyberspace*, ed. Mark Smith and Peter Kollock, 29–59. London: Routledge.

Doty, Alexander. 1995. There's something queer here. In *Out in culture: Gay, lesbian, and queer essays on popular culture*, ed. Corey K. Creekmur and Alexander Doty, 71–90. Durham, NC: Duke Univ. Press.

Dyer, Richard. 1998. *Stars*. London: British Film Institute.

Faderman, Lillian. 1981. *Surpassing the love of men: Romantic friendship and love between women from the Renaissance to the present*. New York: William Morrow.

Halperin, David. 1990. *One hundred years of homosexuality and other essays on Greek love*. New York: Routledge.

Haraway, Donna. 1991. A cyborg manifesto: Science, technology, and socialist-feminism in the late twentieth century. In *Simians, cyborgs and women: The reinvention of nature*, 149–81. New York: Routledge.

Henderson, Samatha, and Michael Gilding. 2004. "I've never clicked this much with anyone in my life": Trust and hyperpersonal communication in online friendships. *New Media and Society* 6:487–506.

Hills, Matt. 2002. *Fan cultures*. London: Routledge.

Isilya. 2004. Not based on a true story. Available at: http://www.juppy.org/santa/stories.php?ForAuthorID=101&Year=2004 (accessed June 1, 2006)

Jenkins, Henry. 1992. *Textual poachers: Television fans and participatory culture*. New York: Routledge.

Lamb, Patricia Frazer, and Diane Veith. 1986. Romantic myth, transcendence, and *Star Trek* zines. In *Erotic universe: Sexuality and fantastic literature*, ed. Donald Palumbo, 236–55. Westport, CT: Greenwood Press.

Ludlow, Peter, ed. 1996. *High noon on the electronic frontier: Conceptual issues in cyberspace*. Cambridge, MA: MIT Press.

Penley, Constance. 1992. Feminism, psychoanalysis, and the study of popular culture. In *Cultural studies*, ed. Lawrence Grossberg, Cary Nelson, and Paula A. Treichler, 479–500. New York: Routledge.

Rheingold, Howard. 1993/2000. *The virtual community: Homesteading on the electronic frontier*. Cambridge, MA: MIT Press.

Rojek, Chris. 2001. *Celebrity*. London: Reaktion.

Schechner, Richard. 1988. *Performance theory*. New York: Routledge.

Sedgwick, Eve Kosofsky. 1985. *Between men: English literature and male homosocial desire*. New York: Columbia Univ. Press.

Smith-Rosenberg, Carol. 1985. The female world of love and ritual: Relations between women in nineteenth-century America. In *Disorderly conduct: Visions of gender in Victorian America*, 53–76. New York: Alfred A. Knopf.

Smol, Anna. 2004. "Oh ... oh ... Frodo!" Readings of male intimacy in *The Lord of the Rings*. *Modern Fiction Studies* 50:949–79.

Stacey, Jackie. 1991. Feminine fascinations: Forms of identification in star-audience relations. In *Stardom: Industry of desire*, ed. Christine Gledhill, 141–63. London: Routledge.

Turkle, Sherry. 1995. *Life on the screen: Identity in the age of the Internet*. New York: Simon and Schuster.

Turner, Graeme. 2004. *Understanding celebrity*. London: Sage.

PART IV
MEDIUM AND MESSAGE: FAN FICTION AND BEYOND

---

10. Writing Bodies in Space
Media Fan Fiction as Theatrical Performance
Francesca Coppa

ABSTRACT.—I argue that that fan fiction develops in response to dramatic, not literary, modes of storytelling and therefore can be seen to fulfill performative rather than literary criteria. By recognizing drama instead of prose as the antecedent medium for fan fiction, and by examining fan fiction through the lens of performance studies, three highly debated things about fan fiction become explicable: (1) fan fiction's focus on bodies; (2) fan fiction's repetition; and (3) fan fiction's production within the context of media fandom. Fan fiction, whether written in teleplay form or not, directs bodies in space: readers come to fan fiction with extratextual knowledge, mostly of characters' bodies and voices, and the writer uses this to direct her work. In theatre, there's a value to revisiting the same text in order to explore different aspects and play out different scenarios; in television, we don't mind tuning in week after week to see the same characters in entirely different stories. Similarly, fan fiction retells stories, but also changes them. If traditional theatre takes a script and makes it three-dimensional in a potentially infinite number of productions, modern fandom takes something three-dimensional and then produces an infinite number of scripts. This activity is not authoring texts, but making productions—relying on the audience's shared extratextual knowledge of sets and wardrobes, of the actors' bodies, smiles, and movements to direct a living theatre in the mind.

Introduction

I explore a relatively simple proposition: that fan fiction develops in response to dramatic rather than literary modes of storytelling and can therefore be seen to fulfill performative rather than literary criteria. This may seem obvious, as the writing of fan fiction is most strongly and specifically associated with the nearly forty-year-old phenomenon of media fandom,[1] which is to say, the organized subculture that celebrates, analyzes, and negotiates with stories told through the mass (mainly televisual) media, and whose crossroads has long been the annual MediaWest convention held since 1981 in Lansing, Michigan. But the importance of media fan fiction being written in response to dramatic rather than literary storytelling has been overlooked for at least two reasons: first, that fan fiction is itself a textual enterprise, made of letters and words and sentences written on a page (or, more likely these days, a screen), and it therefore seems sensible to treat it as a literary rather than an essentially dramatic form; and second, that media fandom has its origins in science fiction fandom, which is a heavily textual genre. Media fandom spun off from science fiction fandom as a direct result of the original *Star Trek* television series (1966–1969),[2] and although fans and scholars have catalogued many similarities (in fannish organization, jargon, and interests; even today, most media fans maintain a strong interest in science fiction and fantasy) and differences (most strikingly in terms of gender, but also in attitudes toward profit and professionalization) between the two fannish cultures, the impact of the switch in genre from prose to drama is rarely discussed or even noticed. But whereas fans of literary science fiction often take to writing "original" science fiction themselves, fans of mass media write fan fiction — which, I submit, is more a kind of theatre than a kind of prose.

In making this claim, I should note that I am defining *fan fiction* narrowly as creative material featuring characters that have previously appeared in works whose copyright is held by others. Although the creative expansion of extant fictional worlds is an age-old practice, by restricting the term *fan fiction* to reworkings of currently copyrighted material, I effectively limit the definition not just to the modern era of copyright, but to the even more recent era of active intellectual property rights enforcement. Although fans themselves often seek continuities between their art-making practices and those with a much longer history (Laura M. Hale starts her History of Fan Fic timeline with "0220 The Chinese invent paper"),[3] this conflation of folk and fan cultures may blur important distinctions between them, not least of which is the relatively recent legal idea that stories can be owned. It is only when storytelling becomes industrialized — or, to draw upon Richard Ohmann's definition of mass culture, produced at a distance by a relatively small number of special-ists — that fan fiction begins to make sense as a category, because only then are "fans" distinguished from Ohmann's distant "specialists," just as amateurs are differentiated from professionals (1996, 14; and see Garber 2001).

The line between amateur and professional writing is both sharply defined and frequently crossed in science fiction fandom, because science fiction is a literature itself written by fans of the genre; to be an amateur sci-ence fiction writer is therefore merely a step on the way to becoming a pro-fessional science fiction writer, and professional writers still go to conventions to hobnob. From this perspective, the professional is superior to the amateur, who is serving a kind of apprenticeship. Conversely, Media-West prides itself on being a convention run by fans and for fans, without any paid guests (professional authors, actors, or producers), and fan fiction writers tend to be defiantly amateur in the sense of writing precisely what they want for love alone. In this schema, to be a professional is to write at the command of others for money. There are exceptions to this in creators like Joss Whedon or Aaron Sorkin, who are seen as relatively fannish auteurs trying to make personal shows within the confines of the industry. How-ever, fans mostly shake their heads in bemusement at television shows that can't keep track of basic continuity, or films that miss obvious dramatic opportunities; it's understood that this is the by-product of creating a dra-matic universe for profit and by committee. Bemusement can give way to an angrier sort of frustration when creators visibly command the resources and power necessary for good mass media storytelling and are judged to have botched it anyway (George Lucas and Chris Carter come to mind).

In the infamous "Get a Life" (1986) sketch on *Saturday Night Live,* William Shatner framed his involvement with *Star Trek* as purely profes-sional: "You've turned an enjoyable little job, that I did as a lark for a few years, into a colossal waste of time!" Shatner's professionalism is tied to his refusal to take mass media storytelling seriously. But what of the fan who does take mass media storytelling seriously? What response is available to her? The science fiction fan may challenge her literary forerunners by becoming a professional writer, but the media fan is less likely to become a producer, screenwriter, or director. Science fiction is produced from among "us," but the mass media is still produced at a distance by "them." Few fan fiction writers will ever have access to the means of production for mass media storytelling. The bar is much higher; the funds needed are enor-mous; one still has to move to Los Angeles or Vancouver; the odds of writ-ing a show you like, as opposed to one you're assigned to, are small; until relatively recently, the gender bias in Hollywood was astounding. There is, in short, a very small chance of a fan fiction writer becoming a professional mass media storyteller, even if she was inclined to do so. Defiant amateurism in this case is both realistic and structurally smart, but that doesn't stop some science fiction fans from scoffing at the media fan's refusal to write something potentially salable.

Not only has "derivative" fiction been scoffed at within science fiction fandom, but drama has historically been a belittled category as well.[4] Despite the popular sense of science fiction as a genre with space battles, laser guns, and voyages to the moon, these dramas have been traditionally scoffed at by science fiction writers, whose allegiance is to idea-based narrative fiction. Magazines and novels are at the heart of science fiction fandom, not stage, film, or television (Ohmann 1996; Zimmerman 2003). In January 1976, an essay by Harlan Ellison appeared in the Science Fiction Writers of America newsletter urging the membership to take drama, and the SFWA's Nebula Award for Best Dramatic Presentation, more seriously:

> We haven't been quite as concerned with the Drama Nebulas as with the more familiar categories, chiefly because a small percentage of our membership has been employed in the areas that Nebula touches, and so it has been something of an illegitimate offspring. But sf films and tv shows and stage productions and sf-affiliated record albums reach a much wider audience than even our most popular novels and stories. And to a large degree the public image of sf is conditioned by these mass-market presentations [Ellison 1984, 82].

Ellison pointed out the historic "snobbishness on the part of our older, more print-oriented members toward film and tv" and noted that "everyone else seems to understand the power of film/tv. SFWA doesn't" (84). However, when the group chose not to award a Nebula for drama in 1977, Ellison resigned from SWFA and gave a speech in which he berated his audience for "worrying about a lousy 5 cents a word" while ignoring the much more lucrative fields of stage, television, film, and audio recordings (87–98). But Ellison's concern was for the strategic and financial importance of drama, not for drama's artistic value. In fact, Ellison is blatant about his allegiance to prose: "Tragically, the illiterates keep multiplying, and the audience for books *must* be kept alive! ... Books are *my* first interest, books should be *your* first interest. They count. But the way to support the writing of books is to get some of that film and TV money" (93).

This is hardly an enthusiastic defense of performative storytelling; Ellison merely argued that SFWA members should profit from the current boom in dramatic science fiction — 1977 being, of course, the year *Star Wars* was released. Ellison not only wrote the hands-down most popular episode of *Star Trek,* "City On the Edge of Forever," but is now also famous as a fierce defender of writers' intellectual property. However, the snobbishness against drama Ellison was fighting in the 1970s is still alive and well in the new millennium. Orson Scott Card (2005) celebrated the recent (and surely temporary) death of the *Star Trek* franchise by attacking the original series as mere visual "spectacle" for people who weren't readers of science fiction, although he does end by granting that "screen sci-fi has finally caught up with written science fiction." This is offensive to the female sf fans who created *Star Trek* fandom in the late 1960s; as Justine Larbalestier (2002) has shown, women were always present as readers of sf, though they weren't always visible on the zine letter pages that were the public face of the sf fandom (23–27). In fact, the subset of female sf fans who founded *Star Trek* fandom had multiple literacies and competencies: like many readers (and writers) of science fiction, they were likely not only to be avid readers but also to have advanced degrees in the hard sciences at a time when this was much less common for women (Coppa, "A Brief History of Media Fandom," this volume).

Most media fans still maintain at least a (ritual) allegiance to print over film; the two most recent large-scale media fandoms—*Harry Potter* and *The Lord of the Rings*— are listed at the multifandom archive site Fanfiction.net under "Books" rather than "Movies" even though both fandoms grew exponentially only after film versions appeared. Ask a fan, and she'll generally express a preference for the book over the "movieverse," but over and over, dramatic, not literary, material generates fan fiction. Although creative fannish practices have become familiar enough to be applied to practically every genre of art —fanfic exists about books, movies, television, comics, cartoons, anime, bands, celebrity culture, and political culture — it's only when stories get *embodied* that they seem to generate truly massive waves of fiction.

It is a truth almost universally acknowledged that fan fiction is an inferior art form and worthy of derision — oh, for kids, maybe, sure, to get them reading and writing, but writing fan fiction is nothing that any respectable adult should be doing. Fan fiction, from this point of view, is neither art nor commerce. Instead, it is charged with being derivative and repetitive, too narrowly focused on bodies and character at the expense of plot or idea. That may sound like failure by conventional literary standards, but if we examine fan fiction as a species of performance, the picture changes. Fan fiction's concern with bodies is often perceived as a problem or flaw, but performance is predicated on the idea of bodies, rather than words, as the storytelling medium.

Scholars of performance studies often refer to their object of study as "the movement of bodies in space," and the behavior of those bodies is never unique or "original"; all behavior, as Richard Schechner (2002) explains, "consists of recombining bits of previously behaved behaviors" (28). For this reason, Schechner defines performance as "twice behaved" or "restored" behavior (22), so a focus on the importance of repetition and combination as well as a focus on bodies is intrinsic to performance as a genre. As Schechner explains:

> Restored behavior is living behavior treated as a film director treats a strip of film. These strips of behavior can be rearranged or reconstructed; they are independent of the casual systems (personal, social, political, technological) that brought them into existence. They have a life of their own. The original "truth" or "source" of the behavior may not be known, or may be lost, ignored, contradicted — even while that truth or source is being honored [28].

This decontextualizing of behavior echoes the appropriation and use of existing characters in most fan fiction; in fact, one could define fan fiction as a textual attempt to make certain characters "perform" according to different behavioral strips. Or perhaps the characters who populate fan fiction are themselves the behavioral strips, able to walk out of one story and into another, acting independently of the works of art that brought them into existence. The existence of fan fiction postulates that characters are able to "walk" not only from one artwork into another, but from one genre into another; fan fiction articulates that characters are neither constructed or owned, but have, to use Schechner's phrase, a life of their own not dependent on any original "truth" or "source."

What better tool to apply to studying *Star Trek* and its derivative artistic productions than a form of criticism dedicated to explaining the semiotic value of bodies in space? By recognizing drama and not prose as the antecedent medium for fan fiction, and by examining fan fiction through the lens of performance studies, we are able to begin explaining three highly debated things about fan fiction: (1) Why does fan fiction seem to focus on bodies? (2) Why does fan fiction seem so repetitious? and (3) Why is fan fiction produced within the context of media fandom? What is the relationship between a fanfic writer and her audience?

Embodying the Geek Hierarchy

I begin a more detailed argument about the conflict between textual and embodied meanings with a quick close reading of the Brunching Shuttlecock's "Geek Hierarchy" (Figure 10.1). The Brunching Shuttlecocks are an online comedy troupe popular among a broad spectrum of geeks, nerds, fans, programmers, and hackers. The "Geek Hierarchy" is one of their most . circulated jokes, but a revealing joke, one that gets at something true about fannish hierarchies and social structure.

The Shuttlecocks place "Published Science Fiction *Authors*" at the very top of the chart, to be followed by "Science Fiction *Literature Fans*," "Science Fiction *Television Fans*," "*Fanfic Writers*," "*Erotic* Fanfic

Writers," and "Erotic Fanfic Writers Who Put *Themselves* in the Story" (all italics are my emphasis). To frame it another way, the Shuttlecocks rank the dramatic below the literary and the erotic below the dramatic. The hierarchy supports traditional values that privilege the written word over the spoken one and mind over body. The move down the hierarchy therefore represents a shift from literary values (the mind, the word, the "original statement") to what I would claim are theatrical ones (repetition, performance, embodied action). As we descend, we move further away from "text" and more toward "body," and, at least on the media fandom side of the diagram, toward the female body (because fan writers are likely to be women). At the very bottom of the hierarchy are the "furries," or fans who enjoy media involving anthropomorphic animals. These fans indulge a fantasy of pure body that asserts a connection between our human bodies and animal bodies. The mainstream discomfort with that idea is straight out of Freud's *Civilization and Its Discontents.*

Even the Geek Hierarchy's comparison between "Science Fiction *Authors*" and "Fanfic *Writers*" makes its distinction in terms of embodied action — because writing is a visible physical activity, a verb, while "authoring" (derived from the Latin *auctor,* "creator") is something more complex. To author a text is to have power over it, to take public responsibility for it, regardless of whether or not one did the actual work of selecting words and putting them in order. Authorship is a sign of control rather than creation. This distinction is gendered, because there is a larger tradition of seeing the female writer in terms of body rather than mind. Consider, for instance, Hawthorne's famous denigration of female authors as "scribbling women"; the slur conjures a picture of these women as engaged in frenetic activity, as if women's writing must be more physical than mental. Scribbling women are like *skiing* women, *cleaning* women, *dancing* women — not minds, but bodies in space.

Moreover, Henry Jenkins, in *Textual Poachers* (2002), explains that one of the earliest uses of the word *fan* was in reference to "women theatregoers, 'Matinee Girls,' who male critics claimed had come to admire the actors rather than the plays" (12) — or, to gloss the idea another way, bodies rather than texts, or to have given a somehow wrongful emphasis to the body in space. Similarly, Joan Marie Verba, in her 1996 history of *Star Trek* zine culture, *Boldly Writing,* notes that by 1975, ever-increasing numbers of fans saw *Star Trek* not as science fiction but "as a 'buddy' show, or as a heroic/romantic saga, in which Kirk and Spock were the focus." She continues, "Many of these stories reminded me of the ancient Greek

THE GEEK HIERARCHY

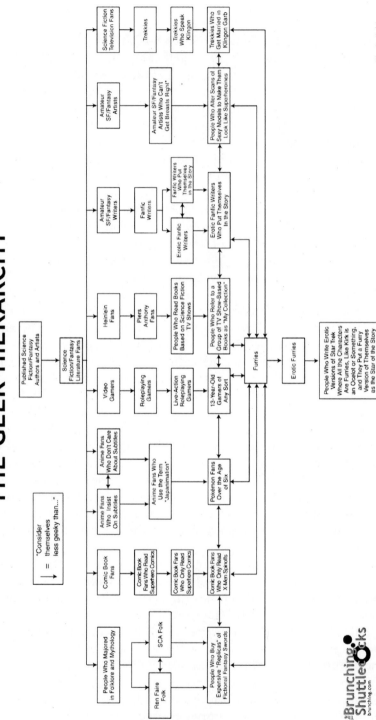

"Consider themselves less geeky than…"

=   →

Published Science Fiction/Fantasy Authors and Artists

People Who Majored in Folklore and Mythology

Ren Faire Folk

SCA Folk

People Who Buy Expensive "Replicas" of Fictional Fantasy Swords

Comic Book Fans

Comic Book Fans Who Read Superhero Comics

Comic Book Fans Who Only Read Superhero Comics

Comic Book Fans Who Only Read X-Men Spinoffs

Anime Fans Who Insist On Subtitles

Anime Fans Who Don't Care About Subtitles

Anime Fans Who Use the Term "Japanimation"

Pokémon Fans Over the Age of Six

Science Fiction/Fantasy Literature Fans

Video Gamers

Roleplaying Gamers

Live-Action Roleplaying Gamers

13-Year-Old Gamers of Any Sort

Heinlein Fans

Piers Anthony Fans

People Who Read Books Based on Science Fiction TV Shows

People Who Refer to a Group of TV Show-Based Books as "My Collection"

Amateur SF/Fantasy Writers

Fanfic Writers

Erotic Fanfic Writers

Fanfic Writers Who Put Themselves in the Story

Erotic Fanfic Writers Who Put Themselves In the Story

Amateur SF/Fantasy Artists

Amateur SF/Fantasy Artists Who Can't Get Breasts Right*

People Who Alter Scans of Sexy Models to Make Them Look Like Superheroines

Science Fiction Television Fans

Trekkies

Trekkies Who Speak Klingon

Trekkies Who Get Married in Klingon Garb

Furries

Erotic Furries

People Who Write Erotic Versions of Star Trek Where All the Characters Are Furries, Like Kirk is an Ocelot or Something, and They Put a Furry Version of Themselves as the Star of the Story

*Nearly all of them

legend of Damon and Pythias, with Kirk and Spock substituted" (23). This allusion is interesting, because practically speaking, the legendary characters aren't so much "characters" as a set of actions, a behavioral script; to offer to exchange places with a comrade who is facing death is to *be* Damon and Pythias, and so this sort of fan fiction "casts" Kirk and Spock as the legendary friends in a performance of the myth. From this viewpoint, Kirk and Spock aren't characters firmly enmeshed in a narrative, but performers whose twice-behaved behaviors might (like Schechner's behavioral strips) be rearranged or otherwise reconstructed. The result of this reconstruction wouldn't be "original" behavior, however, because according to Schechner, there's no such thing. Rather, Kirk and Spock are well cast to perform Damon and Pythias. One set of twice-behaved behaviors is exchanged for another. This emphasis on character, behavior, and relationships is often framed as a female value; it's certainly a theatrical one.

We can see these theatrical and performative values in the very earliest creative contributions to *Star Trek* zines. The first *Star Trek* fanzine, *Spockanalia* (1967, edited by Devra Langsam and Sherna Comerford), included the creative artwork "The Territory of Rigel," by Dorothy Jones (Figure 10.2). In *Boldly Writing,* Verba describes this as a "poem," but it is, in fact, a song with an explicit stage direction that tells us it's a *ni var* to be performed by two voices and a Vulcan harp, no doubt influenced by the scene in the *Star Trek* episode "Charlie X" where Uhura sings while accompanied by Spock. Perhaps some readers actually sang the song with their friends, or perhaps the reader was merely supposed to direct the performance of the song in her head — but the key thing is that the reader of this song can do these things because she has an image of Leonard Nimoy as Spock with a Vulcan harp accompanying a singer. The performance of this song has already been cast; we know the behaviors of both singers and harpist. To read this song is therefore to supplement the written words with the mental image of the appropriate bodies. This "text" is overtly performative and relational; two voices, *ni var,* two people singing; as the songwriter explains, *ni var* means "two form," comparing and contrasting two aspects of the same thing (Verba 1996, 11). This *ni var* features two people singing, a third if the Vulcan harpist isn't one of the singers, and a fourth if you, the reader/director, isn't part of the performance. It's not a poem, it's a party; it's an artwork that implies a community.

Opposite **Fig. 10.1. Brunching Shuttlecock's "Geek Hierachy." Available at http://www.brunching.com/geekhierarchy.html (accessed June 1, 2006). Used with permission.**

The Territory of Rigel
(A *ni var* to be performed by two voices and Vulcan harp)

First Voice	*Second Voice*
	Dark and silent
Rigel in the scanner,	
blue-white and crystalline,	is the field of space.
shining. Light	
born in the corona	
pours into space.	The bridge is empty.
	The time, three hundred.
The instruments whisper,	
the panel lights flicker.	The instruments tell little.
The stars are still and clear.	The computer absorbs in silence
	trivial patterns meaning nothing.
Their song is deliberate,	
long years to a cadence.	
Dust in their paths	
moves in their wake like water.	Three-twenty.
	The night is very long.
and Rigel shines.	
	In the dark gulf is the ship.
The stars like ancient trees.	in the sleeping ship is the bridge
heavy with planets, blazing with life.	on the bridge am I,
	silence upon silence,
	as quiet as memory,
	and dark as death.
I wander the bright roads	
whom no planet claims:	I am far
live in the open Galaxy	from my beginning and my end.
I have clarity before me,	Four hundred and the watch is changed.
and Rigel full of light.	I leave the bridge and go
	from darkness into darkness.

Figure 10.2. "The Territory of Rigel," by Dorothy Jones, From *Spockanalia I* © 1967, edited by Sherna Comerford and Devra Michele Langsam. Available in Verba (1996, 2). Used with permission.

Similarly, some fan fiction has been written in script or teleplay form, often by fans who aspired to write for the produced show (and there is a perception among fans that a greater proportion of these script-writing fans have been men [Cynthia Walker and Laura Hale, personal communications, June 8, 2005]). An actual theatrical play based on *Star Trek* was put on at the Denham Springs Community Theatre in 1971; the fact was widely reported in zines, as was Gene Roddenberry's approving letter: "I have no objection to plays similar to *Star Trek* or even identical to *Star Trek* if done by students or community groups on a non profit basis as long as the appropriate credit is given to the source material and individuals. Or as long as a production remains a community theatre venture" (Verba 1996, 6). Roddenberry's coda insists on the play's nonprofit status; then as now, to write in script form would be a sign of a writer's aspiring professionalism. Although some fan teleplays were probably written as spec scripts for the industry, others ended up published in zines, and when online fan fiction archives became popular in the mid-1990s, the fiction was categorized not only as "gen," "het," or "slash," but by such categories as "romance," "drama," "humor," "poetry," "filk," or "teleplay." But the script form has always been unpopular among readers, so a fan whose primary audience was other fans rather than the television industry was more likely to tell her dramatic story in prose. Arguably, the teleplay form declined as media fandom broke away from science fiction fandom, becoming more defiantly amateur as television writing grew more professionalized, but the current fracturing of the television market due to competition from cable, satellite, DVD, video games, and the Internet seems to be reversing this trend once again. Newer shows (and older shows that have had time to evaluate the creative and economic value of their fan base) increasingly invite the creative participation of fans, and many seem to want to blur the lines between amateur and professional, fan and specialist. As an example, the Web site for the television series *The Dead Zone,* a show helmed by longtime *Star Trek* writer and producer Michael Piller, offers to fans not only free copies of the aired scripts, but a writer's guide for the show and explicit instructions on how to send in your teleplay for professional consideration. In this climate, fans may become professional movie or teleplay writers while still maintaining their identities as fans and while writing fan fiction.

The existence of the teleplay and other performative forms helps to demonstrate fan fiction's roots as an essentially dramatic literature, but the larger part of my argument is that fan fiction directs bodies in space even when it's not overtly written in theatrical form. Readers come to fan fiction with extratextual knowledge, mostly of characters' bodies and voices. Jane Mailander (2005) argues that fan fiction is an ideal medium for erotica because "the audience knows the characters; they've walked that mile in their shoes, they are *primed*. The dynamic between these two people is clear to the audience." A fan fiction writer has "the challenge of expressing that dynamic, of taking it to a place that would make the producers blush — but a place that must follow logically from that baseline development." Mailander is talking about character, but she might as well be talking about bodies; we know who these characters are because we know the actors who play them, and we bring our memories of their physicality to the text, so the reader is precharged, preeroticized. But the actor's body, as much as the words on the page, is the medium of even nonerotic fannish storytelling. In making her point that we come to fan fiction "primed," Mailander also identifies something we might correlate with Schechner's twice-behaved behavior. We're primed because we've met these characters already, and now we're seeing them again. In theatre, we call that a *production*, and it isn't a problem.

Repetition and the Derridean Supplement

From a literary perspective, fan fiction's unusual emphasis on the body seems like a thematic obsession or a stylistic tic, but in theatre, bodies are the storytelling medium, the carriers of symbolic action. Similarly, in literary terms, fan fiction's repetition is strange; in theatre, stories are retold all the time. Theatre artists think it's fine to tell to tell the same story again, but differently: not only was Shakespeare's *Hamlet* a relatively late version of the tale (previous versions include the "Amleth" of Saxo Grammaticus, its translation by Francois de Belleforest, and the *Ur-Hamlet* attributed to Thomas Kyd), but we're happy to see differently inflected versions of the tale. Moreover, there's no assumption that the first production will be definitive; in theatre, we want to see *your* Hamlet and *his* Hamlet and *her* Hamlet; to embody the role is to reinvent it. We also want to see new generations of directors and designers recast the play without regard for authorial intent or historicity, putting *Hamlet* into infinite alternative universes. What if Hamlet was a graduate student? What if Hamlet had an (entirely ahistorical) Oedipal complex? What if Hamlet was a street kid in the Bronx? Hamlet has been portrayed as an action hero/medieval warrior (Mel Gibson, dir. Franco Zefferelli, 1990), the avenging son of a Japanese CEO (*The Bad Sleep Well;* Toshiro Mifune, dir. Akira Kurosawa, 1960), an angry young man (Peter O'Toole, dir. Laurence Olivier, Old Vic, 1963), and a university student home on break (Alex Jennings, dir. Matthew Warchus at the RSC, 1997).

In theatre, there's a value to revising the same text in order to explore different aspects and play out different behavioral strips; similarly, in television, we don't mind tuning in week after week to see the same characters in entirely different stories. We don't mind new versions of *Hamlet* the way we don't mind new episodes of *Star Trek*. We don't say, "Oh, *Star Trek* again? We had *Star Trek* last week!" We don't mind if Kirk and Spock visit — as they did on the aired series — a planet based on Roman gladiator culture, or Native American culture, or America during the Great Depression. Most people happily watch televised repeats—identical replayings of dramatic action. How much more interesting would different performances of the same scripts be if the actors and directors explored the limitations of the text and tried to elicit different readings, different embodied meanings? And because fan fiction is an amateur production accountable to no market forces, it allows for radical reimaginings: plots, themes, and endings that would never be permitted on network television. One could imagine *Star Trek* by David Lynch, *Star Trek* by Stanley Kubrick, *Star Trek* by Woody Allen — and what I'm getting at here is that that's what fan fiction *is.*

But you don't even have to attend multiple productions to understand doubling and repetition in theatre. Most productions were scripts first: theatre is an art form where we read something with the goal of making something else out of it. The script isn't the final product in theatre; in fact, one of the questions that theatre theorists have had to debate is the location of the work of art. Is it in the author's original script? Probably not; the original script goes through innumerable changes in performance and is rarely seen outside of library archives. The published script of a theatrical or teleplay is usually a postproduction draft that takes into account changes that were made during production by actors, director, and designers; far from being evidence of a single authorial vision, a published play is one of the most collaborative genres in existence. And most theatre works never result in a published script at all, so it's difficult to argue for text as the central object in a theatrical art experience.

Far from being a sacred text, a play's script is more like a blueprint for a production — a thing used to make another thing. Like any architectural blueprint, a script provides the directions for building something three-dimensional and situated in space. But one can't point to theatrical production as the center of dramatic art either, because the question then becomes: which production? A script isn't simply directions for building something in space, but also in time — not just a single production, but a potentially infinite series of productions. Marvin Carlson (1985) theorizes the complicated relationship between all the multiple and vastly different works of art that can be associated with a single dramatic story in terms of the Derridean supplement, and the supplement also serves as an excellent model for fan fiction as well (see Derecho [this volume], who uses the Derridean term *archontic* to describe this same supplementarity).

The best way to explain a supplement is by pointing to a concrete example of one; Roger Laport used a French dictionary, but let me substitute for that the more familiar example of an encyclopedia. When you buy an encyclopedia, you buy a complete set, volumes A–Z. But the world keeps progressing, and knowledge keeps expanding, and so this "complete" set of encyclopedias is outdated the second you buy it; it doesn't include today's news and discoveries. So when you buy an encyclopedia, they generally also include a yearly supplement — 2005, 2006, and so on — that you can slot into your bookcase after "Z." So with that image in mind, consider what the supplement does: it reveals the original thing, the encyclopedia, in this case, as incomplete, but also prophesies future supplements. In fact, a supplement suggests that completeness is actually impossible, as the presence of a 2005 supplement suggests the need for one in 2006, 2007, 2008, and on into the future, indefinitely.

We can apply this concept to theatrical performance, and then to fan fiction as performance. In theatre, a working script becomes a staged performance, but as Carlson explains, "A play on stage will inevitably display material lacking in the written text, quite likely not apparent as lacking until the performance takes place, but then revealed as significant and necessary. At the same time, the performance, by revealing this lack, reveals also a potentially infinite series of future performances providing further supplementation" (1985, 10). Fan fiction works much the same way. Once a story supplements canon — giving us something the original source did not by filling in a missing scene, getting inside a character's head, interpreting or clarifying or departing from the story as originally told — future supplements become inevitable, and they aren't any more redundant than multiple productions of *Hamlet*.

A conservative critic might argue that Shakespeare can support that level of interpretation and invention, whereas your average — or even better than average — television show simply can't. We tell certain stories over and over because they're brilliant and continue to be relevant. I don't share that point of view. I agree with Alan Sinfield when he argues that Shakespeare seems relevant because he is constantly interfered with (1994, 4–5). It is Shakespeare's endlessly creative fans — be they theatre practitioners carrying the stories on their bodies or literary critics teasing out new textual interpretations — who keep Shakespeare going. An endless number of Shakespearean productions supplement the texts, adding meanings that Shakespeare never intended and making them meaningful to twenty-first-century audiences. There's no reason not to see this as a perfectly valid artistic activity; and if it is so for theatre, why is it not for television?

Before a Live Audience

The third theatrical quality I want to discuss in terms of fan fiction is the need for a live audience. A live audience has always been a precondition for fandom. Longtime fanzine editor and archivist Arnie Katz (n.d.) explains that science fiction magazines— particularly their letter pages— were essential to the genesis of science fiction fandom. As Katz notes, "Science fiction and fantasy were widely available for many years before fandom erupted.... Those who wanted to be more than readers couldn't do much while books remained the main delivery vehicle for science fiction. It's hard to interact with a book, other than to write a letter to the author in care of the publisher." Science fiction fans have a saying: "fandom is a way of life"— which is to say, science fiction literature fandom is more than a celebration of texts; it's a series of practices. This may be why most academic works on fandom are ethnographies, or analyses of social organizations and cultural performances. As Katz points out, fandom is essentially interactive in a way beyond the traditional reader-writer relationship.

Fan fiction, too, is a cultural performance that requires a live audience; fan fiction is not merely a text, it's an event. Whether published in a zine, on a mailing list, to an archive, or to a blog like LiveJournal.com, there's a kind of simultaneity to the reception of fan fiction, a story everyone is reading, more or less at the same time, more or less together. Over the years, technology has allowed television viewers to reconstitute themselves as an audience; now, you can watch television while you post to the boards at TelevisionWithoutPity.com, or sit in an IRC channel, or send updates to your mailing list; you don't have to wait for the next issue of a zine to be mailed. Similarly, fandom gathers together a live, communal audience for stories, and fans have adopted and adapted every mode of communication in an effort to ensure that fan fiction quickly reaches its target audience.

Compare this to John Ruskin's definition of a "true" book:

> A book is essentially not a talked thing, but a written thing; and written, not with the view of mere communication, but of permanence. The book of talk is printed only because its author cannot speak to thousands of people at once; if he could, he would — the volume is mere multiplication of his voice.... But a book is written, not to multiply the voice merely, not to carry it merely, but to perpetuate it [1985, 259–60].

Most books— including most mass market fiction — are not "true books" by this standard. Most books merely convey the storytelling voice to an audience that cannot be gathered together to listen simultaneously, as they do in theatre. A book's audience is generally dispersed over both space and time; people in different places read a book at different times, and reading is— at least in the last hundred or so years— a pretty solitary activity. This didn't used to be so; the line between reading and theatre was thinner in the days when a family patriarch might read aloud to his family after dinner, or a group of middle-class women might stage a tableau based on a favorite text. Ironically, the rise of literacy and the greater availability of printed matter are largely responsible for fracturing the communal reading audience and encouraging the solitary consumption of stories. Consider Isaac Asimov's prophetic description of "the perfect entertainment cassette":

> A cassette as ordinarily viewed makes sound and casts light. That is its purpose, of course, but must sound and light obtrude on others who are not involved or interested? The ideal cassette would be visible and audible only to the person using it.... We could imagine a cassette that is always in perfect adjustment; that starts automatically when you look at it; that stops automatically when you cease to look at it; that can play forward or backward, quickly or slowly, by skips or with repetitions, entirely at your pleasure.... Must this remain only a dream? Can we expect to have such a cassette some day? We not only have it now, we have had it for many centuries. The ideal I have described is the printed word, the book, the object you now hold.... Does it seem to you that the book, unlike the cassette I have been describing, does not produce sound and images? It certainly does.... You cannot read without hearing the words in your mind and seeing the images to which they give rise. In fact, they are your sounds and images, not those invented for you by others, and are therefore better [quoted in Ellison 1984, 51–52].

Asimov, writing years before VHS, let alone DVD, frames the book as an improvement over other forms of dramatic storytelling ("sounds and images") precisely because it's more individualized ("visible and audible only to the person using it"). Asimov's prophetic description illustrates how the book, taken as a technology, anticipates the virtual reality so feared by those who worry about the effects of video games and the Internet on children; it's interesting that those same parents are often keen to encourage immersive reading of the kind Asimov is valorizing. But immersive reading is generally not the kind encouraged by literature departments, which teaches students to attend to language. To read critically is to see a text not as "sounds and images" but as specific words placed on a page in a particular order; to closely read a text is to make meaning out of those particular words and no others. To look at, rather than through, the specifically defined words on the page is to see a story as a written rather than a "talked" thing.

Fan fiction is Ruskin's "talked" thing, or Asimov's "perfect entertainment cassette." Fan fiction writers generally use a relatively transparent style of prose conducive to an immersive reading experience. There are marvelous exceptions: many fan fiction writers are great prose stylists or even poets. But historically the fan fiction writer has tried not to get in the way of the reader's view of the characters, and in this, fan fiction writers are part of a more general literary trend. In an article in the *Washington Post*, Linton Weeks (2001) complains about the "No-Style style" of many best-selling authors and quotes book reviewer Pat Holt as noticing that "the style of commercial fiction has shifted over to a television mentality," with "short paragraphs, a lot of switching of locations and lots of dialogue," without ever questioning to what extent this might make it not simply "inferior" prose but prose put to a different and nonliterary purpose. In her introduction to the forthcoming *Reconstructing Harry: "Harry Potter" Fan Fiction on the World Wide Web,* Jane Glaubman observes J. K. Rowling's "transparent" prose style without judgment, concluding that "the impression of transparency must stem in part from continuities with visual culture" and these continuities "call on devices ubiquitous in commercial media that themselves aspire to transparency." Certainly, Rowling's visual style may explain why the *Harry Potter* books were adopted by media fandom; they share fan fiction's theatrical values. For instance, Glaubman notes the unusual extent to which Harry was embodied in Rowling's text: "An awareness of the body is everywhere in these books.... Rowling expresses [Harry's] feelings somatically, 'his heart twanging like a giant elastic band,' 'as though he'd just been walloped in the stomach.' ... By giving us immediate access to his sensations, she contributes ... to the effect of transparency."

Harry Potter comes to us as the embodied protagonist of a series of stories that retell Harry's adventures during a series of school years. By the time of the fourth installment, *Harry Potter and the Goblet of Fire,* the simultaneous, worldwide release of the book was the occasion for something very like a public festival, with people coming out at midnight, sometimes in costume, not simply to purchase the book but also to formally constitute themselves as an audience. The ongoing series of novels was then made into an ongoing series of films. In all of these ways, the *Harry Potter* books resist the status of "finished literary text" made up of particular words in a particular order, and instead construct themselves as the open-ended inspiration for future performative supplements that will allow its audience to reconstitute itself on a regular basis. *Harry Potter* has already resulted numerous translations, four sequels, three films, and, as of June 13, 2005, at least 190,994 fan fiction stories—so far.

Why stop there? *Can* it be stopped there? This is no longer a phenomenon within a single author's control; "Harry Potter" is now an entire creative universe within which millions of people are writing, reading, drawing, reporting, discussing, analyzing, criticizing, celebrating, marketing, filming, translating, teaching, theorizing, playacting. Although Rowling may be responsible for putting together a initial series of words in a particular order, only in the legal sense is she the "author" of all of these other creative productions. Or, to put it another way, she's the *author* in the sense of taking responsibility for these productions, but she's not the *writer* of those specific other expressions of the idea of a boy wizard at school. There are other creative players involved, some paid (the artists who illustrated the text; the scholars who are writing the critical studies of the series) and some unpaid (the fans who participate in heated analytical discussions on *Harry Potter* Web sites or mailing lists, fan fiction writers). Similarly, a film like *Star Wars* or a television show like *Buffy the Vampire Slayer* have become rich art worlds quite apart from the authorial or auteurial efforts of George Lucas or Joss Whedon.

One last word about the complex relationship between the author, these other creative writers, and the audience: in traditional literary studies, the author is dead, and has been for some time. The phrase alludes to Roland Barthes's essay "The Death of the Author" and to Barthes's argument that "as soon as a fact is narrated ... the voice loses its origin, the author enters into his own death, writing begins" (1977, 142). From this perspective, language always means more than an author intends, and we cannot evaluate writing as an expression of a "person's" ideas or thoughts. Rather, we should look at writing as a separately existing linguistic performance that does/says more than any one person ever could. Barthes concludes by saying that what meaning there is to a text is made by the reader, and "the birth of the reader must be at the cost of the death of the Author" (148).

But not the writer. In fandom, the author may be dead, but the writer — that actively scribbling, embodied woman — is very much alive.[5] You can talk to her; you can write to her and ask her questions about her work, and she will probably write back to you and answer them. She might enjoy discussing larger plot, style, and characterization points with you if you engage her in critical conversation. You can tell her that her story is bad and hurt her feelings, or you can flame her as someone who shouldn't be writing at all. Moreover, the writer may well have worked with a team of editors or beta readers; the fiction might well be not only derivative of an author, but written collaboratively by a group, or crafted as a birthday present for a fellow fan — in short, the writer is part of an interactive community, and in this way, the production of fan fiction is closer to the collaborative making of a theatre piece then to the fabled solitary act of writing.

I believe that fandom is community theatre in a mass media world; fandom is what happened to the culture of amateur dramatics. In the days before television, people often made theatre in their homes, for fun, and in fandom, we still make theatre together, for fun, except we cast the play from our televisions sets. Theatre — actual, three-dimensional theatre that moves bodies in space — is expensive and requires tremendous social capital; you've got to have the power to make those bodies move under your direction and at your command. We discover women's poetry in attic trunks and women's novels written under male pseudonyms, but we still find that women are underrepresented in the roles that orchestrate and dictate the actions of (male) bodies in performance. Consider the ongoing underrepresentation of women playwrights, composers, directors, and symphony conductors. If traditional theatre takes a script and makes it three-dimensional in a potentially infinite number of productions, modern fandom takes something three-dimensional and then produces an infinite number of scripts. This is not authoring texts, but making productions—relying on the audience's shared extratextual knowledge of sets and wardrobes, of the actors' bodies and their smiles and movements—to direct a living theatre in the mind.

Notes

1. Media fandom, although probably best the known and most studied as a result of the popularity of the mass media it is based around, is not the only kind of fandom. Comics, anime, and gaming each have well-established fandoms with different histories. However, the Internet has encouraged crossover among these groups.

2. Or possibly as a result of the double whammy of *Star Trek* and *The Man from U.N.C.L.E.* (1964–1968), another television series that was hugely popular with science fiction fans; see Walker (2001) and my own "A Brief History of Media Fandom" (this volume).

3. When possible, I have chosen to cite the online work of fan-critics and fan-historians rather than the published scholarly works of professional academics. As a fan, I am wary of "distanced professional expertise," even my own; the position of the media fan is one of defiant amateurism. In that spirit, I therefore note that fandom has always done an excellent job of explaining itself to itself, producing its own canon of theoretical literature, its own roster of fannish scholars, and its own critical apparatus for reviewing, analyzing, and recommending fan fiction.

4. Although the social value of live theatre has historically been greater than that of mass media dramatic forms, both have been marginalized. Literature and theatre are often grouped together as "high art" against film and television, but in practice, textual values are often opposed to performative ones. Drama has been seen as appealing to the working classes, women, children, and illiterates; also, until recently, there was no way to record and distribute it. In the specific context of science fiction, plays like Karel Capek's *RUR* (1920), which introduced the word *robot* into the world's languages, are often left out of the sf canon, even though they antedate the rise of prose magazine fiction.

5. I am indebted to my conversations with Georgina Paterson for these insights.

References

Barthes, Roland. 1977. The death of the author. In *Image-music-text*, 142–48. New York: Noonday Press.

Card, Orson Scott. 2005. Strange new world: No *Star Trek*. *LA Times*, May 3.

Carlson, Marvin. 1985. Theatrical performance: Illustration, translation, fulfillment, or supplement. *Theatre Journal* 37:5–11.

Ellison, Harlan. 1984. *Sleepless nights in the procrustean bed: Essays by Harlan Ellison.* Ed. Marty Clark. San Bernardino, CA: Borgo Press.

Garber, Majorie. 2001. *Academic instincts.* Princeton, NJ: Princeton University Press.

Glaubman, Jane, ed. Forthcoming. *Reconstructing Harry: "Harry Potter" fan fiction on the World Wide Web.* Durham, NC: Duke Univ. Press.

Hale, Laura M. 2005. A history of fan fic. Fanzine.

Jenkins, Henry. *Textual poachers: Television fans and participatory culture.* New York: Routledge.

Katz, Arnie. N.d. The philosophical theory of fanhistory. http://www.smithway.org/fstuff/theory/phil1.html (accessed June 1, 2006).

Larbalestier, Justine. 2002. *The battle of the sexes in science fiction.* Middletown, CT: Wesleyan Univ. Press.

Mailander, Jane. 2005. The advantages of erotic fan fiction as an art form. http://members.aol.com/janemort/erotic.html (accessed June 1, 2006).

Ohmann, Richard. 1996. *Selling culture: Magazines, markets, and class at the turn of the century.* London: Verso.

Ruskin, John. 1985. On king's treasuries. From *Sesames and lillies,* in *Unto this last and other writings,* 255–87. London: Penguin Classics.

Schechner, Richard. 2002. *Performance studies: An introduction.* New York: Routledge.

Sinfield, Alan. 1994. *Cultural politics — Queer reading.* Philadelphia: Univ. of Pennsylvania Press.

Verba, Joan Marie. 1996. *Boldly writing: A Trekker fan and zine history, 1967–1987.* 2nd ed. Minnesota: FTL Publications. http://www.ftlpublications.com/bw.htm (accessed June 1, 2006).

Weeks, Linton. 2001. Plotting along: Best-selling authors are richer than ever. So why is prose from these pros so poor? *Washington Post,* November 18.

Zimmerman, Diane Leenheer. 2003. Authorship without ownership: Reconsidering incentives in a digital age. *DePaul Law Review* 52:1121–70.

11. "This Dratted Thing"
Fannish Storytelling Through New Media
Louisa Ellen Stein

ABSTRACT.— I link together three avenues of thought relating to online fan texts: (1) new media theory's focus on technology, specifically understandings of interface — that is, the point of interaction between a user and a computer at the level of the software with which we engage with new media; (2) genre theory's conception of genre discourse as shared, shifting, cultural category; and (3) fan studies' focus on fans as users and authors of media texts, who engage with and build on already existing media texts in various ways. I propose that, through the merging of these three avenues of inquiry, we can find a new, more tangible, way to understand fan engagement with new media and popular media texts. From the interplay among fan culture, genre discourse, and new media interfaces, fan-created fiction and art are born. The histories and traditions of fan fiction intersect with broader cultural (generic) discourses as fandom moves online. In turn, as fans use the tools of new media to write and share fannish narratives, new forms of fan creative expression come into being. I look at how this trifold process is exemplified in two fannish uses of interface to create new modes of storytelling: diary-based fan fictions that use interactive blogging sites such as LiveJournal.com to create daily diaries kept by fictional characters; and fictional narratives created by fans out of images from *The Sims,* a computer game where players create characters and control various aspects of their lives.

245

Introduction

One wouldn't expect Harry Potter's school yard bully, Draco Malfoy, to be an introspective, memoir-writing type, nor would one expect him to be particularly technologically savvy; and yet, as it turns out, he does indeed keep an online diary, in which he records his thoughts, hopes, and dreams. Among his first words in cyberspace were, "Time to tweak around a bit with this dratted thing. I do hope they have my colours in stock. Or however you're awarded your combo ... leave it to a Muggle device to make your decisions for you" (Dracolicious, LiveJournal.com [LJ], February 26, 2003). To translate for the uninitiated, the Muggle (nonmagical) device he complains about is a Web-accessing PDA, from which he is posting to his online journal. His complaint focuses on the limitations of technology, which "makes your decisions for you." However, as he better learns to use this technology, he succeeds in setting his PDA appropriately to Slytherin green, thus making his voice known on the Web in true Malfoy style.

Truth be told, this is only one of many Draco Malfoys online, all of whom share cyberspace with a variety of Buffy Summerses, Spikes, Mulders, and the like. Even Darth Vader has a blog. These fictional online voices are part of new developments in fan storytelling spurred by the rapid growth of online media culture. Such new narrative forms build on traditions within fan fiction and at the same time are shaped by the technologies of the new media with which they are created and shared. They also draw on generic structures within popular media and culture in general, as well as within fan fiction specifically.

To explore the shifting and layered terrain of these new modes of fannish storytelling (including, but not limited to, online diary-based narratives), in this essay, I link together three avenues of thought relating to online fan texts: (1) new media theory's focus on technology, specifically understandings of interface — that is, the point of interaction between a user and a computer at the level of the software we use to engage with new media; (2) genre theory's conception of genre discourse as shared, shifting, cultural category; and (3) fan studies' focus on fans as users and authors of media texts, who engage with and build on already existing media texts in various ways.[1] I propose that, through the merging of these three avenues of inquiry, we can find a new, more tangible, way to understand fan engagement with new media and popular media texts.

Out of the interplay of these three cultural forces—fan culture, genre discourse, and new media interfaces—fan-created fiction and art are born in various forms. As fan cultures and fan creative texts evolve online, the histories and traditions of fan fiction intersect with broader cultural (generic) discourses. In turn, as fans use the tools of new media to write and share fannish narratives, new forms of fan creative expression come into being. This trifold process is exemplified in two fannish uses of interface to create new modes of storytelling: diary-based fan fictions that use interactive blogging sites such as LJ to create daily diaries kept by fictional characters, and fictional narratives created by fans out of images from *The Sims,* a computer game in which players create characters and families and control various aspects of their lives.[2]

Within the many diverse forms of fan creativity online, we can identify a central tension between two defining fannish concerns: expansiveness and limitation. On the one hand, fannish imaginings and creativity both draw on and create a sense of expandability. Fan creative texts expand the world of the source text in potentially infinite directions, and, as Roberta E. Pearson (2003) has argued, fans often focus on texts that have expandability built into their structure. On the other hand, fannish authorship is also driven by a sense of limitation and restriction, as fannish storytelling plays out in relation to the original source text on which it is based. This negotiation between limitation and expansiveness shapes fan creativity. Both the source text and culturally shared codes of genre provide structures and limitations within which fans write and from which fans draw. As fandom and fan fiction have grown in the cultural spaces carved out by new media in the past two decades, new media interfaces provide another layer of limitation and expansiveness, and it is within this context that fan creativity flourishes online. I consider how the dynamics of online fan creativity play out in specific fan texts, exploring instances in which new media interfaces are especially crucial in the shaping of emergent modes of fannish storytelling.

Impetus and Limitation: Canon, Fantext, Genre, Interface

Fan fiction is always created in relation to an outside media text; however, to say that fan fiction is derivative oversimplifies the relationship between the fan fiction and the source text. At the most obvious level, fans write fan fiction in relation to canon. In their fan fiction, authors play with the limitations and possibilities offered by their source text of choice. Obviously, canon comes in many forms and is found across media. In turn, the many different fan creative texts which circulate online compose what fans and fan scholars call the *fantext,* the combined, flexible whole of the fan imagination (related to but not quite the same as *fanon*, which carries with it the negative connotation of overused cliché). All of these fan texts, which together make up the larger fantext, build on and move beyond canon to different degrees. Canon restrictions are used as both creative impetus and delineation. Some authors write carefully within canon, valuing fan fiction that fills in canonical spaces without breaking any canonical characterization or plot. However, other authors define their fan fiction precisely as it breaks from canon, as is most evident in the fan understood category of the alternate universe (AU), in which fan authors take recognizable characters and place them in noncanonical contexts, so that the protagonists are recast as Roman gladiators or undercover agents.[3] But even when the expectations created by canon are disregarded, fantextual or fanon understandings of characters and relationships often provide a new set of limitations within which an author must work. For example, the various fan-favored romantic pairings develop their own set of specific fantextual expectations as well as perceived limitations or restrictions that fan authors then follow or break: *Smallville* slash fans' investment in the romantic union between teenage alien/Superman-to-be Clark Kent and young billionaire Lex Luthor comes complete with its own set of expectations and even clichés.

Such fantextual expectations often extend beyond specific fannish investments in a particular pairing or character. Instead, they draw on larger fan concerns that surface across fandoms. If we take a step back, we can also see the proliferation of pairings and similar characterizations in fan fiction as part of broader textual expectations that we might understand as genre discourse. Indeed, the ever-shifting fantext stretches beyond specific fandoms, drawing on and establishing widely shared generic structures in fan-specific ways. This in turn provides a new set of expectations and limitations to be followed. For example, labels such as "slash" or "het" signal fantextual expectations that cut across fandoms and pairings. Thus, within fan culture, these terms function as generic discourse that is used to categorize, to distinguish, and to communicate expectations.

Indeed, genre itself functions in a similar way to canon and fantext in terms of restriction and impetus; shared understandings of generic codes and tropes contribute story possibilities and yet also limit the ranges of types of stories told. For example, both *Smallville* and *Harry Potter* fan fiction draw on fantasy, romance, and adolescent angst, invoking elements associated with the teen genre in their stories' conflict and resolution. Fan fiction narratives evolve from this interplay of canonical, fantextual, and generic expectations. A slash author pairing Draco with Harry may break both canonical and generic expectations—for example, forgoing Draco as bully — to embrace him in a different, if related, role as bratty yet ultimately sympathetic romantic hero. A fan fiction with Lex Luthor at its center may shed any vestiges of the character's supervillainy in favor of the misunderstood, thoughtful, but alcoholic Lex favored by *Smallville* fans of slash and het alike, many of whom have transformed Lex into a redemptive figure, someone who, like Draco, has lost his way. In such a transformation, varying levels of generic and fantextual codes are brought into play, ranging from broader cultural generic constructs like teen romance and redemption narratives to fan-specific generic constructs like *domesticfic.*

But what of the tools used to create and share fan texts? Fan authors use a range of technologies, interfaces, and forms in their creative authorship, from the word-processing program Microsoft Word to write fan fiction, to Photoshop to create icons and manipulated figures, to pen, paper, and a digital camera to capture hand-drawn illustrations. In so doing, the original canon/fantext relationship is now compounded not only by the broader structures of genre but also by the varying technologies, software, and interfaces used by the fan author. Of course, restrictions in terms of medium existed before the digital age; the limitations of communication through writing rather than images, for example, has always been at issue for fans writing about nonliterary media texts such as television series and movies. Similarly, the VCR presented its own set of technological limitations as rudimentary video-making technology.[4] In fact, one could argue that such limitations of technology and interface were (and are) as crucial to the specific dynamics of fan creativity as the stimulating restrictions of canon.

In the introduction to this volume, Kristina Busse and Karen Hellekson note the importance of "the creation of free, easy-to-use online tools that permit easy authoring of beautiful and accessible sites with little technical expertise" (16). At this moment, fans creating and sharing fan art and fiction online have the extensive layers of limitations and possibilities offered by a range of technologies and software — personal Web page creation tools, Photoshop, Premiere, digital games that lend themselves to fannish use such as *The Sims,* and online community forums such as LJ, FanForum.com, TelevisionWithoutPity.com, and EzBoard.com. The interplay between the limitations and possibilities of varying interfaces and the limitations and possibilities of the fan authors' relationship to canon and fantextual expectations intersect in the creation of online fan texts and fannish modes of storytelling. Superimposed on this synthesis, we have the fluctuating structures of generic discourse, which provide a shifting yet culturally shared set of possibilities and limitations. Together, all three lenses focus the process of fantextual creation.

Character Diary Networks as Storytelling

As Francesca Coppa notes in her "Brief History of Media Fandom" (this volume), over the past few years, online journaling sites such as LJ and JournalFen.net have become increasingly central forums for fan engagement and have all but replaced older forms of interactions for large parts of many fandoms. LJ facilitates the construction not only of personal journals but also of communities that link together participants, thus creating shared personal spaces. Although some use LJ primarily as a space to keep a traditional diary of their daily experiences or to stay in touch with friends and family, others use it pseudonymously to participate in virtual communities. Fan communities in particular have found many uses for the LJ interface, and LJ has in turn changed and shaped forms of fannish storytelling and creativity. Authors post stories as works in progress in their journals and receive ongoing feedback from readers through LJ's commenting system, which in turn may be incorporated into the writing process. Communities for fan fiction written in specific alternate universes or with specific themes or rules, such as drabbles (comprising exactly one hundred words), flourish in the LJ framework.[5] The narrative mode I'm concerned with here is the diary-based multiauthored fan fiction network.

Busse and Hellekson's introduction to this volume provides an overview of terms used in the LJ blogsphere, but let me quickly run down the features of the software relevant to my argument. LJ offers a space for a user to post her own diary entries and, if she chooses to post her journal publicly or semipublicly, to engage in conversation with her readers by using the comments function. Journals appear in chronological order of posting on one's *friendslist*. Clearly the use of the term *friend* to name the relationship between different LJ users suggests a social networking dimension to the LJ experience; other journal sites, such as Diaryland and Blogger, do not emphasize this to the same extent. This social networking facilitates the interpersonal engagement necessary for the process of group authoring. Such social dimensions of the LJ interface also translate into the depiction of fictional social networks in online fictional journal communities.[6]

Online diary-based fan fiction uses LJ to create first-person fragmented narratives told in many voices and written by many authors. These journal networks create unfolding, serial, expansive universes where fannish narratives play out. One might at first primarily associate such communities with role-playing games (RPGs), which have evolved from a Dungeons and Dragons gaming heritage to encompass a wide scope of computer-based and live-action interactive gaming.[7] Certainly some participants do think of these projects as specific incarnations of RPGs, but others contest such labeling. They prefer to call their process of storytelling *interactive fiction.* However, online diary-based fictional journaling communities, whether they call themselves RPGs or not, also owe much of what they are to traditions of fan fiction — in concerns, theme, narrative structure, and creative process. The dynamics of group or shared writing has a long history in fan fiction, including feedback, round robins, fiction author partnerships, shared alternate universes, and team-written alternate television seasons or virtual seasons. LJ diary-based fictions thus merge practices of fannish role playing with traditions of fan fiction cowriting, creating a synthesis that is part game, part narrative, with the boundary between game and story blurry at best.

Online diary/journal-based networks vary greatly from project to project, but virtually all function as unfolding fiction. Some are intended to be followed only by the writers themselves; others are followed by a broad audience of readers. Several such communities exist for *Harry Potter,* as do countless RPGs for a wide range of media sources, including *Buffy the Vampire Slayer, Angel, Smallville,* and *The Lord of the Rings.* Each of these diary-based fictions or RPGs is quite specific in its mode of storytelling and in its use of chosen interface. Within LJ, some RPG fiction projects use the LJ interface to provide an opportunity for readers to interact with the characters; others do not make use of the comments function, or use comments only for interaction between characters, with separate communities set up for readers to comment on the unfolding narrative.

The interface of LJ contributes to readers' experience of these narratives as unfolding, serial, and everyday. Interested readers can follow the narrative by "friending" Harry, Draco, Hermione, and even Narcissa. Each character's periodic journal posting then appears on one's friendslist, alongside personal narratives of the nonfictional sort, as well as quizzes, fan reviews, fan art, and other more traditional installments of fan fiction. In fact, characters sometimes post the quizzes and memes that are informally circulating in LJ communities, thus further confusing the boundary between the fictional and nonfictional: the diaries appear exactly as if a person, not a narrative construct, were posting. Depending on the RPG, readers may also be able to interact with the characters as they do with the other LJ users on their friendslist, giving them support and advice or chastising them for self-destructive behavior. Sometimes they may receive comments from the characters, thus interacting with fictional characters as if they were other LJ users. Alternatively, a reader coming upon an RPG fiction with an established history can read all the previous posts by moving through the archive, which organizes posts and comments by date. Although this removes the narrative from its nonfictional LJ counterparts, it still frames the narrative within real time, and the constant links to other journals contextualize each thread within the whole of the RPG fictional network, if not the whole of LJ.

The Draco example with which I opened this essay is a part of an RPG fiction that takes advantage of LJ's capacity for capturing and communicating the periodic unfolding of everyday experience. Readers of this RPG follow the evolving interactions between Harry, Draco, and their family and friends as they post, comment, and engage in conversation on their LJs. The added dimension of hyperlinks leading to images related to the narrative, as well as to other characters' LJs, creates a sense of verisimilitude, providing details that function to emulate the expansiveness of real-life experience. Readers who have Harry and Draco on their friendslist can also watch as their conversations (or, as often is the case, arguments) unfold in the comments after each post, moving from no comments to more than two hundred comments over the course of a few hours across multiple threads. These threads explore character depth, showcase Harry and Draco's romantic relationship, and advance the plot. They do so at times nonlinearly; plot elements unfold within one journal in multiple threads, or in multiple journals, extending even beyond both Harry and Draco's journal into Blaise's, Snape's, or Ron's. Within this context, even the role of magic itself becomes infused with the everyday and the domestic: the major narrative thrust of this RPG includes the marriage of Draco and Harry, followed by Draco's magically enabled pregnancy and the birth and growth of their daughter.

In this instance, we can see clearly how canon, fantext, genre, and interface come together in the narrativization of Draco's experiences of pregnancy. The daily nature of LJ interweaves mundane concerns with the fantasy inherent to *Harry Potter* canon, with fantasy used to explore the everyday. Not only do Draco and Harry's magically enhanced life narratives appear on one's friendslist alongside other, nonfictional, journal entries, but also the magical elements of Draco and Harry's life instigate real-life concerns connected to pregnancy and child rearing, such as decorating a nursery and hearing a baby's heartbeat for the first time. The following excerpt exemplifies this concern with the everyday, the patterns of daily posting, and the emotional content of the narrative being told. The use of the LJ mood listing to signify Draco's current emotional state at the time of posting (he specifies his mood as "lonely") indicates how the emotion and experience centered cultural uses of the LJ interface shape the nature of Draco's narrative.

Current mood: lonely

Update, of sorts.

I feel rather foolish bothering with this "updating" business, as I've no business of any sort to report. I simply want communication. I'm lonely. And this is tedious. Someone leave me a note before I go mad.

While I wait, I suppose I should catalogue my day in full, for anyone who may care.

I woke promptly at one o'clock in the afternoon, vomited into the dustbin, and staggered to the bath, where I cat-napped for some time, and returned to bed to suffer the heat in semi-comfort. However, this quickly proved boring [Dracolicious, LJ, July 18, 2003].

In this entry, Draco narrates the events of his day, even as he insists he has "no business of any sort" to report — the result of limitations incurred because of his pregnancy. This recounting of the everyday experience of pregnancy uses the LJ interface, with its emphasis on transitory emotional states and the periodic posting of everyday experience, to convey the serial experience of pregnancy.

The role of genre here is evident; in addition to the romance and adolescent angst affiliated with teen generic discourse, we also have the fan-specific generic construct of the domesticfic, as well as the domestic possibilities inherent in the fantastic element of male pregnancy (in fan terms, an *Mpreg*), a generic trope that cuts across fandoms and that raises complex issues of gender, identity, and experience.[8] More broadly, we can see the fantastic elements of the situation as enhancing the possibilities of realism inherent in the cultural uses of the LJ interface, with realist social issues evoked through metaphor. Hyperbolic epic narratives (the magical birth of a daughter to Harry and Draco) play out through the intervention of fantasy and magic, but they produce everyday concerns such as Draco's worry about gaining weight with the pregnancy, which he communicates in the daily, interpersonal context of LJ.

The inclusion of fantasy in this RPG enables a magical yet domestic coming-of-age narrative, and with it an extensive exploration of character depth, as we see Harry and Draco struggle to become fathers and adults. The extended serial narrative created out of the combination of (and interplay between) character journals facilitates the daily development of characters and relationships, and the expansive comments allow for less linear character exploration. In this way, the various cultural uses of the LJ interface intersect with fannish traditions intertwining domesticity and fantasy as well as with the fannish focus on character development. As a result, through the interplay of generic discourse, fantext, and the LJ interface, the narrative created by this RPG explores and expands on already established fannish foci.

Expansive Domesticity:
The Sims *as Fannish Storytelling*

To further elucidate the relationship between canon, fantext, genre, and interface, I turn my attention next to a significantly different interface: the popular cross-platform video game, *The Sims. Sims* players create characters and guide or micromanage their lives. Whereas some players approach *The Sims* as a strategy game, it lends itself to the creation of narrative and the telling of that narrative.[9] Some players do play *The Sims* as a linear game with a goal, if not an end point, and certainly many strategy guides have been written from this viewpoint. But it almost seems as if such a use of *The Sims* is working against its implicit design. Indeed, *Sims* creator Will Wright has called *The Sims* a sandbox game rather than a game with a singular goal or way to win.[10] In fact, the newer version of the game, *The Sims 2 (TS2)*, features a category called storytelling, which facilitates the capturing, ordering, and textual narrativizing of *Sims* images. Like LJ, *The Sims* is a home well fit for expansive fannish imaginings.

Fans have put both versions of *The Sims* to use, creating fannish universes and characters and playing out fannish narratives. The differences between the two versions of the program have led to varying types of fannish play and narrative construction. Both versions encourage the creation of unique characters. The first edition of *The Sims* enables characters to be created from photographs of people, thus lending itself to media fandoms—that is, a player can use the face of an actor in the creation of a sim avatar, also known as a sim skin. *TS2* skins are not based from photographs, and therefore a realistic look is more difficult to attain. However, the game provides the tools to create a nuanced, if not realistic, avatar, as one can choose from a vast selection of facial features and wardrobe. Because of this, *TS2* lends itself to literary fandoms where the characters exist visually only in the imagination of the reader, and it also encourages the creation of fantextual versions of televisual and cinematic fan-favored characters who may not look exactly like the canon incarnation on whom they are based.

Because *The Sims* doesn't actually depict the workplace, many of the narratives created in both editions are domestic, with the majority of character interactions taking place within the home. In this way, the fan generic category of domesticfic, with its concern with the everyday and the familial, finds a good fit in *The Sims,* just as it did within LJ. Although in the first edition of *The Sims* the players created characters as either children or adults, with children staying permanently young, in the newly released *TS2,* avatars age from birth to death and are connected to one another through extensive family trees. This new focus on aging characters and family relationships to some degree shapes the nature of the narratives created by *Sims* players, so that many fan stories are devoted to creating networks of families and documenting their developing relationships. As with the minutiae of daily lives played out in LJ, here too is a concern with the serial and the everyday, the familial and the communal. And while *TS2* has essentially turned on the sands of time, rather than trading in a sense of expansiveness for a linear single narrative, the emphasis on multiple families and generations transforms *Sims* family narratives into something we could almost see as navigable space in the form of the family tree. Thus, *TS2* molds to fannish concerns in a variety of ways.[11]

The first expansion pack for *The Sims 2*, entitled "University," depicts university life, creating a new age category, "young adult," and introducing new spaces such as the dorms, the cafeteria, and the frat house. This plays into fannish imagination and already existing fannish categories, as what fans refer to as *collegefic* can now be depicted through *The Sims*. *Sims* fan stories now often draw on adolescent generic themes such as leaving home, making college friends, joining a fraternity or sorority, and graduating. Along the same lines, *TS2* includes an element that fits all too well into the *Smallville* slash fantext: men can become pregnant when abducted by aliens, which has, perhaps unsurprisingly, led to a profusion of abducted and then pregnant Kent-Luthor domestic partners.

But creating a fannish world in *The Sims* is only the first step. The telling of the story engages with yet another level of interface. *TS2* interface provides one mode of storytelling, as I mentioned; one can share images at the official site for *TS2*, taking from the infinite database of possible snapshots to create a smaller selection of images, out of which one then creates a narrative with the addition of text. However, for many reasons (not least of which is the presence of already existing fan-created spaces for shared *Sims* storytelling, combined with the lack of ability to community-build within the design of the official *TS2* "story exchange"), *Harry Potter* fan communities, and fan communities in general, rarely use *The Sims'* official site, but instead use LJ to share their stories. Fans have set up journals and communities to share their fannish *Sims* narratives. These communities define themselves in different ways in relation to canon, fantext, and the projects of fan fiction. One LJ community dedicated to the representation of literary sims posits as its central rule that participants need to have created *The Sims* skins themselves, thus valuing a sense of authorship and individuality in interpretation of canon text. Another community created for the posting of *Harry Potter* sims has no such rule, stating only that one does not need to replicate the film actors in one's imagining of the characters, thus emphasizing the expansiveness of fan imagination rather than the limitations of canon, specifically overthrowing any reign of the *Harry Potter* films as canonical for characters' physical appearances.

What types of narratives are told within these spaces? How do they position themselves in relation to canon and to their specific new media context? How do the various intervening interfaces (of *The Sims* and LJ) affect the nature of the story being told? As one might suspect, many *Sims* fan narratives focus on family and domesticity. For example, one story with a large readership documents the "Marauders" generation, depicting the adolescence of Harry's parents and their friends Sirius Black and Remus Lupin. With the introduction of the "University" expansion pack, the Marauders went to college; Sirius and Remus formed a college band and rehearsed in their dorm's common area. Thus, the *TS2* interface guides the narratives that are told, but at the same time, the story draws extensively on various fantextual foci. Similarly, *Smallville* slash *Sims* stories tend to focus on domesticfic, with Clark and Lex raising little green babies, learning how to change their diapers, and otherwise engaging in the trials of parenthood as envisioned by *TS2.*

Other *Sims* authors push more at the limitations of *TS2,* as in one user's re-creation of the first book of *Harry Potter,* chapter by chapter, through *The Sims.* Although from a fan fiction perspective such a canonical recreation might seem predictable, from a *Sims* authorship perspective, this task is both impressive and inventive. This specific re-creation of the *Harry Potter* narrative closely follows the book's storyline and its structure: it re-creates the book's very chapter breakdown. Sections of the book that can't be represented by the game (such as a snake speaking to Harry in snake language, called Parseltongue) are filled in through text rather than image—what we could perhaps think of as fans scribbling in the margins of their own text, although in this case, the scribbling is necessary to re-create canon as closely as possible given the limitations of *The Sims.*[12]

However, this *Sims* author also includes what she calls outtakes, which show things that her *Harry Potter* sims did on their own while she was trying to re-create the *Harry Potter* canon narrative. That is, while she was attempting to set up her careful re-creation, her sims did things that didn't fit in the careful canonical narrative she was creating, and she recorded these moments. The humor of these outtakes is found when sims do something out of character—for example, the normally dour and scary Professor Snape dances in front of his class. Such an instance creates a sense of narrative spontaneity that is amusing precisely in its absurd relation to canon. However, humor is also consistently born when the sims themselves (or, rather, the unpredictable gameplay as carried out through the actions of the sims characters) seem to re-create fantextual patterns rather than simply straying from canon. So when Harry and Draco spontaneously hug rather than fight, their actions affirm a fantextual slash vision of the characters and the sense that the fantextual characters have lives of their own — lives that may even override canon.

Mia Consalvo (2003) investigates how the quality of emergent gameplay in the first version of *The Sims* creates an awareness of the possibility of queerness as it disassociates sexuality from identity, making sexuality an act rather than a self-defining (or sim-defining) factor. This possible queerness of *The Sims* through the unpredictability of its gameplay certainly facilitates the easy rendering of slash narratives. But more generally, *The Sims'* quality of unpredictability contributes to a perception of the independent existence of *Sims*-created characters beyond the original source text, and beyond even the specific captured narrative being told through *Sims* images. As Sara Gwenllian Jones (2000) and Roberta E. Pearson (2003) have pointed out, this sense of character depth is of vital importance to fannish engagement. In this way, *The Sims* beautifully fills fannish concerns through its creation of characters who seem to have lives of their own.

In LJ-based RPG fan fiction, the LJ interface itself contributes to a perception of verisimilitude, encouraging daily posting in real time, thus creating a sense of the expansive, everyday existence of fictional characters. In contrast, in the case of fannish storytelling through *The Sims,* authors use LJ to narrate and share their fannish interpretations of *Sims* gameplay and images, with verisimilitude coming more from *The Sims* than LJ. *Sims*-created, LJ-shared fannish narratives are made of two layers: the images, and the author's commentaries explaining and narrativizing those images. Through this interplay, another character comes to the fore: *The Sims* author, who comments on, interprets, and sets the tone for the unfolding *Sim*-based narrative. The database of possible *Sims* images functions as an expansive palette onto which the *Sims* author can dip her brush, but at the same time, it also provides the type of restrictions and specific limitations against which fannish creativity blossoms. We can see this fruitful tension play out at the micro level in the dialogue between a *Sims* image and the author's textual narration.

Conclusion

Media phenomena around which fandoms thrive often center on media texts that mix genres and that incorporate fantasy. Jones (2002) points to the prominence of the fantastic as a reason why programs like

Xena and *Buffy* are often slashed, suggesting that fantasy increases the possibilities of representations of otherness. Although I would argue here that the possibilities of both fantasy and queerness can instead lead to representations of the everyday and domesticity, the understanding that fantasy contributes new possibilities of character development and interrelationships remains sound. Similarly, as I mentioned before, Pearson (2003) speaks of the expansiveness of cult television metatexts, arguing that the fantastic possibilities of cult television contribute to fannish nonlinear exploration of character. From this perspective, we can see how both LJ and *The Sims* serve as welcome homes for new articulations of fannish concerns. Both are similarly expansive in nature, well suited to the exploration of fannish themes and to the affirmation of a sense of fully developed characters, and yet at the same time replete with the types of challenges and restrictions within which fannish play flourishes.

Just as Draco initially encountered difficulties programming his PDA but soon found a way to inscribe what he perceived as an expression of identity through the technological options available, so fan authors encounter and then use the interface of LJ to express a creative and expansive vision of the fictional characters with whom they are engaged. Similarly, through *The Sims,* fans create fannish universes in which, as a result of the unpredictability of gameplay, the characters seem to have full existences, enabled by — but not fully controlled by — *The Sims* player/author. In turn, *Sims* authors inscribe narratives by capturing, reorganizing, and building on these *Sims*-created images. These *Sims* narratives are shaped by the foci, limitations, and possibilities of *The Sims,* just as they draw on canonical, fantextual, and generic structures. Thus in both cases fans draw on and are guided by each interface to create new narrative forms and complex imaginative universes that engage and expand on already existing fannish concerns.

Notes

1. On new media's concern with technology and interface, see Manovich (2001). Jenkins's *Textual Poachers* (1992) is the seminal work in fan studies focusing on fans as media users. See the general bibliography in this volume for contemporary work from this approach. For work on genre as discourse, see Mittell (2004); and Naremore (1998).

2. I draw on a range of online fan texts. I do not give specific URL references to LJ spaces out of consideration for the maintenance of these spaces as fan spaces and the privacy of the participants. For a discussion of methodological issues involved in studying online communities, see King (1996) and Boehlefeld (1996).

3. Alternative universes are but one of many ways in which authors play with and at times reject various levels of canon; another example would be the recasting of

Harry Potter's Draco as actor Boyd Holbrook by a subcommunity of fans who reject the *Harry Potter* films as canon, favoring the casting of Holbrook because he suits their fan-textual vision of Draco better than Tom Felton, the actor cast in the film.

   4. See Jenkins (1992, 223–49) on fan vids made with VCRs.

   5. In addition, LJ uses open-code software, and other, similar sites have sprung up in its wake, such as GreatestJournal.com and JournalFen.net. The latter is specifically envisioned as a space for fans and for journal-based role-playing games.

   6. Dana Boyd's (2004) study of Friendster provides a similar analysis of how an interface encourages and/or discourages social networking among individual users.

   7. Lancaster (2001) considers fan role-playing games as performance; and Mackay (2001) explores the role of performance in face-to-face fantasy role-playing games.

   8. The fantasy component of the story plays a crucial function here in terms of gender, placing the voice of the female experience of pregnancy into the male subject. Fan fiction's female authorship — specifically the fact that mostly straight-identified women write slash — has been the subject of much comment by scholars of fandom and by fan authors themselves. In the case of Dracolicious, we have a female experience — pregnancy — being written onto a male body, by way of an interface that encourages a soap opera–like seriality, with no evident narrativewide closure, as the emergent nature of LJ suggests no end to this narrative of experience. Modleski's (1982) much-contested work on soap operas suggests that the serial structure of soap operas mirrors female experience; and Mumford (1995) argues that soaps' excessive closing gestures have ideological implications. The ideological implications of this RPG may come precisely from the combination of form, theme, and gendered subjectivity. Although such an analysis is beyond the scope of this essay, this is exactly the type of work that a methodology combining fan studies with genre and new media studies should pursue.

   9. The question of the role of narrative in games has been much debated. Some game theorists, such as Frasca (2003), have argued against the focus on narrative in the study of games, proposing instead that we consider games as "simulation." Whether or not we consider games themselves as narrative, we can understand each instance of gameplay in *The Sims* as constructing a narrative that the player to some degree both follows and authors. Even more so, we can understand fannish reconstructions and reformulations of gameplay through screencaps and text/intertitles as a form of story-telling, in which the player becomes author to an audience of fellow fans. As such, these *Sims*-based fan stories come close to Cassell's (1999) vision for a future of games as interactive storytelling. See also Jenkins (2004) for an overview of these debates on ludology versus narratology and for a discussion of the narrative possibilities in *The Sims*. For more on the relationship between story and game, see also Wardrip-Fruin and Harrigan (2004).

   10. For a discussion of *The Sims* as sandbox game, see an interview with Will Wright, "Will Wright Speaks Simlish" (http://pc.gamespy.com/pc/the-sims-2/591767 p7.html, accessed June 1, 2006).

   11. See Jenkins (2002) on *Sims* fan storytelling as part of a new participatory culture that redefines the relationship between media consumers and media producers. Also see Mia Consalvo's (2003) work on queerness as an emergent quality in *The Sims*.

   12. An expansion pack for the first edition of *The Sims*, "Making Magic," enabled the easy representation of magic, as the name suggests. However, even before the release of the expansion pack, *Sims* users had made objects such as flying brooms for use in *Harry Potter* sims gameplay. Although to date *TS2* has no such magic-oriented expansion pack, this does not stop fans from creating a representation of the *Harry Potter* Simsverse that incorporates magic; they only need to be creative in how they represent it. Sometimes they fill in blanks with words in order to communicate what *Sims* images cannot represent.

References

Boehlefeld, Sharon Polancic. 1996. Doing the right thing: Ethical cyberspace research. *Information Society* 12:141–52.

Boyd, Dana. 2004. Friendster and publicly articulated social networks. Presented at the Conference on Human Factors and Computing Systems (CHI 2204), Vienna, ACM, April 24–29.

Cassell, Justine. 1999. Storytelling as a nexus of change in the relationship between gender and technology: A feminist approach to software design. In *From Barbie to Mortal Kombat: Gender and computer games,* ed. Justine Cassell and Henry Jenkins, 298–322. Cambridge, MA: MIT Press.

Consalvo, Mia. 2003. It's a queer world after all: Studying *The Sims* and sexuality. Glaad Center for the Study of Media and Society, http://www.glaad.org/programs/csms/papers.php (accessed June 1, 2006).

Frasca, Gonzalo. 2003. Simulation versus narrative: Introduction to ludology. In *The video game theory reader,* ed. Mark J. P. Wolf and Bernard Perron. New York: Routledge, 221–34.

Jenkins, Henry. 1992. *Textual poachers: Television fans and participatory culture.* New York: Routledge.

_____. 2002. Interactive audiences: The "collective intelligence" of media fans. *The new media book,* ed. Dan Harries, 157–70. London: British Film Institute.

_____. 2004. Game design as narrative architecture. In *First person: New media as story, performance, game,* ed. Noah Wardrip-Fruin and Pat Harrigan, 118–30. Cambridge, MA: MIT Press.

Jones, Sara Gwenllian. 2000. Starring Lucy Lawless? *Continuum* 14:9–22.

_____. 2002. The sex lives of cult television characters. *Screen* 43:79–90.

King, Storm. 1996. Researching Internet communities: Proposed ethical guidelines for the reporting of results. *Information Society* 12:119–27.

Lancaster, Kurt. 2001. *Interacting with "Babylon 5."* Austin: Univ. of Texas Press.

Mackay, Daniel. 2001. *The fantasy role-playing game.* Jefferson, NC: McFarland.

Manovich, Lev. 2001. *Language of new media.* Cambridge, MA: MIT Press.

Mittell, Jason. 2004. *Genre and television: From cop shows to cartoons in American culture.* New York: Routledge.

Modleski, Tania. 1982. *Loving with a vengeance.* New York: Methuen.

Mumford, Laura. 1995. *Love and ideology in the afternoon.* Bloomington: Indiana Univ. Press.

Naremore, James. 1998. *More than night: Film noir in its contexts.* Berkeley: Univ. of California Press.

Pearson, Roberta E. 2003. Kings of infinite space: Cult television characters and narrative possibilities. *Scope* (August). http://www.nottingham.ac.uk/film/journal/articles/kings-of-infinite-space.htm (accessed June 1, 2006).

Wardrip-Fruin, Noah, and Pat Harrigan, eds. 2004. *First person: New media as story, performance, and game.* Cambridge, MA: MIT Press.

12. From Shooting Monsters to Shooting Movies
Machinima and the Transformative Play of Video Game Fan Culture
Robert Jones

ABSTRACT.—Machinima represents one of the most important out-growths of video game fan culture. Through the manipulation of video game engines (the architectural code of a video game), players take control of the characters and use them to create short animated films within the game's 3D virtual environment. These films are then distributed and shared over the Internet. Creators of machinima films engage in trans-formative play, an act of altering the rules and structures of designated play spaces to suit their individual needs. The video game possesses unique qualities that separate it from traditional forms of media. The video game's interactive nature creates a different relationship between consumers and producers, which requires the reconsideration of previ-ous theories of fan cultures that were based on traditionally passive rela-tionships to media (such as film and TV). Because gamers are capable of fundamentally manipulating the medium of the video game in ways that other fans of traditional media cannot, notions of fan "resistance" must be reexamined within this new context. Moreover, transformative play (a term borrowed from game design theory) offers new ways of understanding consumer-producer relationships.

Introduction

What is machinima? Is it filmmaking? Animation? Gaming? Or just the latest form of fan-produced media that owes its roots to fan fiction and resembles the more recent fan films? As one of new media's more recent manifestations— some might even say mutations— machinima poses some interesting questions regarding our understanding of the medium of the video game and our conceptualization of its fans. The term itself is a portmanteau of *machine* and *cinema*— some say *animation* as well — that designates "animated filmmaking within a real-time 3D environment" (Marino 2004, 1). Although much of the popular discourse on this burgeoning group of gaming/filmmaking fans has been enthusiastic, the understanding of what it is has not found much consensus. Mirapaul (2002, E2) refers to it as "animation as improvised performance." Bloom (2002, 6) calls it "a cross between Fritz Lang and anime." And Azhar (2003, 21) says, "The format is still experimental and reflects its gaming roots. Science-fiction plots with action and overly excitable camera work seem commonplace."

Despite machinima's ambiguous status as a new medium, the fans who enjoy making it and watching it know precisely what it means to them. Most would agree that it is a form of filmmaking; more specifically, it is a form of 3D animation. At its center, machinima relies on the manipulation of video game engines, or the core software that allows developers to construct the characters and the environments, as well as to determine the rules that govern how characters and environments interact. These engines also enable players to control those characters on the screen. Through the manipulation of these engines, video game fans can create animated films without any animation skills (see Busse and Hellekson's introduction to this volume for a sketch of fans' use of technology to fannish ends). After adding music and voice-overs for the characters, the result is an animated film that usually — although not always— resembles the game used to create it.

The production of these machinima films by video game fans offers a new direction in the study of fan cultures, one aspect of which is the stark contrast in the gender difference between the producers of machinima and the producers of fan fiction. As documented by Coppa in "A Brief History of Media Fandom" (this volume), the history of media fandom has been largely populated by the production of texts by women. Although a full investigation into the nature of this gender divide exceeds the scope of this chapter, a tentative answer can be found in the literature on gender and video games. Many of the explanations for the gender divide among video game players draws from the developmental literature on gendered play spaces. Jenkins (1998) suggests a logical progression from E. Anthony Rotundo's notion of "boy culture" (outlined in *American Manhood*, 1993) as an escape from the domestic setting to the exploration made possible through video games. Cassell and Jenkins (1998) propose that lack of access to computer technology also plays a large part in the lack of participation on the part of women. However, Bryce and Rutter (2005, 302) contend that too much of the research on participation by girls and women in video games has "consistently taken a media effects or text-based research perspective that fails to interrogate the every day practices of being a 'computer gamer' or being excluded from being so." Moreover, Yates and Littleton (1999, 567) insist that focusing research on the lack of female gamers "ignores the voices of those women and girls who do engage with computer games." And although most of these studies draw from data suggesting that a majority of video games are played by boys and men, the most recent surveys released by the Entertainment Software Association state that girls and women account for 43 percent of all game players (http://www.theesa.com/facts/top_10_facts.php, accessed October 22, 2005).

So when we talk about machinima as a primarily male-dominated form of fandom, it is important to separate it from video game fandom. Because machinima began from the first-person shooter (FPS) genre (Bryce and Rutter 2002), known for being overrun with male players, it makes sense that the majority of machinima would come from men. In addition, the technical skills necessary to manipulate a video game engine in order to produce machinima also presents the same barrier to potential female producers of machinima as does the entry into male-dominated arenas of computer programming. Graner Ray (2004, 11) suggests that this is because women "are more comfortable working *with* machines rather than attempting to master them." This mastery over computers serves as a defining quality of hacker culture, which is a precursor to the fan culture of machinima. Therefore, the discrepancy between the large number of women who participate in fan fiction and the lack thereof in machinima can be explained by mere access alone. The skill set necessary to write fan fiction does not pose the same barriers as the technical skills needed to make machinima. However, the recent creation of user-friendly technologies has begun to change this (see Stein, this volume; http://www.sim-movies.com, accessed June 1, 2006).

In addition to the gender difference, machinima also makes us reconsider fandom within the age of new media, particularly in interactive media.

As an interactive medium, the video game requires the participation of the gamer. This disrupts the normal relationship between the media consumer and media producer. Although typical consumers of traditional media products have maintained this paradigm, fan cultures have sought to change this by becoming actively engaged in their own production of their favorite cultural products. Jenkins's crucial study, *Textual Poachers* (1992), refers to these as "participatory cultures" that engage in textual poaching for their own purposes. The participation on the behalf of the fan exceeds mere consumption and transforms the object of fandom; slash fan fiction, where the sexual orientation of characters is altered from straight to gay to suit the fan's needs, is perhaps one of the more common examples. It is important not to conflate this kind of fan participation with the interactivity of a video game. When players make choices within games, the rules and narratives within those games confine them. Although a level of authorial control exists for the player, it is not the same as participation exercised by an author of slash fiction. These choices constitute *play* within the system of the game, what Salen and Zimmerman (2004, 300) define as "the free movement within a more rigid structure." When players alter the game so that the game is different for others, they call this *transformative play*. Through the use of advanced skills, gamers can modify, or *mod*, a game to suit their needs (for example, removing the clothes of a character like Lara Croft), or they can use those skills to manipulate the game engine and create machinima. Both serve as instances of transformative play and can also be understood as forms of participatory culture.

I want to suggest that this model of transformative play, which explains how machinima came about, offers not just insight into the nature of the video game medium and its users, but also a new way of understanding more traditional fan cultures. If we assume that the typical consumption of old media like TV and film allows for a certain amount of play through interpretation, as Fiske (1989) suggests—a level of interpretation made possible through the polysemic nature of mass media texts—then the participatory exercise of fan fiction would be an act of *transformative play*. Video games, however, differ from traditional media in that they build this element of transformative play into their design. Through tracing the history of machinima and transformative play's role in that history, I hope to provide a useful explanation about consumer/producer relationships as the medium of the video game reconfigures them, thus extending the definition of fan culture. This analysis will, I hope, offer other scholars of fan cultures new ways to understand how power gets relocated when we talk about audiences of new media, such as video games, and how they differ from traditional audiences.

Demos, Mods, and Machinima

The history of machinima began in the late 1970s and early 1980s with the *demoscene* (Tasajärvi 2004; http://www.freax.hu, accessed June 1, 2006). Hackers on Commodore 64 and Amiga personal computers would "tag" software they had cracked with introductory sequences they called *intros.* So that those who used it would know who hacked it, hackers manipulated the code to produce visual effects containing their names at the beginning of the software. Hacker teams like Future Crew, Pulse, and Haujobb became increasingly competitive in these displays of technical prowess, to the extent that they would bypass hacking the software altogether and just create the intros. Because these intros served as a demonstration of a hacker's ability, they later became known as *demos,* and they spawned hacker communities solely dedicated to creating them. As the technology grew and visual graphics evolved, demos became more complex and garnered fan followings. Once 3D virtual environments became more advanced, teams made more elaborate demos; some even used the form to construct their own little narratives. These narratives were the first primitive machinima films in that they used virtual 3D space to construct their narratives; however, they differed in their construction. Although demos began to take the shape of short animations and music videos, akin to the machinima produced today, they were built by hackers from the code. Casual computer users could not create these texts; in fact, the driving force behind most of the hacker teams in the demoscene was the prospect of creating a demo that exceeded the abilities of all other hackers (Thomas 2002). These displays of digital dexterity marked the beginning of the performative quality of computing that would pave the way for gamers to show their stuff through demos.

As the demoscene continued, hackers became (among other things) new media artists; meanwhile, a small software company called id Software, founded by John Carmack and John Romero, began developing a game engine for a 3D FPS (Kushner 2003). *Wolfenstein 3D,* released in May 1992 and an update of the 2D original, proved to be a milestone in game development, offering a three-dimensional world for the player to navigate from the first-person perspective. Although FPS as a genre of video games dates as far back as the 1970s, id Software's update of *Wolfenstein* set the standard for how shooters look and play today (Galloway 2006). However, not satisfied with the "realism" of the game, Carmack and the id Software designers decided to develop a better engine. This new engine had a modular design so that gamers could edit and create their own levels, as well as fast networking capabilities for multiplayer gaming, and it featured the famous "deathmatch" mode that permitted competitions. In December 1993, id Software released *DOOM*. It changed the face of computer gaming: gamers could both *play* the game and *play with* the game's design:

> id Software didn't stop there, the team of innovators also made *DOOM*'s source code available to their fan base, encouraging would-be game designers to modify the game and create their own levels, or "mods." Fans were free to distribute their mods of the game, as long as the updates were offered free of charge to other enthusiasts. The mod community took off, giving the game seemingly eternal life on the Internet. In fact, id discovered many of their current employees and development partners based on mods that were created and distributed over the Internet [id Software 2005].

The ability to create these *mods* enthralled gamers on a new level and tapped into their hacker sensibility, enabling them to demonstrate their mastery of code as they had done previously, during the demoscene (Figure 12.1).

Mods reveal one of the unique qualities of the video game as a medium — one that separates it from traditional forms of audio/visual media. Although the primary function of a game may be to play through the levels as they are designed, in effect following the path provided by the designer the same way that readers read and filmgoers watch, the ability to freely play with the medium presents a challenge to previous notions of how audiences conventionally behave. The authorial shift that occurs between gamers and designers differentiates it from other traditional media and thus positions the video game as an important site of investigation into fan cultures. Gamers' freedom to *play with* and *repurpose*[1] the video game text through modification permitted as a direct result of the game's design evokes Jenkins's (1992) notion of textual poaching: it is an instance of a fan's altering — or in this case *modding* — the object of his obsession. The

two, however, diverge on two separate accounts. First, Jenkins's formulation of the textual poacher relies on a metaphor of resistance borrowed from De Certeau's (1984) model of consumer appropriation in which consumers use "tactics" as a

Fig. 12.1. *DOOM*, id Software (1993).

means of popular resistance to the stronger "strategies" used by producers. This resistance model of fan appropriation has since been problematized by a number of critics (Scodari 2003; Hills 2002; Abercrombie and Longurst 1998). Scodari in particular insists that "the very act of fans creatively laboring to adjust commercial texts to their interest is remarkable, but their particular adjustments or the motives behind them are not always resistive, despite the fact that much of the incipient work tends to frame such reservations as minor caveats rather than as emphatic claims" (113).

Because modding a video game like *DOOM* becomes part of the producer's intended use of the product — as indicated by the source code being made available to gamers— such activity hardly seems resistive. In fact, the case could be made that id Software's move to make the source code available was an ingenious marketing strategy that galvanized interest in their product. However, inviting gamers to alter the game does not mean that there is no resistance. Video game modding artists like Jodi (an acronym formed by joining the first names of the group's two members, Joan Hemskerk and Dirk Paesmans) perform acts of countergaming by creating mods that challenge the nature of the medium in a way that Galloway (2006) finds comparable to the counter cinema of French filmmaker Jean-Luc Godard (Bosama 2002; http://www.jodi.org, accessed October 22, 2005; Wollen 1982). So although resistance may not be inherent in the act of creating mods, the potential is certainly made available through the unique technologies of video games, particularly their open-source code design. The second and perhaps most profound way that mods diverge from Jenkins's textual poaching focuses on the means of production. For Jenkins and De Certeau, the power that producers hold over consumers derives from their exclusive access to the means of production. Therefore, the move that fans make from being consumers to producers (as is the case in fan fiction) represents an act of empowerment for Jenkins. Hills points out that this may not be the case for De Certeau: "It seems too rigid to deal helpfully with any blurring of consumer and consumer-as-producer identities. De Certeau denies the possibility that the consumer can occupy an official and production-based space (since spatialisation belongs to strategy, while 'tactical' consumption strays across the territory of the other without making any space or place of its own)" (2002, 39).

The degree to which fans empower themselves by becoming producers has since become highly contested within the literature on fan cultures (Hills [2002] provides a comprehensive discussion of these tensions). Rather than siding with any one position, I propose to complicate the matter even further. Because most literature on fan culture has focused on traditional media such as film and TV, the power that fans maintain over their chosen media products seems marginal at best. Fan fiction certainly offers a creative outlet to those looking to expand and explore the narratives of their favorite films and TV shows. Fan films take this creative exploration even further in that these new narratives try to replicate the production as an audiovisual medium (Jenkins 2003). Nevertheless, in both cases, the original medium stays intact. Within video games, the means of production are placed within the hands of the consumer because as software, video games function as both tool and product. So when players create mods for *DOOM*, they do not just alter their own experience of the medium; they also potentially alter the experience of others—mods for *DOOM*, as well as many other games, are available throughout the Internet (for example, http://planetdoom.gamespy.com, accessed June 1, 2006). Armed with the actual means of production — in the case of *DOOM*, the source code that created it — players become producers in a way that is arguably far more empowered than that of fanfic writers or fan film producers (Postigo 2003; Schleiner 2005).

Although mods complicate how we understand consumers and producers within the context of fan research — and this is an area that requires further investigation — they are only part of the story of machinima. The *DOOM* game engine offers far more than just the ability to mod the game's design. More instrumental to the development of machinima is the capacity to record gameplay. This provides an opportunity for seasoned gamers to capture their runs through the various levels of the 3D virtual world and save their gameplay as files that can be reviewed. These demo movies,[2] known as *speedruns,* function as highlight reels among the game's fan base. Because the game's networking capabilities allow for multiplayer play, competitive play is fierce, and the ability to record these "deathmatches" fuels competition further. Matches carry more than just boasting rights against defeated opponents; they are instances of true performance that engender unprecedented spectatorship and that live on in recorded form. As is the case with most FPSs, *DOOM* requires high levels of manual dexterity and often requires extensive practice. Speedruns of exceptional players offer newcomers insight into the tricks of the game. Demo movies of top players also elevate their status within the gaming community; this eventually led to the formation of the *DOOM* Honorific Title (DHT) Program in 1994. The DHT, created to determine the best *DOOM* players by distributing their demos (also called LMPs, named after Little Movie Processing, the format for recording gameplay) online, offers even more reason for gamers to record their gameplay:

The DOOM Honorific Titles, based on LMP recording with an authentication mechanism, are the means by which good players can objectively prove to the world that they are as good as they claim. The DHT system also has the beneficial side effect of promoting the production of amazing LMPs— if you want to see some superior DOOM action, turn to the ever-growing repository of DHT exam files [http://www.cl.cam.ac.uk/~fms27/dht/dht5/ #dht5, accessed June 1, 2006].

The creation of the DHT demonstrates the type of cultural exchange that the *DOOM* software invokes as a unique model of gaming. Along with the trading of mods that perpetuates the game's life beyond the initial release, these demo movies foster what Manovich (2001) calls a cultural economy. Implementing De Certeau's (1984) notion of "strategies" and "tactics," Manovich explicates the relationship between the *DOOM* fans and the game's designers: "The producers define the basic structure of an object and release a few examples as well as tools to allow the consumer to build their own version, to be shared with other consumers" (245). Demo movies are seen as a currency within these fan communities: greater status is awarded to gamers who perform the most amazing runs. This interactive exchange permitted innovations to quickly develop. This led to the evolution of the game and how it was played, followed by the growth of mods, and eventually to the transformation of what constituted the medium through the emergence of *DOOM* demo movies. The moment when gamers began recording their play is crucially important — not just for history of machinima, but also for the medium of the video game. Although it is easy to reduce the definition of what a video game is to mere software, the nature of the video game as a medium is far more complex. Because of its interactive quality, the end product becomes a variable outcome, one that embodies performance on par with theater (see Coppa, "Writing Bodies in Space," this volume).

Within gaming communities — and particularly the competitive tournaments for which *DOOM* has become famous — this sort of spectatorship reveals the ephemeral quality of this end product. Before the ability to record gameplay, gaming spectators had to be in the room to witness these performances. The demo movies, and later machinima, mark a distinct shift in this mode of spectatorship. Players transformed from mere players into the producers of tangible media: they used the game not just as a medium but also as a tool. Manovich (2001, 258) is particularly sensitive to this quality of not just video games but new media in general: "In the case of new media, we should look not only at the finished objects but first of all at the software tools, their organization and default settings. This is particularly important because in new media the relation between production tools and media objects is one of continuity; in fact, it is often hard to establish the boundary between them." If we understand the video game not merely as a medium of consumption but also as a means of production, the communities it prompted — demoscene, mods, machinima — seem inevitable.

Although the release of *DOOM* set the stage for what would become machinima, the demos that were produced by the game's record function were all in first person. This perspective seemed natural to gamers: it was the vantage point they had grown accustomed to as they navigated three-dimensional space. However, although such first-person navigation seemed natural to players— Manovich (2001) suggests that the process of navigating space is a defining characteristic of new media — it did not adhere to the viewing expectations of the watchers. In his chapter on "Gamic Vision," Galloway (2006) traces the history of the first-person perspective in film, what he identifies as the "subjective shot," citing early examples like *The Lady in the Lake* (1946) and *Dark Passage* (1947). He goes on to say: "Further, more often than not, this type of shot is used to show the vision of criminals, monsters or killer machines. This analysis shows that the merging of camera and character in the subjective shot is more successful if the character in question is marked as computerized in some way" (12). So although the subjective shot used in FPSs like *DOOM* felt natural as a mediated experience of navigation for the player, the cultural viewing habits as perpetuated through traditional Hollywood cinema, which relies on third-person perspective , required one last modification in order for them to become something that could be watched rather than played. The demo movies made famous in the *DOOM* community were shot from the perspective of the player; therefore, seeing as a shooter also meant seeing as a camera. Once gamers realized that they could use their character purely as the camera within the 3D virtual environment, capturing the images of other players from the more traditional third-person perspective, machinima was born. A group of gamer-hackers known as The Rangers was the first to do this, following the release of id Software's next big contribution to machinima history: *Quake.*

The Rangers were the first group to take advantage of the many improvements id Software had made to the *DOOM* game engine. *Quake* was the richest 3D virtual environment to date; it also offered the capacity to set up client-server networking, thus enabling multiplayer gameplay over the Internet. Before id Software released production tools that enabled modifications for players, such as *QuakeC* and *QuakeEd*, The Rangers created their own hacks to allow them to make a demo captured from the perspective of traditional Hollywood cinema (Figure 12.2). The result was the now-famous "Diary of a Camper." According to Paul Marino (2004), this was the first machinima film:

The Rangers choreographed the players as actors, hitting their marks while another player acted as the camera, recording the actors as the scene progressed. The actor playing also typed in dialogue that appeared in the recording. (This is also a feature of the multiplayer game — the ability to send text messages to the players that appear on screen.) Once completed, the demo served as the very first Machinima film — a narrative story told within the game space [6].

This important shift from the first-person perspective of a *player* to what essentially becomes the first-person perspective of a *director,* shooting and recording the action of other players, reflects the transition from the demo movie as a cultural product designed to broadcast a player's gaming prowess to a mediated form of storytelling. These narratives, which were originally referred to as "*Quake* movies" before becoming machinima, were acts of performance and displays of technical skill. But the move to storytelling rather than showing off reassigns the role that spectatorship plays within gaming communities. The *DOOM* speedruns were esoteric, competitive forms of media targeted specifically to the members of that community. Machinima offered a potential for expression that would appeal to an audience beyond the gaming communities. This attention to audience concerns (the move from first to third person and the addition of narrative) indicated a need to expand the gaming community. More importantly, machinima films represent quite literally a transformation of the medium from an interactive game that is played to a more traditional film that is watched. Although the final product does not take the shape of an interactive game, the process of creating a machinima film constitutes an act of play. It represents the culmination of the performative aspects indicative of the medium of the video game. By exploring the notion of transformative play within machinima, we stand to gain a better understanding of video game fans in particular and fan cultures in general.

Fig. 12.2. "Diary of a Camper," The Rangers (1996).

"The Magic Circle" and Transformative Play

In 1950, Huizinga wrote, "All play moves and has its being within a playground marked off beforehand either materially or ideally, deliberately or as a matter of course" (10). Although he offers many ways to describe this demarcated space of play (card tables, stages, tennis courts), the universality of his use of the "magic circle" is a useful metaphor for discussing the boundaries between areas of play and nonplay. Salen and Zimmerman (2004, 94), building from Steve Sniderman's notion of *frame* (a way of delineating between the artificial world of play and the real world), use the magic circle as way of discussing the negotiation between these distinct spaces: "It is responsible not only for the unusual relationship between a game and the outside world, but also for many of the internal mechanisms and experiences of a game in play." The magic circle helps us to understand the artificiality of games and the rules that govern them. Playing any sort of game requires agreement on the rules of play. Otherwise, chaos ensues. Players abide by rules so that the game can take shape; they have no other reason to do so. Suits (1990, 34) defines playing a game as "the voluntary effort to overcome unnecessary obstacles." The rules of play thus stand in opposition to rules that govern human behavior (that is, laws, norms, and etiquette) inasmuch as they do not carry the same weighty consequences. Violation of a rule of play merely warrants a penalty within the game — another arbitrary construction — whereas the violation of a "real" rule has consequences that extend beyond the realm of play.

The cultural meaning within a game (inside the circle) is separate from the context (outside the circle) in which the game is situated. Thus, the permeability of the magic circle depends on how games are framed, which determines whether or not the game functions as either a closed or open system (Littlejohn 1989). Salen and Zimmerman offer three contexts for understanding games: games as rules (closed systems), games as play (open or closed systems), and games as culture (open systems). The last category provides the most useful way of thinking about transformative play. Salen and Zimmerman (2004, 97) note, "The internal functioning of the game is not emphasized; instead, as a cultural system the focus is on the way that the game exchanges meaning with the culture at large." The transformative play inherent in the design of architecture-enabled open-system video games like *DOOM* and *Quake* requires that we consider them as cultural systems, which allow players to freely traverse the space between the inside and the outside of the magic circle. Salen (2002, 1) states that transformative play occurs when "the free movement of play alters the more rigid structure in which it takes shape. The play doesn't just occupy the interstices of the system, but actually transforms the space as a whole."

Game designers who learned from the open-system models pioneered by innovators like id Software began to realize the importance of transformative play because it allowed players to participate in the construction of these increasingly complex game systems. The open-system approach not only saved the designers money on extensive beta testing (see Karpovich, this volume), but also created brand loyalty among their fans by allowing the players to actively participate in the production of the games. This new philosophy in game design encapsulates what Salen and Zimmerman (2004) refer to as the *player-as-producer paradigm*. It is important to understand this notion of the player as producer differently from earlier discussions of the performative quality of gameplay. Video games differ from traditional forms of media in that the actions of the player produce what is on the screen; these performances only existed in the moment until the recording of *DOOM* demo movies. The player-as-producer paradigm goes beyond these acts of performance to the level of actually changing the game (for example, the many mods produced for *DOOM*). Whereas in the performative model players are behaving as players, the role gets flipped in the latter model, where players function as designers. Not all video games fall within the player-as-producer paradigm; only games that function as open systems posses this quality.

The open-system game design thus proposes a radically different relationship between media producers and media consumers. Despite the video game's unique interactive quality, which already separates it from traditional forms of media, the open-system design of games like *DOOM* and *Quake,* which paved the way for machinima, shifted the power from the producer to the consumer. Salen and Zimmerman, aware of this important shift, insist that open-system games are important because "the permeability of the magic circle feeds innovation, resulting in rich systems of cultural production and new forms of creative expression" (2004, 544). The potential of these rich systems through the technology of open-system game design may seem utopian — a charge that also plagues Jenkins's optimistic view of participatory cultures. Critics could challenge the notion that the player-as-producer paradigm primarily functions as a marketing strategy designed to induce a false sense of autonomy within consumers as a means of galvanizing their commitment to the brand. At the end of the day, gamers are still just buying a piece of software and playing with it.

These same criticisms leveled at the consumer-as-producer model of resistance put forth by Jenkins, which most would agree are valid, do not hold up as well with the transformative play model of video games. As previously discussed, the video game as a medium functions in ways incomparable to traditional media. Although the differences in this new medium are hardly unassailable, they require that theories of consumer and fan cultures need to be reexamined with a thorough understanding of how new media function in ways previously unimagined. Studies of fan cultures online have provided the most recent forms of exploring these recent relationships with new media. Consalvo's (2003) study of *Star Trek* and *Buffy the Vampire Slayer* fans in online communities offers a skeptical view of the freedom that this new technology offers fan cultures: "They provide telling examples and evidence of how that new media environment is changing and how users are limited by increasing control of the Web. The architecture of the Web allows fans some 'resistant' activities but, at the same time, works to constrain these activities in important ways" (68). Consalvo continues by arguing that the Internet's architecture operates within structures designed by corporate interests, which work against any emancipatory potential offered to fans. She draws on Lawrence Lessig's (1999) argument about restrictive capabilities written into the foundational code of the Internet. Both Consalvo's and Lessig's concerns about the illusions of autonomy that are generated through new media technologies like the Internet could apply to the open-system game design that makes machinima possible. Although these concerns hold some weight with respect to video games, the ability of hackers and gamers to overcome such restrictive barriers has demonstrated itself through the history of the medium, beginning with the demoscene and on through mods and machinima. The model of transformative play as a case of fan cultures merging with new technology thus withstands criticism that such online communities as documented by Consalvo may not.

Not Just Playing Anymore

The Rangers's 1996 release of "The Diary of a Camper" spawned a new breed of video game fan and marked a turning point in the history of the medium. These innovators, distinguished by their penchant for play and their appetite for control, redefined the boundaries of gaming. And although the creation of these first films dates back nearly a decade, machinima has only recently made a blip on the radar of mainstream media (Thompson 2005; Bray 2004; Buchanan 2003). But machinima is growing. In fact, in March 2002, Paul Marino (cofounder the ILL Clan, a group of machinima artists) and several other members of the machinima community established the Academy of Machinima Arts and Science (http://www.machinima.org, accessed June 1, 2006). On the Web site for the 2005 Machinima Film Festival (http://festival.machinima.org/modules.php?name=Content&pa=show-page&pid=3, accessed June 1, 2006), Marino states, "It is our goal to both

make the current cre-
ative industries aware
of Machinima as well
as bring support and
credibility to inde-
pendent Machinima
productions as a
whole." In efforts to
garner this support,
the academy held the
first annual Machin-
ima Film Festival later
in 2002 in Mesquite,
Texas (home of id
Software). Although

Fig. 12.3. *Anachronox: The Movie*, Jake Hughes (2002).

the majority of the entries were the typical short film length, Jake Hughes
debuted his feature-length sci-fi opera, *Anachronox: The Movie* (Figure
12.3), which won for best picture that year. Hughes, originally a student of
film, found that the machinima format offered him possibilities otherwise
not available to him: "I sort of always thought it would be neat to make a
space opera, but I don't have $100 million. Suddenly I was able to create
this story. You can make any story you want, and it doesn't cost you thousands or millions of dollars" (Slagle 2002, 4).

Video game fans and fledgling filmmakers are not the only ones who
have harnessed the affordability of machinima. During preproduction for
his film *A.I.*, Steven Spielberg used the game engine of a popular FPS,
Unreal Tournament, to block scenes and camera movements that, had
conventional computer animation been used, would have otherwise taken
more time (Wilonsky 2002). These games—demonstrated to be powerful tools capable of constructing entire 3D virtual worlds—have moved
beyond the mere play of gamers and hackers. The fact that an established
icon within the Hollywood elite has adopted a professional use for game
engines testifies to the empowering capability that open-system games
offer to its fans. Despite Spielberg's use of *Unreal Tournament,* machinima has not yet found a home within Hollywood. Perhaps the closest
to commercial success for machinima so far came in 2003 when Fountainhead Entertainment produced a machinima music video for the
band Zero 7's song "In the Waiting Line." Fountainhead used the *Quake III
Arena* game engine in conjunction with proprietary software developed in
house, called Machinimation (http://www.fountainheadent.com, accessed
June 1, 2006), and created characters in a world that hardly resembled

the game's original design. In March 2005, they released Machinimation 2, which uses *DOOM III,* currently the most advanced game engine available and lauded for its advanced ability to render graphics. Like the original version, Machinimation 2 gives users who have little or no skill in hacking the ability to create machinima (Figure 12.4).

The history of machinima has demonstrated that although the producers of these films were primarily consumers, these gamers possessed talents that enabled them to transform their play into these narratives. So although the case can certainly be made that gaming fans had the tools to make these films presented to them by open-system game design, a threshold of programming knowledge still separated those early innovators from casual gamers. The people at Fountainhead Entertainment recognized this and decided to make a piece of software that no longer functioned as a game, but rather as a specific tool whose sole purpose is to create machinima. In addition to the formation of the Academy of Machinima Arts and Sciences, the release of the Machinimation software illustrates the machinima community's attempts at legitimacy (Figure 12.4).

As the audience for machinima grows, legitimacy will follow. However, once machinima becomes profitable, the freedom that gaming fans are currently experiencing may cease to exist. Video games represent a multibillion-dollar industry, and the open-system games that allow for players to function as producers have persisted only because they do not run contrary to the fiscal needs of the software companies. When and if that does happen, Consalvo's (2003) skepticism about the nature of the computer code may rear its ugly head. As it stands, current primary concerns have to do with intellectual property rights. Fans have long since fought producers along these lines for their appropriation of texts to create their own forms of popular culture. Machinima introduces new concerns to this ongoing dialogue

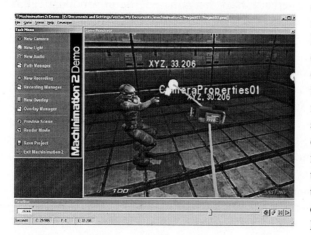

Fig. 12.4. Machinimation 2, Fountainhead Entertainment (2005).

because the product itself functions as a tool of production. Machinima producers like Fountainhead Entertainment use game engines to create music videos (a commercial purpose), which is different from the hundreds of machinima films that can be found for free on the Internet at sites such as http://www.machinima.com (accessed June 1, 2006). Both benefit from the work of the game designers who developed the *Quake III Arena* engine used to make the film. Paul Marino spoke about these issues at the Signal or Noise 2k5 Conference sponsored by Harvard Law School. Although the industry wants to protect itself from others profiting commercially from their labors, it seems to be willing to work with the machinima community because it is aware that machinima has had a positive effect on the gaming industry. These concerns will become more pressing as machinima develops as a medium, particularly as audiences expand. Consumers becoming producers with large audiences may also draw the attention of the game designers. Once the machinima audiences expand beyond the gaming community, the commercial potential will very likely be reconsidered. The most widely popular machinima series to date is *Red vs. Blue,* a series of films first released in 2003 (available at http://www.machinima.com). The series, created with the Xbox game console using the game *Halo,* boasts a staggering audience — more than 900,000 downloads a week (Allen 2004). Although an audience of this size does not represent the majority of audiences that machinima films draw, the potential power that machinima offers consumers seeking to be producers is undeniable.

By repurposing the game engine and using it as a means of animation/film production, machinima producers take transformative play to its most extreme level. If the machinima phenomenon were merely the result of forward-thinking filmmakers looking for a cheap alternative to the growing appetite for 3D animation, it would not offer much significance to those of us who study fan cultures or video games. As such, I contend that the history of machinima is not the story of filmmaking innovators, but rather of gamers as insatiable fans. That is to say, the development of machinima was an inevitability of the medium because of the very nature of the relationship formed between game designers and gamers. The transformative play that became a defining quality of the modern video game offered both the opportunity and the invitation to drastically change the medium. More importantly, the player-as-producer paradigm proposed by open-system games offers tremendous potential for fan cultures across all media. The agency afforded to players and the need that it fills within this relationship is perhaps telling of all audiences and their relationship to their chosen media — the body of work on fan cultures certainly supports this. So as machinima grows and becomes more widespread within mainstream culture, it will be interesting to see what the outgrowths may be for both fan cultures and the medium of the video game. In addition to learning from the study of new media such as the video game, where audiences get reconceptualized, the model of transformative play offers a great deal to scholars of fan cultures. Because transformative play insists that cultural production is an ongoing organic process that ebbs and flows between producers and consumers, it presents a new theoretical approach to fans that requires further exploration.

Notes

1. Admittedly, the use of *repurpose* here could be problematic for some inasmuch that the end results do not deviate that far from the game's original design. The mods that change the avatars and add levels to a game do not necessarily equate to the kinds of "modifications" that fanfic writers use. The mods that I discuss here in relation to *DOOM* represent only a portion of the kind of modding that takes place within the gaming community. The countergaming movement uses these tactics to political or social ends (Galloway 2006).

2. It is important to distinguish the use of *demo* here in the *DOOM* demo movies from that of the earlier discussed *demos* of the demoscene. Both visually represent a person's ability; however, *demos* were displays of hackers' ability to hack code, whereas the *demo movies* were a visual record of a player's ability. The former is a display of intellectual capacity; the latter depicts the agility of hand-eye coordination. Regardless, they are both bound as performative expressions of competition.

References

Abercrombie, Nicholas, and Brian Longhurst. 1998. *Audiences: A sociological theory of performance and imagination.* London: Sage.

Allen, Greg. 2004. Virtual warriors have feelings, too. *New York Times,* November 4.

Azhar, Azeem. 2003. Play it again, Sam: Forget Hollywood special effects, hip film makers are using PCs to create a new type of cinema. *Guardian,* November 20.

Bloom, David. 2002, Gamers fine-toon new pic form in machinima. *Variety,* August 12–18.

Bosama, Josephine. 2002. JODI and the cargo cult. In *INSTALL.EXE — JODI,* ed. C. Verlag, 91–94. Publication accompanying exhibition.

Bray, Hiawatha. 2004. Inspired animation tools from an uninspired sitcom. *Boston Globe,* March 17.

Bryce, Jo, and Jason. Rutter. 2002. Spectacle of the deathmatch: Character and narrative in first-person shooters. In *ScreenPlay: Cinema/videogames/interfaces,* ed. G. King and T. Krzywinkska, 66–80. New York: Wallflower Press.

_____. 2005. Gendered gaming in gendered space. In *Handbook of computer game studies,* ed. Joost Raessens and Jeffrey Goldstein, 301–9. Cambridge, MA: MIT Press.

Buchanan, Levi. 2003. Underground machinima is making waves. *Chicago Tribune,* August 9, 23.

Cassell, Justine, and Henry Jenkins. 1998. Chess for girls? Feminism and computer games. In *From Barbie to Mortal Kombat: Gender and computer games*, ed. Justine Cassell and Henry Jenkins, 2–45. Cambridge, MA: MIT Press.

Consalvo, Mia. 2003. Cyber-slaying media fans: Code, digital poaching, and corporate control of the Internet. *Journal of Communication Inquiry* 27:67–86.

De Certeau, Michel. 1984. *The practice of everyday life.* Berkeley: Univ. of California Press.

Fiske, John. 1989. *Reading the popular.* New York: Routledge.

Galloway, Alex. 2006. *Gaming: Essays on algorithmic culture.* Minneapolis, MN: Univ. of Minnesota Press.

Graner Ray, Sheri. 2004. *Gender inclusive game design: Expanding the market.* Hingham, MA: Charles River Media.

Hills, Matt. 2002. *Fan cultures.* London: Routledge.

Huizinga, Johan. 1950. *Homo ludens: A study of the play-element in culture.* Boston: Beacon Press.

id Software. 2005. id Software backgrounder. http://www.idsoftware.com/business/history (accessed June 1, 2006).

Jenkins, Henry. 1992. *Textual poachers: Television fans and participatory culture.* New York: Routledge.

_____. 1998. "Complete freedom of movement": Video games as gendered play spaces. In *From Barbie to Mortal Kombat: Gender and computer games*, ed. Justine Cassell and Henry Jenkins, 262–97. Cambridge, MA: MIT Press.

_____. 2003. Quentin Tarantino's *Star Wars*? Digital cinema, media convergence, and participatory culture. In *Rethinking media change*, ed. David Thorburn and Henry Jenkins, 281–312. Cambridge, MA: MIT Press.

Kushner, David. 2003. *Masters of DOOM: How two guys created an empire and transformed pop culture.* New York: Random House.

Lessig, Lawrence. 1999. *Code: And other laws of cyberspace.* New York: Basic Books.

Littlejohn, Stephen W. 1989. *Theories of human communication.* 3rd ed. Belmont, CA: Wadsworth Publishing.

Manovich, Lev. 2001. *The language of new media.* Cambridge, MA: MIT Press.

Marino, Paul. 2004. *3D game-based filmmaking: The art of machinima.* Scottsdale, AZ: Paraglyph.

Mirapaul, Matthew. 2002. Computer games as the tools for digital filmmakers. *New York Times*, July 22.

Postigo, Hector. 2003. From *Pong* to *Planet Quake*: Post-industrial transitions from leisure to work. *Information, Communication and Society* 6:593–607.

Salen, Katie. 2002. *Quake! DOOM! Sims!* Transforming play: Family albums and monster movies. Walker Art Center, October 19. http://www.walkerart.org/archive/7/A57 36D3C789330FC6164.htm (accessed June 1, 2006).

Salen, Katie, and Eric Zimmerman. 2004. *Rules of play: Game design fundamentals.* Cambridge, MA: MIT Press.

Schleiner, Anne-Marie. 2005. Game reconstruction workshop: Demolishing and evolving PC games and gamer culture. In *Handbook of computer game studies*, ed. Joost Raessens and Jeffrey Goldstein, 405–14. Cambridge, MA: MIT Press.

Scodari, Christine. 2003. Resistance re-examined: Gender, fan practices, and science fiction television. *Popular Communication* 1:111–30.

Slagle, Matt. 2002. Software creates new genre; part cinema, part video game, films made on PCs. *Chicago Tribune*, September 2, 4.

Suits, Bernard Herbert. 1990. *The grasshopper: Games, life, and utopia.* Boston: David R. Godine.

Tasajärvi, Lassi. 2004. A brief history of the demoscene. In *Demoscene: The art of realtime*, ed. Lassi Tasajärvi, 11–32. Even Lake Studios.

Thomas, Douglas. 2002. *Hacker culture.* Minneapolis: Univ. of Minnesota Press.

Thompson, Clive. 2005. The Xbox auteurs. *New York Times,* August 7.

Wilonsky, Robert. 2002. Joystick cinema: It's man vs. machinima when video games become, ahem, movies. *Scene Entertainment Weekly,* August 14.

Wollen, Peter. 1982. *Readings and writings: Semiotic counter-strategies.* New York: Routledge.

Yates, Simeon J., and Karen Littleton. 1999. Understanding computer game cultures: A situated approach. *Information, Communication and Society* 2:566–83.

Contributors

Kristina Busse has a PhD in English from Tulane University. She is an independent scholar who has been reading and writing on fan fiction since 1999.

Francesca Coppa is an associate professor of English at Muhlenberg College, where she teaches twentieth-century dramatic literature, sexuality theory, and performance studies. She is the editor of a three-volume collection of playwright Joe Orton's early works, and her *Casebook on Joe Orton* was published by Routledge in 2003. She is currently coediting a book on stage magic and coteaching a course on *Buffy the Vampire Slayer*.

Abigail Derecho is a PhD candidate in comparative literary studies at Northwestern University. She received a BA in modern thought and literature and an MA in humanities from Stanford University.

Catherine Driscoll is a senior lecturer and convenor of graduate studies in the Department of Gender and Cultural Studies at the University of Sydney. She has published in the fields of philosophy, cultural theory, modernism, and youth studies. Her book *Girls: Feminine Adolescence in Popular Culture and Cultural Theory* was published by Columbia University Press (2002). Her current research projects include ethnographic research on fan fiction communities.

Karen Hellekson is a full-time freelance copyeditor specializing in the scientific, technical, and medical market. She has a PhD in English from the University of Kansas and remains active as an independent scholar in the fields of science fiction and media studies. Her *Science Fiction of Cordwainer Smith* was published by McFarland in 2001.

Robert Jones teaches at New York University. His PhD work focuses on machinima and mods as instances of transformative play within video game culture. He is also interested in digital cinema as participatory culture, Hollywood's convergence with the gaming industry, and the social and political implications of video games.

Deborah Kaplan is a graduate of both the Center for the Study of Children's Literature and the Graduate School of Library and Information Sciences at Simmons College. She has been reading fan fiction since 1988, but only writing it since 1999.

Angelina Karpovich's PhD thesis, written for the Department of Theatre, Film and Television Studies, University of Wales Aberystwyth, is about social interaction in online fan fiction communities.

Eden Lackner holds an MA in English with a specialization in nineteenth-century British literature. Her first and most beloved fandom is *The Lord of the Rings*, which she discovered at age eleven and returned to with the release of the first of Peter Jackson's films in 2001. Her interest and specialization in fan culture stems from her status as a fan: she has been actively participating in online slash fandoms since 1999. She writes *LotR* FPS and RPS, maintains a LiveJournal, and comoderates several online communities, all from her Calgary, Alberta, Canada, home.

Barbara Lynn Lucas has an MA in English with a concentration in British Renaissance literature. Although she has been a fan since her early teens, she is a latecomer to fandom itself. Although she has dabbled in some other fandoms, *The Lord of the Rings* fictional person slash (FPS) and real person slash (RPS) are her main fandoms, and she is the comoderator of Sons of Gondor, a *LotR* slash fiction community. She currently resides in a suburb of Cleveland, Ohio.

Robin Anne Reid is a professor of literature and languages at Texas A&M University, Commerce. She has an MA in creative writing and a PhD in English with specializations in critical theory and marginalized twentieth-century American literatures. She teaches courses in creative writing, popular culture, Tolkien, and critical theory, especially gender/queer theory. She is currently developing essays on fan fiction. She became active in fandom in 1977 in Outpost 13 of the Puget Sound Star Trekkers and was a member of APA-5 until the early 1990s. She rejoined fandom through the Internet in 2003. She writes *LotR* FPS (AU) and RPS.

Mafalda Stasi is an independent scholar who lives in Paris, France. Her active involvement in slash fiction dates to 1994. Her overarching theoretical interest is in discourse transposition: she has published a book and a number of articles on the dynamics of discourse, ideology, and practice across cultural, gender, and national lines. Her PhD is in English from the University of Texas at Austin, where she worked in the division of Rhetoric and Composition.

Louisa Ellen Stein is an assistant professor at San Diego State University in the School of Theatre, Television, and Film. She recently completed her dissertation at NYU on genre discourse in teen/fantasy television and online fan culture.

Ika Willis is a faculty lecturer in reception at the University of Bristol. Her research is centered around theories of reception and textuality. She is currently working on a book (provisionally titled *Rome and the Teletechnology of History*) on the relationship between political sovereignty and literary transmission/reception in the context of Roman imperial and contemporary globalizations.

Elizabeth Woledge completed her PhD at the University of Chester (UK). She is currently working at Liverpool, Chester, and Manchester Metropolitan Universities while rewriting her thesis for publication. Her interest and involvement with K/S fandom, where she is known as an artist rather than a writer, predate her academic endeavors by several years.

Index